Reimagining Reparations in Human Rights

International Studies in Human Rights

VOLUME 149

The titles published in this series are listed at *brill.com/ishr*

Reimagining Reparations in Human Rights

The Evolving Concept of Reparations in International Human Rights Law

Edited by

Otto Spijkers, Iakovos Iakovidis, Pierre Thielbörger and Elena Abrusci

BRILL | NIJHOFF

LEIDEN | BOSTON

The views and opinions expressed in this publication herein are those of the author and should not be attributed to the institutions they are associated with.

The Library of Congress Cataloging-in-Publication Data is available online at https://catalog.loc.gov
LC record available at https://lccn.loc.gov/2026902864

Typeface for the Latin, Greek, and Cyrillic scripts: "Brill". See and download: brill.com/brill-typeface.

ISSN 0924-4751
ISBN 978-90-04-71673-5 (hardback)
ISBN 978-90-04-71674-2 (e-book)
DOI 10.1163/9789004716742

This book is printed on acid-free paper and produced in a sustainable manner.

Contents

CHAPTER 1

Mapping the Evolution of Reparations across the Transforming Human Rights Regime

Otto Spijkers, Iakovos Iakovidis, Pierre Thielbörger and Elena Abrusci

1 Introduction

Return of looted shipwreck treasures to countries of origin as reparation for slavery,[1] and calls in the Caribbean for restorative justice for slave trade from former colonies;[2] these are only some of the news items that hit the front page over the last years on the topic of reparations.

Moreover, the recent jurisprudence of international judicial organs,[3] United Nations General Assembly resolution 60/147,[4] as well as significant other initiatives, such as the creation of the Trust Fund for Victims (TFV) in the framework of the International Criminal Court (ICC),[5] hint at interesting new directions in the field of international reparations.

It becomes henceforth clearly understood that the principles set by the Permanent Court of International Justice in the *Chorzów Factory* case in 1928[6] have since then fundamentally evolved and the landscape of the inter-

1 Dalya Alberge, 'Return looted shipwreck treasures to countries of origin as reparations for slavery, says lawyer', published in the *Guardian* on 12 January 2025, https://www.theguardian.com/world/2025/jan/12/return-looted-shipwreck-treasures-to-countries-of-origin-as-reparations-for-slavery-says-lawyer.

2 Verene Shepherd, 'The Caribbean calls for restorative justice', published in the UNESCO Courier on 3 July 2024, https://courier.unesco.org/en/articles/caribbean-calls-restorative-justice.

3 Among other rulings, see *The Prosecutor v Thomas Lubanga Dyilo* (Decision Establishing the Principles and Procedures to be Applied to Reparations) ICC-01/04–01/06–2904 (7 August 2012), *Prosecutor v Ahmad Al Faqi Al Mahdi* (Reparations Order) ICC-01/12–01/15–236 (17 August 2017), and *The Prosecutor v Germain Katanga* (Order for Reparations pursuant to Article 75 of the Statute) ICC-01/04–01/07–3728-tENG (24 March 2017).

4 United Nations General Assembly, 'Basic Principles and Guidelines on the Right to a Remedy and Reparation for Victims of Gross Violations of International Human Rights Law and Serious Violations of International Humanitarian Law' (2005) UN Doc A/RES/60/147.

5 The Trust Fund for Victims was created in 2004 by the Assembly of States Parties, in accordance with article 79 of the Rome Statute, https://www.icc-cpi.int/tfv.

6 Permanent Court of International Justice, *The Factory at Chorzow* (*Germany v. Poland*), Merits, 13 September 1928, p. 47.

 | DOI:10.1163/9789004716742_002

national law on reparations has undergone a profound transformation over recent decades, especially in the field of human rights.[7] This collection has the ambition to explore how reparations have evolved across various human rights systems, reflecting on their legal, social, and cultural dimensions.

The journey that led to this book began in the late summer of 2023. On the 30th of August 2023, we convened the annual pre-conference workshop of our European Society of International Law (ESIL) Interest Group on International Human Rights Law. The workshop took place in Aix-en-Provence (France), and addressed the topic of 'Reparations in International Human Rights Law: A Critical Reflection'. Ten authors came from all over the world to Aix-en-Provence and contributed to our workshop.

Earlier, we had issued a call for papers where we invited scholars to critically reflect on the normative evolution of reparations, with a focus on human rights law and institutions. In particular, we welcomed contributions that explore the ways in which traditional forms of reparation (restitution, compensation, and satisfaction) have been (re)interpreted and applied in fields reflecting broader community values, including human dignity. We also invited contributions that explore new forms of reparations such as rehabilitation and collective reparations. Finally, we invited submissions on recent efforts to repair historical wrongs – such as reparations for colonial times, slavery, oppression – and the ways in which the legal principle of reparation has been conceptualized in support of these claims.

The reasons why we chose to focus our workshop on the topic of reparations were manifold. First of all, we felt that the emergence of international human rights law and the designation of the individual as bearer of rights and obligations under international law had created a new dynamic in the international law of reparation. Reparation has been recognized as part of a victim's right to a remedy and enshrined in treaties like the Rome Statute of the ICC. This codification builds upon the practice of many states after World War II, which provided reparations to war victims by establishing public compensation schemes, restitution of property, satisfaction through criminal trials, the building of monuments, and the creation of national days of remembrance. Across the Americas, a wave of reparations was implemented as part of transitional justice processes in numerous states, including Argentina, Chile, and Colombia. The Inter-American Court of Human

7 For an overview of the evolution of reparations in a general sense, see Otto Spijkers, Julie Fraser, Emmanuel Giakoumakis (editors), *Reparations in International Law: A Critical Reflection*, Netherlands Yearbook of International Law, volume 2022, Springer, 2025.

Rights (IACtHR) continues to award tailored and progressive reparations to victims.

At the same time, we noticed that soft law instruments began to adopt a novel approach to the topic, actively contributing to shaping the contemporary law of reparation. The United Nations General Assembly Resolution 60/147 set out the Basic Principles and Guidelines on the Right to a Remedy and Reparation for Victims of Gross Violations of International Human Rights Law and Serious Violations of International Humanitarian Law. The Human Rights Council has through various channels undertaken the task of further studying the issue. The Special Rapporteur on the Promotion of Truth, Justice, Reparation, and Guarantees of Non-occurrence has launched a call for inputs on the financing of reparations owed to victims of serious violations of human rights and humanitarian law. In response to such developments, scholars and practitioners have argued that there is a need to reassess the basic principles and rules relating to reparation, and we hoped our workshop could make a modest contribution to that.

In response to our call for papers, we received over thirty abstract proposals, of which we selected ten. The selected authors were invited to Aix-en-Provence to present their paper at our workshop. Almost all of the authors then developed their paper into a chapter for this book. We asked a few other scholars, not present at Aix-en-Provence, to provide additional chapters. The result is the collection of papers in this book.

2 Overview of the Chapters

Let us give an overview of the chapters, before identifying some common themes.

Deborah Casalin in her chapter, entitled 'Developing International Law on Reparations for Displacement: Foundational Cases from Four Corners of the International Human Rights System', examines the gradual recognition by inter-state forums for international law-making and adjudication of arbitrary displacement of people from their homes as a wrongful act which could give rise to a right to reparation. She provides an analysis of landmark cases from different jurisdictions, including the *Moiwana v. Suriname* case before the Inter-American Court of Human Rights, the *Doğan and Others v. Türkiye* case before the European Court of Human Rights, the *Endorois v. Kenya* case before the African Commission on Human and Peoples' Rights, and the *I.D.G. v. Spain* case before the United Nations Committee on Economic Social and

Cultural Rights. She highlights the pivotal role played by these regional and international human rights bodies in shaping reparations for displaced populations. By situating these cases within broader legal trends, Casalin demonstrates how human rights mechanisms have begun to develop a framework for addressing displacement-related claims.

Diana Odier-Contreras Garduno's contribution, entitled 'Translating Principles into Practice: Collective Reparation and Harm Assessment across International Tribunals', addresses collective reparations. These are a key response to gross human rights violations, central to the jurisprudence of courts like the Inter-American Court of Human Rights, the International Criminal Court (ICC), and the Extraordinary Chambers in the Courts of Cambodia (ECCC). Despite their importance, collective reparations lack a clear definition, and their scope is determined on a case-by-case basis. Courts assess collective reparations based on alleged harm and victims' needs, yet standards for proving harm and valuing damages remain inconsistent. Diana examines how these courts assess moral, material, and collective harm, arguing that collective reparations is often justified on humanistic and pragmatic grounds rather than clear evidentiary standards.

Giulio Bartolini contributed a chapter entitled 'Reparation in Inter-state Disputes: Preliminary Lessons from the Practice of Human Rights Bodies'. In his chapter, he delves into the complexities of reparations in inter-state disputes involving human rights violations. His chapter explores whether individual victims can be direct beneficiaries of reparation measures when claims are brought by states on behalf of their nationals against other states. He also examines various procedural and substantive challenges in ensuring that reparations serve those affected by *erga omnes* violations.

Juliette Rémond-Tiedrez's contribution, entitled 'Listening to What Victims Want: The Search for, Exhumation, Identification and Return of Remains of the Disappeared', addresses the exhumation, identification, and return of remains of victims of human rights violations as a form of reparation. While states initially prioritized financial compensation, growing dissatisfaction among victims led regional human rights courts and other such bodies to recognize other forms of reparation, including satisfaction measures. Among these, the exhumation, identification, and return of remains have emerged as crucial, particularly in cases of enforced disappearances. The plight of Yazidi families seeking the remains of loved ones disappeared during the 2014 genocide by the so-called Islamic State of Iraq and Syria underscores the profound significance of this measure.

Marina Aksenova authored a paper entitled 'Is There Room for Creative Reparations in International Criminal Law?' She explores the potential for creative reparations within international criminal law, as a means to translate legal judgements into the language of art. Her focus is on the International Criminal Court (ICC). Acknowledging that there are inherent limitations in the system of international criminal justice, she nonetheless persuades us that it is a compelling testing ground for legal innovation, especially when it comes to addressing mass violence. She investigates how symbolic reparations – such as artistic expressions and memorialization – can address the deeper structural causes of mass violence and contribute to healing for affected communities. Aksenova's work raises critical questions about the limitations of legal judgments in fully capturing victims' grievances.

Nina Bries Silva and Laura Triana Gallego contributed a paper entitled 'A Song to Nature: Traditional Wiwa Music as Relational Reparation to Indigenous Communities and Their Territory'. They introduce a groundbreaking perspective on relational reparations through the lens of the Wiwa Indigenous community in Colombia. Their chapter highlights how traditional Wiwa music serves as a form of reparation not only for the community but also for their territory, recognized as a living entity harmed by armed conflict. Based on fieldwork done by the authors themselves, the chapter underscores the significance of music for the Wiwa Indigenous community in Colombia, and its potential to be recognized as a new form of reparation to both the communities and the territory.

Patricia Grazziotin Noschang drafted a paper entitled 'Human Rights Violations Caused by Climate Change: Who Repairs Whom?' In this chapter, she examines the intersection of human rights and climate change law, and how this has impacted climate litigation. As climate litigation gains traction in human rights courts, she discusses the challenges of assigning reparations for environmental harm also to individuals affected by climate-related rights violations. By analysing emerging cases, primarily before the European Court of Human Rights, she explores whether existing legal frameworks can adequately address these new frontiers of reparative climate justice.

Prosper Simbarashe Maguchu wrote a chapter entitled 'Rethinking Development/Reparations Programmes and the Role of Third States in Transitional Justice'. In this chapter, he critically rethinks the conventional separation between reparations and development in post-conflict societies. He explores how recovered assets from human rights violators, channelled through international agencies, can fund development projects in Africa, thereby serving as a form of reparative justice. In his chapter, he advocates for a more integrated approach that combines reparations and development efforts.

Sotirios-Ioannis Lekkas wrote a chapter entitled 'Reparations for Armed Conflict Related Atrocities in Inter-state Proceedings: The *Armed Activities* (DRC v Uganda) Judgment on Reparations and Its Legacy'. In this chapter, the author provides an in-depth analysis of the reparations judgment of the International Court of Justice (ICJ) in the *Armed Activities* case between the Democratic Republic of the Congo and Uganda of 2022. This decision represents the Court's most complex reparations ruling to date, addressing large-scale harm. The author's main point is that the law of state responsibility does require reparations to accurately reflect the wrongdoer's responsibility and address victims' harm, but that institutional and evidentiary limitations can distort outcomes in cases involving mass claims arising from armed conflict.

Finally, *Veronica Botticelli* authored a paper entitled 'Fitting a Square Peg in a Round Hole? Challenges and Prospects of Inter-state Human Rights Complaints as (Overlapping) Avenues for Individual Reparations' Human Rights Violations'. In it, she complements the paper by Giulio Bartolini, and explores the challenges of using inter-state complaints as avenues for securing reparations for individuals. She assesses the limitations of existing mechanisms and considers whether international law can evolve to better serve victims of human rights violations within State-centred dispute frameworks.

3 Identifying Common Themes

One of the key themes emerging from these contributions is a trend of broadening reparations beyond financial compensation to encompass also symbolic, relational, culture-specific, and environmental forms of redress. Juliette Rémond-Tiedrez highlights how victim-centred approaches have led to various contexts-specific forms of satisfaction such as the search for, exhumation, identification, and return of remains in cases of enforced disappearances, particularly in the context of the Yazidi genocide. Marina Aksenova explores the potential for more creative forms of reparation at the ICC, including symbolic and artistic expressions. In her view, these may be more suitable to address reparations for mass violence and they can better reflect victims' experiences. Nina Bries Silva and Laura Triana Gallego go even further, and extend the concept of reparations by considering the Wiwa Indigenous people's use of traditional music to heal both their community and their territory, which they see as a living entity harmed by conflict.

Another recurring theme is the way in which inter-state mechanisms can respond to the needs of individuals seeking justice. The contributions addressing this issue see much room for improvement. Giulio Bartolini examines whether victims can be direct beneficiaries of reparations when claims are brought by states against other states. Sotirios-Ioannis Lekkas, critically analysing the reparations judgment of the ICJ in the Armed Activities case between the Democratic Republic of the Congo and Uganda of 2022, highlights administrative and procedural challenges faced by an inter-state court when awarding reparations that are ultimately meant for individuals. More generally, Veronica Botticelli explores the limitations of inter-state complaints as a means of providing reparations for individual victims of human rights violations, questioning whether international law can evolve to better address these challenges.

Several contributions challenge traditional, Western-centric approaches to reparations and introduce perspectives rooted in non-Western cultures and traditions. Nina Bries Silva and Laura Triana Gallego argue that territory itself should be recognized as a victim of harm, aligning with the Wiwa Indigenous community's worldview. Prosper Simbarashe Maguchu, in his exploration of how recovered assets from human rights violators can be channelled through international agencies to ensure transitional justice in the Global South, criticizes the rigid separation between reparations and development, advocating for a model that integrates both. This challenges the traditional view, i.e. that provision of reparations for harm and provision of official development assistance need to be neatly separated.

Almost all contributions analyse how various international, regional, and domestic courts and other dispute settlement bodies have developed new and more innovate legal frameworks for reparations. Deborah Casalin's work traces the evolution of reparations for displacement, showing how international and regional courts have recognized displacement as a wrongful act warranting redress. Patricia Grazziotin Noschang examines the emerging role of human rights courts in reshaping reparations through climate litigation. As efforts to address responsibility for environmental degradation increasingly intersect with human rights, she explores whether existing legal frameworks can provide the appropriate reparations.

Despite progress, the practical and legal implementation of reparations remains fraught with challenges. Many of our authors have identified such challenges. Sotirios-Ioannis Lekkas critiques the ICJ's methodology in its reparations judgment, noting its shortcomings in proving causation, valuing damage, and determining payment modalities. Giulio Bartolini explores the procedural complexities involved in implementing reparations for individual victims in inter-state disputes, particularly when identifying beneficiaries and enforcing compliance.

Taken together, we believe these contributions have done a thorough job at mapping the evolving landscape of reparations within international human rights law. They challenge existing paradigms, introduce novel approaches, and advocate for a more victim-centred and less traditional, more holistic understanding of justice in the wake of human rights violations, thus balancing the scales of justice.

CHAPTER 2

Developing International Law on Reparations for Displacement: Foundational Cases from Four Corners of the International Human Rights System

Deborah Casalin

1 Introduction

Despite the immense negative impacts of mass population displacement on societies and individuals worldwide, the multilateral forums which engaged in developing international law relating to peace, security and human rights in the 20th century – as well as associated inter-state adjudication forums – have been slow to view displacement as an internationally wrongful act giving rise to a right to reparation.[1] An important exception can be found in international and regional human rights courts and commissions. Especially over the past 25 years, these bodies have served as venues for the reparation claims of displaced people who could not obtain a domestic remedy and have ordered or recommended reparation in an increasing range of displacement situations. In doing so, they have attempted to address an issue which presents particular complexities for reparative efforts, given the multifaceted impacts of displacement on affected people and societies, as well as its connections to questions of property, land and territory. However, the role of the jurisprudence of human rights bodies in developing international human rights law on reparations for displacement has remained relatively underexamined in legal literature on displacement and reparations respectively.[2] This chapter will exam-

1 See further D Casalin, 'Reparations for Displacement since Chorzów: Moving from the "Problems of Displacement" to the "Problems of the Displaced" via International and Regional Human Rights Bodies' (2024) 53 Netherlands Yearbook of International Law 15. Otherwise, parts of the current chapter draw on analysis in the author's doctoral dissertation: D Casalin, 'The role of international (quasi-)judicial mechanisms in ensuring reparation for arbitrary displacement' (University of Antwerp Faculty of Law 2022), https://hdl.handle.net/10067/1875990151162165141.

2 For discussions of reparation in the context of broader themes in legal literature on displacement, see e.g. W Kälin, *Internal Displacement and the Law* (Oxford University Press 2023) 236–284; E Katselli Proukaki, 'The Right to Return Home and the Right to Property Restitution under International Law', in E Katselli Proukaki (ed) *Armed Conflict and Forcible*

 | DOI:10.1163/9789004716742_003

ine the key contributions that these bodies have made to the development of international human rights law on reparations for displacement through highlighting the innovations brought about by emblematic decisions from the African, European, Inter-American and UN human rights systems. The cases have been selected for the novelty, significance, and relative comprehensiveness of their approach to framing displacement as a human rights violation and developing context-appropriate reparative measures.

Following the present introduction (Section 1), Section 2 will address the approach of the Inter-American Court of Human Rights (IACtHR) to reparations for conflict displacement in *Moiwana v. Suriname*. Section 3 contrasts this with the judgments of the European Court of Human Rights (ECtHR) in *Doğan and others v. Turkey*. Section 4 turns to examine the African Commission on Human and Peoples' Rights' (ACHPR) engagement in remedying development-induced displacement in *Endorois v. Kenya*; while Section 5 explores the Committee on Economic, Social and Cultural Rights' (CESCR) handling of a context of mass mortgage evictions in *I.D.G. v. Spain*. Finally, Section 6 draws conclusions regarding the key contributions of these cases (as well as the lines of jurisprudence which they inspired within and beyond their respective systems) to developing international human rights law on reparations for displacement.

Displacement: Individual Rights under International Law (Routledge 2018), 51–61; D J Cantor, 'Returns of Internally Displaced Persons during Armed Conflict: International Law and its Application in Colombia' (Brill 2018) 69–73. On regional and international human rights bodies' approaches to reparation in contexts of widespread violence/mass human rights violations, incorporating various displacement cases from this perspective, see F E Torres, 'The State, the assailant? Guaranteeing economic and social rights after widespread violence through the Inter-American Court of Human Rights', (2022) 40 Netherlands Quarterly of Human Rights, 12; F E Torres, 'Economic and Social Rights, Reparations and the Aftermath of Widespread Violence: The African Human Rights System and Beyond', (2021) 21 Human Rights Law Review 935; F E Torres, 'Reparations: To What End? Developing the State's Positive Duties to Address Socio-economic Harms in Post-conflict Settings through the European Court of Human Rights', (2021) 32 European Journal of International Law 807; L Oette, 'Bringing Justice to Victims? Responses of Regional and International Human Rights Courts and Treaty Bodies to Mass Violations', in C Ferstman, M Goetz (eds), *Reparations for Victims of Genocide, War Crimes and Crimes against Humanity: Systems in Place and Systems in the Making* (Brill 2020). On Cyprus, see V Tzevelekos, 'Reparation of the Rights to Property and Home of Displaced Persons Arising from Armed Conflict under the European Convention on Human Rights: Falling Short of the Exigencies of International Law and the Humanistic Purpose of Human Rights?' in E Katselli Proukaki (ed) *Armed Conflict and Forcible Displacement: Individual Rights under International Law* (Routledge 2018).

2 *Moiwana v. Suriname:* Inter-American Court of Human Rights

This 2005 judgment of the Inter-American Court of Human Rights, which was seminal in many respects, addressed the prolonged displacement of massacre survivors by applying their rights to collective property as a tribal people; freedom of movement and residence (and to enter their own country); and to physical, mental and moral integrity. This judgment was particularly significant for the development of international human rights law on reparation for displacement, as it constituted an early recognition of prolonged displacement in itself as giving rise to a right to reparation, and developed innovative reparative measures specific to the context of mass displacement.

2.1 *The Case and Its Findings*

The claim in *Moiwana v. Suriname* arose from the context of a conflict between Suriname's military regime and the *Jungle Commando* armed opposition group in the 1980s and early 1990s. The applicants – mainly the displaced survivors of a massacre – were members of the *N'djuka Maroon* Afro-descendant tribal people, for whom a relationship with traditional land plays a crucial role in cultural survival. In November 1986, state forces attacked Moiwana village. They killed and wounded civilians, burned the village, and forced survivors to leave. Over 100 villagers fled to French Guyana or within Suriname, where they lived in conditions of deprivation. Even after peace accords were concluded, Moiwana survivors considered that they could not return safely, as the incident had never been investigated, perpetrators had not been brought to justice, and their homes were still destroyed. Given the situation of impunity, the survivors feared further violence, as well as spiritual repercussions for failing to obtain justice for the dead.[3]

As Suriname had ratified the American Convention on Human Rights (ACHR) a year after the massacre and the community's initial displacement, the IACtHR found that it could not assess or order reparation for this incident as such, as this fell outside of its temporal jurisdiction. However, it did assess allegations of violations of a continuing nature in connection with the community's ongoing displacement and inability to return, as well as the absence of an investigation.[4] The IACtHR took into account the *N'djuka Maroon* tribal

3 *Moiwana v. Suriname*, Series C No. 124 (IACtHR, Judgment, 15 June 2005) paras 86(6)–86(24); F MacKay, *Moiwana zoekt gerechtigheid: de strijd van een Marrondorp tegen de staat Suriname* (KIT Publishers, 2006); R Price, *Rainforest Warriors: Human Rights on Trial* (University of Pennsylvania Press, 2011) 83–103.

4 *Moiwana v. Suriname* (n 3) para 43.

people's multi-faceted relationship to their traditional land and collective concept of ownership.[5] Consequently, even though the community and its members had no formal legal title to their lands,[6] the Court found that Suriname had "violated the right of the Moiwana community members to the communal use and enjoyment of their traditional property".[7] On its own initiative, the IACtHR also considered the applicants' continued displacement, as well as its consequences and the circumstances contributing to its prolongation. It found that the obstruction of the survivors' attempts to obtain justice – resulting in fear of return, separation from traditional land and inability to honour the dead – had caused suffering to a degree that constituted a violation of the right to respect for physical, mental and moral integrity (ACHR, Article 5(1)).[8] The IACtHR also considered investigation of the massacre and prosecution of perpetrators to be indispensable in creating conditions for safe, dignified and voluntary return. Given Suriname's failure in this regard, the IACtHR found a violation of the right to freedom of movement and residence in respect of internally displaced persons (IDPs) (ACHR, Article 22(1)), and the right to enter one's country in respect of those displaced to French Guyana (ACHR, Article 22(5)).[9]

In particular, the following reparation measures were ordered to address the applicants' displacement: individual compensation; effective investigation of the massacre; security guarantees for returnees; securing of the community's collective property rights; and establishment of a development fund for health, housing and educational programmes.[10]

2.2 *Recognizing Prolonged Displacement as a Human Rights Violation Giving Rise to a Right to Reparation*

Moiwana v. Suriname was the first judgment where the IACtHR engaged with the phenomenon of internal displacement and confirmed that IDPs are entitled to reparation for a state's failure to take steps to resolve their situation.[11] In particular, the IACtHR's interpretation of the right to freedom of move-

5 Ibid, paras 131–134.
6 Ibid, para 130.
7 Ibid, para 135.
8 Ibid, paras 90–103.
9 Ibid, paras 110–121.
10 Ibid, paras 187–217.
11 T Antkowiak, 'Moiwana Village v. Suriname: A Portal into Recent Jurisprudential Developments of the Inter-American Court of Human Rights', (2007) 25 Berkeley Journal of International Law 268, 274–275; see also *Moiwana v. Suriname* (n 3) Separate Opinion of Judge A.A. Cançado Trindade.

ment in light of the Guiding Principles on Internal Displacement (Guiding Principles) – the first reference to this instrument in any regional human rights judgment or decision – was lauded as a pioneering move.[12] One notable aspect was the IACtHR's endorsement of the Guiding Principles' articulation of a positive duty of competent authorities to establish conditions and provide the means for displaced persons' safe, dignified and voluntary return or resettlement.[13] This served as a key precedent for the IACtHR's approach to reparation for internal conflict displacement in Colombia,[14] which was also carried over into judgments on conflict displacement against El Salvador and Guatemala.[15]

Beyond internal displacement, Judge *Cançado Trindade* more generally highlighted the significance of the IACtHR applying the Convention to address the "contemporary and growing tragedy of uprootedness",[16] whether within or across borders. Indeed, the *Moiwana v. Suriname* judgment addressed the situation of both IDPs and survivors displaced to French Guyana, without drawing distinctions between them in terms of reparation. This demonstrated that the migration status or current location of displaced persons has little relevance in attributing state responsibility or determining reparations for human rights violations connected to their initial displacement or its prolongation. This approach corresponds to that of the Pinheiro Principles, adopted the same year, which address housing, land and property restitution and "apply equally to all refugees, internally displaced persons and to other similarly situated displaced persons".[17] A similar approach is visible in later regional deci-

12 T Antkowiak (n 11) 273.

13 *Moiwana v. Suriname* (n 3) para 111; see Guiding Principles on Internal Displacement, Principle 28(1).

14 T Antkowiak (n 11) 274–275. See *Mapiripán Massacre v. Colombia*, Series C No. 134 (IACtHR, Judgment, 15 September 2005) paras 167–179; *Ituango Massacres v. Colombia*, Series C No. 148 (IACtHR, Judgment, 1 July 2006) para 209; *Operation Genesis v. Colombia*, Series C No. 270 (IACtHR, Judgment, 20 November 2013) paras 284, 349; *Santo Domingo v. Colombia*, Series C No. 259 (IACtHR, Judgment, 30 November 2012) para 256.

15 *Rio Negro v. Guatemala*, Series C No. 250 (IACtHR, Judgment, 4 September 2012) paras 172–184; *El Mozote v. El Salvador*, Series C No. 252 (IACtHR, Judgment, 25 October 2012) paras 187–188.

16 *Moiwana v. Suriname* (n 3) Separate Opinion of Judge A.A. Cançado Trindade, para 23.

17 UN Commission on Human Rights (Sub-commission), 'Final report of the Special Rapporteur Paulo Sérgio Pinheiro: Principles on housing and property restitution for refugees and displaced persons (Pinheiro Principles)' (28 June 2005) UN Doc. E/CN.4/Sub.2/2005/17, Principle 1(2); see also K Hassine and S Leckie, 'The United Nations Principles on Housing and Property Restitution for Refugees and Displaced Persons ('The Pinheiro Principles'): A Commentary' (Brill 2016) 8–16.

sions on reparations addressing both internal and cross-border displacement, or situations where international borders were contested.[18]

Furthermore, the recognition of the community's ongoing displacement as a continuing violation was instrumental in allowing the IACtHR to order any kind of reparation at all, owing to the limitations on its temporal jurisdiction.[19] Thus, the judgment laid significant groundwork for the IACtHR's approach in other cases where displacement had initially taken place before the state concerned had ratified the ACHR.[20]

2.3 *Pioneering Specific Forms of Reparation for Mass Displacement*

Moiwana v. Suriname was an early example of a case dealing with violations affecting a whole community, and particularly one made up of indigenous or tribal people who are the holders of collective rights in international law. As such, the IACtHR was required to develop innovative reparative measures which could benefit the community by addressing the collective damage caused, and which would take into account the particular harms of displacement in a context where connection to particular lands is fundamental to the community's cultural and physical survival.[21] Applying the general principle that integral reparation should be made as far as possible, the IACtHR therefore elaborated context-specific collective forms of reparation of a restitutive nature, as well as explicitly taking displacement-related harm into account in determining other reparative measures.

The main collective restitutive measure was the order to take legislative or administrative measures to secure the community's rights to its traditional lands. This effectively extended to similarly situated groups, as it required

18 *El Mozote v. El Salvador* (n 15) para 187; ACommHPR, *Sudan Human Rights Organisation (SHRO) & Centre on Housing Rights and Evictions (COHRE) v. Sudan*, 27 May 2009, Comm No 279/03–296/05, paras 67, 190, 229; *Đokić v. Bosnia*, (ECtHR, Judgment, 2010) para 44.

19 T Antkowiak (n 11) 269–270; F MacKay (n 3) 20–21; P A Ormachea, 'Moiwana Village: The Inter-American Court and the Continuing Violation Doctrine', (2006) 19 Harvard Human Rights Journal, 283–288.

20 *Sawhoyamaxa v. Paraguay*, Series C No 146, (IACtHR, Judgment, 29 March 2006) paras 131–141, 163–166; *Xákmok Kásek v. Paraguay*, Series C No. 214 (IACtHR, Judgment, 24 August 2010) paras 112–116, 214–217.

21 T Antkowiak (n 11) 269–270. On the requirements for collective reparation (collective beneficiary, collective harm and violation of international law in relation to the collective), see D Shelton, 'Remedies in International Human Rights Law' (Oxford University Press 2015), 252.

creation of a mechanism for demarcation, delimitation and titling of all indigenous and tribal land.[22] This was underpinned by the IACtHR's extension of its recognition of indigenous peoples' collective ownership of traditional land to tribal peoples as well. Had this not been the case, the Court may not have had grounds to recommend such far-reaching collective measures. The latter were visibly informed by the Court's approach of going beyond property rights to address the particular effects of the victims' separation from their land through displacement and their inability to return.[23] In this sense, facilitation of the victims' safe, dignified and voluntary return to their land was a clear underlying objective of measures such as the establishment of a community development fund, investigation of the massacre, and security guarantees for returnees.[24] To the extent that these measures served as guarantees of non-repetition or applied in respect of similarly situated communities, it could also be considered that they were for the benefit of the society as a whole.[25]

As for the IACtHR's supplementary order of individual monetary compensation, this explicitly took specific displacement-related material damage into account, as the IACtHR referred to community members' loss of homes, possessions and customary livelihoods, as well as their situation of deprivation while in displacement.[26] Regarding moral losses, the IACtHR also considered the aggravated suffering caused by the victims' separation from their traditional lands.[27] The reparative measures ordered in this case have inspired similar orders in later mass displacement cases before the IACtHR – in particular, those including forms of reparation which aim to make displaced people's voluntary choice of return or resettlement feasible in the particular context, such as security guarantees,[28] development programmes to ensure

22 T Antkowiak (n 11) 279–280; F MacKay (n 3) 23.

23 G Torres, 'Indigenous peoples, Afro-indigenous peoples and reparations', in F Lenzerini (ed.), *Reparations for Indigenous Peoples: International and Comparative Perspectives* (Oxford University Press 2008) 130.

24 See e.g. *Moiwana v. Suriname* (n 3) paras 209, 212–213.

25 On this function of reparative measures at the IACtHR, see J Schönsteiner 'Dissuasive Measures and the "Society as a Whole": A Working Theory of Reparations in the Inter-American Court of Human Rights' (2007–2008) 23 American University International Law Review 127.

26 *Moiwana v. Suriname* (n 3) paras 185–187.

27 *Moiwana v. Suriname* (n 3) para 191–196, 201.

28 *Mapiripán Massacre v. Colombia* (n 14) para 313; *Ituango Massacres v. Colombia* (n 12) para 404.

dignified living conditions at the site of return or resettlement,[29] and effective investigations and prosecutions of perpetrators.[30]

In recognizing prolonged displacement as a human rights violation and elaborating context-appropriate forms of reparation, the Inter-American Court's decision in *Moiwana v. Suriname* was at the forefront of broader normative developments on reparation for displacement. The following sections will illustrate how largely consistent developments manifested in decisions of other human rights bodies, as well as in differing contexts of displacement.

3 *Doğan and Others v. Turkey*: European Court of Human Rights

In this pair of mid-2000s judgments within a series of similar cases on internal conflict-related displacement in Turkey, the ECtHR assessed the state's compliance with the rights to peaceful enjoyment of possessions and respect for family life and the home. These judgments were notable in the European context for recognizing displaced people's right to restitution in principle; globally, they provide a landmark endorsement and articulation of states' duties to facilitate durable solutions for IDPs, irrespective of the state's involvement in their displacement.

3.1 *The Case and Its Findings*

The claim in *Doğan and others v. Turkey* arose from the situation of conflict in south-eastern Turkey between state security forces and the Workers' Party of Kurdistan (PKK) in the 1980s and 1990s – in particular, a context of heightened tensions near the village of Boydaş in 1994. The applicants – a group of former village inhabitants – alleged that security forces had forcibly evicted them and destroyed their homes, and that state authorities continued to deny them access to the village.[31] Turkey denied the security forces' involvement, claiming that residents had left because of PKK intimidation.[32]

The ECtHR decided not to rule on the initial displacement from the village, owing to insufficient evidence on this issue. Instead, the ECtHR focused on the state's denial of repeated requests to access the village. It found that this

29 *Río Negro v. Guatemala* (n 15) paras 284–285.

30 *El Mozote v. El Salvador* (n 15) paras 319–321; *Chichupac v. Guatemala*, Series C No. 328 (IACtHR, Judgment, 30 November 2016), para 285.

31 *Doğan and others v. Turkey*, App nos 8803–8811/02, 8813/02 and 8815–8819/02 (ECtHR, Judgment (merits), 29 June 2004) paras 11–18.

32 Ibid, para 22.

had interfered with the applicants' right to peaceful enjoyment of their possessions, as it had deprived them of livelihood resources and substantially affected their property ownership.[33] This was deemed disproportionate to the state's expressed security aims, as the applicants had consequently lived in extreme poverty for over ten years. State assistance was deemed inadequate and ineffective, as the village remained in ruins and the applicants had received only minimal financial aid. As such, the ECtHR found violations of the right to peaceful enjoyment of possessions (Protocol 1 to the European Convention on Human Rights (ECHR), Article 1), as well as the right to respect for family life and the home (ECHR, Article 8).[34] The state was also found to have violated the right to effective remedy (ECHR, Article 13), as it had not demonstrated that any domestic procedures could address the applicants' claim regarding their continuing displacement.[35]

In its just satisfaction judgment, the ECtHR framed its orders in the context of the state's duty to make integral reparation for human rights violations, i.e. restore the applicant's prior situation as far as possible. The ECtHR emphasized Turkey's discretion to choose the means to accomplish this, while asserting the Court's own competence to order appropriate reparation to the extent that domestic law did not permit this.[36]

The Court correlated the duty of integral reparation to a duty to establish the conditions and provide the means for IDPs to return to their homes or resettle elsewhere in the country, as expressed in the Guiding Principles. It observed that allowing the applicants to return and compensating them for losses caused by their prolonged displacement would align with this duty. However, noting that the applicants did not wish to return, the ECtHR ordered compensation for losses related to their inability to access their homes and property, such as damage to houses and barns (owing to deterioration), loss of earnings (in the context of a rural land-based livelihood) and the cost of alternative accommodation.[37] The ECtHR did not award any compensation for loss of the property as such, since the applicants remained the legal owners or possessors.[38] Reparation for non-pecuniary loss was limited to

33 Ibid, para 143.

34 Ibid, paras 153–160.

35 Ibid, paras 161–164, c.f. paras 106–108.

36 *Doğan v. Turkey*, App nos 8803–8811/02, 8813/02 and 8815–8819/02 (ECtHR, Judgment (just satisfaction), 13 July 2006) paras 45–46.

37 Ibid, paras 47–57.

38 *Doğan v. Turkey* (merits) (n 31) para 146.

declaration of a violation, as the state had in the meantime made efforts to remedy the situation of the applicant and others similarly situated.[39]

3.2 *Recognizing a Right to Restitution in Principle in Displacement Contexts*

The cases arising from claims of people displaced by the conflict in south-eastern Turkey were the first in which the ECtHR addressed the phenomenon of internal displacement. Although *Doğan v. Turkey* was not the first in this line of cases, it aptly illustrates the ECtHR's overall approach of recognizing the state's duty to make integral reparation as far as possible in displacement contexts, including a right to restitution in principle. This case was also the first to explicitly frame the underlying issue as one of internal displacement.[40] In contrast to the IACtHR's approach of specifically ordering comprehensive restitutive measures (as in *Moiwana v. Suriname*), the ECtHR's approach has been characterized by, on the one hand, recognizing a right to restitution in principle where this is possible, subject to the state's discretion in implementation; and on the other, compensating displaced people for losses incurred during displacement and recognizing the continued validity of their property rights.[41]

The ECtHR's repeated recognition of a state duty to make integral reparation in displacement contexts, operationalized through asserting the survival of displaced people's property rights (to preserve the possibility of restitution) coupled with compensation for other harms caused by displacement, was broadly significant for the development of international law regarding internal displacement. A right to restitution for displaced people, as outlined in the Guiding Principles, was not yet firmly established at that point,[42] and this

---

39 *Doğan v. Turkey* (just satisfaction) (n 36) para 61.

40 D Kurban, 'Human Rights Watch, Kurdish Human Rights Project, and The European Court of Human Rights on Internal Displacement in Turkey', in D Kurban et al. (eds), *Coming to Terms with Forced Migration: Post-Displacement Restitution of Citizenship Rights in Turkey* (TESEV 2007), 135–136.

41 See e.g. *Selçuk & Asker v. Turkey*, App nos 23184–23185/94 (ECtHR, Judgment, 24 April 1998) paras 104–125; *Menteş and Others v Turkey*, App no 58/1996/677/867 (ECtHR, Judgment (just satisfaction), 24 July 1998), paras 13–24. For cases where the retention of property rights is implicit (potentially because restoration of rights was not specifically claimed), see *Bilgin v. Turkey* App no 23819/94 (ECtHR, Judgment, 16 November 2000) paras 138–156; *Dulaş v. Turkey*, App no 25801/94 (ECtHR, Judgment, 30 January 2001), paras 84–104.

42 C Phuong, 'The International Protection of Internally Displaced Persons' (Cambridge University Press 2004) 64; R C Williams, 'Guiding Principle 29 and the right to restitution', (2008) GP10 Forced Migration Review 23–24.

jurisprudence of the ECtHR – along with similar decisions by other regional courts – was considered key in its consolidation.[43] The ECtHR maintained this overall approach not only in cases arising from the same context of south-eastern Turkey,[44] but also in conflict-related displacement cases against Turkey relating to the situation in Cyprus,[45] as well as similar cases against Russia, Armenia, and Azerbaijan.[46] In the Armenia/Azerbaijan cases in particular, the ECtHR elaborated on the issue of restitution by referring to regional standards developed since the *Doğan v. Turkey* case by the Parliamentary Assembly of the Council of Europe (PACE). In particular, these decisions cited a PACE Resolution endorsing the prioritization of restitution, given its role in ensuring that displaced persons retain a choice between return, local integration or resettlement.[47] The context in these cases differed from *Doğan* in that applicants had not necessarily expressed that they did not wish to return, but rather accepted that this was not yet feasible in light of the ongoing conflict.[48] In this light, the ECtHR cited Pinheiro Principle 21.1 on compensation as relevant (i.e. framing compensation as a supplementary, yet integral part of the restitution process),[49] and proceeded to award compensation on this basis.[50]

3.3 *Addressing State Duties to Facilitate Durable Solutions*

Doğan was the first – and to date, only – case in which the Guiding Principles have been explicitly referred to by the ECtHR.[51] Similarly to the Inter-American Court in *Moiwana*, the European Court employed Guiding Principle

---

43 S Bagshaw, 'Property restitution for IDP s: developments in the normative framework', in S Leckie (ed) *Returning Home: Housing and Property Restitution Rights of Refugees and Displaced Persons* (Transnational Publishers 2003).

44 See e.g. *Özkan v. Turkey* App no 21689/93 (ECtHR, Judgment, 6 April 2004) para 489.

45 See e.g. *Demades v. Turkey* App no 16219/90 (ECtHR, Judgment (just satisfaction), 31 July 2003), para 24.

46 *Esmukhambetov v. Russia* App no 23445/03(ECtHR, Judgment, 29 March 2011) paras 217–219.

47 Parliamentary Assembly (PA), 'Solving property issues of refugees and displaced persons', Resolution 1708 (2010), para 4, cited in *Chiragov v. Armenia* App No 13216/05 (ECtHR, Judgment (merits)) para 100; *Sargsyan v. Azerbaijan* (ECtHR, Judgment (merits)) para 100.

48 ECtHR, *Chiragov and others v. Armenia* App No 13216/05 (Judgment (just satisfaction), 12 December 2017) para 59; *Sargsyan v. Azerbaijan* App No 40167/06 (Judgment (just satisfaction), 12 December 2017) para 42.

49 *Chiragov v. Armenia* (merits) (n 47) para 98; *Sargsyan v. Azerbaijan* (merits) (n 47) para 96.

50 *Chiragov v. Armenia* (just satisfaction) (n 48) para 59; *Sargsyan v. Azerbaijan* (just satisfaction) (n 48) para 42.

51 *Doğan and others v. Turkey* App nos 8803–8811/02, 8813/02 and 8815–8819/02 (ECtHR (Third Section Judgment (just satisfaction), 13 July 2006) para 154; see further D Casalin,

28 – asserting a state duty to facilitate safe, dignified and voluntary return or resettlement within the country – to address resolution of displacement through durable solutions, of which reparation is one reinforcing element.[52] Notably, this was another element of the Guiding Principles that was deemed to represent a progressive development of international law at the time of drafting.[53]

Over and above the reference to the Guiding Principles, the Court's decision in this sense was viewed as ground-breaking in its recognition of positive state obligations to resolve displacement and ensure an adequate standard of living for displaced people.[54] This represented a broadening of the Court's analysis of displacement situations, which in previous cases had focused more narrowly on the right to access property.[55] According to Kurban, the judgment's broader tackling of the displacement situation characterizes it as a "pilot judgment" highlighting systemic issues with the state's programme to facilitate return.[56] However, unlike the Inter-American Court, the European Court did not address positive obligations in the operative part of its judgment by directly ordering measures to facilitate return or resettlement. Rather, as outlined by Torres, the Court's judgment regarding positive measures to facilitate durable solutions was based on a "complete diagnosis of the root causes of violations"[57] and provided specific recommendations on the remedial steps to be taken, with the legally binding status of this guidance playing a secondary role. This approach – also followed in the subsequent Armenia/Azerbaijan cases – was potentially taken with a view to fostering state cooperation in the implementation phase, especially given the socio-economic nature of the reparative measures and the need to coordinate them with broader development strategies.[58]

'The Guiding Principles in International Human Rights Courts' (2018) 59 Forced Migration Review, 42–43.

52 See UN General Assembly, Report of the Special Rapporteur on the human rights of internally displaced persons, UN Doc. A/73/173, 17 July 2018, paras 33–37, 42; Inter-Agency Standing Committee, *Framework on Durable Solutions for Internally Displaced Persons* (Brookings-Bern Project on Internal Displacement 2010) 43.

53 W Kälin (n 2) 84.

54 F E Torres, 'Reparations: To What End?' (n 2) 830–831.

55 W Kälin (n 2) 246.

56 D Kurban, 'Human Rights Watch, Kurdish Human Rights Project, and The European Court of Human Rights on Internal Displacement in Turkey' in D Kurban et al (eds) (n 40) 134–136.

57 F E Torres, 'Reparations: To What End?' (n 2) 831.

58 Ibid, 830–832. On specificity of remedial recommendations manifesting in follow-up processes rather than the text of the judgment, see R Murray and C Sandoval, 'Balancing

In this regard, the Court's subsequent judgment on just satisfaction noted that in the interim, the state had passed a law introducing compensation commissions for displaced people denied access to their homes and possessions. In an admissibility decision on a similar case arising from the same context, but considered by the Court after this law had been passed, the Court had assessed the law and concluded that the state had fulfilled its duty to address the systemic issue identified in *Doğan* and provide and effective remedy. The application was therefore found inadmissible.[59] However, the Court did not link this law to the state's duty to facilitate durable solutions or evaluate it in this light. From this perspective, the compensation law reportedly did not cover "the costs of medical, legal, social and other services" or "post-displacement costs of living",[60] and thus did not remedy inadequacies in material assistance to facilitate return, or the lack of integration support for IDP s choosing to remain in urban areas.[61]

4 *Endorois v. Kenya*: African Commission on Human and Peoples' Rights

In this 2009 decision, the ACHPR found violations of a number of collective rights in the African Charter (namely, to collective property, religion and culture, development, and natural resources) regarding a pastoralist community evicted from their traditional land for the creation of a nature reserve. This remains one of few cases where a human rights treaty has been interpreted and applied to address development-induced displacement, as well as formulate reparative measures while taking into account legitimate state and societal interests in development.

Specificity of Reparation Measures and States' Discretion to Enhance Implementation', (2020) 12 Journal of Human Rights Practice 101. See also section 5.2. Below on CESCR's approach to state policy space in making socio-economic remedial recommendations.

59 *Doğan v. Turkey* (just satisfaction) para 6 (c.f. *İçyer v. Turkey* App no 18888/02 (ECtHR, Decision (admissibility), 12 January 2006) para 73–87. For a broader critique of this law and details on the circumstances around its adoption, see D Kurban, *Reparations and Displacement in Turkey: Lessons Learned from the Compensation Law* (International Centre for Transitional Justice 2012).

60 D Kurban, *Reparations and Displacement in Turkey* (n 59) 14.

61 Ibid, 9; D Kurban et al, 'Towards a Solution to Turkey's Internal Displacement Problem: Social Reconciliation and Rehabilitation', in D Kurban et al (eds) (n 40) 318–319.

4.1 *The Case and Its Findings*

The African Commission decision in *CEMIRIDE & Minority Rights Group (on behalf of the Endorois Welfare Council) v. Kenya* addressed the eviction of the Endorois pastoralist community from their traditional land in the 1970s to make way for a game reserve.[62] After their eviction, the Endorois dispersed into different locations near the reserve. They were unable to secure their livelihoods or perform key cultural and religious rites, as their access to grazing land and other resources in the reserve, as well as their sacred lake, was heavily restricted.[63] Their land was subsequently exploited and alienated without benefit accruing to them – first, as a game reserve, and later on, through demarcation and sale of parts of the land and the granting of ruby mining concessions.[64]

The Commission examined the Endorois' eviction and ongoing situation of displacement in light of a number of collective rights under the African Charter. The separation of the Endorois from sacred land and their relocation to an area unsuitable for herding were deemed to breach their rights to religious freedom and culture.[65] The Commission also found the Endorois' rights and interests in their traditional lands, as well as the benefits thereof, constituted property under the African Charter,[66] and that the continuing and severe interference was "not proportionate to any public need".[67] As the legality or public interest of granting concessions over the Endorois' natural resources had not been assessed, the Endorois' rights over these resources were also found to have been violated by the subsequent use of their land.[68] Finally, various aspects of the eviction process breached the right to development, namely: negation of the Endorois' choice of residence; inadequate information on their eviction; denial of their participation and consultation via their

---

62 *Centre for Minority Rights Development and Minority Rights Group on behalf of Endorois Welfare Council (Endorois) v. Kenya*, Comm No 276/03 (ACommHPR, 25 November 2009) para 3–7, 16; Kenya Truth, Justice and Reconciliation Commission (TJRC), 'Final Report: Vol. IIB, Chapter 2', para 410–412, https://digitalcommons.law.seattleu.edu/tjrc-core/5/.

63 *Endorois v. Kenya* (n 62) para 16–17, 80, 99, 115, 126; see also the testimonies of Toyoi Tekamoi and Kipteroi Kibet (Endorois community members) and Charles Kamuren (then Endorois Welfare Council chairman), in Witness et al, 'CEMIRIDE & Minority Rights Group, Endorois' Struggle for Justice' (video documentary), 2007, 4:25–4:45, 8:50–9:40, https://www.youtube.com/watch?v=kl6XSG6quMo&t=113s.

64 *Endorois v. Kenya* (n 62) para 7, 13–14, 111, 124, 227, 297. See also the testimony of Richard Arap Yegon (Endorois community elder), in Witness et al (n 63) 9:45–11:05.

65 *Endorois v. Kenya* (n 62) para 173, 251.

66 Ibid, para 187.

67 Ibid, para 238.

68 Ibid, para 267–268.

chosen representatives (the Endorois Welfare Committee); and inadequate compensation for appropriation of their land or benefit-sharing from its subsequent use.[69] This specific interpretation and application of the right to development is a key contribution of this case to the development of international human rights law on reparations in development-induced displacement contexts.[70]

Consequently, the Commission recommended the following collective reparation measures: restitution of the Endorois' ancestral land; granting of access to sites for grazing and religious/cultural rites; compensation for losses suffered; community benefit-sharing in economic activities on their land; and registration of the Endorois Welfare Committee.[71]

4.2 *Putting Development-Induced Displacement on the Reparations Map*

Endorois was the first ACHPR decision on development-induced displacement. Especially given the prevalence of displacement and relocation linked to development projects in Africa, *Endorois* was significant in interpreting and applying states' human rights obligations under the African Charter to these phenomena – including obligations to make reparation to displaced people. The Kampala Convention – an African Union regional treaty on the protection and assistance of internally displaced persons – has since become a central point of reference on development-induced displacement in Africa.[72] However, the Commission's decision – which predates the Convention's entry into force in 2012 – remains an important precedent for human rights analysis of development-induced displacement in Africa, especially regarding states which have not ratified or domesticated the Kampala Convention. Further-

69 Ibid, para 279–298.

70 Regarding the right to development, the African Charter on Human and Peoples' Rights provides that "[a]ll peoples shall have the right to their economic, social and cultural development with due regard to their freedom and identity and in the equal enjoyment of the common heritage of mankind" (African Charter on Human and Peoples' Rights, adopted June 27, 1981, OAU Doc. CAB/LEG/67/3 rev. 5, 21 ILM 58 (1982), adopted 27 June 1981, entered into force 21 October 1986, Article 22(1)). The UN Declaration on the Right to Development holds that "every human person and all peoples are entitled to participate in, contribute to, and enjoy economic, social, cultural and political development, in which all human rights and fundamental freedoms can be fully realized" (UN General Assembly, Declaration on the Right to Development, General Assembly Resolution 41/128, 4 December 1986, Article 1(1)).

71 *Endorois v. Kenya* (n 62) recommendations 1(f) – (g) & 2.

72 Kampala Convention, Article 10; see further R Adeola, 'The Legal Protection of Development-Induced Displaced Persons in Africa' (2017) 10 African Journal of Legal Studies 91.

more, the African Commission's interpretation of the African Charter may need to be read and applied in conjunction with the Convention.[73]

In this case, the Commission approached development-induced displacement from the perspective of peoples' rights expressed in the African Charter. It carefully navigated controversies around indigenous rights in an African context by contextualizing them within the framework of peoples' rights more broadly and focusing on current marginalization and exclusion, as well equality with other groups. This was a positive step in counteracting increasing pressure on marginalized groups from exclusionary development projects.[74] In terms of protection from and reparation for displacement, it is especially significant that the Commission recognized indigenous peoples' rights to collective ownership of their land (rather than merely access), as well as their rights to natural resources and the requirement of their free, prior and informed consent to any development or investment activity with a major impact on their land.[75]

The Commission also defined human rights-based criteria for balancing the interests of indigenous and marginalized peoples and the state regarding economic development activities.[76] In this sense, the Commission's interpretation of the right to development is particularly relevant for contexts of development-induced displacement and relocation, as it highlights that states are obliged to include indigenous people both in development processes (through consultation and participation) and development outcomes (through benefit-sharing).[77] Thus, the Commission concretely aimed to reconcile indigenous peoples' rights and conservation activities, which have often been viewed in opposition to each other in a context of frequent eviction of marginalized communities for conservation and tourism in African states.[78] As the right to

---

73 See e.g. ibid, 99–101, on consultation and participation.

74 *Endorois v. Kenya*, para 149. D Inman, D Cambou and S Smis, 'Evolving Legal Protection for Indigenous Peoples in Africa: Some Post-UNDRIP Reflections', (2018) 26 African Journal of International and Comparative Law, 339, 363–364; A Korir Sing'Oei and J Shephard, "In Land We Trust": The Endorois' Communication and the Quest for Indigenous Peoples' Rights in Africa', (2010) 16 Buffalo Human Rights Law Review 57, 70–76.

75 A Korir Sing'Oei and J Shephard (n 75) 77–82; D Inman et al (n 70) 362–364; G Lynch, 'Becoming Indigenous in Pursuit of Justice: The African Commission on Human and Peoples' Rights and the Endorois' (2011) African Affairs 111/442, 24–45.

76 A Korir Sing'Oei and J Shephard (n 75) 80.

77 J Gilbert, 'Litigating Indigenous Peoples' Rights in Africa: Potentials, Challenges and Limitations' (2017) 66 International & Comparative Law Quarterly 657, 663–664; Inman et al (n 70) 364; A Korir Sing'Oei and J Shephard (n 75) 81–82; G Lynch (n 76) 40.

78 C Morel, 'Conservation and Indigenous Peoples' Rights: Must One Necessarily Come at the Expense of the Other?' (2010) 17 Policy Matters, 174, 180–181; J Gilbert (n 78) 663–664.

development does not only apply to indigenous peoples, the principles developed here may be applied to other marginalized collectives with a particular attachment to their lands which face displacement in the context of development activities.

4.3 *Recommending Reparation in the Context of State/Societal Interests in Development*

Beyond attempting to reconcile community and state/societal interests on the merits, the Commission sought to strike a similar balance in justifying its remedial recommendations aimed at redressing the Endorois' eviction and dispossession – particularly, restitution and benefit-sharing.

Regarding restitution, the Commission had to respond to state arguments that measures to allow access to the land sufficed as a restitutive measure, and that recognition of the community's ownership rights was therefore unnecessary.[79] The Commission justified the particular importance of recognizing ownership rights in this context by pointing to a state duty to protect indigenous peoples' rights from further violations and ensure that they could actively engage with the state and third parties.[80] Furthermore, the Commission referred to the community's willingness and ability to cooperate on conservation.[81]

In response to the Endorois' claim regarding denial of financial benefits from the use of their land,[82] the Commission also recommended that the state pay royalties to the Endorois and ensure they would benefit from employment opportunities at the game reserve.[83] The Commission justified this by interpreting "just compensation" in the African Charter to include a right to "reasonably share in the benefits made as a result of a restriction or deprivation of their right to the use and enjoyment of (…) traditional lands and of those natural resources necessary for (…) survival."[84]

---

79 See *Endorois v. Kenya*, paras 178–180 (state position) & recommendations (a) & (b); on the state's position, see further: National Assembly of Kenya, 'Response by James Orengo, Minister of Lands', *Questions by private notice: property rights for pastoralists /marginalized groups*, Official Report, 18 January 2011, 18, https://info.mzalendo.com/hansard/sitting/national_assembly/2011-01-18-14-30-00.

80 *Endorois v. Kenya*, paras 188, 191, 202, 204.

81 Ibid, para 235.

82 Ibid, para 99, 124.

83 Ibid, recommendation (d).

84 Ibid, para 295. See also African Charter on Popular Participation in Development and Transformation, 1990, Part I, para 7, https://www.ircwash.org/sites/default/files/70-UNECA90–7322.pdf; UN Declaration on the Right to Development (n 67) Article 2(3).

Thus, the Commission contextualized both restitution and benefit-sharing not only as means to redress the community's losses, but also as mechanisms to ensure that the rights and participation of a currently marginalized group were protected and promoted. Simultaneously, it acknowledged broader state and societal interests of an economic and ecological nature in conservation and wildlife tourism.[85] Thus, the Commission set a precedent for later reparation decisions in cases where forest-dwelling peoples had been evicted for conservation, both in its own jurisprudence and that of the African Court on Human and Peoples' Rights.[86]

5 *I.D.G. v. Spain*: Committee on Economic, Social, and Cultural Rights

In this first merits decision issued by CESCR under its individual communications procedure in 2015, the right to adequate housing – as well as a corresponding state duty to take measures to protect this right – was applied in the context of widespread mortgage evictions in Spain. This case provides a relatively exceptional example of a state being held accountable at the international level for protecting the right to adequate housing against third parties – in particular, through the issuing of remedial recommendations in the forms of structural guarantees of non-repetition.

5.1 *The Case and Its Findings*

I.D.G. v. Spain addressed a context of widespread mortgage foreclosures and evictions which was brought to a head by the global economic crisis of 2008.[87] The applicant's claim related to her situation of impending eviction as a result

85 On the importance of benefit-sharing in balancing these interests with the rights of local communities in Kenya, see P Kameri-Mbote, 'Wildlife conservation and community property rights in Kenya', in P Kameri-Mbote et al (eds), *Law | Environment | Africa* (Nomos 2019) 221–246, at 226–228, 233–235; World Bank Group, *Kenya's Tourism: Polishing the Gem – Finance and Private Sector Development, Africa Region, Final Report* (World Bank Group 2010) pp. 14–44.

86 See e.g. *ACommHPR v. Kenya* Application 006/2012 (ACtHPR, Judgment, 26 May 2017 and Judgment (Reparations), 23 June 2022); L Claridge, 'Litigation as a Tool for Community Empowerment: The Case of Kenya's Ogiek', (2018) 11 Erasmus Law Review, 57; *Minority Rights Group and Environnement Resources Naturelles et Développement (on behalf of the Batwa of Kahuzi-Biega National Park, DRC) v. Democratic Republic of Congo*, Comm No 588/15 (ACommHPR, 21 April – 13 May 2022).

87 *Report of the Special Rapporteur on adequate housing as a component of the right to an adequate standard of living, Miloon Kothari, Addendum – Mission to Spain*, A/HRC/7/16/Add.2, 7 February 2008, para 50–56.

of a special mortgage enforcement procedure, in a context where 400 000 evictions and foreclosures had been carried out over the seven preceding years.[88]

After the applicant had missed a number of mortgage payments on her home owing to financial difficulties, the lending bank had launched an executive foreclosure procedure in 2012. Following unsuccessful attempts to notify I.D.G. in person at her home address, the court enforcement service affixed the notification at the court. I.D.G. claimed she had only become aware of the foreclosure after auction proceedings were initiated. At that point, her home was to be auctioned in fifteen days and she had no alternative accommodation.[89]

The applicant alleged that the failure to notify her adequately of the proceedings had violated her right to a defence and to effective legal protection, in particular because notification should have only taken place via the court's notice board if other measures had been exhausted.[90]

As a reparative measure, I.D.G. requested that the state reverse the enforcement proceedings to the point of the initial notification, to allow her to defend her right to adequate housing before the courts. More broadly, in addition, she requested that the state adopt appropriate legislative measures to guarantee the right to adequate housing.[91]

In reaching its findings, the CESCR declined to examine the adequacy of the state's legislation, as it found that the outcome would depend on whether the notification procedure followed had actually affected I.D.G.'s ability to defend her rights.[92] It found that the state had not exhausted all reasonable means to notify I.D.G. in before proceeding to public posting, and that I.D.G. had in fact been deprived of the possibility to defend herself and access an effective remedy. The Committee therefore concluded that the state had violated her right to adequate housing.[93]

88 *I.D.G. v. Spain*, CESCR, Comm. 2/2014, 17 June 2015, paras 3.1.–3.6.

89 Ibid, para 2.2–2.6; J Solís, 'No puede haber un modo privilegiado de notificar las demandas de los bancos', Voz Populi, 4 October 2015, https://www.vozpopuli.com/actualidad/sociedad/Desahucios-ONU-Derechos-Naciones_Unidas-ejecuciones_hipotecarias-hipotecas-Fernando_Ron-abogado-ley_espanola-ley_hipotecaria_0_849515042.html.

90 *I.D.G. v. Spain* (n 94) paras 2.7–2.8; J Solís (n 95).

91 *I.D.G. v. Spain* (n 94) para 3.6 (see para 3.3. re the non-material damage alleged).

92 Ibid, para 13.5.

93 Ibid, para 13.3, 14–15.

In respect of the individual author's situation, the CESCR recommended that the auction procedure be suspended until due procedural protection and due process were made available.[94] Regarding the broader situation, general measures were recommended to ensure accessibility of legal remedies for people facing mortgage enforcement procedures; strict limitation of notification by public posting; and alignment of residential eviction or auction procedures with the right to adequate housing.[95]

5.2 *Holding States Accountable for Ensuring Protection against Arbitrary Evictions*

I.D.G. v. Spain was not only the CESCR's first decision on evictions, but the very first merits decision that it issued overall. By focusing on procedural aspects of the right to adequate housing rather than reviewing policy decisions, this decision struck a delicate balance between respecting state policy space and promoting accountability for protection of economic, social and cultural rights. State accountability was reinforced by emphasizing effective remedy for interference with the right to adequate housing, as well as detailed interpretation of procedural requirements in mortgage eviction contexts.[96]

Regarding the right to an effective remedy, the CESCR applied this for the first time in a context of mortgage enforcement and confirmed that, just as in other eviction situations, this is immediately applicable to people whose right to adequate housing might be affected.[97] Furthermore, by focusing on the regulation and enforcement of fair procedures and access to remedy, the CESCR seized a crucial opportunity to clarify states' obligations to exercise

94 Ibid, para 16.

95 Ibid, para 17.

96 S Liebenberg, 'Between Sovereignty and Accountability: The Emerging Jurisprudence of the United Nations Committee on Economic, Social and Cultural Rights Under the Optional Protocol' (2020) 42 Human Rights Quarterly 48, 65, 68, 82–84; S Sun, 'Five Years after the Entry of Force of the Optional Protocol to the International Covenant on Economic, Social and Cultural Rights: Some Observations' (2018) 17 Journal of Human Rights 625, 633; B Porter, 'Reasonableness and Article 8(4)', in M Langford et al (eds), *The Optional Protocol to the International Covenant on Economic, Social and Cultural Rights: A Commentary* (Pretoria University Law Press 2016) 173–202, 199; J C Benito Sánchez, 'The UN Committee on Economic, Social and Cultural Rights' Decision in *I.D.G. v. Spain*: the right to housing and mortgage foreclosures' (2016) European Journal of Human Rights 320,333–339; E Durojaye, 'Bringing justice to the disadvantaged: a commentary on CESCR's decision in IDG v Spain (Communication No. 2/2014)' (2015) 16 ESR Review: Economic and Social Rights in South Africa 10, 11.

97 *I.D.G. v. Spain*, para 11.4.

due diligence in displacement contexts where private economic actors are the key players impacting individuals' rights.[98]

The decision also further clarified procedural obligations in foreclosure situations by setting standards for the serving of notices.[99] In this regard, the CESCR outlined that all reasonable steps should be taken to ensure proper and effective notice of judicial or administrative proceedings, to allow the affected person to participate and defend their rights.[100] Thus, the CESCR set concrete parameters for regulating and applying mortgage eviction procedures in conformity with the right to adequate housing, as well as offering a relatively uncommon example of how a state's responsibility can be engaged where it fails to protect economic and social rights against third parties in displacement contexts.[101]

5.3 *Developing Structural Guarantees of Non-repetition for Widespread Evictions*

I.D.G. was also the CESCR's first opportunity to exercise its broad discretion to craft remedial recommendations. In addition to individual remedial recommendations, the CESCR notably opted for broader structural recommendations as well. The latter aimed not only to remedy the situation of the individual complainant but also to address underlying systemic issues.[102] In this case, these issues flowed from application of a special express mortgage enforcement procedure. Given the high prevalence of foreclosures at the time, the CESCR's structural recommendations regarding access to effective remedy, limitation of public posting of notifications and legislative incorporation of

98 E Durojaye (n 103) 10–11; M Langford, 'Substantive Obligations', in M Langford et al (eds) (n 103) 223.

99 J C Benito Sánchez (n 103) 333–336, 339; M Langford (n 103) 223–225.

100 *I.D.G. v. Spain*, paras 12.2–12.4.

101 On the more common employment of due diligence obligations to investigate violations of civil and political rights and/or a requirement of state collusion in displacement cases involving non-state actors, see respectively F E Torres, 'Economic and Social Rights, Reparations and the Aftermath of Widespread Violence' (n 2) 943–946; F E Torres, 'The State, the Assailant?' (n 2) 20–23.

102 S Sun, 'Five Years after the Entry of Force' (n 103) 637–639; V Krsticevic and B Griffey, 'Remedial Recommendations', in M Langford et al (eds) (n 95), 331–333, 341–346, 356; R Izquierdo and A L Ugalde, 'La actividad cuasi-judicial del sistema de protección universal del Comité de Derechos Económicos, Sociales y Culturales, Comité para la Protección de los Trabajadores Migrantes y Comité para la Protección de las Personas Discapacitadas: alcance y limitaciones', in H Olásolo Alonso et al (eds), *Alcance y limitaciones de la justicia internacional*, Vol. 4 (Tirant Lo Blanch 2018), 221–252, 230–232.

other procedural protections were relevant beyond the individual claimant's situation as guarantees of non-repetition in favour of the broader society.

As a quasi-judicial body whose general recommendations cannot directly effect changes in the domestic policy space, the CESCR has significant scope to elaborate on the structural aspects of a situation which domestic measures need to address to guarantee non-repetition of violations of socio-economic rights.[103] In response to a large number of subsequent claims relating to the Spanish eviction crisis, the CESCR has had the opportunity to progressively elaborate and expand the general recommendations in *I.D.G.* to address additional structural issues relating to the right to adequate housing (as well as differently situated claimants, such as tenants and occupiers without title) in this context. Such recommendations have included the reform of legislation which did not ensure adequate protection from or access to remedy for forced eviction; measures to ensure the provision of adequate alternative accommodation for evictees; the development of a plan to ensure sufficient availability of social housing; and the repeal of exclusions from social housing based on previous occupation of housing without title.[104] In this way, the CESCR has developed a range of guarantees of non-repetition which address the specificities of displacement situations resulting from widespread judicialized evictions that are carried out in terms of domestic law, but nevertheless linked to inadequate protection of the right to adequate housing.

---

103 For discussion on the binding nature of UN human rights treaty bodies' recommendations at the domestic level, especially in the Spanish context, see Tribunal Supremo – Sala Tercera, de lo Contencioso-Administrativo, STS 1263/2018, 17 de julio de 2018, Part II, para 5; J C Benito Sánchez, 'Los pronunciamentos del Comité DESC sobre derecho a la vivienda relativos a España' (2019) 9 Lex Social 584, 597; K Casla, 'Supreme Court of Spain: UN Treaty Body individual decisions are legally binding', EJIL: Talk!, 1 August 2018, https://www.ejiltalk.org/supreme-court-of-spain-un-treaty-body-individual-decisions-are-legally-binding/.

104 For recommendations regarding rental evictions, see *Ben Djazia & Bellili v. Spain*, CESCR, Comm. No. 5/2015, UN Doc. E/C.12/61/D/5/2015, 20 June 2017, para 18–21; *Gómez-Limón Pardo v. Spain*, CESCR, Comm. No. 52/2018, E/C.12/67/D/52/2018, 5 March 2020, para 13–14. Regarding occupants without title, see *López Albán v. Spain*, CESCR, Comm. No. 37/2018, E/C.12/66/D/37/2018, 11 October 2019, para 14–17; *El Goumari & Tidli v. Spain*, CESCR, Comm. No. 85/2018, E/C.12/69/D/85/2018, 18 February 2021, 14–17; *El Ayoubi & El Azouan Azouz v. Spain*, CESCR, Comm. No. 54/2018, E/C.12/69/D/54/2018, 19 February 2021, para 14–17.

6 Conclusion

The above analysis offers insights into how the broader jurisprudence of regional and UN human rights judicial and quasi-judicial bodies has consolidated key points of international human rights law on reparations in contexts of displacement. In response to the claims of displaced people, these bodies have recognized the right of displaced people to restitution and developed supplementary forms of reparation. They have also broken new ground by addressing a growing range of concrete displacement situations, from conflict displacement to development-induced displacement to widespread judicialized evictions. The contribution of this jurisprudence has converged across systems regarding the framing of displacement as a human rights violation, which in principle gives rise to an individual or communal right to reparation, where this had not yet been explicitly addressed in the underlying human rights treaties. This has overall strengthened the consolidation of progressive developments which had been introduced in the Guiding Principles – in particular, their recognition of a right to restitution for internally displaced people. In these decisions, regional and international human rights bodies have also developed context-specific reparative orders/recommendations aiming to address and prevent the recurrence of the particular harms of displacement.

The Guiding Principles were explicitly invoked and endorsed in the cases dealing with conflict displacement (*Moiwana* and *Doğan*, before the IACtHR and ECtHR respectively). However, this was not the case in the decisions dealing with development-induced displacement (*Endorois*, ACHPR) and evictions (*I.D.G.*, CESCR), even though the Guiding Principles' scope is broad enough to encompass such situations. Instead, the latter two decisions respectively employed the right to development and the right to adequate housing to frame the impacts of displacement and the interests at stake beyond a balancing of property rights.

Thus, regional and international human rights bodies have contributed to consolidating and elaborating international human rights law on reparations for displacement through application and interpretation in concrete cases. Despite striking convergence in principle on restitution and other forms of reparation for displaced people, these decisions inevitably exhibit some differences in how they address these matters more concretely with an eye to implementation. This is to be expected given the differing nature and practice of the bodies from which they emanate. However, this does not detract from these decisions' value as rich precedents which are flexible enough to be adapted to inform and underpin various types of reparation efforts at different levels. At the same time, they offer interpretations of principles of international human rights law on reparation which can be more broadly applied beyond the regional and UN human rights bodies, including to forms of arbitrary displacement that have not yet been addressed in regional or international claims.

CHAPTER 3

Translating Principles into Practice: Collective Reparation and Harm Assessment across International Tribunals

Diana Odier-Contreras Garduno

1 Introduction

Collective reparations, also known as transformative or administrative reparations, are the most common response to address the consequences and harm caused by gross violations of human rights and egregious international crimes.[1] As such, these measures have become the hallmark of international human rights courts, such as the Inter-American Court of Human Rights (IACtHR),[2] as well as international criminal tribunals such as the International Criminal Court (ICC) and the Extraordinary Chambers of the Court of Cambodia (ECCC), when granting reparations to victims of such serious crimes.[3] Admittedly, the difference in the nature of these courts influence the form in which CR are implemented.

Collective reparations (CR) commonly take the form of social projects (i.e., housing, educational, and health programmes), infrastructural projects (i.e., improvements on road and water systems), community development programmes (i.e., construction of community centres or community funds) and symbolic measures (i.e. memorials, renaming a street). There are compelling arguments in favour of the use of CR by judicial and non-judicial bodies adju-

1 This response has been embraced by governments and non-judicial bodies, such as truth commissions and mass claims processes See: Diana Odier-Contreras Garduno, *Collective Reparations: Tensions and Dilemmas Between Collective Reparations with the Individual Right to Receive Reparations* (Intersentia 2018) 4–5; International Center for Transitional Justice, 'The Rabat Report: The Concept and Challenges of Collective Reparations' (ICTJ 2009); Pablo de Greiff (ed) *The Handbook of Reparations* (OUP 2006).

2 Elizabeth Odio Benito, 'Development and Interpretation of Principles of Reparation: the Case Law of the IACHR and its Possible Contributions to the Jurisprudence of the ICC' in Chile Eboe-Osuji (ed), *Protecting Humanity: Essays in International Law and Policy in Honour of Navanethem Pillay* (Nijhoff 2010).

3 Christoph Sperfeldt, *Practices of Reparations in International Criminal Justice* (CUP 2022); Nadia Tapia Navarro, 'Collective Reparations and the Limitations of International Criminal Justice to Respond to Mass Atrocity' (2018) 18 International Criminal Law Review.

 | DOI:10.1163/9789004716742_004

dicating serious crimes. First, gross violations of human rights often affect groups or substantial number of victims, impacting communities and disrupting their social structure. Contrary to individual measures, collective reparations can address the collective dimension of harm caused by serious crimes.[4] In this context, CR aim to transform and reconstruct the social reality of marginalised victims including groups and serve as a symbolic expression of solidarity with affected groups or communities.[5] CR are moreover, seen as a feasible response to the key challenges in these cases, such as the large number of victims, lack of evidence, and limited resources.[6] In addition, they are believed to have the potential to *transform* or, at the very least contribute to, the *transformation* of structural disparities and underlying causes of victimisation.[7]

Despite their justifications, CR possesses several dangers. To begin with, they do not equally address the material loss and individual suffering experienced by victims as a result of gross violations of human rights. CR can be easily mistaken for humanitarian aid, development programmes, or the states' obligations to provide basic social rights necessary for a minimum standard of dignified living. When reparations are formulated as social projects, there exists a potential risk of obscuring the distinction between social assistance and reparations, and the risk of diminishing the alleviation of victims' suffering as they are not specifically aimed at victims.[8]

While some of the dangers when using CR may be prevented, their use also raises ethical dilemmas. Firchow argues that distinguishing collective remedial measures from other state obligations and development programmes is possible. First of all, states must recognise the human rights violations suffered by victims, and then ensure their active participation in the implementation of the CR awarded. Yet, collective reparations may imply that marginalised

4 Frédéric Mégret, 'The Case for Collective Reparations before the International Criminal Court', in Jo-Anne M. Wemmers (ed), *Reparations for Victims of Crimes against Humanity: The Healing Role of Reparation* (Routledge 2014) 180.

5 Ibid.

6 Lisa Magarrell, 'Reparations in Theory and Practice, Reparative Justice Series' (ICTJ, 2007) 6; Rodrigo Uprimny Yepes, 'Transformative Reparations of Massive Gross Human Rights Violations: Between Corrective and Distributive Justice' (2009) 27 Netherlands Quarterly of Human Rights 4.

7 Ruth Rubio-Marín, 'The Gender of Reparations in Transitional Societies' in Ruth Rubio Marín (ed), The Gender of Reparations: Unsettling Sexual Hierarchies While Redressing Human Rights Violations (CUP 2009) 63, 66.

8 CR may eventually benefit non-victims and even perpetrators are they target communities. See The Rabat Report (n 1) 11.

communities must 'bleed' to receive basic social services.[9] Moreover, it is important to highlight that CR have gained widespread acceptance as means of *repairing* the harm and *addressing* the consequences endured by victims of widespread human rights violation, but their reparative effect can be questioned.[10]

Uprimny, however, sees CR as a way to bridge social services and provide redress to those victims of serious human rights violations who generally live in conditions characterised by widespread poverty.[11] According to him, CR have the potential to transform inequalities and complement broader development policies in a given place. In practice, the risk nevertheless exists that social services may only be provided for a limited period, as collective reparations are often framed as short-term projects. This makes them appealing alternatives for the permanent provision of services that governments are obligated to deliver.[12] Therefore, if granted as temporal substitutes for social services, CR may even exacerbate the harm experienced by victims.[13]

The use of collective reparations was first implemented in transitional justice processes across Latin America, which were typically referred to as 'Domestic Administrative Programmes'.[14] This approach was found to be the

9 Pamina Firchow, 'Must our communities bleed to receive social services? Development projects and collective reparations schemes in Colombia' (2013) 8 Journal of Peacebuilding and Development 50, 50–63.

10 Diana Contreras-Garduno, 'Defining Beneficiaries of Collective Reparations: The experience of the IACtHR' (2012) 4 *Amsterdam Law Forum 3*, 48 citing Malarino: "Only when putting a lot of effort, one could argue that the construction of a sewage system, a water system or improving roads, to cite a few examples, 'repair' the victims of a massacres". See: Ezequiel. Malarino, 'Activismo Judicial, Punitivización y Nacionalización. Tendencias Antidemocráticas y Antiliberales de la Corte Interamericana de Derechos Humanos', in Grupo Latinoamericano de Estudios sobre Derecho Penal International, *Sistema Interamericano de Protección de los Derechos Humanos y Derecho Penal Internacional* (Konrad-Adenauer-Stiftung 2010) 69.

11 Uprimny refers to collective reparations in the form of social services as transformative reparations. See: Uprimny Yepes (n 6) 625–647.

12 Pamina Firchow, 'The Implementation of the Institutional Programme of Collective Reparations in Colombia' (2014) 6 Journal of Human Rights Practice, 356–357.

13 *The Prosecutor v Dominic Ongwen* (Reparations Order) ICC-02/04-01/15 (28 February 2024) para. 619.

14 Some examples include the reparation programs established by the government of Chile and Guatemala as well as those established by truth commissions in Morocco, Liberia, Peru, and Sierra Leone in Diana Odier-Contreras Garduno, 'Collective reparations in Colombia: a tool for the non-repetition of violations?' in Michiel Luchtman et al. (eds), *Of Swords and Shields: Due Process and Crime Control in Times of Globalization. Liber Amicorum Prof.dr. J.A.E. Vervaele* (Eleven 2023) 741–742; Cristian Correa, 'Reparation Programs for Mass Violations of Human Rights: Lessons from Experiences in Argentina,

most victim-friendly method of reparations as it could be labelled as a 'good enough' effort to provide symbolic recognition to a large number of victims.[15] Although CR were constructed outside the legal framework that prioritises individual rights, they entered the international judicial arena in 1993 in the *Aloeboetoe case* before the Inter-American Court of Human Rights.[16] Since then, the IACtHR has continuously awarded collective reparations as an adequate means of fulfilling the right to reparation for large numbers of victims.[17]

The IACtHR accordingly serves as the starting point for this analysis due to its significant role in shaping the international legal standards for CR. The IACtHR has developed a robust approach centred on state responsibility for human rights violations, emphasising transformative justice to address structural inequalities affecting marginalised communities. Its approach has set a precedent for other supranational bodies,[18] a fact frequently highlighted in academic literature on the broader international law of reparations.[19]

The use of CR extended beyond the realm of human rights courts into international criminal tribunals, such as the ICC. As the first permanent international criminal tribunal with jurisdiction over individuals, the ICC addresses severe crimes such as genocide, war crimes and crimes against humanity, focusing on individual accountability. Offering a distinct perspective on awarding CR,[20] the ICC is also guided by Article 21(3) of the Rome Statute, which mandates alignment with internationally recognised human rights,[21]

Chile and Peru' in Felix Reategui (ed), *Transitional Justice Handbook for Latin America* (Brazilian Ministry of Justice Amnesty Commission 2011) 409–413.

15 Brandon Hamber, 'The Dilemmas of Reparations: In Search of a Process-driven Approach' in K De Feyter, S Parmentier, M Bossuyt and P Lemmens (eds), *Out of the Ashes: Reparations for Victims of Gross and Systematic Human Rights Violations* (Intersentia 2005) 135, 137.

16 Sylvain Aubry and María Isabel Henao-Trip, 'Collective Reparations and the International Criminal Court'(2011) Briefing Paper 2, Essex Transitional Justice Network.

17 OAS, *Principal Guidelines for a Comprehensive Reparations Policy* (Doc. No. OEA/Ser/L/V/II.131, 2008), para. 1.

18 *Ahmadou Sadio Diallo (Republic of Guinea v Democratic Republic of the Congo)* (Compensation Judgment) ICJ No. 103 (19 June 2012) paras. 13, 18, 24, 33, 40, 49, 56; *The Prosecutor v. Kaing Guek Eav* alias *'Duch' (Case 001)* (Appeal Judgment) ECCC No. 001/18–07–2007–ECCC/SC (3 February 2012) paras. 417, 431–444, 517, 647, 652, 661, 676, 683.

19 Juan-Pablo Perez-Leon-Acevedo, 'Reparations in environmental cases: should the International Criminal Court consider the Inter-American Court of Human Rights' jurisprudence?' (2024) 15 Journal of International Dispute Settlement 378.

20 The ICC has the power to grant reparations including restitution, compensation, rehabilitation and collective awards against the convicted person. See: ICC, arts. 75, 79; ICC's RoPE, rule 98.

21 ICC, art 21 (3).

and incorporates elements of the IACtHR's reparations framework.[22] As Pérez-León-Acevedo highlights, this integration positions the IACtHR's reparations jurisprudence as a key reference point for evaluating the ICC's reparative practices, underscoring the relevance of a comparison between the two courts.[23]

The ECCC provides a third dimension that enriches this comparative analysis, offering a unique perspective on reparative justice in the context of historical mass victimisations. The ECCC operates as a hybrid court combining national and international elements, and focuses on symbolic reconciliation and historical remembrance for victims of Cambodia's Khmer Rouge regime.[24] Compared to the IACtHR and ICC, the ECCC takes a more modest, objective, and pragmatic approach, and its mandate is limited to collective reparations with a special emphasis on symbolic award, rather than material compensation.[25] Given the narrower scope of its reparative framework and the limited literature available, the evaluation of ECCC is less extensive in this discussion.

Despite the variations in their mandates, protecting human rights, addressing international crimes, and prosecuting historical atrocities, this comparative analysis highlights the value of judicial cross-fertilisation in shaping consistent jurisprudential principles and fostering a coherent international law of reparations.[26] It aims to provide a comprehensive understanding of the relationship between harm assessment and the awarding of collective reparations across these interrelated yet distinct courts. By examining how the IACtHR, ICC, and ECCC approach these issues, this study sets the stage for a deeper exploration of how international courts assess harm and apply evidentiary standards, contributing to the broader discourse on international reparative justice.

While there is no single accepted meaning of these collective remedial measures within international law, their 'adequate' content appears to be determined on a case-by-case basis. International courts have asserted that

22 *see The Prosecutor v Thomas Lubanga Dyilo* (Decision establishing the principles and procedures to be applied to reparations) ICC-01/04–01/06–2904 (7 August 2012) paras. 33–43.

23 Perez-Leon-Acevedo (n 19) 380; Dinah Shelton, *Remedies in International Human Rights Law* (OUP 2015) 228–232.

24 Helen Jarvis, 'Trials and Tribulations: The Long Quest for Justice for the Cambodian Genocide' in Simon M Meisenberg and Ignaz Stegmiller (eds), *The Extraordinary Chambers in the Courts of Cambodia: Assessing their Contribution to International Criminal Law* (TMC Asser Press 2016) 25.

25 Ibid, 32.

26 Perez-Leon-Acevedo (n 19) 400, 402.

the two key elements in determining the 'adequate' content of collective reparations are the assessment of alleged harm and the wishes and needs of the affected victims and communities.[27] This raises several questions about the tests and thresholds that victims and communities must meet to prove alleged harm, the methodology courts use to assess this harm, and how this assessment influences the content of collective reparations awarded by international tribunals. This study compares and analyses the different evidentiary standards as well as rules and techniques employed by the IACtHR, the ICC, and the ECCC in assessing alleged moral, material, and collective harm in relation to serious crimes giving rise to CR.

This contribution is divided into three parts. The first section discusses the common basic substantive principles and standards that guide international human rights and criminal courts in determining the types of reparations deemed adequate to fulfil victims' longstanding right to reparation. This includes the principle of restoring the victim to the situation before the violation occurred (*restitutio in integrum*), the principle of adequacy which relates to what are the appropriate measures of reparations in a given case, and the principle of proportionality which ensures reparation awards be proportional to the seriousness of the violation and harm caused.[28] The second section moves into a discussion of how the IACtHR, the ICC, and the ECCC assess material, moral, and collective harm. The third section analyses the procedural principles and evidentiary requirements for these courts when granting collective reparations. Finally, conclusions are provided as to the unclear link between the harm assessment conducted by these courts and the granting of collective reparations, as well as the lack of legal certainty with regard to evidentiary requirements.

2 Substantive Guiding Principles for Determining Reparations

There are several substantive basic principles of reparations, including *restitutio in integrum* (restoring victims to their original situation);[29] the adequacy or appropriateness, and proportionality of the remedies to the gravity of vio-

27 Odier-Conteras Garduno (n 1) 143–144, 173–174, 209–211.

28 There exists more substantive principles guiding courts when granting reparations. However, international human rights courts and criminal tribunals not always refer and elaborate. Moreover, the principles under study in this contribution are those most closely related to determining the content of awards. See: Odier-Contreras Garduno (n 1) 95–96, 190–192.

29 *Factory at Chorzów* (*Germany v. Poland*) (Indemnity Order) PCIJ Series A No. 17 (26 July 1927) 21.

lations and harm suffered;[30] the effectiveness and promptness of remedies;[31] due recognition of victimhood, which encompasses effective victim participation,[32] non-discrimination,[33] and gender-sensitive.[34] However, this section focuses on those principles closely related to determining the content of awards and which are commonly used by international human rights courts and criminal tribunals: *restitutio in integrum,* adequacy, and proportionality.

2.1 *Restitutio in Integrum Principle*

Victims' right to reparations is widely recognised under public international law, international human rights law, and international criminal law.[35] The right to reparation has also become a growing customary practice in transitional processes, further reinforcing its importance in addressing systematic human rights violations.[36] In the judicial sphere, reparations can take the form of restitution, compensation, rehabilitation, satisfaction, or guarantees of non-repetition, and can be granted individually or collectively.[37]

The jurisprudence of the International Court of Justice (ICJ) and other human rights courts have been instrumental in clarifying the goals of reparations and the functions of its various forms.[38] The foundational principle of

30 Basic Principles and Guidelines on the Right to a Remedy and Reparation for Victims of Gross Violations of International Human Rights Law and Serious Violations of International Humanitarian Law (UNGA Resolution 60/147, 2005) Principle 2 c); Lubanga-2012 (n 22) para. 242–243.

31 Ibid.

32 Declaration of Basic Principles of Justice for Victims of Crime and Abuse of Power (UNGA Resolution 40/34, 1985) Principle 6 a); Lubanga-2012 (n 22), para. 203.

33 Octavio Amezcua-Noriega, 'Reparations Principles under International Law and their Possible Application by the International Criminal Court: Some Reflections' (2011) Briefing Paper 1, Essex Transitional Justice Network, 7; *Lubanga-2012* (n 22), para. 187–192.

34 Rubio-Marín (n 7).

35 *Factory at Chorzów* (n 29) 21; 2005 Basic Reparation Principles (n 30); American Convention on Human Rights (ACHR) (as adopted on 22 November 1969, entered into force 18 July 1978) art. 63 (1); Rome Statute of the International Criminal Court (adopted 17 July 1998, entered into force 1 July 2002) 2187 UNTS 3 (ICC's RS) art. 75; Rules of Procedure and Evidence of the International Criminal Court (adopted 9 September 2002, immediately in force) ICC-ASP/1/3 (ICC's RoPE) rules 94–98; ECCC Internal Rules Revision 9 (2015) (ECCC's Internal Rules) rules 23*quinquies*, 80*bis*.

36 International Center for Transitional Justice, 'Reparations in Theory and Practice' (Reparative Justice Series 2007) 2,5–6; United Nations, 'Guidance Note of the Secretary-General: United Nations Approach to Transitional Justice' (UN, March 2010) 8–9.

37 2005 Basic Reparation Principles (n 30) Principle 18.

38 Gentian Zyberi, 'The International Court of Justice and applied forms of reparation for international human rights and humanitarian law violations' (2011) 7 Utrecht Law Review, 204–215.

restitutio in integrum was first asserted by the ICJ's predecessor in 1927, establishing that reparations, under international law, should eliminate all effects of the wrongdoing.[39] This concept, which posits that reparations should, as far as possible, restore victims to the position they were in before the violation occurred, is rooted in longstanding private law principles.[40] Given the nature of private law litigation, restoring victims to their status *quo ante* is possible in the majority of cases. However, in cases of (gross) human rights violations, *restitutio in integrum* is frequently impossible. Despite being unachievable, human rights courts continue to uphold and evolve this principle.[41]

The IACtHR in particular has consistently recognised *restitutio in integrum* as the goal and guiding principle of reparations since its first judgement.[42] According to the Court, this principle consists of three criteria; i) the restoration of the *quo ante* situation of the victim, ii) the reparation of the consequences of the violation, and iii) the compensation of the harm (materially, morally, and emotionally).[43] However, in practice, the Court focuses on the last two criteria following Judge Cançado Trindade's suggestion that in the context of human rights, reparations should also aim to alleviate the ongoing negative consequences of violations,[44] as restoration is in most cases impossible to achieve.

This has led the IACtHR to adopt the concept of *integral reparations,* which consist of a combination of individual and collective measures that are considered adequate and proportional to the violation and harm suffered.[45] Under this umbrella of *integral reparations,* the IACtHR has provided progressive and innovative forms of reparations including material, symbolic, and collective measures.[46] Unsurprisingly, the Court's jurisprudence in this regard

39 *Factory at Chorzów* (n 9) 21.

40 Odier-Contreras Garduno (n 1) 315.

41 *Velásquez-Rodríguez v Honduras* (Reparations and Costs, Judgment) IACtHR Series C No. 07 (21 July 1989) para. 26; *Papamichalopoulos and Others v Greece (Article 50)* (Judgment) ECtHR 14556/89 (31 October 1995) para. 34.

42 *Velásquez-Rodríguez* (n 41) para. 26.

43 Ibid.

44 *Sadio Diallo* (n 18) (Separate Opinion of Judge Cançado Trindade, Compensation Judgment) ICJ No. 103 (19 June 2012) para. 26.

45 Jorge Calderón Gamboa, *La reparación integral en la jurisprudencia de la Corte Interamericana de Derechos Humanos: estándares aplicables al nuevo paradigma mexicano* (Instituto de Investigaciones Jurídicas, Suprema Corte de la Nación 2013).

46 Shelton (n 23).

has served as a source of inspiration for other international courts dealing with reparations for serious human rights violations.[47]

In cases of gross violations of human rights and mass victimisation, the IACtHR has prioritised collective reparations over individual awards. This approach aims to address the conditions of poverty and social exclusion in which the victims lived prior to the human rights violations.[48] These reparations often take the form of social service programs, including healthcare, education, and psychological support, aimed at addressing systemic harm. By improving access to essential services, these measures provide both symbolic and tangible redress for affected communities. Social services offer a pragmatic solution to the complexities of large-scale violations – such as the difficulty in identifying victims, limited resources, and the marginalised status of many victims.[49] However, they also raise concerns regarding the principle of proportionality, which becomes challenged when communities are required to 'bleed' in order to access basic services, even if these services are permanent.[50] This raises profound questions. Firstly, what is the relationship between the access to these services and the physical, emotional, and psychological toll that victims of gross human rights violations experience? Furthermore, how can service-centred measures adequately acknowledge the material and moral harm that results from a violation, especially one that is considered serious? And how building an educational centre or sewage system 'repair' victims of serious human rights violations?[51]

---

47 The ICC has referred to the IACtHR's reparations jurisprudence extensively in its reparation orders. See: *The Prosecutor v. Ahmad Al Faqi Al Mahdi* (Reparations Order) ICC-01/12-01/15 (17 August 2017) para. 85.

48 Odier-Contreras Garduno (n 1) 327.

49 Simeon Gready, 'The Case for Transformative Reparations: In Pursuit of Structural Socio-Economic Reform in Post-Conflict Societies', 16 Journal of Intervention and Statebuilding 2, 182–201.

50 The Court has granted collective reparations both on a permanent basis or based on a specific budget devoted to their operation.

51 Diana Contreras-Garduno, 'Defining Beneficiaries of Collective Reparations: The experience of the IACtHR' (2012) 4 *Amsterdam Law Forum 3*, 48 citing Malarino: "Only when putting a lot of effort, one could argue that the construction of a sewage system, a water system or improving roads, to cite a few examples, 'repair' the victims of a massacres". See: Ezequiel. Malarino, 'Activismo Judicial, Punitivización y Nacionalización. Tendencias Antidemocráticas y Antiliberales de la Corte Interamericana de Derechos Humanos', in Grupo Latinoamericano de Estudios sobre Derecho Penal International, *Sistema Interamericano de Protección de los Derechos Humanos y Derecho Penal Internacional* (Konrad-Adenauer-Stiftung 2010) 69.

Similarly, the ICC has approached collective reparations in a forward-looking fashion.[52] Although the ICC has never directly referenced *restitutio in integrum*, it has upheld that reparations should not only address the aftermath of violations, but should also mitigate the underlying injustices victims suffered before the crimes took place.[53] It has thus made the *transformation* of underlying injustices a key factor in assessing the *adequacy* of reparations. Although progressive, this remedial approach must also be proportional to, and appropriate for, the harm caused.[54]

Within this forward-thinking framework, the ICC has granted collective reparations in the form of service-based projects, with a duration of two or four years, such as housing, income-generating activities, education, and psychological rehabilitation projects.[55] However, one may question the extent to which these short-term projects can effectively address, and even transform, deep-seated structural inequalities and underlying injustices such as poverty and historical inequality. These are usually wide-nation problems unlikely to be alleviated by temporal projects awarded to the victims of a given case.[56] Similarly, the question of whether reparations should be proportional to the severity of international crimes remains unresolved.

In addition to this *transformative* element, the ICC has emphasised the promptness of reparations implementation as a significant factor in determin-

52 A backward-looking approach focuses on addressing past violations and placing marginalised victims back into positions of marginalisation following serious harm. A forward-looking approach, on the other hand, seeks to both address the past violations and improve the conditions of marginalisation that victims endured before the human rights violations.

53 *Lubanga*-2012 (n 22) para. 192; *The Prosecutor v Thomas Lubanga Dyilo* (Judgment on the appeals against the "Decision establishing the principles and procedures to be applied to reparations" of 7 August 2012 with AMENDED order for reparations (Annex A) and public annexes 1 and 2) ICC-01/04–01/06–3129 (3 March 2015) para. 17; *The Prosecutor v Germain Katanga* (Ordonnance de réparation en vertu de l'article 75 du Statut) ICC-01/04–01/07–3728 (24 March 2017) para. 310.

54 *Lubanga*-2012 (n 22) para. 242; *Lubanga-2015* (n 53) paras. 44, 48; *Katanga-2017* (n 53) paras. 15, 268.

55 *The Prosecutor v Thomas Lubanga Dyilo* (Filing on Reparations and Draft Implementation Plan, Annex A) ICC-01/04–01/06-Red (3 November 2015) paras. 61–94, (hereinafter *Lubanga DIP-2015*); *Katanga-2017* (n 53) paras. 302, 304; *The Prosecutor v Bosco Ntaganda* ICC (Reparations Order) ICC-01/04–02/06 (8 March 2021) para. 240 (hereinafter *Ntaganda-2021*); *The Prosecutor v Bosco Ntaganda* (Judgment on the appeals against the decision of Trial Chamber II of 14 July 2023 entitled "Addendum to the Reparations Order of 8 March 2021, ICC-01/04–02/06–2659") ICC-01/04–02/06–2908-Red (1 November 2024), para. 492 (hereinafter *Ntaganda-2024*).

56 Odier-Contreras Garduno (n 14) 745.

ing adequacy. This was established in the *Ongwen* reparations' order. The Court first noted that in the previous cases of *Katanga* and *Lubanga*, the inclusion of individual (and symbolic) reparations ordered next to CR led to significant delays in the implementation of reparations. Similarly, the Court believed that in the *Ntaganda* case, the specific content of the CR was still not fully approved after three years, primarily due to the individualised components.[57] Accordingly, the Court awarded CR without any individualised component, and continued to emphasise the transformative value of such awards.[58]

In contrast, the ECCC, at first glance, seems to diverge from the general principles of reparations by adopting a more modest, objective, and pragmatic approach. While the IACtHR and ICC can issue individual awards as well as material or service-based collective reparations, the ECCC is limited to granting only collective reparations with a special emphasis on symbolic awards.[59] These reparations serve the primary aim of acknowledging the harm suffered by victims as a result of the crimes committed by the convicted individual and providing symbolic redress.[60] And thus the content of the CR awarded by the ECCC has been limited to psychological assistance projects[61] and memory-related measures,[62] like public memorials and community-building efforts.

The ECCC believes that collective reparations not only have a symbolic significance, but they also serve to acknowledge and address the harm suffered by victims as a result of the crimes committed by the convicted individual.[63]

The tribunal's refusal to grant service-based reparations is due to a number of pragmatic considerations:[64] the indigence of the accused, the ECCC's lim-

57 *Ongwen* (n 13) para. 801; *Ntaganda-2021* (n 55) paras. 9, 246.

58 *Ongwen* (n 13) para. 637.

59 It is important to note that the ECCC's legal framework refers to moral awards instead of symbolic ones. See ECCC's Internal Rules, Rule 23*quinquies*; *The Prosecutor v Nuon Chea and Khieu Samphan (Case 002/01)* (Judgment) ECCC No.002/19–09–2007/ECCC/TC (7 August 2014) para. 1114.

60 Ibid.

61 *Chea and Samphan* (n 59) paras. 1131–1133, 1135–1137.

62 *Chea and Samphan* (n 59) para. 1161.

63 ECCC's Internal Rules, Rule 23*quinquies* (1); *Chea and Samphan* (n 59) para. 1114.

64 Including the need to adopt measures aimed to benefit as many victims as possible, avoid possible tensions between communities considered victims with those not considered as such and the likelihood of defendants not having enough funds to pay individual reparations. See: ECCC's Internal Rules, Rules 23*quinquies*, 80*bis*; *The Prosecutor v. Nuon Chea et al. (Case 002)* (Appeals on Civil Party Applications) ECCC No. D404/2/4 (24 June 2011) para. 70; *Duch-2012* (n 18) para. 659.

ited resources and financial constraints, and the fact that service based measures require cooperation from national authorities. Although reparations can be funded by third parties, the ECCC has highlighted the need of different governmental authorities for their implementation. Whilst the ECCC cannot oblige them, those authorities are free to agree to cooperate.[65] The question of whether this approach is better than that of the ICC and the IACtHR is beyond the scope of this contribution. However, the ECCC's cautious and modest approach to reparations may help manage victims' expectations about the potential content of reparation orders in international criminal proceedings.

2.2 *Adequacy and Proportionality Principles*

The legal concept of reparation is framed in such a way that it suggests that harm caused by human rights violations must be *adequately* remedied. However, in practice, the reparations, regardless of their form, are unlikely to fully achieve this objective, especially in cases of gross human rights violations or international crimes. One might initially resort to the goal of restoring victims to their *status quo ante* as the primary criterion for determining an adequate remedy. Yet, it is materially impossible to bring victims who have been killed, tortured, or raped to their original position.[66] And it is morally inappropriate to return marginalised and impoverished communities who were victimised to their previous state of vulnerability.[67]

In essence, reparations considered 'fair' or 'adequate' must involve a combination of financial and non-financial measures, as well as of individual and collective measures.[68] In addition, they must be tailored to the specific nature, gravity, and extent of the harm, as well as to the circumstances surrounding the violation.[69] When collective reparations are pursued, the principle of adequacy gains further complexity, as it requires courts to ensure that these reparations sufficiently address the collective dimension of the harm suffered

65 *Chea and Samphan* (n 59) paras. 1124–1140.

66 *Blake v Guatemala* (Reparations and Costs, Judgment) IACtHR Series C No 48 (22 January 1999) para. 42.

67 Yepes (n 6) 638–639.

68 Odier-Contreras Garduno (n 1) 10; Letschert, R. and van Boven, T., 'Providing Reparation in Situations of Mass Victimization: Key Challenges Involved', in R. Letschert et al. (eds.), *Victimological Approaches to International Crimes: Africa* (Cambridge, Intersentia 2011)) 182.

69 *Avena and other Mexican nationals* (*Mexico* v. *United States of America*) (Judgment) ICJ No. 128 (31 March 2004) para. 119.

while remaining proportional to the scale and impact of the violation. While specific remedies sought by claimants may also be considered when determining the 'adequacy' of a remedy,[70] it is essential for courts to both define and quantify the victims' suffering and losses. Consequently, the principle of adequacy is closely related to how proportional the remedy is to the violations and their consequences.[71]

In theory, proportionality may warrant a higher award of damages or an increased number of reparation measures when a violation is gross, as such violations tend to have a greater impact at the individual and community level. However, calculating damages in these scenarios is anything but an easy task. Translating material, moral, and collective harm into remedies, including compensation, is already a complex task, and additional constraints related to resources, evidence, and marginalisation add further challenges. Thus, a certain degree of flexibility is necessary,[72] where equitable considerations are taken into account to ensure that reparations do not result in either enrichment or impoverishment of victims.[73]

In determining the 'adequacy' principle for collective reparations, the IACtHR, the ICC, and the ECCC place emphasis on different factors, shaping unique outcomes for collective reparations. The IACtHR primarily considers the following factors: the gravity of the violation, the views and wishes of the victims, the conditions of the victims (gender, vulnerability, needs, age), the likelihood of certain measures to alleviate the effects of the violations, and all the relevant social and cultural circumstances of the victim, especially when dealing with indigenous and tribal peoples. The Court's jurisprudence reveals that it finds CR an adequate means for states to comply with their obligation to reparation in cases dealing with group victims, such as indigenous people, and in cases dealing with mass victimisation.

To uphold the principle of adequacy, the IACtHR has adopted a flexible approach to reparations, particularly in addressing the complexities of mass victimisation.[74] In its seminal ruling *La Oroya* in 2023, the Court clarified that it

70 Chester Brown, *A Common Law of International Adjudication* (Oxford, OUP 2007), 192.

71 Odier-Contreras Garduno (n 1) 56.

72 Odier-Contreras Garduno (n 1) 172–173, 330.

73 *"Street Children" (Villagrán-Morales et al.) v Guatemala* (Reparations and Costs, Judgment) IACtHR Series C No. 77 (26 May 2001) para. 63; *Varnava and others v Turkey* ECtHR (Judgment) Cases Nos. 16064/90, 16065/90, 16066/90, 16068/90, 16069/90, 16070/90, 16071/90, 16072/90 and 16073/90 (18 September 2009).

74 Odier-Contreras Garduno (n 1) 141, 143–145.

also takes account of the individual or collective nature of the right violated.[75] Therefore, adequacy is usually established on a case-by-case basis.[76] This is because what may be adequate for some would not necessarily be adequate for others. Since reparations need to be proportional to the nature, gravity, and scope of the injury, it can be assumed that the IACtHR determines the adequacy and proportionality principle simultaneously. Moreover, the Court has relied on CR to ensure remedies remain effective, particularly in cases where victims are identified years after a ruling. While this approach has enabled some form of redress for late-identified victims, it has limitations. For instance, when issuing rulings without specific knowledge of the vulnerabilities or needs of these individuals, the reparations risk serving as broad, general relief rather than tailored, adequate remedies. Finally, the IACtHR has maintained that reparations are to be proportional to the harm caused and gravity of the violation.[77] However, it has failed to outline how this is achieved.[78]

In contrast, the ICC approaches the concept of adequacy in a distinct manner, with a stronger focus on assessing the harm caused, the number of victims, and the rights of the defendants. While the ICC also considers victims' wishes, this does not seem to be the main criteria for deciding reparations orders. If the number of victims in a given case is large, collective reparations are preferred above individual awards, to ensure that those awards only benefit victims of crimes for which the defendant was convicted.[79] For instance, in the *Al-Madhi* case, the Court explicitly acknowledged that 'the overwhelming number of eligible victims' was the primary reason collective reparations were the appropriate response.[80] In the *Ntaganda* case the Court also acknowledged that CR, which were part of the victims' reparations requests, ensures a 'more efficient, prompt, and practical approach' and avoids the time-consuming task of ruling on each individual application for reparations.[81]

75 *Habitantes de La Oroya v Peru* (Excepciones Preliminares, Fondo, Reparaciones y Costas, Judgment) IACtHR Series C No. 511 (27 November 2023) para. 324.

76 Odier-Contreras Garduno (n 1) 173.

77 *Castillo Petruzzi et al. v Peru* (Merits, Reparations and Costs) Series C No. 52 (30 May 1999, para. 51.

78 Odier-Contreras Garduno (n 1) 100.

79 ICC's RS, art.75 (1); ICC's RoPE, Rule 97 (1). The defendant is given the opportunity to challenge the scope of reparations, eligible victims and types of reparations, see *Ongwen* (n 13) para. 586.

80 *Al Mahdi* (n 47) para. 577.

81 *Ntaganda-2021* (n 55) paras. 9, 194, 196.

With regards to the matter of proportionality, similarly to the IACtHR, the ICC claims that the modalities of reparation must be proportional to the harm suffered, but has not clarified how this is determined.[82] Moreover, the ICC's claim on the proportionality of its reparation awards is refuted by the Court's own legal framework and practice where pragmatic considerations are decisive in shaping reparation orders. Collective reparations are preferred when the number of victims in a case is large without any discussion on their proportionality to the harm and gravity of the crimes suffered by the victims. Furthermore, the ICC has also endorsed CR as it considers that individual reparations may run against the principle of non-discrimination towards victims. In some contexts, they could create 'tensions, jealousy, or animosity' among them.[83] This is attributed to the potential for individual reparations to establish a hierarchy of victims as they aim to consider the unique individual consequences of international crimes.

The ECCC takes a notably different approach. Its Internal Rules bestow the tribunal with full discretion to decide when collective reparations in the form of material (social projects) or symbolic measures, or both, should be deemed adequate, and no specific guidelines are provided within its legal framework. Contrary to the IACtHR and the ICC, the ECCC has not claimed that the reparations must be proportional to the gravity of the crimes and harm of the victims.

Finally, it must be noted that non-legal requirements can also be held as significant by the courts when determining the 'adequacy' of reparations. For example, the IACtHR has acknowledged that in some contexts, reparations may put the victims in a dangerous or vulnerable position. As such, it is a moral responsibility of courts to consider the potential adverse consequences of granting certain forms of reparations. For instance, in the *Plan de Sánchez* case, which involved the massacre of over two hundred and fifty individuals, the IACtHR ordered the government of Guatemala to provide individual compensation of USD 25,000 to nearly two hundred victims.[84] The majority of these individuals were members of the Maya indigenous community in Guatemala, who lived in a marginalised area. Given that the annual minimum

82 *The Prosecutor v Germain Katanga* (Draft implementation plan relevant to Trial Chamber II's order for reparations of 24 March 2017 (ICC-01/04-01/07-3728)) ICC-01/04-01/07 (25 July 2017) para. 80 (*Katanga DIP-2017*).

83 *Ntaganda-2021* (n 55) para. 194; *Ongwen* (n 13) para. 584.

84 *Plan de Sánchez Massacre v Guatemala* (Reparations, Judgment) IACtHR Series C No. 116 (19 November 2004) paras. 74–76, 88–89.

wage in Guatemala was approximately USD 140 in 2004,[85] when the court's decision was upheld, and considering ongoing insecurity issues, the compensation was a substantial sum of money for local standards. Unfortunately, after receiving their monetary compensation, several victims were robbed.[86] This is something they could consider in future judgements.

The ICC has adopted a similar approach through the 'do no harm' principle. This ensures that the reparation measures will not result in secondary victimisation, put victims at risk, or lead to stigmatisation. The ICC has pointed out that CR allows victims of sexual crimes to receive benefits without being publicly identified as victims, which can lead to social rejection and stigma within their communities.[87] Additionally, the ICC emphasises the importance of ensuring collective reparations complement, rather than duplicate, services already provided by the government.[88] This to avoid that CR could be seen as temporal substitutes for social services as this has the potential to exacerbate the harm experienced by victims.[89] The ECCC on the other hand, has been silent about the danger that some form of reparations could present to victims, most likely because of its limited reparation mandate.

3 Assessment of Harm to Establish Reparations

In civil domestic law and public international law, the assessment of both material and non-material harm is equally important to determine the measures and quantum of reparations. Similarly, human rights and international criminal law acknowledge harm assessment as a precondition for reparations. In contrast to tort law, international law has no guidelines and rules to assess alleged harm. Moreover, the fact that international courts like the ICJ and IACtHR rarely delegate damage assessments to experts[90] raises the question of whether judges should be required to possess a certain level of expertise in

85 'El salario mínimo sube en Guatemala' (*Datosmacro.com* (*expansion.com*), 2004) <https://datosmacro.expansion.com/smi/guatemala?anio=2004#:~:text=El%20salario%20m%C3%ADnimo%20sube%20en,mayor%20parte%20de%20los%20pa%C3%ADses> accessed 30 March 2023.

86 Christian Evans, *The Right to Reparation in International Law for Victims of Armed Conflict* (CUP 2012) 72.

87 *Ntaganda-2021* (n 55) paras. 51, 195.

88 *Ongwen* (n 13) para. 619.

89 Ibid.

90 For instance, the ICJ has only asked experts to conduct the assessment of harm in two cases, *Sadio Diallo* (n 18) and *Corfu Channel* (*United Kingdom of Great Britain and Northern Ireland v Albania*) (Merits) No. 001 (9 April 1949). Before the IACtHR, a few cases can

damage quantification. Without such expertise, one could argue that international law grants judges full discretion in determining the factors and methods used to assess and quantify harm. This could result in a lack of transparency and foreseeability, negatively impacting the parties involved in the proceedings and undermining the legitimacy of international courts themselves.

The following sections aim to first clarify the different and commonly recognised types of harm and then discuss how courts tend to assess and quantify them. The IACtHR, the ICC, and the ECCC have all recognised three different categories of harm: material, moral, and collective harm.[91] Despite the general perception that material harm is simpler to quantify than moral harm, it will be demonstrated that both are similarly complex to assess.

3.1 *Material Harm*

Material harm consists of loss of or damage to possessions or property, loss of earnings, loss of savings, any costs incurred by relatives, and any financial damage caused in connection from the violation, such as loss of opportunities, including education, employment, social security, and benefits.[92] In assessing and quantifying harm, the IACtHR primarily exercises reasonable judicial discretion and the principle of equity.[93] In exercising such judicial discretion, the Court has failed to disclose any methodology guidelines that it may use to quantify material and non-material damage. The Court has, however, highlighted different factors that it considers to calculate material harm

---

be identified where the Court delegated such assessments. For instance, *Miguel Castro-Castro Prison v Peru* (Merits, Reparations and Cost, Judgment) IACtHR Series C No. 160 (25 November 2006) and *Chaparro Álvarez and Lapo Íñiguez v Ecuador* (Objections, Merits, Reparations, Costs Judgment) IACtHR Series C No. 170 (21 November 2007). The ICC however has extensively relied on experts since its Katanga reparations order in 2017, *Katanga-2017* (n 53).

91 The IACtHR usually label material harm as pecuniary damage and moral harm as a non-pecuniary damage. On the other hand, the ICC usually employs the term of material harm but subdivides moral harm into two categories: physical and psychological harm. However, in the *Al Mahdi* case, the ICC went into dividing material harm into damage to the protected buildings and consequential economic loss. Finally, following its Rule 23 (2), the ECCC recognizes physical, material and psychological harm, *Street Children* (n 73) para. 63; *Al Mahdi* (n 47) paras. 42, 60, 76, 97; *Duch-2010* (n 91) para. 640.

92 Dinah Shelton (n 23) 42–44, 146–456; *Garífuna Triunfo de la Cruz Community and its Members v Honduras* (Merits, Reparations and Costs, Judgment) IACtHR Series C No. 305 (8 October 2015) para. 289.

93 *19 Merchants v Colombia* (Merits, Reparations and Costs, Judgment) IACtHR Series C No. 109 (5 July 2004) para. 116; *Mayagna (Sumo) Awas Tingni Community v Nicaragua* (Merits, Reparations and Costs, Judgment) IACtHR Series C No. 79 (31 August 2001) para. 1687.

including the age, health, living conditions, life expectancy and place of residence of the victim.[94] These are 'carefully examined' on the basis of information provided by the parties in a case.[95]

Although the IACtHR has claimed that determining the quantum for material harm requires a higher burden of proof,[96] its case law demonstrates some flexibility. When parties fail to provide sufficient evidence, or any evidence at all, the Court has the discretion to presume the material harm claimed.[97] In such cases, the IACtHR may calculate the harm based on equity,[98] taking into account factors such as the country's average life expectancy[99] and the minimum wage established by national law.[100] In some cases, the Court has even adjusted the minimum wage in its calculations if it deems the figure too low.[101]

However, while the Court seems to adopt a flexible approach to assessing material harm in order to protect victims' right to reparations, its application is not consistent. For example, there is a significant disparity in the amounts determined for the loss of earnings, despite the lack of supporting evidence to justify those amounts. In some cases, the IACtHR adopts a more flexible approach, awarding a higher quantum based on equity. In other cases, however, the quantum is lower due to the claimant's failure to provide sufficient evidence.[102] This inconsistency in approach, especially towards similar cases, is made without clear explanation.

---

94 *Las Palmeras v Colombia* (Reparations and Costs, Judgment) IACtHR Series C No. 96 (26 November 2002) paras. 56, 58.

95 *El Amparo v Venezuela* (Merits, Judgment) IACtHR Series C No. 19 (18 January 1995) para. 49; *Members of the Village of Chichupac and Neighboring Communities of the Municipality of Rabinal v Guatemala* (Preliminary Objections, Merits, Reparations and Costs, Judgment) IACtHR Series C No. 328 (30 November 2016) para. 66.

96 *Atala Riffo and Daughters v Chile* (Merits, Reparations and Costs) IACtHR Series C No. 239 (24 Feb 2012) para. 292.

97 For an overview of the common presumptions used by the Court to assess material harm see: Odier-Contreras Garduno (n 1) 159–161.

98 *White Van* (*Paniagua-Morales* et al.) *v Guatemala* (Reparations and Costs, Judgment) IACtHR Series C No. 76 (25 May 2001) para. 119.

99 *Caracazo v Venezuela* (Reparations and Costs, Judgment) IACtHR Series C No. 95 (29 August 2002) para. 29.

100 *Street Children* (n 73) para. 79.

101 *Neira Alegria v Peru* (Reparations and Costs, Judgment) IACtHR Series C No. 29 (19 September 1996) paras. 49–50.

102 Clara Sandoval, Two steps forward, one step back: Reflections on the jurisprudential turn of the Inter-American Court of Human Rights on domestic reparations programmes, *22 The International Journal of Human Rights,* (2017) 6, referring to the cases of *Bamaca* and *Chitay* against Guatemala.

The IACtHR has also been inconsistent in its victim-friendly approach and tends to be more lenient when dealing with gross violations of human rights, such as massacres, than in cases of mass victimisation involving indigenous peoples. For instance in *El Mozote*, a massacre case, the court understood the difficulties of victims to bring evidence since three decades had elapsed between the time when the violations took place and the judgement. It therefore stated that despite the lack of 'evidence to prove the loss of earnings and the consequential losses suffered by the victims in this case', it was logical to presume that the nature of the violations entailed serious pecuniary consequences. As a result, the Court calculated the compensation of that damage on equity. Interestingly, in this case, the Court arrived at a quantum that was supposed to cover material and moral damage without explaining how much was awarded for each type of harm.

In contrast, the IACtHR is less willing to assert and fix a quantum for the material losses in cases dealing with indigenous group's deprivation of land. In these cases, the Court has either sidestepped the quantification of material losses,[103] or awarded low sums of money that contrast the amounts of awards for moral damages.[104] An example of this is the *Saramaka* case, where the state of Suriname was ordered to pay USD 75,000 for the material harm suffered for the timber extracted in their lands by a state-granted concession.[105] In contrast, the Saramaka tribe received USD 650,000 as compensation for the moral harm resulting from the mining activities.[106] However progressive, this approach implies that the value of collective land has a symbolic, but not material value. This raises important questions about whether vulnerable groups are treated equally in reparations proceedings before the Court, which is known for having the most comprehensive approach towards reparations. Finally, the Court has consistently awarded compensation for the expenses and costs related to the judicial proceedings in cases dealing with both group victims and gross violations of human rights.[107]

103 *Sawhoyamaxa Indigenous Commmunity v Paraguay* (Merits, Reparations, and Costs, Judgment) IACtHR Series C No. 146 (29 March 2006) para. 198.

104 Odier-Contreras Garduno (n 1) 139–140.

105 *Saramaka People v Suriname* (Preliminary Objections, Merits, Reparations and Costs, Judgment) IACtHR Series C No. 172 (28 November 2007) para. 199.

106 This money was granted as a community development fund devoted to finance educational, housing, agriculture and health projects among others. *Saramaka* (n 105) para. 200–201.

107 *Norín Catrimán et al. (Leaders, members and activist of the Mapuche Indigenous People) v Chile* (Merits, Reparations and Costs, Judgment) IACtHR Series C No. 279 (29 May 2014) para. 444; *Massacres of El Mozote and nearby places v El Salvador* (Merits, Reparations and Costs, Judgment) IACtHR Series C No. 152 (25 October 2012) para. 393.

As far as the ICC is concerned, it is their responsibility to determine the harm that needs to be remedied. However, it may delegate its assessment to the Trust Fund for Victims (TFV). The ICC has delegated the assessment of harm to experts only once, in its first case *Lubanga*, where experts assisted the TFV in this task.[108] On the contrary, in both the *Katanga* and the *Al Mahdi* cases, the ICC conducted the assessment of harm itself. While the ICC conducted the assessment in *Katanga* without the help of experts, it was helped by experts in *Al Mahdi*.[109] In the *Katanga* case, the Court did not assess harm on an individual basis, but instead used a mass claims technique with standard valuation, grouping harm types and calculating compensation accordingly. This approach was feasible primarily due to the tangible nature of the material damages, such as the destruction of houses, pillaging of livestock, and household goods. Notably, this technique was proposed by both the victims and the defence representatives, which may have influenced the Court's selection of this method.[110] In the *Al Mahdi case,* while the order of reparations acknowledged the economic loss and damage of buildings and property, the ICC did not conduct an extensive analysis of the harm resulting from it. Instead, it relied on expert reports that quantified both material and moral harm.[111]

In its latest reparations order, the ICC took a two-step approach to assess the material harm inflicted. Initially, it relied on presumptions to determine the harm, then used the available evidence, observations of the parties, and participants to assess the extent of such harm.[112] Similar to the IACtHR, the ICC usually acknowledges the difficulties victims encounter in obtaining evidence as a result of the absence of official records, displacement, or the passage of time between the commission of crimes and their prosecution. Consequently, the ICC has lowered the standard of evidence required from victims in determining and quantifying alleged harm.[113] Finally, in respect of the ECCC, the tribunal has avoided any discussion of material harm, and has only tangentially suggested that victims may have suffered such harm.[114]

---

108 *Lubanga-2015* (n 53) para. 58.

109 *Al Mahdi* (n 47) paras. 7, 57; *Katanga-2017* (n 53) para. 191.

110 Odier-Contreras Garduno (n 1) 228.

111 *Al Mahdi* (n 47) paras. 84–108.

112 *Ongwen* (n 13) paras. 556, 771.

113 *Ongwen* (n 13) paras. 518–519.

114 *Duch-2010* (n 91) para. 641–643.

3.2 *Moral Harm*

Moral harm refers to the non-financial consequences of a violation, such as the pain, suffering, anxiety, and sadness experienced by the victims and their families[115] as well as any disruption to their lifestyle.[116] The IACtHR usually considers factors such as the vulnerability of the victim,[117] the extent of anxiety suffered by the victims and their relatives,[118] and the passing of time in which the violation enjoyed impunity,[119] to calculate moral damage. Interestingly, in a few cases, the Court has also held that the acknowledgement of responsibility has a twofold consequence to moral harm. First, such recognition may be sufficient to establish and remedy the moral harm suffered by victims,[120] potentially eliminating the need for further calculation of this harm.[121] In cases of indigenous peoples, such as the *Moiwana* case, the IACtHR has taken into account the victims' culture and traditions to evaluate any harm to their 'spiritual integrity'[122] and specific culture.[123] It has nevertheless failed to explain how these factors play a role in its quantification of harm. In cases of ancestral lands, while often unwilling to quantify the material value of economic losses, the Court has been generous in quantifying the non-pecuniary harm arising from such land deprivation.[124] This suggests that the impact on the victims' way of life is considered more significant than the material value of the land itself. Notably, those generous awards, which can

115 *Cantoral-Benavides v Peru* (Reparations and Costs, Judgment) IACtHR Series C No. 88 (3 December 2001) para. 53; *Caracazo v Venezuela* (n 99) para. 50.

116 *Members of the Village of Chichupac and Neighboring Communities* (n 95) para. 324.

117 *Street Children* (n 73), para. 91 (b).

118 Jo M Pasqualucci, "Victim Reparations in the Inter-American Human Rights System: A Critical Assessment of Current Practice and Procedure" (1996)18 Michigan Journal of International Law, 6.

119 *Ibsen Cárdenas And Ibsen Peña v Bolivia* (Merits, Reparation, and Costs) IACtHR Series C No. 217 (1 September 2010) para. 283; *Las Palmeras* (n 94) para. 55.

120 *Aloeboetoe et al. v Suriname* (Reparations and Costs, Judgment) IACtHR Series C No. 15 (10 September 1993) para. 52.

121 *El Amparo v Venezuela* (Reparations and Costs, Judgment) IACtHR Series C No. 28 (14 September 1996) para. 34; *González et al. ("Cotton Field") v Mexico* (Preliminary Objection, Merits, Reparations, and Costs, Judgment) IACtHR Series C No 205 (16 November 2009) para. 584.

122 *Moiwana Community v Suriname* (Preliminary Objections, Merits, Reparations and Costs, Judgment) IACtHR Series C No. 124 (15 June 2005) para. 195.

123 *Plan de Sánchez Massacre* (n 84) para. 49 (12).

124 *Yakye Axa Indigenous Community v Paraguay* (Merits, Reparations and Costs, Judgment) IACtHR Series C No. 125 (17 June 2005) para. 205.

exceed USD 1 million,[125] are often devoted to guarantee social-service projects, in other words, collective reparations.[126]

Given the challenges of quantifying moral harm, it is not surprising that international judicial and non-judicial bodies typically calculate non-material damage on an equitable basis and rely heavily on presumptions.[127] This is because moral damage cannot be calculated mathematically using a fixed formula.[128] Further, while the equity criterion is arguably a subjective notion, it implies a degree of fairness,[129] and aligns with the recognition that moral harm has occurred, rather than providing 'financial comfort or sympathetic enrichment'.[130] However, the application of the principle of equity can vary from judge to judge. Without consistent legal reasoning from judges or the adoption of clear Court guidelines, the principle of equity fails to provide legal certainty and foreseeability.

The IACtHR in particular relies significantly on presumptions to streamline and justify assessments of moral harm. This is grounded in the recognition that suffering is an inherent and inevitable consequence of gross human rights violations.[131] Notably, the IACtHR engineered *rebuttable* presumptions (*iuris tantum*), which automatically assume moral harm for the relatives of victims of gross human rights violations.[132] This places an obligation on the state to provide evidence to disprove such harm.[133] In addition, the IACtHR has consistently awarded higher compensation amounts to immediate relatives, such as spouses and children. In cases involving mass victimisation, the Court often reduces individual compensation amounts for victims and their relatives. And instead opts for collective reparations as a more comprehensive means of addressing harm. However, the Court does not typically provide detailed reasoning for this shift, leaving some ambiguity in its proportionality rationale.[134]

125 *The Kaliña and Lokono Peoples* v. *Suriname* (Merits, Reparations and Costs, Judgment) IACtHR Series C No. 309 (25 November 2015) para. 298.

126 Odier-Contreras Garduno (n 1) 140.

127 *Cantoral-Benavides* (n 115) para. 53; *Sadio Diallo* (n 44) para. 33.

128 Pasqualucci (n 118) 34.

129 Szilvia Altwicker-Hámori et al, 'Measuring Violations of Human Rights: An Empirical Analysis of Awards in Respect of Non-Pecuniary Damage under the European Convention on Human Rights' (2016) 76 Heidelberg Journal of International Law 1, 15.

130 *Varnava and others* (n 73) para. 225.

131 *Cantoral-Benavides* (n 116) para. 21.

132 *Aloeboetoe* (n 120) paras. 71, 76; *Valle Jaramillo et al. v Colombia* (Merits, Reparations and Costs) IACtHR Series C No. 192 (27 November 2008) para. 119.

133 *Peasant Community of Santa Bárbara v Peru* (Preliminary Objections, Merits, Reparations and Costs, Judgment) IACtHR Series C No. 299 (1 September 2015) paras. 274–276.

134 Odier-Contreras Garduno (n 1) 153–154.

Finally, in a few cases, the Court has relied on expert reports to assess the harm of a violation, and applied the equity principle to decide on the *quantum* for compensation for moral harm.[135]

As previously discussed, the ICC delegated the assessment of all harm to the TFV in the *Lubanga* case, but it retained judicial oversight. In this regard, the ICC followed the IACtHR and presumed psychological harm suffered by the victims.[136] Likewise, in all subsequent orders of reparations, the ICC has presumed moral harm of victims.[137] Having presumed this harm, the Court has clarified that its quantification is independent of the economic situation of the location where the violation occurred,[138] and takes account of the views of the parties.[139] This suggests that the victims' own calculations on the quantification of their (moral) harm influences the ICC's own assessment. Nonetheless, the ICC has declined to disclose any guidelines on other factors influencing its assessment. Similarly, the assessment of moral harm before the ECCC remains equally unclear. The ECCC has sustained that moral harm is essentially presumed on discretionary basis,[140] because it is a natural consequence of the crimes under the jurisdiction of this tribunal.[141] Its quantification, however, remains a matter of judicial discretion.

3.3 *Collective Harm*

Unlike other international courts such as the ICJ, these three understudied tribunals have recognised the existence of collective harm in relation to gross human rights violations and mass victimisation. Scholars have long held that collective reparations aim to redress collective harm, without further elaborating on what that harm may involve.[142] The jurisprudence of IACtHR,

---

135 *Las Palmeras* (n 95) para. 50; *Santo Domingo Massacre v Colombia* (Preliminary Objections, Merits, Reparations and Costs, Judgment) IACtHR Series C No. 259 (30 November 2012) paras. 242, 244; *Plan de Sánchez Massacre* (n 84) para. 78.

136 *Lubanga DIP-2015* (n 55) para. 71.

137 *Katanga-2017* (n 53); *Al Mahdi* (n 47); *Ntaganda-2021* (n 55); *Ongwen* (n 13).

138 *Katanga-2017* (n 53) para. 189.

139 This included the victims, the convicted person and the TFV as this would ultimately implement the reparations; *The Prosecutor v Germain Katanga* (Observations in response to the Trial Chamber's order of 15 July 2016 with Public redacted version of Annex A: Index of annexes, and public annexes 1–5 and 7–14) ICC-01/04-01/07-3714-Red (30 September 2016).

140 *Chea et al. Appeals on Civil Party Applications* (n 64) Separate and Partially Dissenting Opinion of Judge Marchi-Uhe) para. 68.

141 *Chea et al. Appeals on Civil Party Applications* (n 64) para. 93.

142 Friedrich Rosenfeld 'Collective Reparations for Victims of Armed Conflicts' (2010) 92 International Review of the Red Cross 731, 732.

the ICC, and the ECCC has shed some light on this type of harm. It encompasses the suffering of the members of a group or community where the violations took place, as well as the negative effects on the social fabric of such communities and groups.[143] Consequently, this harm is understood to be non-material in nature. Collective harm implies the recognition of a collective victim, whether a group,[144] a community,[145] or mass victimisation.[146] If collective harm is determined, the IACtHR typically grants collective reparations without attempting to quantify the extent of the harm.[147] Notably, victims are not per se obliged to prove their collective harm, as the Court generally assumes its existence in cases involving gross violations and when the victim happens to be a group or community.[148]

Both the ICC and the ECCC have acknowledged the existence of collective harm in all their reparations orders, but do so without providing further explanation on its concept and quantification. However, the ICC has mirrored the practice of the IACtHR by recognising collective harm if the victims of a case are a group/community or happen to be numerous. While the ICC has recognised the importance of reparations to address collective harm,[149] the ECCC has only acknowledged that collective harm, as opposed to individual harm, is a realistic harm to be proved and established. However, the ECCC has not specified how victims are expected to substantiate such claims.[150] To date, it remains unclear whether these two international criminal tribunals consider collective harm as an inherent consequence of international crimes. Similarly,

143 *Plan de Sánchez Massacre* (n 84) para. 110; *Afro-Descendant Communities displaced from the Cacarica River Basin (Operation Genesis) v Colombia* (Preliminary Objections, Merits, Reparations and Costs, Judgment) IACtHR Series C No. 270 (20 November 2013) para. 473; *The Prosecutor v. Germain Katanga* (Report on applications for reparations in accordance with Trial Chamber II's Order of 27 August, Annex 1) ICC-01/04-01/07-3512-Anx1-Red2 (21 January 2015) para. 74; *Lubanga*-2012 (n 22) para. 88; *Al Mahdi* (n 47) paras. 83, 141; *Chea et al. Appeals on Civil Party Applications* (n 64) para. 77.

144 *Xákmok Kásek Indigenous Community v Paraguay* (Merits, Reparations and Costs, Judgment) IACtHR Series C No. 214 (24 August 2010) para. 278.

145 *The Kichwa Indigenous People of Sarayaku v Ecuador* (Merits and Reparations, Judgment) IACtHR Series C No. 245 (27 June 2012) para. 284; *Moiwana Community* (n 122) para. 176.

146 *Ituango Massacre v Colombia* (Preliminary Objections, Merits, Reparations and Costs, Judgment) Series C No.148 (1 July 2006) para. 276.

147 *Mayagna (Sumo) Awas Tingni v Nicaragua* (n 51) Operative para. 173 (1–7); *Aloeboetoe* (n 120) paras. 83–84; *Plan de Sánchez Massacre* (n 84) para. 110; *Operation Genesis* (n 143) paras. 459, 476.

148 Odier-Contreras Garduno (n 1) 175.

149 *Lubanga*-2015 (n 53) para. 33; *Katanga report on applications* (n 143) para. 74; *Katanga*-2017 (n 53) para. 274.

150 *Chea et al. Appeals on Civil Party Applications* (n 64) para. 77.

it remains unclear if claims of collective harm from victims and expert witnesses play a role in the ICC's willingness to recognise it.

4 Collective Reparations and Evidentiary Standards: A Critical Look

4.1 *Collective Reparations*

In addition, when dealing with mass victimisation, courts are challenged by several factors, such as the irreparable nature of the violations, the far-reaching consequences for individuals, society, and communities, the difficulty in identifying the perpetrators and the extent of their culpability, and the challenges of identifying and acknowledging victims. Moreover, the limited capacity and resources of both the state and individuals responsible for these violations complicate these efforts.[151] To address these challenges, collective reparations have been implemented as a pragmatic and somewhat innovative solution. These reparations were first adopted under transitional justice processes and were crafted as a symbolic measure of social solidarity.[152] Subsequently, they were incorporated into the judicial sphere, initially within the realm of international human rights law and later in international criminal law.

Collective reparations are often considered the preferred response to international crimes and gross human rights violations. However, courts have been notably reluctant to define collective reparations. It is possible that this reluctance stems from the nature of these reparations, which tend to be characterised by a high degree of *flexibility* in both their content and the methods used to shape such content. Despite this flexibility, collective reparations typically encompass a range of service-based measures, infrastructure projects, and community development programmes.

While prioritising victims' immediate needs, CR aims to both reduce their vulnerability and address some of the root and structural causes of given violations. Regardless of their commendable goal, their reparative and transformative effects are neither evident nor always achievable. They set a higher bar of structural and systemic transformation which is commonly at odds with political feasibility.[153] In the case of the *Pueblo Bello Massacre*, which involved

151 Odier-Contreras Garduno (n 1) 4, 54.

152 De Greiff, 'Justice and Reparations' in de Greiff (n 1).

153 Odier-Contreras Garduno (n 1) 142; Margaret Urban Walker, 'Transformative Reparations? A Critical Look at a Current Trend in Thinking about Gender-Just Reparations' (2016) 10 International Journal of Transitional Justice 108, 110–111.

the killing of six persons and the enforced disappearance of thirty seven others by paramilitary groups in Colombia, the IACtHR ordered the state to implement collective reparations in the form of a housing programme for the affected families. These CR were intended to help displaced victims return to the village of Pueblo Bello, and help address their socio-economic situation.[154] However, it is debatable whether these collective reparations ordered in 2006, could effectively transform the structural injustices in a country that was still experiencing an ongoing internal conflict, which only ended nation-wide in 2016 with the signing of a peace agreement.[155]

Receiving collective reparations and having access to permanent social programmes may lead victims to perceive them as a pragmatic and cheaper substitute for individual reparations, provoking disappointment rather than redress.[156] Following the principle of *restitutio in integrum*, victims are entitled to individual reparations in conjunction with collective measures, such as satisfaction and guarantees of non-repetition.[157] Against this background, the ICC and the IACtHR have attempted to provide individual reparations, in addition to collective ones, when adjudicating mass victimisation. These individual awards have been inherently symbolic, thereby diluting their aim to repair the individual suffering and material loss resulted from the violation. Cases in point are *Katanga* and *Ongwen*, where the ICC awarded individuals USD 250 and EUR 750, respectively, as monetary compensation.[158]

While transitional justice may well justify CR as a gesture of social solidarity, remedies awarded by international courts are, in theory, bound to meet certain principles. This ensures they can be considered a legitimate way to fulfil the right to reparation. Additionally, it is widely accepted that mass violence justifies the adoption of extraordinary measures and policies, including collective reparations, that may not be applied in typical legal contexts. It is also worth noting that the IACtHR, the ICC and the ECCC have advocated for collective reparations as the adequate means of addressing collective harm. The following sections aim to explore the evidentiary requirements for these courts to both grant collective reparations and consider them adequate.

---

154 *Pueblo Bello Massacre v Colombia* (Merits, Reparations and Costs, Judgment) IACtHR Series C No. 140 (31 January 2006) paras. 275–276.

155 Final Agreement to End the Conflict and Building a Stable and Lasting Peace, 2016 <https://www.refworld.org/legal/agreements/natlegbod/2016/en/121520> accessed 20 April 2024.

156 Catalina Díaz Gómez (ed), *Tareas Pendientes: Propuestas para la formulación de políticas públicas de la reparación en Colombia* (ICTJ 2010) 273–280.

157 Odier-Contreras Garduno (n 1) 172.

158 *Katanga-2017* (n 53) paras. 112–113; *Ongwen* (n 13) para. 621.

4.2 *Evidentiary Standards*

In contrast to tort law, international law does not prescribe common evidentiary requirements for reparations, which limits the sources from which human rights and international criminal tribunals can draw inspiration. The main evidentiary rules under international law are nonetheless the standard of proof and causation.[159] However, while Courts are often willing to refer to those requirements, they do not always elaborate on how they apply them when granting reparations. Instead, they tend to adopt a flexible approach to evidentiary rules such as the burden and standard of proof.[160] In fact, this flexible approach is considered a procedural principle of reparation.[161]

The ICJ has long clarified that victims bear the burden of proof with regard to the harm and causal link between the violation and such harm.[162] Regardless, the *onus probandi* is applied with some degree of flexibility in reparation proceedings by both the IACtHR and the ICC. Unsurprisingly, reparations for widespread and gross human rights violations face numerous obstacles, including the difficulty for victims to obtain evidence as a result of the absence of official records, displacement, or the passage of time between the commission of crimes and their prosecution.

4.2.1 Standard of Proof

The standard of proof refers to the amount and quality of evidence required to establish a claim. It implies a test that a court applies to evaluate the evidence presented by the parties. Therefore, the standard of proof directly influences the assessment of the court.

Although the IACtHR's legal regime does not specify the burden and standard of proof required for reparations, its case law provides some clarity. To begin with, the court has adopted a principle called '*sana crítica*' (also referred as 'sound judicial discretion') to guide the assessment of evidence. This principle allows judges to evaluate evidence using their logic and experience, ensuring their conclusions are well-reasoned, clearly articulated, and effec-

---

159 John Barker, 'The different forms of reparation: compensation' in J Crawford, S Olleson, A Pellet (eds), *The Law on International Responsibility* (OUP 2010) 603.

160 Anna Riddell, 'Evidence, Fact-Finding, and Experts' in K Alter, C Romano, Y Shany (eds), *The Oxford Handbook of International Adjudication* (OUP 2015) 852.

161 Amezcua-Noriega (n 33) 6.

162 *Application of the Convention on the Prevention and Punishment of the Crime of Genocide (Bosnia and Herzegovina v Serbia and Montenegro* (Judgment) ICJ No. 91 (26 February 2007) para. 462.

tively substantiated.[163] According to Paúl, this principle is adopted within civil law traditions, when tribunals are not provided with specific evidentiary rules.[164] Secondly, the Court embraces the principle of the burden of proof being on the claimant. Yet, it has shifted it, especially when determining moral harm,[165] to allow for a more fair equality of arms between the parties.[166] Unlike human rights courts, both the ICC and the ECCC do not apply a flexible approach towards the burden of proof. This always rests on the claimant throughout the entire process, including the reparations stage.[167] Recognising the challenges victims face in obtaining evidence,[168] the ICC has demonstrated a willingness to lower the standard of evidence required, rather than shifting the burden of proof onto the victims.

4.2.1.1 *Balance of Probabilities or Sufficient Evidence?*

As mentioned previously, international tribunals are often flexible in relation to the standard of proof, and in some cases, they may refrain from mentioning the standard used in their ruling.[169] Yet, it is possible to identify two common standards that international courts apply in reparations: the 'balance of evidence'[170] and 'the sufficiency of evidence'.[171] The former requires the claimant to demonstrate that the harm is 'more likely than not to be true', and the letter demands the claimant to present convincing or persuading evidence related to affirmation.[172]

A look at the official rules of the IACtHR unveils that the standard of proof required is 'sufficiency of evidence'.[173] Yet, the Court adopts an informal and case-by-case approach in applying it.[174] In most of its judgments related to gross violations, there is simply no explicit mention of a standard of proof

163 Álvaro Paúl, 'Sana Crítica: The System for Weighing Evidence Utilized by the Inter-American Court of Human Rights' (2012) 18 Buffalo Human Rights Law Review, 193.

164 Ibid, 205.

165 *Aloeboetoe* (n 120) paras. 71, 76.

166 Odier-Contreras Garduno (n 1) 152.

167 *Katanga-2017* (n 53) para. 59; *Duch-2012* (n 18) para. 33.

168 *Lubanga*-2015 (n 53) para. 22; *Ongwen* (n 13) paras. 518–519.

169 Álvaro Paúl, 'In search of the standards of proof applied by the Inter-American Court of Human Rights' (2012) 55 Revista Instituto Interamericano de Derechos Humanos, 62, 75.

170 It is also called the 'preponderance of evidence, 'more likely than not', and 'more probable than not'.

171 Also known as '*l'intime conviction du juge*'.

172 Odier-Contreras Garduno (n 1) 63.

173 *Norín Catrimán et al.* (n 107) para. 113.

174 *Velásquez Rodríguez v Honduras* (Merits, Judgment) IACtHR Series C No. 04 (29 July 1988) para. 128.

used when assessing harm.[175] This omission may be understandable in cases where the state has acknowledged its responsibility, though such instances are more the exception than the rule. In some cases, particularly those involving material harm, the Court has indirectly implied a standard of 'sufficiency of evidence' by using terms such as 'satisfactory and convincing explanation of evidence'[176] or 'sufficient evidence'.[177] However, it has not clarified what types or levels of evidence meet these criteria for substantiating specific claims.

Notably, if the nature of the case makes it difficult for victims to bring enough evidence or evidence at all, the Court usually shifts from the standard of 'sufficient evidence' to the use of presumptions to establish material harm.[178] In relation to moral harm, the IACtHR often recalls that excessive burden of proof is incompatible within human rights.[179] As a result, the Court often presumes moral harm for both victims and their close relatives.[180] Similarly, the Inter-American Court has long presumed collective harm in two types of cases: 1) in those involving gross violations affecting a large number of victims and 2) when the victim happens to be a group or a community, such as an indigenous one.[181] Victims in these cases are therefore not required to prove the existence of collective harm.

In the recent case of *Community of La Oroya,* the IACtHR added a third category where collective harm can be presumed. This is when 3) the collective nature of the right has been violated. In this case, the Court specifically acknowledged the collective dimension of the right to a healthy environment and the collective harm that results as an inherent consequence of its violation. Further the court asserted that CR are the adequate form to address such harm.[182] Bearing in mind that *La Oroya* had been exposed to high levels of pollution for over a century, it was logical to conclude that the damage caused was of a great magnitude, affecting every aspect of the lives of both individuals and the entire community.[183] Given the difficulties of the community to prove

175 *Rochela Massacre v Colombia* (Merits, Reparations, and Costs, Judgment) IACtHR Series C No. 163 (11 May 2007); *Xákmok Kásek Indigenous Community* (n 144).

176 *Miguel Castro-Castro Prison* (n 48) para. 273.

177 Operation Genesis (n 143) para. 285.

178 Jo M Pasqualucci, *The Practice and Procedure of the Inter-American Court of Human Rights* (CPU 2013) 194.

179 *Sawhoyamaxa Indigenous Commmunity* (n 103) para. 21.

180 *Members of the Village of Chichupac and Neighboring Communities* (n 95) para. 324.

181 Nevertheless, the Court has not consistently applied this criteria to determine this harm. See Odier-Contreras Garduno (n 1) 156, 170.

182 *La Oroya* (n 75) paras. 44, 324.

183 *La Oroya* (n 75) para. 56.

all single individual and collective damages resulting from the mining activities in the community, the Court found the existence of heavy metals in the communities' territory constituted 'sufficient evidence'.[184] All in all, it is clear that the IACtHR is prepared to lower evidential burdens, adopting a 'relaxed approach' in cases where claimants may not have access to evidence – a common situation in cases of gross violations of human rights.[185]

On the other hand, the ICC and the ECCC have consistently referred to the standard of proof applied when grating reparations. The two tribunals have adopted the standard of *balance of probabilities*.[186] According to the ICC, this standard is compatible with the inherent challenges of bringing justice to international crimes, as these are generally committed within a conflict situation and therefore, evidence may be destroyed or unavailable by the time a case reaches a tribunal.[187]

Considering that this standard allows for a wide use of presumptions, both the ICC and the ECCC have included the presumption test when determining harm. Similar to the IACtHR, the ICC employs presumptions in relation to the identification of indirect victims and their alleged harm.[188] Specifically, the ICC has presumed psychological harm in relation to the close relatives of direct victims.[189] Furthermore, it has also presumed the existence of moral harm as a consequence of victims having proved a given material harm,[190] hereby mirroring the practice of human rights courts.[191] Likewise, the ECCC uses presumptions,[192] especially in respect to the psychological harm suffered by the relatives of direct victims and the members of their local community.[193] When the relatives are unable to prove a close relationship with the direct victim, the ECCC presumes collective harm as a natural consequence of the

184 *La Oroya* (n 75) para. 263.

185 Odier-Contreras Garduno (n 1) 111.

186 *Lubanga*-2012 (n 22) para. 253; *Katanga-2017; Ntganda-2021* para. 136, 140 (n 55) para. 50; *Duch-2012* (n 18) paras. 523–531; *Al Mahdi* (n 47) para. 44; *Ongwen* (n 13) para. 433; ECCC's Internal Rules, Rule 23*bis* (1) (b); *Chea et al. Appeals on Civil Party Applications* (n 64) paras. 56–57.

187 *Lubanga*-2012 (n 22) paras. 251–252; *Lubanga*-2015 (n 53) para. 22; *Katanga-2017* (n 53) para. 84; *Ntaganda* (n 55) paras. 136–138.

188 *Katanga-2017* (n 53) para. 61.

189 *Lubanga*-2015 (n 53) para. 58; *Katanga-2017* (n 53) para. 113; *Ongwen* (n 13) para. 556.

190 *Katanga-2017* (n 53) para. 297.

191 *Firstov v Russia* (Judgment) ECtHR No. 42119/04 (7 July 2014) para. 49.

192 *Duch-2012* (n 18) para. 444.

193 *Chea et al. Appeals on Civil Party Applications* (n 64) Separate and Partially Dissenting Opinion of Judge Marchi-Uhe para. 68.

kind of crimes under its jurisdiction.[194] This suggests that for the ECCC, international crimes have a collective nature, thereby resulting in collective harm.[195] On the whole, both the ICC and the ECCC have shown willingness to adopt a victim-friendly and relaxed standard of proof in their reparations proceedings.

4.2.1.2 *Which Method of Proof?*

Before the IACtHR, evidence and arguments brought by the parties are essential to the assessment of harm.[196] The Court however is free to obtain (more) evidence on its own motion.[197] From its jurisprudence, it is evident that the most common evidence is presented in the form of documentation, written and/or oral expert and witnesses testimonies,[198] and circumstantial evidence and presumptions.[199] When related to the existence of gross violations, the Court has also been open to use national truth commissions to determine facts such as systematic patterns.[200]

The IACtHR has adopted a victim-friendly approach towards the admissibility and assessment of evidence, especially in cases involving group and mass victimisation. Attempting to find evidence to prove material harm in these cases is almost impossible.[201] This is due to several factors, including the nature of the violation (i.e. displacement), the destruction of evidence due to the significant period between the violation and the adjudicating proceeding, and the specific cultural perspectives of certain victim groups. For instance, indigenous peoples' understanding of life, damage, and justice are cultural-

194 *Chea et al. Appeals on Civil Party Applications* (n 64) para. 93; *Ieng Sary et al.* (*Case File 002*) (Decision on Appeals against Orders of the Co-Investigating Judges on the admissibility of civil party applications) ECCC Pre-Trial Chamber 10–09–2007-ECCC/OCIJ (24 June 2011) para. 93.

195 *Chea et al. Appeals on Civil Party Applications* (n 64) para. 86.

196 *19 Merchants* (n 51) para. 236; *Yakye Axa Indigenous Community* (n 124) para. 193; *La Cantuta v Peru* (Merits, Reparations and Costs, Judgment) IACtHR Series C No. 162 (29 November 2006) para. 213; *Garífuna Triunfo de la Cruz Community* (n 92) para. 289.

197 Rules of procedure of the Inter-American Court of Human Rights (November 2009) art 58.

198 *Ituango Massacre* (n 104) para. 6.

199 *Rodríguez Vera et al.* (*The disappeared from the Palace of Justice*) *v Colombia* (Preliminary objections, Merits, Reparations and Costs, Judgment) IACtHR Series C No. 287 (14 November 2014) paras. 1, 230.

200 *Río Negro Massacres v Guatemala* (Preliminary Objections, Merits, Reparations and Costs, Judgment) IACtHR Series C No. 250 (4 September 2012) paras. 56–67, 82–85.

201 *Mapiripán Massacre v Colombia* (Merits, Reparations and Costs, Judgment) IACtHR Series C No. 134 (15 September 2005) paras. 266.

driven. In addition, their language is not always a written one. Requiring specific documentation would render their right to substantive justice illusory. Consequently, the Court has adopted a 'relaxed' and somewhat humanistic approach that allows statements of community leaders, together with two more people, to identify victims and their harms.[202] In doing so, the IACtHR has respected the cultural features of certain groups, and prevented evidentiary issues undermining the right of victims to reparations.

Significantly, in the cases of indigenous people, the Court has given significant weight to expert opinions in understanding these communities' unique cultural features and way of living. However, it has not called on experts to help them with the quantification of the damages inflicted when their lands have been taken away. For instance, in the *Awas Tingni* case, which deals with the state failure to ensure the property rights of an indigenous community to its ancestral lands and natural resources, the Court relied on expert reports to determine the collective personality of the group, their understanding of collective land, their legal entitlement to their ancestral lands despite not having title deeds, and the geographical extent of such lands.[203] However, after having found a violation of the right to property, the Court did not call on experts to quantify the material and moral damage inflicted to the Awas Tingni community. Instead, the Court took a very confusing road. It concluded that material damages were not proven by the commission,[204] but presumed the moral damage which it assessed in equity to be of USD 50,000. This sum was ordered to be invested in social services of collective benefit for the community.[205] Decisions like this contradict the relaxed and humanistic approach of the IACtHR towards evidence, as they implicitly require victims to provide evidence they are unable to produce to prove material harm.

Turning to the ICC and the ECCC, both tribunals have been mindful of the difficulties victims face in providing evidence, especially in relation to their harm. It is worth noting that the ICC has stated it has a broad discretion in assessing the reliability of any piece of evidence.[206] Accordingly, the ICC has adopted a certain degree of flexibility in the type of evidence it accepts. For example, it accepts 'circumstantial evidence',[207] as well as both official and

202 *Moiwana Community* (n 122) para. 178.

203 *Mayagna (Sumo) Awas Tingni Community* (n 93) para. 103.

204 *Mayagna (Sumo) Awas Tingni Community* (n 93) para. 105.

205 *Mayagna (Sumo) Awas Tingni Community* (n 93) paras. 167, 173 (6).

206 *Situation in Uganda* (Decision on Victims' Applications for Participation a/0010/06, a/0064/06 to a/0070/06, a/0081/06, to a/0104/06 and a/0111/06, a/0127/06) ICC-02/04 (10 August 2007) para. 13.

207 *Katanga*-2017 (n 53) para. 61.

unofficial documentation (voting or refugee cards, ID certificates, certificates attesting to the loss of an ID card). It also allows statements as long as they are signed 'by two credible witnesses establishing their identity',[208] and even United Nations official reports,[209] and other forms of identity verification.[210] Contrary to the IACtHR, the ICC has relied on experts to determine the quantum of the harm. This prevents the ICC from exercising full discretion in its orders. Interestingly, the ICC has clearly stated that when granting collective reparations, the burden of victims proving their individual claims is of lesser relevance, and the Court will instead rely on presumptions.[211] Finally, similar to the ICC, the ECCC accepts direct and indirect evidence capable of supporting claims. The ECCC's approach appears more burdensome when reparations are to be funded by the convicted party. However, if collective reparations are financed through external resources, the tribunal is more flexible with the evidentiary requirements.[212]

4.2.2 Causation

The principle of reparation refers to the nexus between a violation and the harm caused.[213] Its main goal is to avoid repairing any harm that is considered to be remote from the wrongdoing.[214] The most common tests applied by domestic and international tribunals for reparations are: 1) 'directness', 2) 'foreseeability', and 3) 'proximity'.[215] However, the application and understanding of these three tests is not universally agreed. This has shaped causality into a flexible and context-specific requirement. In general, the causal link

208 *Lubanga*-2012 (n 22) para. 198; *Lubanga*-2015 (n 53) para. 57; *Katanga*-2017 (n 53) paras. 71–72,104.

209 Haydee Dijkstal, 'Destruction of Cultural Heritage before the ICC: The Influence of Human Rights on Reparations Proceedings for Victims and the Accused (2019) 17 Journal of International Criminal Justice 391, 406 citing the Bennoune Report.

210 *Ntaganda-2021* (n 55) para. 137.

211 *Ntaganda-2021* (n 55) para. 140–141.

212 However, when the reparations are funded by external means, civil parties are not required to provide evidence of their own harm before the ECCC. This is because contrary to the ICC, reparations before this tribunal can be either made against the convicted or funded with external resources, thus unrelated to any criminal liability. See: *Chea and Samphan* (n 59) para. 1110.

213 ILC, 'Articles on State Responsibility' (2001) art 31 (2).

214 *Aloeboetoe* (n 120) paras. 48–49.

215 C McCarthy, 'Reparation for Gross Violations of Human Rights law and International Humanitarian Law at the International Court of Justice' in C Ferstman et al (eds), *Reparations for Victims of Genocide, War Crimes and Crimes Against Humanity: Systems in Place and Systems in the Making* (Brill | Nijhoff, 2009) 291–292.

required may depend of the nature of the violation,[216] and on the type of reparations sought. The ICJ, for instance, requires a *direct* causal link between the alleged harm and the actual violation to award compensation. However, it adopts a lower causal link for the measure of satisfaction as a remedy.[217]

While the IACtHR's foundational document and rules do not explicitly mention causality as a precondition for granting specific types of reparations, the Court has asserted the imperative of a causal connection between the harm and the actual violation,[218] as well as between the harm and the type of reparations sought by the victim.[219] In the majority of cases, the Court has nonetheless refrained from elaborating on the causality test required for the harm suffered from a given violation. In cases where the state acknowledges its responsibility,[220] this omission seems to be logical. On occasion, the Court does address causality, but its approach is inconsistent. While the proximity test is the most frequently causation requirement applied for material harm,[221] the Court tends to use the presumption test for moral harm and collective harm.[222] The jurisprudence on group victims confirms that approach. Although in cases concerning gross violations of human rights, such as massacres, the Court adopts a more victim-friendly approach. And, it has been willing to presume both material and moral harm due to challenges faced by victims in gathering and presenting evidence.[223]

Although the IACtHR has put forward that there must be a causal link between the harm suffered and the reparation sought, it has not provided any explanation specifically regarding the required causal link between collective reparations and collective and moral harm. The court has granted CR in cases where collective harm was determined and when it was not. A possible explanation is that the Court takes into account victims' wishes when granting collective reparation. However, this hypothesis is not supported by its jurisprudence. In cases concerning gross violations of human rights, such as the *Pueblo Bello* massacre case, the victims did not request CR but received

216 ILC, 'Commentaries to the Articles on State Responsibility' (2001) para. 10.

217 *Bosnia and Herzegovina v Serbia and Montenegro* (n 162).

218 *19 Merchants* (n 51) para. 236; *Yakye Axa Indigenous Community* (n 124) para. 193.

219 *Ticona Estrada* et al. *v Bolivia* (Merits, Reparations and Costs, Judgment) IACtHR Series C No. 191 (27 November 2008) para. 110; *Cotton Field* (n 121) paras. 450–451.

220 *Trueba Arciniega* et al *v Mexico* (Friendly Settlement Agreement) IACtHR Series C No. 369 (27 November 2018).

221 The second test most commonly used is that of directness.

222 Odier-Contreras Garduno (n 1) 154.

223 *El Mozote* (n 107) para. 383.

them in the form of a housing programme.[224] Similarly, in the cases of *Aloeboetoe* and *Awas Tingni*, the victims did not request CR but were granted them regardless.[225]

Like the IACtHR, the legal framework of the ICC does not specify a causality test for reparations.[226] Their jurisprudence has however clarified the causality required. Bearing in mind that reparations must be related to the individual criminal liability of the convicted,[227] the ICC has held that the exact causality is defined on a case-by-case basis.[228] Through all its case law, the ICC has consistently adopted the 'proximity' test to establish the nexus between the material and moral harm experienced by the victims and the crimes for which the reparations were awarded.[229] In contrast to the IACtHR, a defendant's admission of guilt does not dilute the causation requirement.[230] This emphasises a stricter causation requirement than that of human rights law. However, it is unclear how this standard is attained in practice, given that the ICC has also presumed the existence of material and moral harm, particularly in the case of *Ongwen*.[231] One can infer from this ruling that the ICC also applies presumptions as its second preferred causality test.

When it comes to collective harm, however, the ICC tends to avoid engaging in a discussion on causality. In the *Al Mahdi* case, the Court not only held the existence of collective harm against the Malian state,[232] but also against the international community represented by UNESCO, for the destruction of cultural heritage in Timbuktu. In this ruling, the ICC avoided any analysis on the causal link between the harm and victimhood, as well as between the collective harm and the reparations ordered.[233] The ICC however reiterated that collective harm was suffered by victims across Timbuktu, a city of approximately 70,000 people around the time of the attack, and thus warranted collective reparations.[234] In the same case, the Court also acknowledged that

224 *Pueblo Bello Massacre* (n 154) para. 276.

225 Odier-Contreras Garduno (n 1) 174.

226 Yet Rule 85 of the ICC's RoPE establishes that legal persons claiming to be victims of crimes must be proving 'direct harm'.

227 *Lubanga*-2015 (n 53) paras. 65, 118.

228 *Katanga*-2017 (n 53) para. 166.

229 *Lubanga*-2015 (n 53) paras. 59, 129; *Katanga*-2017 (n 53) para. 162; *Al Mahdi* (n 47) paras. 75, 87, 102; *Ntaganda-2021* (n 55) para. 132 and *Ongwen* (n 13) para. 192.

230 *Al Mahdi* (n 47) paras. 1, 44, 50.

231 *Ongwen* (n 13) para. 556.

232 *Al Mahdi* (n 47) paras. 83,141.

233 Oumar Ba, 'Who are the Victims of Crimes Against Cultural Heritage?' (2019) 41 Human Rights Quarterly 578, 590.

234 *Al Mahdi* (n 47) paras. 52, 67.

individual reparations awards, in the form of compensation, required victims to effectively prove their material and moral harm. This thereby implies a higher standard of proof and a stronger causal link is necessary for moral and material harm.[235]

On the other hand, the ECCC's legal framework mandates a higher causality than that embraced by the ICC. Rule 23bis (1)(b) requires that the harm suffered is a 'direct consequence' of at least one of the crimes for which a person has been convicted.[236] Consequently, in the *Duch* case, the Extraordinary Chambers applied 'direct causality'[237] and dismissed the majority of claims from civil parties in the trial. This causal link is almost impossible to meet for victims of mass crimes. This is perhaps the reason why in its second reparations case, the *Nuon Chea and Khieu Samphan* case, the tribunal avoided any discussion or reference to the matter of causality. Another reason for this avoidance may be that victims requested reparation projects to be funded by external sources, rather than related to the criminal liability of convicted individuals.[238]

5 Conclusions

This contribution has sought to unveil the link between the assessment of harm and the granting of collective reparations by international courts. The current approach of the IACtHR, the ICC, and the ECCC does not support any serious and clear link between collective harm and the granting of CR.

Regarding evidentiary criteria, the IACtHR takes a relaxed approach, as demonstrated by its constant reliance on presumptions and indirect evidence, and its adoption of the principle of equity in calculating damage.[239] However, its application of presumptions and equity has been highly inconsistent. In addition, the Court has failed to clarify how it quantifies awards or assesses the adequacy of reparations, often leaving these decisions to broad judicial discretion. This approach provides victims with little legal certainty regarding the proof required to establish harm or how their rights will be redressed in

235 *Al Mahdi* (n 47) para. 81, 89.

236 ECCC's Internal Rules.

237 *Duch-2010* (n 91) para. 642; *Duch-2012* (n 18) paras. 642–643.

238 Yet, it must be noted that the requirement of direct causality was used by the ECCC in the *Nuon Chea and Khieu Samphan* case regarding victims' participation. See: *Chea* et al. *Appeals on Civil Party Applications* (n 64) para. 71.

239 *Katanga*-2017 (n 53) para. 191.

judicial proceedings. This inconsistency is allegedly based on the fact that the IACtHR is not obliged to follow its precedents, instead deciding reparations on a case-by-case basis.[240]

The IACtHR has clearly influenced the ICC, who has also not been shy in using presumptions to establish moral harm[241] and to determine that collective reparations are the adequate form of reparations for moral harm suffered by the victims.[242] The ICC's reliance on the jurisprudence of the IACtHR, whose practice is unlikely to pass a legal scrutiny examination, appears risky. However, in comparison, the ICC has relied on experts to determine the quantum of harm, thereby showing more transparency and less judicial discretion.

For determining the standard of proof and causation, the three tribunals adopt a flexible approach to the rules, thereby preventing a *probatio diabolica*.[243] However, the exact requirements for proof and causation in relation to collective reparations remain unclear. Such flexibility seems victim- friendly and has allowed the tribunals to overcome procedural obstacles that could otherwise prevent victims from obtaining reparations.

Finally, the justification for collective reparations across all three tribunals primarily reflects pragmatic considerations rather than a detailed evaluation of collective harm. Although the IACtHR, ICC, and ECCC invoke the concept of collective harm to support the rationale for such reparations, their practices indicate that the primary objective is to address the challenges of large-scale victimisation effectively. Accordingly, the IACtHR grants collective reparations in five scenarios: i) when all victims have not been identified, ii) when there is a lack of evidence of the harm due to the nature of the case, iii) when the victim is a community/group, iv) when victims request them, and v) when a collective right has been violated.[244] Similarly, the ICC and ECCC's practices mirror three of these criteria: i) the number of victims is large,[245] and happens to be a community/group,[246] ii) when victims have not been identified at the

240 *El Amparo* (n 121) para. 34.

241 *Katanga*-2017 (n 53) paras. 48, 57, 61.

242 *Al Mahdi* (n 47) para. 85.

243 *Sawhoyamaxa Indigenous Commmunity* (n 103) Separate Opinion by Judge Cançado Trinade, para. 21.

244 Odier-Contreras Garduno (n 1) 148–157; In the *La Oroya* case the Court recalled the collective nature of the right to a healthy environment. See: *La Oroya* (n 75) paras. 44, 324.

245 *Ongwen* (n 13) paras. 636, 577; *Duch-2012* (n 18) para. 659.

246 *Al Mahdi* (n 47) paras. 83, 141.

time of its judgment, iii) when the victims' wish for them.[247] In this light, it is submitted that international courts usually find the justification of granting CR on pragmatic and humanistic grounds, rather than in the assessment of harm of each individual case.

References

Books

Brown C, A *Common Law of International Adjudication* (Oxford University Press 2007)

Díaz Gómez C (ed), *Tareas Pendientes: Propuestas para la formulación de políticas públicas de la reparación en Colombia* (ICTJ 2010)

De Greiff P, (ed) The Handbook of Reparations (Oxford University Press 2006)

Evans C, *The Right to Reparation in International Law for Victims of Armed Conflict* (Cambridge University Press 2012)

Odier-Contreras Garduno D, (2018) *Collective Reparations: Tensions and Dilemmas Between Collective Reparations with the Individual Right to Receive Reparations* (Intersentia 2018)

Pasqualucci JM, *The Practice and Procedure of the Inter-American Court of Human Rights* (Cambridge University Press 2013)

Shelton D, *Remedies in International Human Rights Law* (Oxford University Press 2015)

Sperfeldt C, *Practices of Reparations in International Criminal Justice* (Cambridge University Press 2022)

Book Chapters

Barker J, 'The different forms of reparation: compensation' in Crawford J, Olleson S, Pellet A, (eds) *The Law on International Responsibility* (Oxford University Press 2010)

Correa C, 'Reparation Programs for Mass Violations of Human Rights: Lessons from Experiences in Argentina, Chile and Peru' in Felix Reategui (ed), *Transitional Justice Handbook for Latin America* (Brazilian Ministry of Justice Amnesty Commission 2011)

Calderón Gamboa J, *La reparación integral en la jurisprudencia de la Corte Interamericana de Derechos Humanos: estándares aplicables al nuevo paradigma mexicano* (Instituto de Investigaciones Jurídicas, Suprema Corte de la Nación 2013)

247 *Lubanga*-2012 (n 22) para. 274.

de Greiff P, 'Justice and Reparations' in de Greiff P (ed), *The Handbook of Reparations* (Oxford University Press 2006)

Hamber B, 'The Dilemmas of Reparations: In Search of a Process-driven Approach' in De Feyter K, Parmentier S, Bossuyt M and Lemmens P (eds), *Out of the Ashes: Reparations for Victims of Gross and Systematic Human Rights Violations* (Intersentia 2005)

Jarvis H, 'Trials and Tribulations: The Long Quest for Justice for the Cambodian Genocide' in Simon M Meisenberg and Ignaz Stegmiller (eds), *The Extraordinary Chambers in the Courts of Cambodia: Assessing Their Contribution to International Criminal Law* (TMC Asser Press 2016)

Letschert, R. and van Boven, T., 'Providing Reparation in Situations of Mass Victimization: Key Challenges Involved', in R. Letschert et al. (eds.), *Victimological Approaches to International Crimes: Africa* (Cambridge, Intersentia 2011)

Malarino E, 'Activismo Judicial, Punitivización y Nacionalización. Tendencias Antidemocráticas y Antiliberales de la Corte Interamericana de Derechos Humanos', in Grupo Latinoamericano de Estudios sobre Derecho Penal International, *Sistema Interamericano de Protección de los Derechos Humanos y Derecho Penal Internacional* (Konrad-Adenauer-Stiftung 2010)

Mégret F, 'The Case for Collective Reparations before the International Criminal Court', in Jo-Anne M. Wemmers (ed), *Reparations for Victims of Crimes against Humanity: The Healing Role of Reparation* (Routledge 2014)

McCarthy C, 'Reparation for Gross Violations of Human Rights Law and International Humanitarian Law at the International Court of Justice' in Ferstman C, Goetz M, Stephens A (eds), *Reparations for Victims of Genocide, War Crimes and Crimes Against Humanity: Systems in Place and Systems in the Making* (Brill | Nijhoff 2009)

Odier-Contreras Garduno D, 'Collective reparations in Colombia: a tool for the non-repetition of violations?' in Michiel Luchtman et al. (eds), *Of Swords and Shields: Due Process and Crime Control in Times of Globalization. Liber Amicorum Prof. dr. J.A.E. Vervaelei* (Eleven, 2023)

Odio Benito E, 'Development and Interpretation of Principles of Reparation: the Case Law of the IACHR and its Possible Contributions to the Jurisprudence of the ICC' in Chile Eboe-Osuji (ed), *Protecting Humanity: Essays in International Law and Policy in Honour of Navanethem Pillay* (Nijhoff 2010).

Riddell A, 'Evidence, Fact-Finding, and Experts' in Alter K, Romano C, Shany Y (eds), *The Oxford Handbook of International Adjudication* (Oxford University Press 2013)

Rubio-Marin R, 'The Gender of Reparations in Transitional Societies' in Rubio-Marin R (ed), *The Gender of Reparations: Unsettling Sexual Hierarchies While Redressing Human Rights Violations* (Cambridge University Press 2009)

Articles

Altwicker-Hámori S, Altwicker T, Peters A, 'Measuring Violations of Human Rights: An Empirical Analysis of Awards in Respect of Non-Pecuniary Damage under the European Convention on Human Rights' (2016) 76 Heidelberg Journal of International Law 1.

Ba O, 'Who are the Victims of Crimes Against Cultural Heritage?' (2019) 41 Human Rights Quarterly 578

Contreras-Garduno D, 'Defining Beneficiaries of Collective Reparations: The experience of the IACtHR' (2012) 4 *Amsterdam Law Forum 3.*

Dijkstal H, 'Destruction of Cultural Heritage before the ICC: The Influence of Human Rights on Reparations Proceedings for Victims and the Accused (2019) 17 Journal of International Criminal Justice 391.

Firchow P, 'Must our communities bleed to receive social services? Development projects and collective reparations schemes in Colombia' (2013) 8 Journal of Peacebuilding and Development 50.

Firchow P, 'The Implementation of the Institutional Programme of Collective Reparations in Colombia' (2014) 6 Journal of Human Rights Practice 356.

Gready S, 'The Case for Transformative Reparations: In Pursuit of Structural Socio-Economic Reform in Post-Conflict Societies', 16 Journal of Intervention and Statebuilding 2.

Magarrell L, 'Reparations in Theory and Practice, Reparative Justice Series' (ICTJ, 2007)

Pasqualucci J M, 'Victim Reparations in the Inter-American Human Rights System: A Critical Assessment of Current Practice and Procedure' (1996) 18 Michigan Journal of International Law 1.

Paúl A, 'In search of the standards of proof applied by the Inter-American Court of Human Rights' (2012) 55 Revista Instituto Interamericano de Derechos Humanos 57.

Paúl A, 'Sana Crítica: The System for Weighing Evidence Utilized by the Inter-American Court of Human Rights' (2012) 18 Buffalo Human Rights Law Review 93.

Perez-Leon-Acevedo JP, 'Reparations in environmental cases: should the International Criminal Court consider the Inter-American Court of Human Rights' jurisprudence?' (2024) 15 Journal of International Dispute Settlement.

Rosenfeld F, 'Collective Reparations for Victims of Armed Conflicts' (2010) 92 International Review of the Red Cross 731

Sandoval, Clara, 'Two steps forward, one step back: Reflections on the jurisprudential turn of the Inter-American Court of Human Rights on domestic reparations programmes' (2017) 22 The International Journal of Human Rights 1.

Tapia Navarro N, 'Collective Reparations and the Limitations of International Criminal Justice to Respond to Mass Atrocity' (2018)18 International Criminal Law Review.

Urban Walker M, 'Transformative Reparations? A Critical Look at a Current Trend in Thinking about Gender-Just Reparations' (2016) 10 International Journal of Transitional Justice 108.

Uprimny Yepes R, 'Transformative Reparations of Massive Gross Human Rights Violations: Between Corrective and Distributive Justice' (2009) 27 Netherlands Quarterly of Human Rights 4.

Gentian Zyberi, 'The International Court of Justice and applied forms of reparation for international human rights and humanitarian law violations' (2011) 7 *Utrecht Law Review*.

Reports

Aubry S, and Henao-Trip MI, 'Collective Reparations and the International Criminal Court'(2011) Briefing Paper 2, Essex Transitional Justice Network.

Amezcua-Noriega O, 'Reparations Principles under International Law and their Possible Application by the International Criminal Court: Some Reflections' (2011) Briefing Paper 1, Essex Transitional Justice Network.

International Center for Transitional Justice, 'The Rabat Report: The Concept and Challenges of Collective Reparations' (ICTJ 2009)

International Center for Transitional Justice, 'Reparations in Theory and Practice' (Reparative Justice Series 2007)

United Nations, 'Guidance Note of the Secretary-General: United Nations Approach to Transitional Justice' (UN, March 2010)

Online Documents

'El salario mínimo sube en Guatemala' (Datosmacro.com (expansion.com), 2004) < https://datosmacro.expansion.com/smi/guatemala?anio=2004#:~:text=El%20salario%20m%C3%ADnimo%20sube%20en,mayor%20parte%20de%20los%20pa%C3%ADses> accessed 30 March 2023

Justice Yaw Appau, 'Justice of the Court of Appeal in Ghana: Assessment of Damages, Paper Presented at Induction Course for Newly Appointed Circuit Judges at the Judicial Training Institute' (jtighana.org) <https://jtighana.org/old/educational/papers/> accessed 24 March 2023

Final Agreement to End the Conflict and Building a Stable and Lasting Peace, 2016 <https://www.refworld.org/legal/agreements/natlegbod/2016/en/121520> accessed 20 April 2024

UN Documents

General Assembly, *Basic Principles and Guidelines on the Right to a Remedy and Reparation for Victims of Gross Violations of International Human Rights Law and Serious Violations of International Humanitarian Law* (Resolution 60/147, 2005)

General Assembly, *Declaration of Basic Principles of Justice for Victims of Crime and Abuse of Power* (UNGA Resolution 40/34, 1985)

Table of Cases

European Court of Human Rights

Firstov v *Russia* (Judgment) No. 42119/04 (7 July 2014)*Papamichalopoulos and Others v Greece (Article 50)* (Judgment) 14556/89 (31 October 1995)

Varnava and Others v Turkey (Judgment) Cases Nos. 16064/90, 16065/90, 16066/90, 16068/90, 16069/90, 16070/90, 16071/90, 16072/90 and 16073/90 (18 September 2009)

Extraordinary Chambers in the Courts of Cambodia

Case of Ieng Sary et al. (*Case File 002*) (Decision on Appeals against Orders of the Co-Investigating Judges on the admissibility of civil party applications) Pre-Trial Chamber No. *10–09–2007-ECCC/OCIJ* (24 June 2011)

Case of Kaing Guek Eav alias *'Duch'* (*Case 001*) (Judgment) No. 001/18–07–2007-ECCC/TC (26 July 2010)

Case of Kaing Guek Eav alias *'Duch'* (*Case 001*) (Appeal Judgment) No. 001/18–07–2007-ECCC/SC (3 February 2012)

Case of Nuon Chea and Khieu Samphan (*Case 002/01*) (Judgment) No. 002/19–09–2007/ECCC/TC (7 August 2014)

Case of Nuon Chea et al. (*Case 002*) (Appeals on Civil Party Applications) No. D404/2/4 (24 June 2011)

Case of Nuon Chea et al. (*Case 002*) (Appeals on Civil Party Applications, Separate and Partially Dissenting Opinion of Judge Marchi-Uhe) No. D404/2/4 (24 June 2011)

Inter-American Court of Human Rights

19 Merchants v Colombia (Merits, Reparations and Costs) Series C No. 109 (5 July 2004)

Afro-descendant Communities displaced from the Cacarica River Basin (Operation Genesis) v Colombia (Preliminary Objections, Merits, Reparations and Costs) Series C No. 270 (20 November 2013)

Aloeboetoe et al v Suriname (Reparations and Costs) Series C No. 15 (10 September 1993)

Atala Riffo and Daughters v Chile (Merits, Reparations and Costs) Series C No. 239 (24 Feb 2012)

Blake v Guatemala (Reparations and Costs) IACtHR Series C No 48 (22 January 1999)
Cantoral Benavides v Peru (Reparations and Costs) Series C No. 88 (3 December 2001)
Caracazo v Venezuela (Reparations and Costs) Series C No. 95 (29 August 2002)
Castillo Petruzzi et al. v Peru (Merits, Reparations and Costs) Series C No. 52 (30 May 1999)
Chaparro Álvarez and Lapo Íñiguez v Ecuador (preliminary objections, merits, reparations and costs) Series C No 170 (21 November 2007)
El Amparo v Venezuela (Merits) Series C No. 19 (18 January 1995)
El Amparo v Venezuela (Reparations and Costs, Judgment) IACtHR Series C No. 28 (14 September 1996)
Gangaram-Panday v Suriname (Merits, Reparations and Costs) Series C No. 16 (21 January 1994)
Garífuna Triunfo de la Cruz Community and its Members v Honduras (Merits, Reparations and Costs) Series C No. 305 (8 October 2015)
González et al ("Cotton Field") v Mexico (Preliminary Objections, Merits, Reparations and Costs) Series C No 205 (16 November 2009)
Habitantes de la Oroya v Perú (Excepciones Preliminares, Fondo, Reparaciones y Costas) Series C No. 511 (27 November 2023)
Ibsen Cárdenas And Ibsen Peña v Bolivia (Merits, Reparation, and Costs) Series C No. 217 (1 September 2010)
Ituango Massacre v Colombia (Preliminary Objections, Merits, Reparations and Costs) Series C No. 148 (1 July 2006)
La Cantuta v Peru (Merits, Reparations and Costs) Series C No. 162 (29 November 2006)
Las Palmeras v Colombia (Reparations and Costs) Series C No. 96 (26 November 2002)
Massacre Mapiripán v Colombia (Merits, Reparations and Costs) Series C No. 134 (15 September 2005)
Massacres of El Mozote and nearby places v El Salvador (Merits, Reparations and Costs) Series C No. 252 (25 October 2012)
Mayagna (Sumo) Awas Tingni v Nicaragua (Merits, Reparations and Costs) Series C No. 79 (31 August 2001)
Members of the Village of Chichupac and Neighboring Communities of the Municipality of Rabinal v Guatemala (Preliminary Objections, Merits, Reparations and Costs) Series C No. 328 (30 November 2016)
Miguel Castro-Castro Prison v Peru (Merits, Reparations and Costs) Series C No. 160 (25 November 2006)
Moiwana Community v Suriname (Preliminary Objections, Merits, Reparations and Costs) Series C No. 124 (15 June 2005)
Neira Alegria v. Peru, (Reparations and Costs, Judgment) IACtHR Series C No. 29 (19 September 1996)

Norín Catrimán et al. (Leaders, members and activist of the Mapuche Indigenous People) v. *Chile* (Merits, Reparations and Costs) Series C No. 279 (29 May 2014)

Peasant Community of Santa Bárbara v Peru (Preliminary Objections, Merits, Reparations and Costs) Series C No. 299 (1 September 2015)

Plan de Sánchez Massacre v Guatemala (Reparations) Series C No. 116 (19 November 2004)

Pueblo Bello Massacre v Colombia (Merits, Reparations and Costs) Series C No. 140 (31 January 2006)

Río Negro Massacres v Guatemala (Preliminary Objections, Merits, Reparations and Costs) Series C No. 250 (4 September 2012)

Rochela Massacre v Colombia (Merits, Reparations and Costs) Series C No. 163 (11 May 2007)

Rodríguez Vera et al (the disappeared from the Palace of Justice) v Colombia (Preliminary Objections, Merits, Reparations and Costs) Series C No. 287 (14 November 2014)

Santo Domingo Massacre v Colombia (Preliminary Objections, Merits, Reparations and Costs) Series C No. 259 (30 November 2012)

Saramaka People v Suriname (Preliminary Objections, Merits, Reparations and Costs, Judgment) IACtHR Series C No. 172 (20 November 2007)

Sawhoyamaxa Indigenous Community v Paraguay (Merits, Reparations and Costs) Series C No. 146 (29 March 2006)

Street Children (Villagrán-Morales et al) v Guatemala (Reparations and Costs) Series C No. 77 (26 May 2001)

The Kaliña and Lokono Peoples v. *Suriname*, (Merits, Reparations and Costs, Judgment) IACtHR Series C No. 309 (25 November 2015)

The Kichwa Indigenous People of Sarayaku v Ecuador (Merits, Reparations and Costs) Series C No. 245 (27 June 2012)

Ticona Estrada et al v Bolivia (Merits, Reparations and Costs) Series C No. 191 (27 November 2008)

Trueba Arciniega et al v México (Friendly Settlement Agreement) Series C No. 369 (27 November 2018)

Valle Jaramillo et al. v Colombia (Merits, Reparations and Costs) IACtHR Series C No. 192 (27 November 2008)

Velásquez Rodríguez v Honduras (Merits) Series C No. 04 (29 July 1988)

Velásquez Rodríguez v Honduras (Reparations and Costs) Series C No 07 (21 July 1989)

White Van (Paniagua-Morales et al) v Guatemala (Reparations and Costs) Series C No. 76 (25 May 2001)

Xákmok Kásek Indigenous Community v Paraguay (Merits, Reparations and Costs) Series C No. 214 (24 August 2010)

Yakye Axa Indigenous Community v Paraguay (Merits, Reparations and Costs) Series C No. 125 (17 June 2005)

International Court of Justice

Ahmadou Sadio Diallo (*Republic of Guinea v Democratic Republic of the Congo*) (Separate Opinion of Judge Cançado Trindade, Judgment) No. 103 (19 June 2012)

Application of the Convention on the Prevention and Punishment of the Crime of Genocide (*Bosnia and Herzegovina v Serbia and Montenegro*) (Judgment) No. 91 (26 February 2007)

Avena and other Mexican nationals (*Mexico v United States of America*) (Judgment) No. 128 (31 March 2004)

Corfu Channel (*United Kingdom of Great Britain and Northern Ireland v Albania*) (Merits) No. 001 (9 April 1949)

International Criminal Court

Case: None (*Situation only*), *Situation in Uganda* (Decision on Victims' Applications for Participation a/0010/06, a/0064/06 to a/0070/06, a/0081/06, to a/0104/06 and a/0111/06, a/0127/06) ICC-02/04 (10 August 2007)

The Prosecutor v Ahmad Al Faqi Al Mahdi (Reparations Order) ICC-01/12-01/15 (17 August 2017)

The Prosecutor v Germain Katanga (Report on applications for reparations in accordance with Trial Chamber II's Order of 27 August) ICC-01/04-01/07-3512-Anx1-Red2 (21 January 2015)

The Prosecutor v Germain Katanga (Scheduling order for interested States or other interested persons to apply for leave to file submissions according to Article 75 of the Statute) ICC-01/04-01/07-3512-Anx1-Red2 (21 January 2015)

The Prosecutor v Germain Katanga (Observations in response to the Trial Chamber's order of 15 July 2016 with Public redacted version of Annex A: Index of annexes, and public annexes 1–5 and 7–14) ICC-01/04-01/07-3714-Red (30 September 2016)

The Prosecutor v Germain Katanga (Ordonnance de réparation en vertu de l'article 75 du Statut) ICC-01/04-01/07-3728 (24 March 2017)

The Prosecutor v Germain Katanga (Draft implementation plan relevant to Trial Chamber II's order for reparations of 24 March 2017 (ICC-01/04-01/07-3728)) ICC-01/04-01/07 (25 July 2017)

The Prosecutor v Thomas Lubanga Dyilo (Decision establishing the principles and procedures to be applied to reparations) ICC-01/04-01/06-2904 (7 August 2012)

The Prosecutor v Thomas Lubanga Dyilo (Judgment on the appeals against the "Decision establishing the principles and procedures to be applied to reparations" of 7 August 2012 with AMENDED order for reparations (Annex A) and public annexes 1 and 2) ICC-01/04-01/06-3129 (3 March 2015)

The Prosecutor v Thomas Lubanga Dyilo (Filing on Reparations and Draft Implementation Plan, Annex A) ICC-01/04-01/06-Red (3 November 2015)

The Prosecutor v Thomas Lubanga Dyilo, (Décision fixant le montant des réparations auxquelles Thomas Lubanga Dyilo est tenu) ICC-01/04-01/06-3379- Red. (15 December 2017)

The Prosecutor v Bosco Ntaganda (Reparations Order) ICC-01/04-02/06 (8 March 2021)

The Prosecutor v Bosco Ntaganda (Judgment on the appeals against the decision of Trial Chamber VI of 8 March 2021 entitled "Reparations Order") ICC-01/04-02/06-2782 (22 September 2022)

The Prosecutor v Bosco Ntaganda (Judgment on the appeals against the decision of Trial Chamber II of 14 July 2023 entitled "Addendum to the Reparations Order of 8 March 2021, ICC-01/04-02/06-2659") ICC-01/04-02/06-2908-Red (01 November 2024)

The Prosecutor v Dominic Ongwen (Reparations Order) ICC-02/04-01/15 (28 February 2024)

Permanent Court of International Justice

Factory at Chorzów (*Germany v Poland*) (Indemnity Order) Series A No. 17 (13 September 1928)

Table of Instruments

ACHR

American Convention on Human Rights (as adopted on 22 November 1969, entered into force 18 July 1978)

ECCC

ECCC's Internal Rules Revision 9 (as amended 16 January 2015)

IACtHR

Rules of procedure of the Inter-American Court of Human Rights (November 2009)

ICC

Rome Statute of the International Criminal Court (adopted 17 July 1998, entered into force 1 July 2022) 2187 UNTS 3.

Rules of Procedure and Evidence of the International Criminal Court (adopted 9 September 2002, immediately in force) ICC-ASP/1/3.

ILC

Articles on State Responsibility (2001)

Commentaries to the Articles on State Responsibility (2001)

OAS

Principal Guidelines for a comprehensive reparations policy (2008) Doc. No. OEA/Ser/L/V/II.131

CHAPTER 4

Reparation in Inter-state Disputes: Preliminary Lessons from the Practice of Human Rights Courts and Bodies

Giulio Bartolini

1 Introduction

Inter-state proceedings claiming violations of human rights law have started to become commonplace in international law, before human rights courts and bodies,[1] as well as the ICJ.[2] This growing practice has begun to shed light on an under-scrutinized issue, namely how the obligation of reparation could and should be performed in inter-state litigations. Such disputes might thus interact with solutions identified by the International Law Commission (ILC) in its

1 See Isabella Risini, *The Inter-state Application under the European Convention on Human Rights* (Brill 2020). For relevant cases, see infra Section 2.

2 In particular a series of applications have been filled by States parties to human rights treaties in light of the erga omnes of such conventions as for: *Application of the Convention on the Prevention and Punishment of the Crime of Genocide* (*The Gambia v. Myanmar*) (Application Instituting Proceedings and Request for Provisional Measures), 11 November 2019, https://www.icj-cij.org/sites/default/files/case-related/178/178–20191111-APP-01–00-EN.pdf; *Application of the Convention against Torture and Other Cruel, Inhuman or Degrading Treatment or Punishment* (*Canada and the Netherlands v. Syrian Arab Republic*) (Joint Application Instituting Proceedings concerning a Dispute under the Convention against Torture and other Cruel, Inhuman or Degrading Treatment or Punishment), 8 June 2023, https://www.icj-cij.org/sites/default/files/case-related/188/188–20230608-APP-01–00-EN.pdf; *Application of the Convention on the Prevention and Punishment of the Crime of Genocide in the Gaza Strip* (*South Africa v. Israel*) (Application Instituting Proceedings), 29 December 2023, 72, para. 111 <https://www.icj-cij.org/sites/default/files/case-related/192/192–20231228-app-01–00-en.pdf>. Furthermore, a series of proceedings have been brought by States claiming the violation of human rights treaties occurred against citizens of the applicant States. See, for instance,: Application of the International Convention on the Elimination of All Forms of Racial Discrimination (Armenia v. Azerbaijan), Application Instituting Proceedings and Request for Provisional Measures of 16 September 2021, https://www.icj-cij.org/sites/default/files/case-related/180/180–20210916-APP-01–00-EN.pdf: Application of the International Convention on the Elimination of All Forms of Racial Discrimination (Azerbaijan v. Armenia), Application Instituting Proceedings (23 September 2021) https://www.icj-cij.org/sites/default/files/case-related/181/181–20210923-APP-01–00-EN.pdf.

 | DOI:10.1163/9789004716742_005

Article 48(2) on the responsibility of States for internationally wrongful acts (ARSIWA),[3] a provision qualified as 'a measure of progressive development'[4] at the time of its adoption. Indeed, in this provision the ILC maintained how when faced with violations of *erga omnes* obligations, any state other than the injured state 'may claim from the responsible State: (a) cessation of the internationally wrongful act, and assurances and guarantees of non-repetition [...]; and (b) performance of the obligation of reparation [...], in the interest of the injured State or of the beneficiaries of the obligation breached'.

The analysis will focus on some key challenges raised by reparation in such scenarios. First (Section 2), the analysis will investigate the possibility to identify the actual victims of violations as the addressees of reparation measures, including in cases in which inter-state claims are brought to human rights courts and bodies by the state of citizenship. Second (Section 3), key issues related to the performance of the obligation of reparation in favour of the beneficiaries of the *erga omnes* obligations breached could be explored. On the one hand, this might relate to procedural aspects, such as the proper representations by States of the victims' interests or the relationship, at the reparation phase, between parallel claims made by States and the same victims. On the other hand, this could involve analysis on the material content of reparation, taking into account how in such instances relevant measures should be tailored to serve the beneficiaries of the *erga omnes* obligation breached.

In this contribution, following the focus of this book, attention will only be paid to practice related to reparation issues linked to cases addressed by human rights courts and bodies. Therefore, cases brought before the ICJ fall outside of its purview. Nevertheless, the review of practice developed by human rights courts and bodies can be relevant for both providing a preliminary assessment of it and in identifying some trends potentially relevant in pending inter-state disputes at ICJ, as mentioned in the concluding Section 4.

2 The Addressee of the Obligation to Reparation in Inter-state Disputes

A preliminary question that arises concerns the identification of the addressee of the obligation to reparation in inter-state disputes brought in front of human rights courts and bodies. Indeed, following the approach adopted by the ILC

3 ILC, 'Draft Articles on Responsibility of States for Internationally Wrongful Acts with Commentaries' (2001) YILC, vol II (Part Two) 31.

4 ILC, 'Draft Articles' (n 3) 127, para. 12.

mentioned above in its Article 48(2), in case of violations of *erga omnes* obligations any State other than the injured one can request the cessation of the unlawful act and assurances and guarantees of non-repetition, as well as the performance of the obligation of reparation in the interest of the beneficiary of the obligation breached, namely individuals affected by wrongful acts in case of violations of human rights norms. This solution is therefore opposite to the approach adopted in relation to Article 42,[5] aimed at identifying the notion of an 'injured State', namely States specifically affected by a violation of a reciprocal obligation or by rules implying an *erga omnes* or *erga omnes* partes obligation, such as a coastal State affected by pollution occurring on the high seas.[6] In this latter case, indeed, the injured State can request the performance of the obligation of reparation to its own benefit.

In this regard, however, particularly at the time of the adoption of the ARSIWA, one specific scenario has proven controversial among scholars, namely inter-state disputes raised by the State of citizenship of individuals materially affected by the breach of human rights treaties. Indeed, this context is different from other types of inter-state proceedings involving *erga omnes* obligations where no bonds of nationality are present between the actual victims and the State pinpointing to the wrongful act. In this latter instance, no doubts are present on the qualification of this latter as a State other than the injured one under Article 48(2) ARSIWA with the consequence of allowing it the possibility to invoke reparation only in the interest of the beneficiary of the obligation breached. The specific scenario of inter-state disputes raised by the State of citizenship of individuals materially affected by the breach of human rights treaties has conversely been addressed in different ways by academics which have split into three main approaches.

A first group of scholars maintains that the State acting to claim the violation of human rights provisions against its citizens ought to be qualified as an 'injured State' according to Article 42(b)(i) ARSIWA[7] in light of its distinct legal position compared to any other State bound by these rules.[8] Conversely, other

5 According to Article 42 ARSIWA 'A State is entitled as an injured State to invoke the responsibility of another State if the obligation breached is owed to: (a) that State individually; or (b) a group of States including that State, or the international community as a whole, and the breach of the obligation: (i) specially affects that State; or (ii) is of such a character as radically to change the position of all the other States to which the obligation is owed with respect to the further performance of the obligation'.

6 ILC, 'Draft Articles' (n 3), 118–209.

7 On this provision see above n 5.

8 See Bruno simma, 'From Bilateralism to Community Interest in International Law' (1994) 250 RCADI, 217, 296; Karl Zemaneck, 'New Trends in the Enforcement of erga omnes Obli-

scholars underline that its legal position is better framed under Article 48 ARSIWA.[9] According to this latter approach, as human rights rules protect collectives and not merely reciprocal values in light of the *erga omnes* character of the relevant obligations, it would be improper to hypothesize that the State of citizenship of individual victims should be framed as an 'injured State': the mere bond of nationality would not be sufficient to receive such qualification pursuant to Article 42(b)(i) as a breach of human rights can hardly be deemed to offend the individual interest of this State. Finally, a third position holds that the State of citizenship has an option to resort to diplomatic protection and qualify itself as an 'injured State' (Article 42) or act as 'any State other than an injured State' (Article 48). This choice will depend on the preferences of the implicated state and guided by strategic litigation assessments involving, for instance, elements such as management of the exhaustion of domestic remedies or even political evaluations.[10]

However, the proper qualification of the position of the applicant State could finally be crucial for the performance of the obligation of reparation as the possibility to qualify the State of citizenship of victims of human rights abuses under Articles 42(b)(i) or 48 ARSIWA has different implications. Even if the content and purpose of a series of measures to be potentially requested by the State invoking international responsibility for such violations would not be affected by its qualification, as provided for by requests for cessation and assurances and guarantees of non-repetition, the same could not be said for the performance of the obligation of reparation and its addressees. Indeed, a State acting as an 'injured State' under Article 42 ARSIWA can claim reparation

gations', (2000) 4 Max Planck Yearbook of United Nations Law 1, 29; Luigi Condorelli, 'La protection diplomatique et l'évolution de son domaine d'application actuelle', (2003) 86 Rivista di diritto internazionale, 5, 18–23; Riccardo Pisillo Mazzeschi, 'Impact on the Law of Diplomatic Protection', in Menno Kamminga and Martin Scheinin (eds), *The Impact of Human Rights Law on General International Law* (Oxford University Press 2009), 211, 228–230.

9 Giorgio Gaja, 'Is a State Specially Affected when Its Nationals' Human Rights Are Infringed?', in Lal Vohrah et al. (eds), *Man's Inhumanity to Man. Essays on International Law in Honour of Antonio Cassese* (Kluwer 2003), 373; Enzo Cannizzaro, 'Is There an Individual Right to Reparation? Some Thoughts on the ICJ Judgment in the Jurisdictional Immunities Case', in Denis Alland et al. (eds), *Unité et diversité du droit international* (Brill 2014) 495, 498–500.

10 Annemarieke Vermeer-Künzli, 'A Matter of Interest: Diplomatic Protection and State Responsibility *Erga omnes*', (2007) 56 International and Comparative Law Quarterly, 553. Also Pisillo Mazzeschi (n 8) 229–231, regardless of the preference for qualifying this State under Article 42(b)(i) ARSIWA, maintains how it could also act based on Article 48, also in light of some procedural advantages.

from the responsible State for its own benefit, while a claim for reparation made by a State acting under Article 48 ARSIWA is made in the interest of the beneficiaries of the *erga omnes* obligation breached. This issue could have a clear impact in claims brought by States both regarding potential diplomatic settlements or inter-state proceedings in front of the ICJ and, therefore, it could be interesting to appreciate how this issue has been addressed in relation to human rights courts and bodies as to appreciate their approach and positions held by States. In particular, this practice is of interest as all inter-state disputes brought so far in front of human rights courts and bodies are related to claims of violations of human rights involving citizenship of the applicant States.

2.1 *The European Court of Human Rights*

Regarding inter-state complaints brought before universal or regional human rights courts and bodies for violations of relevant treaties, an initial reference could be made to practice at the European Court of Human Rights (ECtHR). While in the first inter-state dispute the applicant State did not claim any measure of reparation,[11] the subsequent *Denmark v. Turkey* case is worthy of mention.[12] The proceedings, relating to alleged acts of torture committed by the Turkish security forces against a Danish citizen of Kurdish origin, ended in 2000 with the dismissal of the case following a friendly settlement between the two States. This agreement, endorsed by the ECtHR, envisaged the adoption of measures aimed at avoiding a repetition of the wrongful act and satisfying the applicant State, for instance through an official apology and the establishment of a political dialogue on human rights issues between the States concerned, and the granting of *ex gratia* compensation to Denmark. However, no indications emerge as to Denmark's subsequent action to transfer compensation to the actual victim.

The position adopted by the ECtHR in the reparation judgment of the *Cyprus v. Turkey* case was much more elaborate and coherent with the approach finally enshrined in Article 48(2) ARSIWA. In this case, the Court rejected the defendant State's position according to which the mechanism of inter-state complaints pursuant to Article 33 of the ECHR 'corresponds to the classical logic of diplomatic protection (a direct State-to-State liability)', with

11 In the *Ireland v. United Kingdom* case, the applicant State did not raise any claim regarding reparation (see footnote 51). It should be specified, furthermore, how, in comparison with the other cases discussed here, this dispute did not directly involve citizens of the applicant State.

12 *Denmark v. Turkey* App no. 34382/97 (ECtHR, Friendly Settlement, 5 April 2000).

the consequence that 'Article 41 of the Convention does not apply to inter-state proceedings except, perhaps, where the violation has caused a direct injury to the complaining State Party'.[13] On the contrary, the Court confirmed the applicability of Article 41 of the Convention, concerning 'just satisfaction', to inter-state disputes, given that 'the overall logic of Article 41 is not substantially different from the logic of reparations in public international law'.[14]

As a consequence, when 'the applicant State denounces violations by another Contracting Party of the basic human rights of its nationals (or other victims)',[15] the ECtHR significantly maintains that 'it is the individual, and not the State, who is directly or indirectly harmed and primarily "injured" by a violation of one or several Convention rights. Therefore, if just satisfaction is afforded in an inter-state case, it should always be done for the benefit of individual victims', also recalling for such purposes the solution recommended by the ILC in Article 19(c) of the draft articles on diplomatic protection where, as well-known, the ILC recommended to transfer compensation to individuals in case of actions carried out as diplomatic protection.[16] On this basis, the ECtHR awarded compensation for moral damages to the applicant State with the caveat that this amount was to be transferred to individual victims as the Tribunal has further specified that 'it must be left to the Cypriot Government, under the supervision of the Committee of Ministers, to set up an effective mechanism to distribute the above-mentioned sums to the individual victims'.[17]

This approach was subsequently confirmed in the *Georgia v. Russia (I)* case, where Russia, albeit in a somewhat unclear manner, tried to reject the applicability of Article 41 to inter-state applications, claiming that reparation 'had to be awarded not to the applicant Government, but to the individuals concerned', with the consequence that 'relevant rules of international law on dip-

13 *Cyprus v. Turkey* App 25781/94 (ECtHR, Just Satisfaction, 12 May 2014) para. 36. Article 41 ECHR, mentioned by the ECtHR, provides that '[i]f the Court finds that there has been a violation of the Convention or the Protocols thereto, and if the internal law of the High Contracting Party concerned allows only partial reparation to be made, the Court shall, if necessary, afford just satisfaction to the injured party'.

14 Ibid, para. 41.

15 Ibid, para. 46.

16 According to the Article 19 of the draft articles on diplomatic protection, 'A State entitled to exercise diplomatic protection according to the present draft articles, should: ...(c) transfer to the injured person any compensation obtained for the injury from the responsible State subject to any reasonable deductions'. See Draft Articles on Diplomatic Protection with Commentaries, in Yearbook of the International Law Commission, 2006, vol. II, Part Two, 53–55.

17 *Cyprus v. Turkey* (n 13), para. 59.

lomatic protection – in particular Article 19 of the United Nations International Law Commission Draft Articles on Diplomatic Protection – were incompatible with Article 41 of the Convention'[18] in the case of reparation granted to Georgia. In this manner Russia, while primarily aiming to avoid providing compensation to the applicant State, indirectly confirmed how in such contexts the addressees of reparation measures ought to be identified as the individual victims. Regardless of such objections, the Court endorsed the solution elaborated in the *Cyprus v. Turkey* case, on the assumption that '[j]ust satisfaction is not therefore sought with a view to compensating the State for a violation of its rights but for the benefit of individual victims', through an approach pinpointing the identification of the applicant State not as acting to vindicate its own rights but to ascertain and remedy the violation of *erga omnes* obligations. Therefore, the ECtHR admitted that 'the applicant Government is entitled to submit a claim under Article 41 of the Convention'[19] for the purpose of claiming reparation for the benefit of individual victims. In this case too, the ECtHR, having established compensation for moral damages, left it to Georgia to set up a mechanism to distribute the above-mentioned sums to the individual victims.

Finally, in the subsequent *Georgia v. Russia (II)* case, the ECtHR confirmed its position, which was not challenged by the respondent Government as the case was decided after the expulsion of Russia from the Council of Europe once Russia decided not to participate in pending cases. In its judgment on just satisfaction the ECtHR reiterated its legal principles developed in past inter-state disputes without further elaboration.[20]

The approach endorsed by the ECtHR will certainly influence the numerous pending inter-state applications[21] as it emphasizes how the *erga omnes* nature of the obligations established by the ECHR has a fundamental impact in the management of the reparation phase in inter-state disputes. As recognized by scholars, this solution confirms that according to the ECtHR 'the State of nationality of the victim of a human rights violation may not be considered as "injured" in its own right as a specially affected State under Article 42 (b) (i) of the ILC Draft Articles on State Responsibility', with the conse-

18 *Georgia v. Russia (I)* App 13255/07 (ECtHR, Just Satisfaction, 31 January 2019) para. 18.

19 Ibid, paras. 24, 26–27.

20 *Georgia v. Russia (II)* App 38263/08 (ECtHR, Just Satisfaction, 28 April 2023), paras. 30–33.

21 For an overview of pending inter-state applications see <https://www.echr.coe.int/Documents/InterState_applications_ENG.pdf>.

quence that it cannot 'claim compensation on its own'.[22] In such circumstances, therefore, as the State of citizenship of the victims would primarily act to protect the collective interests expressed in breached human rights rules, it is not entitled to claim reparation for its own benefit, given that 'the applicant State merely plays the role of a transmission belt' with individual victims.[23]

2.2 *African Commission on Human and People's Rights*

The position ultimately elaborated by the ECtHR is like that endorsed by other human rights monitoring bodies in inter-state complaints prompted by the victims' State of citizenship. Prior to the rulings of the ECtHR, reference could be made to the *Democratic Republic of Congo v. Burundi, Rwanda, Uganda*, where the African Commission on Human and People's Rights (ACHPR) ascertained numerous violations against Congolese citizens in past conflict scenarios. In particular, the Democratic Republic of Congo demanded that 'the countries violating human and peoples' rights in the Democratic Republic of Congo pay just reparation for the damages caused and the acts of looting'[24] but failed to specify the addressees of reparation, namely itself or the actual victims of the violations. Regarding this request, it is worth mentioning how the ACHPR in its decision autonomously demanded that 'adequate reparations be paid, in the appropriate ways, to the Complainant State for and on behalf of the victims of the human rights by the armed forces of the Respondent States'.[25] In its decision, therefore, the ACHPR took care to specify that the reparation invoked must finally be materially addressed to benefit the injured individuals, albeit without detailing the form or amount of reparation. The subsequent inter-state application, namely *Djibouti v. Eritrea*, was finally withdrawn by the applicant State, so no further inputs on this issue could be provided through this case.

---

22 Cesare Pitea, 'The ECHR, Judicial Dialogue and General International Law in Cyprus v. Turkey (Just Satisfaction)' (SIDI Blog 26 May 2014) <http://www.sidiblog.org/2014/05/26/the-echr-judicial-dialogue-and-general-international-law-in-cyprus-v-turkey-just-satisfaction/>.

23 Frederike Kollmar and Jan Martin Hoffmann, 'Fewer Complaints, More Satisfaction: Cyprus v. Turkey' (2014) 3 Cambridge Journal of International and Comparative Law, 1361, 1369.

24 *Democratic Republic of Congo v. Burundi, Rwanda, Uganda* Comm 227/1999 (African Commission on Human and People's Rights, May 2003) para. 11 <https://achpr.au.int/en/decisions-communications/democratic-republic-congo-burundi-rwanda-uganda-22799>.

25 Ibid, para. 21.

2.3 *Inter-American Commission on Human Rights*

More difficult to assess, as not all documents were made publicly available, is the friendly settlement between Ecuador and Colombia, reached in front of the Inter-American Commission on Human Rights (IACHR). This case dealt with the death of an Ecuadorian citizen during an attack carried out by Colombia in Ecuador against a base of the organize armed group Fuerzas Armadas Revolucionarias de Colombia (FARC), and the alleged inhumane treatment of his family, lacking investigations into this event. Notably, Ecuador decided to withdraw from the procedure after reaching 'an agreement for social and economic development and reparations and investment for social compensation along the border', which 'satisfies the claims of the victims and the State of Ecuador'.[26] The IACHR consequently dismissed the case, in accordance with the request of the applicant State.

Although the text of the friendly settlement was not included in the decision, it is nevertheless relevant that the victims' claims were qualified by the IACHR as being satisfied through the measures taken. This is in line with Article 40 of the IACHR's rules of procedure, whose application is extended to inter-state disputes under Article 50. The latter requires that, before the adoption of the report concerning the friendly settlement, 'the Commission shall verify whether the victim of the alleged violation or, as the case may be, his or her successors, have consented to the friendly settlement agreement'.[27] This rule aims to prevent the interests of direct victims, not parties to inter-state proceedings, from being jeopardized by broader political inter-state assessments. In any case, the material content of the friendly settlement reached highlights how the measures agreed by the two States went beyond those of more direct interest to the victims' families. Some measures, such as actions facilitating the economic and social development of border regions, were arranged for the exclusive benefit of the applicant State to bring about the diplomatic agreement required to stop the proceedings.

2.4 *Committee for the Convention on the Elimination of All Forms of Racial Discrimination*

Recently, inter-state complaints have also been presented to the Committee for the Convention on the Elimination of All Forms of Racial Discrimination

26 *Ecuador-Colombia*, Inter-state Case 12.779, Decision to Archive, Inter-American Commission on Human Rights Report No. 96/13 (4 November 2013) <https://oas.org/en/iachr/docs/annual/2013/docs-en/EC-COAR12779EN.pdf>.

27 Inter-American Court on Human Rights, 'Rules of Procedure of the Inter-American Commission on Human Rights' (2013) <https://www.oas.org/en/IACHR/jsForm/?File=/en/iachr/mandate/basics/rulesiachr.asp>.

(CERD), although this procedure is characterized by the distinct conciliatory nature referred to in Articles 11–13 CERD.[28] In the context of proceedings initiated by Qatar, the question of reparation was extremely marginal, as in its application Qatar merely required that the United Arab Emirates adopt 'all necessary steps to end the Coercive Measures'.[29] Further inputs were prevented due to the dismissal of this complaint, as well as the one made against Saudi Arabia.

In contrast, the position expressed by Palestine in its case against Israel was more articulated and progressively switched to emphasize its role as a 'State other than an injured State'. First, Palestine, in its initial application in 2018, regardless of mentioning the *erga omnes* nature of the obligations provided by CERD,[30] emphasized how the victims were 'nationals of the State of Palestine, and Palestine hence being the injured State within the meaning of Art. 42 Articles of State Responsibility'.[31] This position was, subsequently, significantly changed as, in its later documents brought to the attention of the Committee in 2019 in response to replies provided by Israel, Palestine underlined how 'all contracting parties of CERD have a legally protected interest within the meaning of Article 48 ILC Articles on State Responsibility (as having codified customary international law)',[32] with the consequence that 'there is no need to consider whether the State of Palestine needs to be the injured State or not'.[33]

---

28 On this procedure see Patrick Thornberry, *The International Convention on the Elimination of All Forms of Racial Discrimination: A Commentary* (OUP 2016), 55–56.

29 'Communication submitted by Qatar pursuant to Article 11 of the International Convention on the Elimination of all Forms of Racial Discrimination' (8 March 2018), reproduced in *Case Concerning Application of the International Convention on the Elimination of All Forms of Racial Discrimination* (*Qatar v. United Arab Emirates*) (Preliminary Objections of the United Arab Emirates) vol II (29 April 2019) 127, para. 123 <https://www.icj-cij.org/sites/default/files/case-related/172/172-20190429-WRI-01-01-EN.pdf>.

30 'Interstate Complaint under Articles 11–13 of the International Convention for the Elimination of All Forms of Racial Discrimination. State of Palestine versus Israel' (23 April 2018) 24, para. 52, and 341, para. 659 <https://tbinternet.ohchr.org/_layouts/15/treatybodyexternal/Download.aspx?symbolno=INT%2FCERD%2FISC%2F9325&Lang=en>.

31 Ibid, 6, para. 10.

32 'Observations on Israel's Response dated 14 January 2019 relating to the State of Palestine's Complaint under Article 11 CERD' (14 February 2019), 30, para. 113. <https://tbinternet.ohchr.org/_layouts/15/treatybodyexternal/Download.aspx?symbolno=INT%2FCERD%2FISC%2F9337&Lang=en>.

33 'Observations on the OLA Memorandum relating to the State of Palestine's complaint under Art. 11 CERD' (28 August 2019), 5, para. 20 <https://tbinternet.ohchr.org/_layouts/15/treatybodyexternal/Download.aspx?symbolno=INT%2FCERD%2FISC%2F9369&Lang=en>.

This assumption was upheld by the Committee in its 2019 decision on the jurisdiction of the case,[34] where the Committee underlined among the different elements contributing to its positive assessment, '[t]he *erga omnes* nature of the core provisions of the Convention'[35] and the characteristic of its inter-state dispute settlement mechanism 'set up for the common good of all States parties'.[36] This approach has led scholars to maintain both that 'Palestine identified itself as a non-injured State under ICERD'[37] and that the same Committee has confirmed 'the CERD inter-state mechanism as pertaining to collective enforcement, identical to the Inter-state application procedure of the ECtHR'.[38]

This approach, regarding the qualification of the applicant State, might also affect the characteristics of measures to eliminate the consequences of alleged violations of the CERD, although Palestine only mentioned few potential redress measures in its initial 2018 application. Essentially, Palestine referred to Article 35 ARSIWA on *restitutio in integrum* to claim that Israel 'is under an obligation to withdraw those parts of its population from the territory of the occupied State of Palestine' and has an 'obligation to cease these violations of CERD, as well as to provide an assurance and guarantee of non-repetition',[39] while these issues were not further raised in subsequent documents provided to the Committee in light of Palestine's focus on admissibility aspects.

This issue was finally been addressed by the Conciliation Commission appointed in 2021 for this dispute.[40] The Conciliation Commission released its final report in August 2024, in which it made a series of recommendations aimed at contributing to an amicable solution to the dispute between the

34 For an extensive review see Michal Balcerzak, 'Special Character of Human Rights Obligations and the Jurisdiction of the Committee on the Elimination of Racial Discrimination in the Palestine v. Israel Case' (2020) 40 Polish Yearbook of International Law 93.

35 CERD, 'Inter-state Communication Submitted by the State of Palestine against Israel', CERD/C/100/5 (12 December 2019), para. 3.50 and furthermore paras. 3.22–3.25.

36 Ibid, para. 3.25.

37 Dai Tamada, 'Inter-state Communication under ICERD: From ad hoc Conciliation to Collective Enforcement?', (2021) 12 Journal of International Dispute Settlement 405, 421.

38 Ibid, 425. For a similar position see J Eiken, 'Breaking new ground? The CERD Committee's decision on jurisdiction in the inter-state communications procedure between Palestine and Israel' (EJIL: Talk!, 29 January 2020) <https://www.ejiltalk.org/breaking-new-ground-the-cerd-committees-decision-on-jurisdiction-in-the-inter-state-communications-procedure-between-palestine-and-israel/>.

39 Interstate Complaint (n 31) 340, para. 658, and 342, para. 660.

40 Jan Eiken, David Keane, 'Appointment of the Ad Hoc Conciliation Commissions under ICERD' (EJIL: Talk! 13 December 2021) <https://www.ejiltalk.org/appointment-of-the-ad-hoc-conciliation-commissions-under-icerd/>.

States concerned. In particular, in relation to reparations, the Conciliation Commission recommends to Israel, to '[e]nsure that all victims of racial discrimination enjoy full access to justice and reparation or satisfaction for any damage suffered, pursuant to article 6 of the Convention'.[41] In this regard, it could therefore be emphasized how the actual victims of violations are qualified by the Conciliation Commission as the beneficiaries of possible reparation measures related to the claims brought by the State of citizenship, referring to the specific provision in the Convention devoted to reparation[42] and confirming that the applicant State cannot be the beneficiary of reparation sought.

2.5 *Conclusion*

The survey of practice involving inter-state disputes brought in front of human rights courts and bodies by the State of citizenship of the victims thus allows us to draw some conclusions. In particular, in such disputes both relevant bodies and the applicant States have finally maintained how reparation measures are requested for the benefit of victims, regardless of the circumstance that the applicant State vindicated violations suffered by its own nationals. In this respect, therefore, these solutions finally confirm the approach supported by some of the scholars mentioned in paragraph 2, according to which, since human rights rules protect collective values and not merely reciprocal values, given the *erga omnes* nature of the relevant obligations, the mere link of nationality would not be sufficient to qualify the applicant State as the injured party under Article 42, with the ultimate consequence that it could only invoke reparation for the benefit of the victims of reparation.

In this latter regard, nonetheless, some further elements worthy of remarks are scenarios raised by friendly settlements reached by concerned States in relation to applications brought to the attention of human rights courts and bodies. Reference could be made to the abovementioned friendly settlements

41 Committee on the Elimination of Racial Discrimination, Report of the ad hoc Conciliation Commission on the Inter-state Communication Submitted by the State of Palestine against Israel under Article 11 of the International Convention on the Elimination of All Forms of Racial Discrimination, CERD/C/113/3, 21 August 2024, para. 51 (g).

42 According to Article 6 of the Convention 'States Parties shall assure to everyone within their jurisdiction effective protection and remedies, through the competent national tribunals and other State institutions, against any acts of racial discrimination which violate his human rights and fundamental freedoms contrary to this Convention, as well as the right to seek from such tribunals just and adequate reparation or satisfaction for any damage suffered as a result of such discrimination'. On this provision see Thornberry (n 29) 399–429.

in the *Denmark v. Turkey* and *Ecuador v. Colombia* cases, where reparation measures by respondent States unrelated to the direct prejudices suffered by the victims have also been adopted, for example through official apologies to the applicant State, the establishment of a political dialogue on human rights issues or the creation of social and economic development programs, not directly connected to the alleged violations for communities present in the areas affected by the violations. In these proceedings, which exploited the possibilities offered by human rights treaties as regards legitimacy to act, the subsequent political negotiation aimed at reaching a friendly settlement, finally endorsed by the same human rights monitoring bodies, was apparently influenced by the more traditional canons of international responsibility, through solutions also seeking to identify tailored measures of satisfaction for the applicant States in light of legal prejudice suffered from the violations, apart from those benefitting the actual victims. At the same time, as emphasized above, whether the case finally reaches the merits phase, human rights courts and bodies are conversely unequivocal to maintain how reparation measures should finally be tailored only to provide reparation for the benefit of individual victims also in cases involving inter-states disputes.

The qualification of applicant States for the purpose of invoking reparation does not exhaust legal issues related to inter-state disputes related to the violations of human rights. A series of procedural and substantial issues can emerge in this scenario, going to be explored in the subsequent paragraph.

3 Procedural and Substantial Issues Related to the Performance of the Obligation of Reparation for the Beneficiaries of Breached *erga omnes* Obligations

As mentioned above, Article 48(2) ARSIWA confirms how any State bound by *erga omnes* obligations may invoke international responsibility to obtain the cessation of the wrongful act, assurances and guarantees of non-repetition and reparation in the interest of the beneficiaries of the breached obligations. However, the practical implementation of measures aimed at remedying the consequences of wrongful acts in the interest of the beneficiaries of the *erga omnes* obligations breached may raise issues, both procedural and substantive, of the reparation to be provided by the wrongful State, which have not been fully resolved by the ILC. In this respect, too, it may be worthwhile to look at the practice developed by human rights courts and bodies to see whether some contributions can be made to the solutions to be adopted in this area.

3.1 *Procedural Issues*

First, as already analysed at the time of the adoption of the ARISWA, the effective capacity of States invoking responsibility for violations of *erga omnes* obligations to properly represent the victims' interests in the definition of reparation and other relevant measures to their benefit could be a challenging aspect. Although this assessment may be complex, given the 'absence of a valid expression of the wishes of the victim or victims' as originally maintained by Crawford,[43] this element does not seem to represent a fundamental procedural obstacle in inter-state disputes related to the violations of human rights provisions.

In this area, indeed, we already experienced examples of third parties invoking reparation measures to the benefit of direct victims. This can be observed in the Inter-American system, where, prior to the 1996 reform of the rules of procedure of the Inter-American Court of Human Rights, the Inter-American Commission on Human Rights (IACHR) was the only body authorized to submit reparation requests.[44] This was due to the procedural impossibility for the victims themselves to directly make autonomous claims in the reparation stage of the proceedings, as finally admitted in 1996. Therefore, it could be maintained that States claiming violations of human rights provisions could similarly be in the position to represent the interests of affected individuals.

At the same time, however, it is hard to recognize a substantial obligation on States to consult victims on envisaged measures of reparation. Nonetheless, a functional synergy between the victims and the acting State can play a significant role in guaranteeing a proper reparation, especially regarding the acquisition of reliable documentation to support claims. For example, in its assessment on reparation claims in inter-state disputes, the ECtHR specified that it is necessary to verify 'whether the victims could be identified' or there are 'sufficiently precise and objectively identifiable groups of people'[45] having suffered from wrongful acts. Proper synergy between victims and claimant

43 James Crawford, 'Third report on state responsibility' (2000) UN Doc A/CN.4/507, 8, para. 378.

44 Compare Art. 23 of the 1996 Rules of Procedures ('At the reparations stage, the representatives of the victims or of their next of kin may independently submit their own arguments and evidence') with the 1991 version where only the Inter-American Commission was authorized to bring reparation claims. See 'Rules of Procedure of the Inter-American Court of Human Rights', Annual Report of the Inter-American Court of Human Rights (1991) O.A.S. Doc. OEA/Ser.L/V/III.25 doc.7, 18.

45 *Cyprus v. Turkey* (n 13) para. 47; *Georgia v. Russia* (*I*) (n 18), paras. 22, 28; *Georgia v. Russia* (*II*) (n 20), para. 32.

States could therefore be crucial to arrange full reparation for the injury caused by the internationally wrongful act.

Second, a more complex issue concerns the management of reparation in parallel proceedings addressing the same wrongful acts introduced both by States other than the injured one and by actual victims. This scenario has already occurred in the practice of the ECtHR, which is currently based on a twofold approach. On the one hand, faced with parallel individual and inter-state proceedings dealing with the same scenarios, the ECtHR did not assess reparation claims in the judgment on the merits related to the individual applicants on the assumption that 'the question of the application of Article 41 is still pending before the Grand Chamber'.[46] In such scenarios, as exemplified by the *Berdzenishvili and Others v. Russia* case, the individual claims were settled in a separate judgment on just satisfaction adopted in the aftermath of the inter-state judgment. Ultimately, the ECtHR provided compensation exactly in line with the solutions accepted in the parallel *Georgia v. Russia (I)* case, since 'the Court sees no reasons to deviate from these conclusions'.[47]

On the other hand, where the ECtHR had already addressed reparation in relation to past individual applications or the individual claims were still pending, the Court excluded any prejudices connected to these individual applicants from the reparation granted in the inter-state dispute. For example, in the *Cyprus v. Turkey* case, when determining the reparation to be provided, the ECtHR specified that '[t]he applicant Government recognized that out of 1,485 missing persons…some should be excluded…(as)…Nine missing persons were already covered by individual applications in the Varnava and Others case'.[48] This approach was upheld in the subsequent *Georgia v. Russia (I)* case, in which twenty-three individuals were excluded from the list of injured parties presented by the applicant State as 'they have lodged individual applications before the Court'.[49]

This approach is substantially correct, both to avoid an obligation of double reparation for the wrongful State with respect to the same internationally wrongful acts and to pragmatically apply similar solutions in both circumstances. However, it implies an implicit hierarchy between the two proceedings in the reparation phase, with priority being granted to inter-state disputes whose conclusions then infer which measures will be provided in pending individual applications.

---

46 *Berdzenishvili and Others v. Russia* App 14594/07 (ECtHR 20 December 2016) para. 148.

47 Ibid.

48 *Cyprus v. Turkey* (n 13) para. 48.

49 *Georgia v. Russia (I)* (n 18) para. 70.

Third, an additional challenge concerns the handling of positions held by the applicant States in relation to reparation. Indeed, it would be possible to face cases where the acting State decides not to make any requests for reparation, as occurred in *Ireland v. United Kingdom*, where 'the applicant Government had expressly declared that they "[did] not invite the Court to afford just satisfaction..., of the nature of monetary compensation, to any individual victim of a breach of the Convention"'.[50] This approach is admissible as even Article 48 ARSIWA provides States not with an obligation, but with an entitlement to request measures provided for in this provision.

However, in such cases, should the applicant State fail to make a reparation claim it would be necessary to assess whether the court could exercise autonomous power to grant reparation to victims. Although this issue has never been addressed in practice dealing with inter-state disputes, some inputs could be inferred from individual complaints brought before human rights tribunals. In fact, although the most widespread approach by human rights tribunals entails awarding reparation in the absence of requests by the applicants,[51] in some cases both the ECtHR and the Inter-American Court[52] have acted *proprio motu* to grant certain measures of reparation on the assumption that some prejudices are inexorably present and in the light of the 'absolute character'[53] of the rights at stake. It is uncertain whether this approach could be used by human rights tribunals also regarding inter-state disputes but it is clear how this approach could finally permit victims to get reparation and avoid to make the use of inter-state disputes just aimed at assessing violations without addressing their consequences.

---

50 *Ireland v. the United Kingdom* App 5310/71 (ECtHR 18 January 1978) paras. 245–246.

51 See, for instance, *Lombardo v. Italy* App 12490/86 (ECtHR 26 November 1992) para. 25; *Capeau v. Belgium*, App 42914/9 (ECtHR 13 January 2005) para. 32.

52 In the *Kawas-Fernández* case, related to an arbitrary deprivation of life, the Inter-American Court of Human Rights affirmed that 'the non-pecuniary damage inflicted upon the victim is evident. In this regard, and even though no request has been made to this effect by the Commission or the representatives, the Court has decided to order the State to pay compensation' for moral damage. See *Kawas-Fernández v. Honduras*, Merits, Reparations and Costs, Inter-American Court of Human Rights Series C No 196 (3 April 2009) para. 185.

53 See *Mayzit v. Russia* App 63378/00 (ECtHR 20 January 2005). In the judgment, the ECtHR confirmed that, lacking requests by the applicant, it would not award reparation. However, as the case involved degrading treatment, it maintained that 'since this right is of absolute character, the Court finds it possible to award the applicant 3,000 euros by way of non-pecuniary damage' (para. 88).

3.2 *Material Content of Reparation*

Inter-state disputes concerning the violations of human rights can also raise a series of issues concerning the material content of reparation measures to be arranged by human rights courts and bodies. In this regard it is worth mentioning how, once addressing claims for reparation directly invoked by the affected individuals in cases brought against States, human rights courts and bodies have made relevant measures functional to the individual nature of the beneficiaries,[54] according to more innovative and victim-oriented approaches finally reflected in the 2006 UNGA Basic Principles and Guidelines on reparation for gross violations.[55]

In this respect, it could be argued that, also in relation to potential inter-state disputes, such victim-oriented approaches to reparation measures should be reiterated, and therefore measures invoked by applicant States should be tailored to the benefit of individual victims. It could therefore be expected that a number of innovative approaches developed by human rights courts and bodies in their reparations practice, such as the emphasis placed on measures of satisfaction, or the flexible approach to the evidence to be provided by applicants in relation to the assessment of damage, such as the flexibility related to the burden of proof in relation to damage qualified as inherent in grave violations, could be replicated in this context.

So far, inter-state disputes reaching the reparation phase have mainly involved the ECtHR which has largely addressed such issues through lump sums based on the criteria of fairness and reasonableness, without resorting, according to the same ECtHR, to 'a process of calculation or precise quantification'.[56] Indeed, the character of some violations, time passed from events to

---

54 See: Fabian Novak, 'The System of Reparations in the Jurisprudence of the Inter-American Court of Human Rights', (2018) 392 RCADI 9; Dinah Shelton, *Remedies in International Human Rights Law* (OUP 2015), 285–431; Giulio Bartolini, *Riparazione per violazione dei diritti umani e ordinamento internazionale* (Jovene 2009).

55 UNGA, 'Basic Principles and Guidelines on the Right to a Remedy and Reparation for Victims of Gross Violations of International Human Rights Law and Serious Violations of International Humanitarian Law' (15 December 2005) UN Doc A/RES/60/147. See: Theo van Boven, 'Victims' Rights to a Remedy and Reparation: The United Nations Principles and Guidelines', in Carla Ferstaman, Mariana Goetz (eds), *Reparations for Victims of Genocide, War Crimes and Crimes against Humanity: Systems in Place and Systems in the Making* (Brill 2020) 15; Pierre D'Argent, 'Le droit de la responsabilité internationale complété?' (2005) 51 Annuaire français de droit international 27.

56 *Cyprus v. Turkey* (n 13) para. 56. For a similar approach adopted by the ECtHR regarding moral damages see *Georgia v. Russia (I)* (n 18) para. 73. The ECtHR, 'making its assessment on an equitable basis', has provided lump sums for material and non-material damages in *Georgia v. Russia (II)* (n 20) paras. 40–45.

legal ascertainment and the high number of potential victims could made complex to adopt an individualized approach.

At the same time, in the European system, reparation measures decided by the ECtHR do not exhaust the potential series of measures to be adopted by the wrongful State to address consequences of violations of human rights obligations. Indeed, monetary compensation provided by the ECtHR could be complemented by further non-pecuniary measures to be adopted under the supervision of the CoE Committee of Ministers to fully eliminate the consequences of wrongful acts. The reparation process could thus be complex to be fully realized and obviously it could be jeopardized by non-cooperative States, as experienced with the *Cyprus v. Turkey* and *Georgia v. Russia (I)* cases. For instance, while in the *Cyprus v. Turkey* case the CoE Committee of Ministers recognized in its interim resolutions how Turkish authorities finally provided support in determining the fate of Greek Cypriot missing persons, in particular through the assistance provided to the Committee on Missing Persons and the Missing Persons Unit in charge of such activities, it was obliged to recognize several years after the delivery of the judgments on just satisfactions that the payment of monetary compensation have not yet been implemented by respondent States.[57] In cases involving Russia, conversely, the respondent State has totally failed to cooperate in the execution of judgments thus avoiding both to pay for the monetary compensation provided by the ECtHR and to adopt further non-pecuniary measures which could have been required in order to provide a full reparation.[58]

4 Concluding Remarks

The analysis carried out on in relation to reparation issues through the lens of human rights courts and bodies might thus provide some preliminary insights on legal challenges going to play a growing role in front of these same monitoring bodies in light of the increased recourse to inter-state disputes by parties to main human rights treaties. Furthermore, such practice could also play a role in other fora, particularly the ICJ, where a series of pending cases for violations of human rights treaties might finally imply the need for the Court

57 Committee of Ministers, Cyprus v. Turkey, Decision, CM/Del/Dec(2024)1492/H46–33, 12–14 March 2024; Interim Resolution CM/ResDH(2021)201, Cyprus v. Turkey, 16 September 2021.

58 Committee of Ministers, Interim Resolution CM/ResDH(2022)354, Georgia v. Russia (I), 8 December 2022.

to address reparation claims made by the applicant States for the benefit of individual victims.

Indeed, in pending cases before the ICJ related to the invocation of responsibility for violation of human rights treaties, applicant States have already requested the implementation of the obligation of reparation in the interest of victims. For instance, in *The Gambia v. Myanmar* case, the applicant State, maintained in its position in the application submitted to the ICJ that Myanmar 'must cease forthwith any such ongoing internationally wrongful act… must perform the obligations of reparation in the interest of the victims of genocidal acts…and must offer assurances and guarantees of non-repetition of violations of the Genocide Convention'.[59] Similarly, in the *Canada and the Netherlands v. Syrian Arab Republic* case concerning alleged violations of the 1987 Convention against torture, the applicant States jointly requested not only to cease violations, provide appropriate assurances and guarantees of non-repetition, and investigate and prosecute and punish those responsible, but also that Syria 'must provide individual victims full reparation, including compensation and rehabilitation, for the injury they have suffered as a consequence of those internationally wrongful acts'.[60] Finally, this solution was also endorsed by South Africa in its application to the ICJ concerning the alleged violation of the Genocide Convention by Israel, where the applicant State has invoked not only the cessation of the alleged wrongful act but has also requested that Israel '…(*e*) must perform the obligations of reparation in the interest of Palestinian victims, including but not limited to allowing the safe and dignified return of forcibly displaced and/or abducted Palestinians to their homes, respect for their full human rights and protection against further discrimination, persecution, and other related acts, and provide for the reconstruction of what it has destroyed in Gaza…; and (*f*) must offer assurances and guarantees of non-repetition of violations of the Genocide Convention'.[61]

When such cases will reach the reparation phase a series of challenges like the ones raised in front of human rights courts and bodies could be present and, therefore, early elements of interest provided by the practice analysed in this paper could contribute to identify proper legal solutions.

---

59 *Application of the Convention on the Prevention and Punishment of the Crime of Genocide* (*The Gambia v. Myanmar*) (n 2) 58, para. 112.

60 *Application of the Convention against Torture and Other Cruel, Inhuman or Degrading Treatment or Punishment* (*Canada and the Netherlands v. Syrian Arab Republic*) (n 2), para. 60 <https://www.icj-cij.org/sites/default/files/case-related/188/188-20230608-APP-01-00-EN.pdf>.

61 *Application of the Convention on the Prevention and Punishment of the Crime of Genocide in the Gaza Strip* (*South Africa v. Israel*) (n 2), 72, para. 111 <https://www.icj-cij.org/sites/default/files/case-related/192/192-20231228-app-01-00-en.pdf>.

CHAPTER 5

Listening to What Victims Want: The Search for, Exhumation, Identification and Return of Remains of the Disappeared

Juliette Rémond-Tiedrez

1 Introduction

Victims of gross human rights violations have a right to remedy and reparation.[1] Historically, States preferred to provide financial compensation as the sole form of reparation, reflecting the practices of their domestic reparation programs. However, as victims started expressing dissatisfaction with mere compensation,[2] regional human rights courts and international instruments adopted other forms of reparations, including restitution, rehabilitation, satisfaction and guarantees of non-repetition.[3] The adoption of the Basic Principles and Guidelines on the Right to a Remedy and Reparation for Victims of Gross Violations of International Human Rights Law and Serious Violations of International Humanitarian Law (UN Basic Principles) by the United Nations (UN) General Assembly on 15 December 2005,[4] which recognised the five above-mentioned reparation measures, constituted a positive step for victims' rights, providing a "solid, and victim-centred, legal grounding for minimum standards of redress – in the broad sense".[5]

1 Universal Declaration of Human Rights, 10 December 1948, art. 8; International Covenant on Civil and Political Rights (ICCPR), 16 December 1996, art. 2; Convention Against Torture and other Cruel, Inhuman or Degrading Treatment or Punishment, UN Doc. A/RES/39/46; 10 December 1984, art. 14; American Convention on Human Rights, 22 November 1969, art. 25; European Convention on Human Rights, 4 November 1950, art. 13.

2 In the context of enforced disappearances, see Sarah Fulton, *Redress for Enforced Disappearance Why Financial Compensation is not Enough*, Journal of International Criminal Justice, 2014, pp. 769–786.

3 Basic Principles and Guidelines on the Right to a Remedy and Reparation for Victims of Gross Violations of International Human Rights Law and Serious Violations of International Humanitarian Law (UN Basic Principles), UN Doc. A/RES/60/147, 21 March 2006, §§ 18–23.

4 Ibid.

5 Sarah Fulton, *supra* note 2, p. 786.

 | DOI:10.1163/9789004716742_006

Among these various forms of reparations, the search for, exhumation, identification and return of remains[6] of the disappeared,[7] has become a crucial satisfaction measure, especially for the relatives of individuals who were subjected to enforced disappearance,[8] as they have a right to know the truth, but also because receiving the identified remains of the victim puts an end to the uncertainty about their fate, and can enable them to grieve and perform funeral rites (2). The enforced disappearances committed during the 2014 genocide by the so-called Islamic State of Iraq and Syria (ISIS) against the Yazidis, and the families and the community's plight for the search for, exhumation, identification and return of the remains of the disappeared, is one of the latest examples of how important this form of satisfaction is for victims (3).

6 Formulation from the International Convention for the Protection of All Persons from Enforced Disappearances (ICPPED), UN Doc. A/RES/47/133, 23 December 2010, art. 15, "searching for, locating and releasing disappeared persons and, in the event of death, in exhuming and identifying them and returning their remains".

7 For the purpose of this article, disappeared means an individual who has been subjected to enforced disappearance as defined by Article 2 of the International Convention of the Protection of All Persons From Enforced Disappearance. The Committee on Enforced Disappearances (CED) provided further interpretation on the responsibility of non-state actors in the commission of the crime of enforced disappearance. In its 2023 *Statement on non-State actors in the context of the International Convention for the Protection of All Persons from Enforced Disappearances*, it stated that non-state actors may be held responsible for the commission of the crime of enforced disappearance under Articles 2 and 3 of the convention if (1) it was perpetrated in the context of a non-international armed conflict, as defined in international humanitarian law; (2) it was perpetrated by a non-State actor exercising effective control and/or government-like functions over a territory. CED, *Statement on non-State actors in the context of the International Convention for the Protection of All Persons from Enforced Disappearances*, UN Doc. CED/C/10, 2 May 2023, § 18. On the crime of enforced disappearance perpetrated by non-State actors, see further Rome Statute of the International Criminal Court, A/CONF.183/9, 17 July 1998, art. 7(2)(i); ICRC, Jean-Marie Henckaerts and Louise Doswald-Beck, *Customary International Humanitarian Law VolumeI: Rules*, rule 98.

On the enforced disappearance of Yazidis by ISIS, i.e. a non-State actor, the Human Rights Council (HRC) mandated Commission of Inquiry (CoI) on Syria found that "the fact that the fate of thousands of men and boys remains unknown constituted the crime of enforced disappearance". CoI Syria, *"They came to destroy": ISIS Crimes Against the Yazidis*, UN Doc. A/HRC/32/CRP.2, 15 June 2016, § 174.

8 As developed below, relatives of the individual who was subjected to enforced disappearance are considered direct victims. See 2.3 A multi-faceted reparation measure.

2 The Search for, Exhumation, Identification and Return of Remains as a Reparation Measure for Enforced Disappearance

This section will examine the emergence under international human rights law of States' obligation to search for, exhume, identify and return remains of disappeared persons (2.2), as part of a broader diversification of reparation measures for enforced disappearances (2.1). It will outline how the search for, exhumation, identification and return of remains allow all affected persons – the disappeared themselves, their relatives and their community – to obtain reparation (2.3), provided the State adopts a victim-centred approach (2.4). Finally, this section will set out the limitations of such reparation measure (2.5).

2.1 *Diversifying the Types of Reparations for Enforced Disappearances*

Originally, reparation for violations of international law comprised of restitution in kind or financial compensation, when restitution was impossible.[9] However, as individuals became bearers of rights under international law and began advocating for a wider range of reparation measures, human rights bodies, especially the Inter-American Court of Human Rights (IACtHR),[10] started recognising and granting reparations beyond compensation.[11] This culminated in the UN Basic Principles enshrining five different forms of reparations: compensation, restitution, rehabilitation, satisfaction and guarantees of non-repetition.[12]

This wide range of available complementary reparations is particularly welcomed for enforced disappearances, which are "a prime example of a violation that requires broader types of reparations".[13] Enforced disappearance impacts the person who is disappeared, their relatives, who are considered direct vic-

---

9 Permanent Court of International Justice, *Case Concerning the Factory at Chorzów (Claim for Indemnity)*, Merits, Series A No. 17, 13 September 1928, p. 47.

10 Thomas M. Antkowiak, *Remedial Approaches to Human Rights Violations: The Inter-American Court of Human Rights and Beyond*, Colombia Journal of Transnational Law, 2008, pp. 351–419.

11 Leiry Cornejo Chavez, *New remedial responses in the practice of regional human rights courts: Purposes beyond compensation*, International Journal of Constitutional Law, 2017; Gabriella Citroni, *Measures of Reparations for Victims of Gross Human Rights Violations: Developments and Challenges in the Jurisprudence of Two Regional Human Rights Courts*, Inter-American and European Human Rights Journal, Volume 5, 2012, pp. 49–71.

12 UN Basic Principles, §§ 18–23.

13 Sarah Fulton, *supra* note 2, p. 770.

tims of the crime,[14] and their community. It violates a number of different human rights, civil and political, but also economic, social and cultural rights, including (i) the right to recognition as a person before the law, (ii) the right to liberty and security of the person, (iii) the right not to be subjected to torture, (iv) the right to life, (v) the right to an identity, (vi) the right to fair trial and to judicial guarantees, (vii) the right to an effective remedy, (viii) the right to know the truth, (ix) the right to protection and assistance to the family, (x) the right to an adequate standard of living, (xi) the right to health and (xii) the right to education.[15] Finally, enforced disappearance is a continuous crime.[16] To address all these different aspects of the crime, the State needs to provide for complementary forms of reparations.

In its 1997 annual report, the Working Group on Enforced or Involuntary Disappearances (WGEID) examined the issue of compensating victims of enforced disappearances, noting that, in recent years, a number of States had started financial compensation programmes. It found the "aspect of compensation extremely important" but also considered that, in addition to financial compensation and punishment of the perpetrators, victims had the right to medical and psychological care, to rehabilitation, to guarantees of non-repetition, to restoration of personal liberty, family life, citizenship, employment or property, and to return to one's place of residence.[17] In 2013, it reiterated that financial compensation was "not sufficient in itself and should be normally associated with other forms of reparations".[18]

Similarly, Grażyna Baranowska highlighted the importance of compensation as most of the disappeared are the family's breadwinner and their disappearance causes severe economic hardship on the remaining family

14 ICPPED, art. 24(1), "For the purposes of this Convention, 'victim' means the disappeared person and any individual who has suffered harm as the direct result of an enforced disappearance". See further below, 2.3 A multi-faceted reparation measure.

15 OHCHR, *Enforced Disappearances*, Fact Sheet No. 6, UN Doc. 6/REV.4, 31 March 2023, p. 12. See also, Declaration on the Protection of all Persons from Enforced Disappearance (DPPED), UN Doc. A/RES/47/133, 18 December 1992, art. 1(2); Working Group on Enforced or Involuntary Disappearances (WGEID), *Question of the Human Rights of all Persons Subjected to Any Form of Detention or Imprisonment: Question of Enforced or Involuntary Disappearances*, UN Doc. E/CN.4/1990/13, 24 January 1990, § 339.

16 ICPPED, art. 8(1)(b).

17 WGEID, *Report of the Working Group on Enforced or Involuntary Disappearances*, UN Doc. E/CN.4/1998/43, 12 January 1998, §§ 65 and 75.

18 WGEID, *Report of the Working Group on Enforced or Involuntary Disappearances*, UN Doc. A/HRC/22/45, 28 January 2013, § 56. See also, WGEID, *Report of the Working Group on Enforced or Involuntary Disappearances: Mission to the Republic of the Congo*, UN Doc. A/HRC/19/58/Add3, 20 January 2012, § 54.

members. However, she considered that, in light of the grave nature of the violation, financial compensation was insufficient and should be accompanied by other measures, especially relating to the establishment of the disappeared's fate and the punishment of perpetrators.[19]

Sarah Fulton explained that merely granting financial compensation in the Argentinian, Algerian, Brazilian and Moroccan contexts "generated extreme controversy and prove[d] to be particularly problematic for family members of disappeared persons".[20] It was insufficient because it failed to provide redress for the violations of all the above-mentioned human rights and to put an end to the continuous violation. Furthermore, the disappeared person's relatives can see monetary reparations as "blood money", intended to silence them and, therefore, as a betrayal of the memory of their relative. This is especially the case if the State believes it is then absolved of its obligation to investigate and prosecute or to provide other reparation measures because financial compensation put an end to the matter.[21] It can also be guilt-inducing for the victim to accept compensation before the investigation has concluded that the disappeared person is indeed dead or before the remains are identified, as it suggests that they are giving up hope on finding them, and that they are acknowledging their death.[22]

Regional courts and UN bodies have thus ordered a wide-range of measures to States to remedy enforced disappearances, including:

- to investigate, prosecute and punish the perpetrators;[23]
- to criminalise enforced disappearances as such in domestic criminal law;[24]

19 Grażyna Baranowska, *Rights of Families of Disappeared Persons: How International Bodies Address the Needs of Families of Disappeared Persons in Europe*, Intersentia, 2021, pp. 12–13.

20 Sarah Fulton, *supra* note 2, p. 777.

21 As developed below, see 2.5 Limitation to the search for, exhumation, identification and return of remains, States will still have the obligation to investigate and prosecute, irrespective of whether compensation was afforded.

22 Sarah Fulton, *supra* note 2, pp. 777; Brandon Hamber and Richard A. Wilson, *Symbolic Closure through Memory, Reparation and Revenge in Post-conflict Societies*, Journal of Human Rights, Vol. 1, No. 1, March 2002, p. 14.

23 Inter-American Court of Human Rights (IACtHR), *Castro Anzualdo v. Peru*, Judgment (Preliminary Objection, Merits, Reparations and Costs), 22 September 2009, § 118; European Court of Human Rights (ECtHR), *Cyprus v. Turkey*, Judgment, Application no. 25781/94, 10 May 2001, § 135; UN Human Rights Committee (HRCom), *González v. Argentina*, Communication No. 1458/2006, 17 March 2011, § 11.

24 IACtHR, *Trujillo Oroza v. Bolivia*, Judgment (Reparations and Costs), 27 February 2002, § 98.

- to provide medical and psychological care;[25]
- to build public memorials and organise commemorations;[26]
- to train police and armed forces on human rights;[27] and
- to release the disappeared[28] or, if they are deceased, to search for, exhume, identify and return their remains.[29]

According to Sarah Fulton, this last satisfaction measure of search for, exhumation, identification and return of remains is so crucial that she considered it one of the five minimum standards of redress for enforced disappearances.[30]

2.2 *The Emergence of the Search for, Exhumation, Identification and Return of Remains of the Disappeared*

The first human rights instrument to deal with enforced disappearance was the Declaration on the Protection of All Persons from Enforced Disappearance (DPPED), which the UN General Assembly adopted on 18 December 1992.[31] It was followed by Inter-American Convention on the Forced Disappearance of Persons, drafted by the Organisation of American States and signed on 9 June 1994. Neither of these two instruments addressed the exhumation of remains specifically, although the DPPED provides that States shall conduct an investigation for as long as the fate of the disappeared remains unclarified,[32] which suggests the search of the body, although it is not stated explicitly.[33]

Grażyna Baranowska noted that the shift towards the search for, exhumation, identification and return of remains started with the Committee on Miss-

25 IACtHR, *Nineteen Tradesmen v. Colombia*, Judgment (Merits, Reparations and Costs), 5 July 2004, § 278.

26 IACtHR, *La Cantuta v. Peru*, Judgment (Merits, Reparations and Costs), 29 November 2006, § 236.

27 Ibid, § 240; ICPPED, art. 23(1).

28 HRCom, *Boucherf v. Algeria*, Communication No. 1196/2003, 30 March 2006, § 11. See also, ICPPED, art. 15.

29 See below, 2.2 The emergence of the search for, exhumation, identification and return of remains of the disappeared.

30 She puts this measure alongside the right to access to justice, the right to access to all forms of reparations, for relatives to be involved in the reparations process and for the State to respect all its obligations under international human rights law including its obligation to investigate and prosecute. Sarah Fulton, *supra* note 2, pp. 782–783.

31 *Supra* note 15. See also, UN General Assembly, *Resolution on Disappeared Persons*, UN Doc. A/RES/33/173, 20 December 1978.

32 DPPED, art. 13(6).

33 Grażyna Baranowska, *Advances and progress in the obligation to return the remains of missing and forcibly disappeared persons*, International Review of the Red Cross, 2017, p. 716.

ing Persons in Cyprus and the Special Process on Missing Persons in the Territory of Former Yugoslavia.[34] The Committee on Missing Persons is a body that was established by Cyprus and Türkiye under the auspices of the UN in 1981. Its mandate covers only to "draw up comprehensive lists of missing persons of both communities, specifying, as appropriate whether they are alive or dead, and in the latter case approximate time of the deaths".[35] However, in 2006, the Committee started conducting exhumation and identification of the remains as well and, a year later, the first remains were returned to their relatives.[36]

Similarly, the Special Process on Missing Persons in the Territory of Former Yugoslavia (the Special Process), a mechanism under both the WGEID and the Special Rapporteur on Human Rights in the territory of the former Yugoslavia, established in 1994, only had a mandate to clarify the fate and whereabouts of missing persons.[37] Again, the Special Process considered that the mandate should be expanded, and resources allocated for the exhumation of mass graves.[38] Unfortunately, the Special Process' initiative was unsuccessful because it managed to collect only 5 per cent of the amount necessary to conduct such exhumations, and because of the overall lack of political will.[39]

Grażyna Baranowska noted that:

> Although it was not possible to carry out exhumations to the extent that was necessary, the very commitment of the expert to this issue was one of the most innovative elements of the Special Process. It indicates that

34 Ibid, p. 732.

35 Committee on Missing Persons in Cyprus, Terms of Reference, § 13. The Committee was only mandated to look into "cases of persons reported missing in the inter-communal fightings as well as in the events of July 1974 and afterwards", § 7.

36 Grażyna Baranowska, *Rights of Families of Disappeared Persons: How International Bodies Address the Needs of Families of Disappeared Persons in Europe*, *supra* note 19, p. 197; Gülbanu K. Zorba and al., *Forensic identification of human remains in Cyprus: The humanitarian work of the Committee on Missing Persons in Cyprus* (CMP), in Forensic Science and Humanitarian Action: Interacting with the Dead and the Living, 2020.

37 Special Process on Missing Person in the Territory of Former Yugoslavia, *Report submitted by Mr. Manfred Nowak, member of the Working Group on Enforced or Involuntary Disappearances, pursuant to paragraph 4 of Commission resolution 1994/72*, UN Doc. E/CN.4/1995/37, 12 January 1995, § 12(a).

38 Special Process on Missing Person in the Territory of Former Yugoslavia, *Report submitted by Mr. Manfred Nowak, member of the Working Group on Enforced or Involuntary Disappearances, pursuant to paragraph 4 of Commission resolution 1995/35*, UN Doc. E/CN.4/1996/36, 4 March 1996, §§ 76 and 79.

39 Grażyna Baranowska, *Rights of Families of Disappeared Persons: How International Bodies Address the Needs of Families of Disappeared Persons in Europe*, *supra* note 19, pp. 202–205.

> one of the basic needs of families of disappeared persons was recognised – to learn the fate of their disappeared relatives, and if they had died, to receive their remains.[40]

In parallel, the IACtHR developed its case law relating to enforced disappearances to include the search for, exhumation, identification and return of remains as a form of reparation. Early on, in its 1988 *Velasquez-Rodriguez v. Honduras* case, the IACtHR had found that the State had a duty to investigate facts "as long as there is uncertainty about the fate of the person who has disappeared" and to "use the means at its disposal to inform the relatives of the fate of the victims and, if they have been killed, the location of their remains",[41] but fell short of ordering the exhumation of remains.

In its 1996 *Neira Alegria* et al. *v. Peru* case, the Court took that extra step, holding that the State had an obligation to deliver the remains of the victims to their relatives, in addition to locating them. It framed the obligation as a "form of moral reparation".[42] The IACtHR incrementally detailed how the return of the remains should be, namely that relatives could choose where the remains would be returned to, with no additional costs for them,[43] including abroad,[44] so as to be in accordance with their religious beliefs and customs. The Court later expressly added that the expenses of the burial itself, as decided by the next of kin, should be covered by the State.[45] It further clarified the identification process' requirements, namely the need for "suitable techniques and instruments",[46] DNA testing[47] and even "to create and implement a genetic information database to safeguard the information, on the one hand, of the osseous remains that were found and exhumed and, on the other, of the next of kin of the persons".[48]

40 Ibid, p. 205.

41 IACtHR, *Velasquez-Rodriguez v. Honduras*, Judgment (Merits), 29 June 1988, § 181.

42 IACtHR, *Neira Alegria* et al. *v. Peru*, Judgment (Reparations and Costs), 19 September 1996, § 69.

43 IACtHR, *Villagrán Morales and Others v. Guatemala ("Street Children")*, Judgment (Reparations), 26 May 2001, § 102.

44 IACtHR, *Caracazo v. Venezuela*, Judgment (Reparations and Costs), 29 August 2002, § 124.

45 IACtHR, *Goiburu* et al. *v. Paraguay*, Judgment (Merits, Reparations and Costs), 22 September 2006, § 172.

46 IACtHR, *Caracazo v. Venezuela, supra* note 44, §, § 124.

47 IACtHR, *Goiburu* et al. *v. Paraguay, supra* note 45, § 172.

48 IACtHR, *Gudiel Alvarez* et al. *("Diario Militar") v. Guatemala*, Judgment (Merits, Reparations and Costs), 20 November 2012, § 336.

The growing focus on the search for, exhumation, identification and return of remains by the IACtHR, the Committee on Missing Persons and the Special Process paved the way for the 2005 UN Basic Principles and the 2006 International Convention for the Protection of All Persons from Enforced Disappearances (ICPPED).

First, the UN Basic Principles provided that States' obligation to respect, ensure respect for and implement international human rights law and international humanitarian law included the provision of, *inter alia*, reparations. Paragraph 22(c) expands on one of the five types of reparations, satisfaction, as including:

> The search for the whereabouts of the disappeared, … and for the bodies of those killed, and assistance in the recovery, identification and reburial of the bodies in accordance with the expressed or presumed wish of the victims, or the cultural practices of the families and communities.

The independent expert in charge of examining the existing international criminal and human rights framework relating to enforced disappearances, to help with the drafting of the ICPPED, was Manfred Nowak, the expert in charge of the Special Process. Building on his experience with enforced disappearances in the former Yugoslavia, he recommended that the convention should "establish an obligation on States to carry out exhumations, since they constituted one of the most important means of investigation and were sometimes necessary in order to determine the fate of persons who have disappeared".[49] Drafters followed Manfred Nowak's recommendation and article 24(3) of the ICPPED states that "each State Party shall take all appropriate measures to search for, locate and release disappeared persons and, in the event of death, to locate, respect and return their remains".[50] According to the Convention, States shall provide mutual assistance in the search, location

49 Commission on Human Rights, *Report of the intersessional open-ended working group to elaborate a draft legally binding normative instrument for the protection of all persons from enforced disappearance*, UN Doc. E/CN.4/2004/59, 23 February 2004, § 170(c).

50 Unfortunately, however, the Committee on Enforced Disappearances', the body in charge of monitoring the implementation of the ICPPED, urgent action procedure does not provide for the Committee to require the return of the remains if the victim is dead and their body is found. Article 30(3) of the ICPPED only provides for the CED's recommendations to include a request to the State Party to "locate and protect the person" without mentioning the search for, exhumation, identification and return of the remains in case of death; Grażyna Baranowska, *Rights of Families of Disappeared*

and exhumation and return of remains, "with a view to assisting victims of enforced disappearance".[51] Article 24(5)(c) of the ICPPED further enshrines the right to reparation as encompassing "satisfaction, including restoration of dignity and reputation".

The UN Human Rights Committee (HRCom), which initially would not order the search for, exhumation, identification and return of remains, expressly provided for such measures following the adoption of the ICPPED in 2006.[52] In its 2010 *Bashasha v. Libya* case, the Committee found that the State was under the obligation to, among others, hand over the remains of the victims in the event that they were dead.[53] The Committee does not include this measure when it is not a request from the applicants, presumably because they "have not abandoned hope for their loved ones' reappearance".[54]

The European Court of Human Rights (ECtHR) was the last human rights body to order States to search for, exhume, identify and return remains. Traditionally, the European Court limits its reparation measures to financial compensation and leaves the State wide discretion to decide on other non-financial measures.[55] In its *Varnava and others v. Turkey* case, the ECtHR found that the State had a duty to "account for the location of the grave",[56] but when ordering reparation measures, it reiterated that Türkiye remained free to choose which reparations to award.[57] However, in its 2012 *Aslakhanova and Others v. Russia* case, the Court felt "compelled to provide some guidance on certain measures that must be taken [to] address the issue of the systemic failure to investigate disappearances in the Northern Caucasus". The Court's

---

Persons: How International Bodies Address the Needs of Families of Disappeared Persons in Europe, supra note 19, p. 180.

51 ICPPED, art. 15.

52 Grażyna Baranowska, *Advances and progress in the obligation to return the remains of missing and forcibly disappeared persons, supra* note 33, p. 724.

53 HRCom, *Bashasha v. Libya*, Case No. 1776/2008, 20 October 2010, § 9. See also, HRCom, *Mihoubi v. Algeria*, Case No. 1874/2009, 19 October 2013, § 9.

54 Grażyna Baranowska, *Advances and progress in the obligation to return the remains of missing and forcibly disappeared persons, supra* note 33, p. 724.

55 Sarah Fulton, *supra* note 2, p. 780; Grażyna Baranowska, *Rights of Families of Disappeared Persons: How International Bodies Address the Needs of Families of Disappeared Persons in Europe, supra* note 19, p. 103.

56 As summarised in *Aslakhanova and Others v. Russia*, ECtHR, *Aslakhanova and Others v. Russia*, Judgment, Application Nos 2944/06, 8300/07, 50184/07, 332/08, 42509/10, 18 December 2012, § 223, referring to ECtHR, *Varnava and others v. Turkey*, Judgement, Application Nos. 16064/90, 16065/90, 16066/90, 16068/90, 16069/90, 16070/90, 16071/90, 16072/90 and 16073/90, 18 September 2009, § 201.

57 ECtHR, *Varnava and others v. Turkey, supra* note 56, § 222.

suggested measures comprised to locate the grave and "carry out large-scale forensic and scientific work on the ground, including the location and exhumation of presumed burial sites".[58] To date, it is the only judgment in which the ECtHR indicated the specific form a reparation should take in a case of enforced disappearance.[59]

The consecration of States' obligation to search for, exhume, identify and return remains would not have been possible without the sustained advocacy efforts of victims and victims' association, which had been at the forefront of the development of the concept of enforced disappearances more generally. As the crime was widely used by Latin American States in the late 1970s, victims associations and non-governmental organisations (NGOs) multiplied cases before the IACtHR and the HRCom, helping with the development of the human rights bodies' case-law.[60] As early as 1982, the Latin American Federation of Associations for Relatives of the Detained-Disappeared drafted a Convention regarding enforced disappearances[61] to push for the codification of the crime.

Victims associations, including the Latin American Federation and other NGOs, actively participated in the negotiation process leading to the ICPPED[62] where they first advocated for, and then praised the eventual inclusion of the "irrevocable right of families to recover the mortal remains of their loved ones" in the final text.[63] Meanwhile, the Special Process, led by Manfred Nowak,

---

58 ECtHR, *Aslakhanova and Others v. Russia, supra* note 56, §§ 221 and 226.

59 Grażyna Baranowska, *Rights of Families of Disappeared Persons: How International Bodies Address the Needs of Families of Disappeared Persons in Europe, supra* note 19, p. 104.

60 Olivier de Frouville, *Criminalizing or Trivializing Enforced Disappearances? The Issue of 'Non-State Actors'*, 9 March 2021 p. 4; Grażyna Baranowska, *Advances and progress in the obligation to return the remains of missing and forcibly disappeared persons, supra* note 33, p. 732.

61 *Proyecto de Convención sobre desaparecimiento forzado*, available at https://www.museovillagrimaldi.info/icaatom/uploads/r/archivo-villa-grimaldi/a/c/6/ac625b0a185e70f5478145eb53a2f5ff1229a25debefea8a87ab627395918204/1.3.1.18_compressed.pdf (last accessed 1 December 2024).

62 Olivier de Frouville, *La Convention des Nations Unies pour la protection de toustes les personnes contre les disparitions forces: Les enjeux juridique d'une négociation* exemplaire, Droits fondamentaux, n° 6, 2006, pp. 6–7; Commission on Human Rights, *Report of the Intersessional Open-ended Working Group to elaborate a draft legally binding normative instrument for the protection of all persons from enforced disappearance*, UN Doc. E/CN.4/2003/71, 12 February 2003, § 8.

63 Asian Federation Against Involuntary Disappearances and al., *Joint Statement by Associations of families of the disappeared and other supportive NGOs on the occasion of the adoption of the Draft International Convention for the Protection of All Persons from Enforced Disappearances*, 22 September 2005, available at https://view.officeapps.live.co

expanded its mandate to the exhumation of mass graves a few months after mothers of victims from Zagreb started hunger strikes, and the attacks on the International Committee of the Red Cross' (ICRC) office in Tuzla by victims' families to pressure Bosnia and Herzegovina, Croatia and the international community to do just that.[64] Latin American victims associations advocated successfully for the Colombian, Mexican[65] and Peruvian authorities to initiate programmes dedicated to the search for, exhumation, identification and return of remains.[66]

2.3 *A Multi-faceted Reparation Measure*

As noted above, enforced disappearances affect a number of people: the disappeared themselves, their relatives and their community.

First, as noted by Tullio Scovazzi and Gabriella Citroni, the disrespect for the disappeared remains can amount to other inhumane acts.[67] In the *Caracazo v. Venezuela* case, the IACtHR found that the return of the remains "[led] to restor[ing] the dignity of the victims [and] to honor[ing] the value of their memory to those who were their beloved ones".[68]

Secondly, the exhumation should be conducted for the sake of the disappeared's relatives. Traditionally, relatives of victims of human rights violations are considered indirect victims.[69] However in the case of enforced disappearances, they are considered direct victims.[70] Article 24(1) of the ICPPED pro-

---

m/op/view.aspx?src=https%3A%2F%2Fwww.icaed.org%2Ffileadmin%2Fuser_upload%2FJOINT_STATEMENT.doc&wdOrigin=BROWSELINK (last accessed 1 December 2024).

64 Special Process on Missing Person in the Territory of Former Yugoslavia, *Report submitted by Mr. Manfred Nowak, member of the Working Group on Enforced or Involuntary Disappearances, pursuant to paragraph 4 of Commission resolution 1995/35*, *supra* note 38, § 75.

65 Jimena Reyes and al., *Harmonizing Legal Approaches to Enforced Disappearances: Evidentiary Challenges, Emerging Developments, and the Role of Non-State Actors*, Harvard Human Rights Journal, Volume 37, 2024, p. 177.

66 Swiss Peace, *Family Association of Disappeared and Missing Persons: Lessons from Latin America and Beyond*, 2019, p. 23.

67 Tullio Scovazzi and Gabriella Citroni, *The Struggle against Enforced Disappearance and the 2007 United Nations Convention*, Brill, Leiden, 2007, p. 369.

68 IACtHR, *Caracazo v. Venezuela*, *supra* note 44, § 123. See also, IACtHR, *Juan Humberto Sánchez v. Honduras*, Judgment (Preliminary Objections, Merits, Reparations and Costs), 7 June 2003, § 187.

69 International Commission of Jurists (ICJ), *Enforced Disappearance and Extrajudicial Execution: The Rights of Family Members, Practitioners' Guide No. 10*, July 2016, p. 5.

70 More generally, considering the UN Basic Principles' broad definition of victims ("the term 'victim' also includes the immediate family or dependants of the direct victim and persons who have suffered harm in intervening to assist victims in distress or to prevent

vides that victim means "the disappeared person and any individual who has suffered harm as the direct result of an enforced disappearance".[71] Different regional human rights courts and UN bodies have recognised that the relatives are themselves victims of torture, cruel, inhuman or degrading treatment or punishment because of the "anguish and stress"[72] caused by the disappearance, including not knowing the victim's fate, but also because of the State's continued refusal to inform the relatives, or to conduct an effective investigation.[73] In terms of reparations, the DPPED provides that the family of the individual subjected to enforced disappearance can obtain redress, compensation and rehabilitation. In case of death, the individual's dependents are entitled to compensation.[74]

Victims have a general right to know the truth about the human rights violations they suffered.[75] In the case of enforced disappearance, this right has a special dimension as, in addition to the more traditional right to truth about the circumstances and reasons that led to the perpetration of crimes,[76] the WGEID, in its 2011 *General comment on the right to the truth in relation to enforced disappearance*, noted that relatives have the right to know the fate and the whereabouts of the disappeared.[77] This is so because one element of enforced disappearance is for the perpetrator to "conceal[] the fate or where-

---

victimization", § 8), the distinction between a direct and an indirect victim seem to have lost its relevance in the context of reparations. International Commission of Jurists, *Enforced Disappearance and Extrajudicial Execution: The Rights of Family Members*, *supra* note 69, p. 7.

71 See also, DPPED, art. 1(2), referring to the disappeared's family.

72 HRCom, *Case of Maria del Carmen Almeida de Quinteros v. Uruguay*, Communication No. 107/1981, 21 July 1983, § 14.

73 Ibid, § 14, "violation of article 7 of the ICCPR [torture or to cruel, inhuman or degrading treatment or punishment]"; IACtHR, *Baldeón García v. Peru*, Judgment (Merits, Reparations, and Costs), 6 April 2006, §§ 128–130, "inhumane treatment"; IACtHR, *La Cantuta v. Peru*, *supra* note 26, §§ 123 and 129, violation of the "right to personal integrity"; ECtHR, *Kurt v. Turkey*, Judgment, 25 May 1998, Application No. 15/1997/799/1002, §§ 133–134, "ill-treatment".

74 DPPED, art. 19.

75 UN Basic Principles, § 24; Updated Set of principles for the protection and promotion of human rights through action to combat impunity (UN Impunity Principles), UN Doc. E/CN.4/2005/102/Add.1, 8 February 2005, principle 2.

76 Ibid.

77 WGEID, *General comment on the right to the truth in relation to enforced disappearance*, in Report of the Working Group on Enforced or Involuntary Disappearances, UN Doc. A/HRC/16/48, 26 January 2011, § 1. The WGEID also notes that the relatives have the right to know about the progress and results of an investigation and the identity of the perpetrator(s).

abouts of the disappeared person, which place[s] such a person outside the protection of the law".[78] The Working Group found that knowing the fate and the whereabouts of the disappeared is an autonomous,[79] absolute right, without limitation or derogation.[80] It further explained that this right includes

> [W]hen the disappeared person is found to be dead, the right of the family to have the remains of their relative returned to them, and to dispose of those remains according to their own tradition, religion or culture. The remains of the person should be clearly and indisputably identified, including through DNA analysis.[81]

Receiving information about the fate and the whereabouts of the disappeared from the State, which could be itself involved in the enforced disappearance, is not always enough for their relatives.[82] They will have difficulties believing the victim is truly deceased without their remains.[83] For instance, the ICRC's "death certificate programme" in Bosnia and Herzegovina was discontinued in 1997 because "families were unwilling and unable to accept a 'paper death'", considering that such document could not replace the remains of their relatives.[84] As noted by Grażyna Baranowska, "in case of death, the ambiguity of the loss is best addressed through the return of the remains of those who have died".[85] Further, this return of the remains can offer the relatives more closure[86] and allow them to "begin to grieve and to heal".[87]

---

78 ICPPED, art. 2.

79 WGEID, *General comment on the right to the truth in relation to enforced disappearance*, *supra* note 77, p. 1.

80 Ibid, § 4. There is not, however, an absolute right to know the truth about the circumstances of the disappearances as hiding part of the truth can facilitate reconciliation, § 8.

81 Ibid, § 6.

82 Grażyna Baranowska, *Advances and progress in the obligation to return the remains of missing and forcibly disappeared persons*, *supra* note 33, p. 714.

83 ICRC, *Accompanying the Families of Missing Persons, A Practical Handbook*, March 2013, p. 36.

84 Eric Stover and Rachel Shigekane, *The missing in the aftermath of war: When do the needs of victims' families and international war crimes tribunals clash?*, International Review of the Red Cross, 2022, p. 855. Once the ICRC received confirmation from the authorities that a person was deceased, it would issue a death certificate signed by an ICRC delegate to the family.

85 Grażyna Baranowska, *Advances and progress in the obligation to return the remains of missing and forcibly disappeared persons*, *supra* note 33, p. 714.

86 Ibid.

87 Sarah Fulton, *supra* note 2, p. 773.

The exhumation, identification and return of remains also allow the relatives to perform the funeral rites according to their religious and cultural practices. Although the ICPPED only provides for the return of the remains,[88] the UN Basic Principles go further and state that, following the search for, exhumation and identification, the remains should be buried "in accordance with the expressed or presumed wish of the victims, or the cultural practices of the families and communities".[89] Similarly to the return itself of the remains, the possibility to bury the disappeared person can help their relatives, as the disappeared can finally be laid to rest.

Thirdly, Tullio Scovazzi and Gabriella Citroni suggest that the right to the search for, exhumation, identification and return of the remains pertains to the victim's community, as well as the society as a whole, which has "a right to know where the human remains of disappeared people are located and to be sure that they are respected, even if there is nobody who claims their return".[90] Enforced disappearance, although committed against individuals, can be aimed at victimizing a community or a group as such.[91] For instance, the IACtHR found that the enforced disappearance of indigenous leaders demonstrated a State doctrine against a whole group, attempting to dismantle all forms of their political representation.[92] The Inter-American Court recognised that exhumations were important for the community of the disappeared person, in addition to their direct family, in its 2005 *Moiwana Community v. Suriname* case, where it noted that:

> [O]ne of the greatest sources of suffering for the Moiwana community members is that they do not know what has happened to the remains of their relatives, and, as a result, they cannot honor and bury them in accordance with fundamental norms of N'djuka culture.[93]

---

88 ICPPED, art. 24(3).

89 UN Basic Principles, § 22(c).

90 Tullio Scovazzi and Gabriella Citroni, *The Struggle against Enforced Disappearance and the 2007 United Nations Convention*, Brill, Leiden, 2007, p. 369.

91 ICJ, *Enforced Disappearance and Extrajudicial Execution: The Rights of Family Members, Practitioners' Guide No. 10*, July 2016, p. 10.

92 IACtHR, *Chitay Nech* et al. *v. Guatemala*, Judgement (Preliminary Objections, Merits, Reparations, and Costs), 25 May 2010, § 108.

93 IACtHR, *Moiwana Community v. Suriname*, Judgment (Preliminary Objections, Merits, Reparations and Costs), 15 June 2005, § 100.

2.4 *A Victim-Centred Approach to the Search for, Exhumation, Identification and Return of Remains*

States should not only search for, exhume, identify and return the remains of the disappeared, but also ensure that the process is conducted in a victim-centred manner. This entails the full effective participation of the relatives, their protection and the provision of information to the general public.[94]

Regarding the search, the Committee on Enforced Disappearances (CED) clarified that any person with a legitimate interest, including the relatives, have the right to take part in the search and their "input, experiences, alternative suggestions, questions and doubts should be taken into account at all stages of the search".[95]

The 2016 Minnesota Protocol on Investigation of Potentially Unlawful Death provides that, once the remains have been found:

> Family members have specific rights in relation to human remains. When the identity of a deceased person has been determined, family members should be informed immediately and thereafter a notification of death posted in an easily accessible way. To the extent possible, family members should also be consulted prior to an autopsy. They should be entitled to have a representative present during the autopsy. Upon completion of the necessary investigative procedures, human remains should be returned to family members, allowing them to dispose of the deceased according to their beliefs.[96]

According to the IACtHR, the next of kin can be present during the exhumations.[97] In case only a part of the remains are found, the CED's 2019 *Guiding principles for the search for disappeared persons* clarified that the decision to continue the search should take into account the "needs expressed by the family members in the context of their cultural norms concerning funerals"

---

94 WGEID, *General comment on the right to the truth in relation to enforced disappearance*, *supra* note 77, § 6.

95 CED, *Guiding principles for the search for disappeared persons*, UN Doc. CED/C/7, 8 May 2019, principle 5, § 1.

96 OHCHR, Minnesota Protocol on the Investigation of Potentially Unlawful Death: The Revised United Nations Manual on the Effective Prevention and Investigation of Extra-legal, Arbitrary and Summary Executions, UN Doc. HR/PUB/17/4, § 37. See also, Principles on the Effective Prevention and Investigation of Extra-legal, Arbitrary and Summary Executions, 24 May 1989, § 16.

97 IACtHR, *Bamaca-Velasquez v. Guatemala*, Judgment (Reparations and Costs), 22 February 2002, § 82.

but also the "actual chances of identifying more remains".[98] When, following an extensive search and exhaustion of all possible leads, the remains can still not be found, the search can be suspended in a transparent manner with prior informed consent of the relatives.[99]

The CED's *Guiding principles* further provide that remains should be returned "under decent conditions[,] with respect at all times for the fact that they are the mortal remains of a person, and not objects".[100] Similarly, the Inter-American Court, considered that remains have to be respected "for the special relevance that the victims bear to their next of kin".[101] This return is not limited to the handing over of the remains to the relatives. The State should also cover the costs of the burial, according to the relatives' wishes, even if this entails the transfer of the remains to another country.[102]

In addition to the process around the exhumation itself, the CED's *Guiding principles* provide more broadly that the "authorities have a duty to ensure that the victims, including family members, are not subject to stigmatization and other moral ill-treatment or slurs that undermine their dignity, reputation or good name as people, or those of their disappeared relative".[103]

2.5 *Limitation to the Search for, Exhumation, Identification and Return of Remains*

Exhumations can be conducted as a form of reparation, but also for evidentiary purposes. In such case, it might not be necessary for a court or tribunal to identify each individual victim. In genocide investigations, for example, the focus will be on proving that the victim belongs to a certain national, ethnical, racial or religious group and the cause of death.[104] The court or tribunal will not always take the extra step to identify victims. The International Criminal Tribunal for the former Yugoslavia's forensic teams, when operating in Kosovo, reburied the remains of victims after autopsy, without proper identifying markers. This forced the UN Interim Administration Mission in Kosovo

98 CED, *Guiding principles for the search for disappeared persons*, *supra* note 95, principle 7, § 3.

99 Ibid, principle 7, § 4.

100 Ibid, principle 2, § 4.

101 IACtHR, *La Cantuta v. Peru*, *supra* note 26, § 231.

102 CED, *Guiding principles for the search for disappeared persons*, *supra* note 95, principle 2, § 4.

103 Ibid, principle 2, § 3. See also, ICPPED, art. 12(1).

104 Eric Stover and Rachel Shigekane, *supra* note 84, p. 846.

and the International Commission on Missing Persons to later re-exhume the bodies for identification, as a satisfaction measure this time.[105]

Further, even when exhumation is conducted as a form of reparation, relatives can be dissatisfied with the process. The State's obligation to return the remains is an obligation of means and not an obligation of results, as it will not always be possible to find the bodies of all disappeared persons.[106] Most victims will therefore be left without the remains of their loved ones.

Additionally, as noted in the Minnesota Protocol, the remains can only be returned upon completion of the investigation,[107] which can sometime take years. The Inter-American Court further conditioned the remains' release to the family to the fact that they cannot be cremated and could be exhumed again for autopsy purposes,[108] thus limiting the families' choices in funeral arrangements.

Finally, the return of the remains to the relatives will not always lead to closure. As noted by Alexa Hagerty, exhumation can create melancholy:

> One definition of melancholy is finally getting the "desired object" only to find it disappointing. In this sense, exhumation can be nothing other than melancholic: The "desired object" is the missing person – the brother, the daughter, the father – but the "getting", the return, is always only bones.[109]

Although this contribution focuses on the search for, exhumation, identification and return of the remains, a truly victim-centred approach to redress for enforced disappearances shall include other forms of reparations, for example, financial compensation, medical and psychological care, and public apologies and commemorations.[110]

The return of remains does not relieve the State of its obligation to investigate and prosecute human rights violations. This has been made clear by the ECtHR in its 2001 *Cyprus v. Turkey* case, when Türkiye argued that the work of the Committee on Missing Persons in Cyprus, which had compiled a list of

105 Ibid, p. 859.

106 WGEID, *General comment on the right to the truth in relation to enforced disappearance*, *supra* note 77, § 5.

107 Minnesota Protocol, *supra* note 96, § 37.

108 IACtHR, *González* et al. (*"Cotton Field"*) *v. Mexico*, Judgment (Preliminary Objection, Merits, Reparations, and Costs), 16 November 2009, § 305.

109 Alexa Hagerty, *Still Life With Bones: Genocide, Forensics and What Remains*, Crown, 2023, chapter 7.

110 UN Basic Principles, §§ 18–23.

disappeared persons and returned some remains, meant that Türkiye had fulfilled its positive obligation under Article 2 of the European Convention on the right to life. However, the Court found that the Committee's investigatory work did not "meet the standard of an effective investigation required by Article 2", and that further investigations were necessary.[111]

3 Case-Study: The Search for, Exhumation, Identification and Return of Remains of Yazidis Subjected to Enforced Disappearances during the 2014 Genocide

This section will start with presenting the genocide of the Yazidis committed by ISIS in 2014 (3.1), and then examine how the Yazidi community and Yazidi-led NGOs advocated for the search for, exhumation, identification and return of remains of their disappeared community members (3.2), and their successes and challenges in such search, exhumation, identification and return (3.3).

3.1 *The 2014 Genocide of the Yazidis by the Islamic State of Iraq and Syria*

Yazidis, who call themselves Êzidî, are an ethno-religious group,[112] traditionally located in the Sinjar district, in Kurdistan/Northern Iraq. They follow Yazidism and worship one God called *Xwede*, who "created the world and entrusted it to seven angels, led by *Tawuse Malak* or *Malek*, symbolized by a peacock" – sometimes called the peacock angel.[113] Yazidism is not a missionary religion, meaning that one must be born a Yazidi and cannot convert or convert back to Yazidism.[114] Yazidis consider that, prior to ISIS' genocide in 2014, they were subjected to 73 genocides or *firmans*,[115] which were undocumented but orally transmitted through generations in songs.[116]

On 3 August 2014, ISIS attacked and seized numerous towns and villages in Sinjar, abducting women, girls and boys who had not reached puberty,

111 ECtHR, *Cyprus v. Turkey*, *supra* note 23, § 135.

112 Yazidis themselves do not always see themselves as a distinct ethnic group. See CoI Syria, *"They came to destroy": ISIS Crimes Against the Yazidis*, supra note 7, §§ 101–102.

113 Yazda, *Get to Know me First: A Survivor- Informed Guide for Interviewing Yazidis from Sinjar*, September 2023, p. 9.

114 Ibid.

115 *Firmans* refers to the decrees adopted during the Ottoman empire, which often had negative impacts on the Yazidi community.

116 Yazda, *Get to Know me First*, *supra* note 113, p. 12.

and rounding up and killing men and older women. The latter were buried in mass graves. The 10 000 Yazidis who managed to flee to Mount Sinjar were trapped as ISIS laid siege to the mountain, preventing them from accessing or receiving water, food and medical care despite the temperatures reaching 50°C. Meanwhile, abducted women, girls and boys were transferred to ISIS-held cities. They were forcibly converted to Islam. Women and girls were sold and used as sex slaves, while boys were forcibly recruited as child soldiers and indoctrinated into ISIS' ideology. Yazidi shrines and temples were destroyed.[117] According to Yazda, a Yazidi-led NGO, ISIS killed 5,000, abducted 6,800 and caused the forced displacement of 400,000 Yazidis.[118]

In its 2016 report *"They came to destroy": ISIS Crimes Against the Yazidis*, the UN Human Rights Council (HRC) mandated Commission of Inquiry on Syria determined that ISIS had committed the crime of genocide.[119] It found that "ISIS intended to destroy the Yazidis of Sinjar, composing the majority of the world's Yazidi population, in whole or in part", noting, among other elements, that ISIS had declared in its *Dabiq* magazine that the Yazidis' "continual existence to this day is a matter that Muslims should question", and that Yazidis women could be enslaved because they were not "People of the Book", unlike Christians.[120] In addition to the Commission of Inquiry on Syria, the UN Investigative Team to Promote Accountability for Crimes Committed by Da'esh/ Islamic State in Iraq and the Levant (UNITAD),[121] and States such as Armenia, Belgium, France, Germany, Iraq, Luxembourg, the Netherlands, the United Kingdom and the United States recognised that ISIS' crimes against the Yazidis constituted genocide.[122]

---

117 For more, see CoI Syria, *"They came to destroy": ISIS Crimes Against the Yazidis*, supra note 7, §§ 23–99; Free Yezidi Foundation (FYF), *Yezidi Genocide Perpetrated by ISIS (2014-onward)* webpage, available at https://freeyezidi.org/yezidi-genocide-2014/ (last accessed 26 May 2024).

118 Yazda, *Yazidi Genocide* webpage, available at https://www.yazda.org/yazidi-genocide (last accessed 1 December 2024).

119 CoI Syria, *"They came to destroy": ISIS Crimes Against the Yazidis*, supra note 7, § 165.

120 Ibid, §§ 150–163.

121 UNITAD, *The ISIL Attack on Sinjar in August 2014 and Subsequent Acts Committed against the Yazidi Community in Iraq*, 11 September 2024, §§ 513 and ff.

122 FYF, *Netherlands and Belgium Genocide Recognition*, 6 July 2021; Euroasianet, *Armenia Recognizes IS Massacres of Yezidis as Genocide*, 23 January 2018; France's *Assemblée Nationale, Reconnaissance du génocide perpétré par Daech*, 8 December 2016, ordinary session; DW, *German parliament recognizes Yazidi 'genocide' in Iraq*, 19 January 2023; Yazidi Survivors Law No. 8 of 2021, 15 March 2021, art. 7; Yazda, *Joint statement by Yazda & YSN in response to Luxembourg recognition of the Yazidi genocide*, 10 November 2022; UK Foreign, Commonwealth & Development Office, *UK acknowledges acts of genocide*

The Yazidi community has roughly to two types of missing people: the women and children who have been abducted and are still being held captive by ISIS, and the men and elderly women who have been killed and buried in mass graves.[123] While it is assumed that people in that first category are likely to still be alive and thus may and should be saved so that they can return to their family and community, the people in the latter category are probably dead, and their remains should be found, exhumed, identified and returned. These two categories are not set in stone, as some women and children were also murdered and buried in a similar fashion to the men, while their relatives still hope to find them alive, and some men believed to be in mass graves might be alive. Not knowing if their relatives are dead or alive is what is particularly crushing for the relatives and the Yazidi community as a whole. As noted by the Free Yezidi Foundation, another Yazidi-led NGO, "[n]othing is more agonizing and frustrating to the Yezidi community than waiting and wondering about the missing. We are realistic, and we know that not every missing Yezidi is still alive".[124]

3.2 *Yazidis' Call for the Search for, Exhumation, Identification and Return of Remains of Their Community Members*

The Yazidi community and Yazidi-led NGOs, like Yazda and the Free Yezidi Foundation, have repeatedly asked Iraq to comply with its obligation to search for, exhume, identify and return the remains of disappeared Yazidis. For instance, in its 2019 policy paper *10 steps to ensure Justice, Reparations,*

---

committed by Daesh against Yazidis, 1 August 2023; USA Congress, *Expressing the sense of Congress that the atrocities perpetrated by ISIL against religious and ethnic minorities in Iraq and Syria include war crimes, crimes against humanity, and genocide*, 15 March 2016, 114th Congress, 2nd session, resolution 75.

123 Yazda identified the following categories of missing persons: "(1) missing persons whose families have not been able to locate [] since the 2014 genocide; (2) [] Yazidis, who went missing after the 2014 genocide, and were either temporarily identified by their family members or informed of their captivity by other rescued individuals [but whose] location and survival status are unknown at the moment; (3) [] missing people whose families or authorities know their whereabouts but rescuing them has not been possible due to financial or security reasons", Yazda, *The Unknown Fate of Missing Yazidis 8 Years On and Still Waiting*, September 2022, p. 7.

The CoI on Syria considered that the thousands of men and boys whose "fate ... remains unknown" were subjected to the crime of enforced disappearance. CoI Syria, "They came to destroy": ISIS Crimes Against the Yazidis, UN Doc. A/HRC/32/CRP.2, 15 June 2016, § 174.

124 FYF, *Missing Yezidis* webpage, available at https://freeyezidi.org/missing-yezidis/ (last accessed 1 December 2024).

Recovery and Return for the Yazidis, Yazda advocated for the "exhumation of mass graves [to] be done swiftly and with dignity".[125] When analysing how the 2021 Yazidi Survivors Law, examined below, fared one year on, the Free Yezidi Foundation noted that survivors with whom they worked "particularly emphasized … accelerating the exhumation of mass graves".[126] Similarly, in her research on responses to and reparations for conflict-related sexual violence in Iraq and Kurdistan, Güley Bor found that, "survivors prioritized their demands as indirect victims of killings and enforced disappearances committed against their families, rather than their demands as direct victims of [conflict-related sexual violence]".[127] The focus is on restoring the community rather than on individuals needs such as financial compensation and psychosocial support.[128]

Natia Nazrouzov, the Executive Director of Yazda, highlighted that "[t]he issue of missing people is very very critical because a lot of people cannot move on, they are just waiting for their relatives to come back and they are in this 'in between' where they cannot move forward, [they] live in the past and are waiting for their relatives".[129] Similarly, the Free Yezidi Foundation explained that exhumations, identification and return of remains were required to enable collective healing, highlighting that, "[p]roviding a proper resting place for the departed allows survivors to begin their journey towards solace and closure".[130] It further noted that this reparation measure was needed, as the disappeared persons kept in mass graves were being neglected and marginalised "in life and even after death".[131]

Natia Nazrouzov explained that the exhumation, return and reburial of remains is particularly important in Yazidi culture because Yazidism revolves around the binary oppositions of life and death, and light and darkness, and Yazidis believe in reincarnation. A dignified burial thus allows victims to come back in their next form. Furthermore, women traditionally hit their chest and face and shout the name of the deceased during funerals but were not able to

125 Yazda, *10 steps to ensure Justice, Reparations, Recovery and Return for the Yazidis*, 2019, p. 3.

126 FYF, *Iraq's Yezidi Survivors Law: Report on Year One of Reparation Applications*, September 2023, p. 5.

127 Güley Bor, *Iraq's Reparation Bill for Yazidi Female Survivors: More Progress Needed*, 12 June 2019.

128 Interview with Natia Nazrouzov, 28 August 2023.

129 Asymmetrical Haircuts, *Episode 93 – Yazidi Genocide justice with Natia Nazrouzov*, 27 February 2024.

130 FYF, *Burial Ceremony for 41 Yezidi Genocide Victims*, 24 January 2024.

131 FYF, *FYF Provides Support at Hamadan Exhumation*, 6 March 2023.

express their grief in such manner when bodies had not been exhumed and returned for burial.[132]

Practically, unexhumed mass graves also impede displaced Yazidis from returning to their homes,[133] which is also one of the community's priorities, especially considering Iraq's Ministry of Migration and Displacement's announcement that it plans to close internally displaced people's camps in Kurdistan, where Yazidis have been living since 2014.[134]

3.3 *The Search for, Exhumation, Identification and Return of Remains in Iraq*

In September 2017, the UN Security Council requested the Secretary-General to establish an Investigative Team to Promote Accountability for Crimes Committed by Da'esh/Islamic State in Iraq and the Levant (UNITAD), to "support domestic efforts to hold ISIL (Da'esh) accountable by collecting, preserving, and storing evidence in Iraq of acts that may amount to war crimes, crimes against humanity and genocide committed by the terrorist group ISIL (Da'esh) in Iraq".[135] One of UNITAD's key technical assistance projects was to build the capacity of the Iraqi authorities to "conduct forensic work in line with international standards, supporting the return of remains to families". It supported the Iraqi Mass Graves Directorate and the Medico-Legal Directorate in exhuming and identifying remains, by training them,[136] drafting practice manuals, and providing them with equipment and consumables.[137] This equipment included disaster victim identification technology in line with international standards, which enables the Iraqi authorities to process large amounts of data on remains recovered from mass graves.[138]

---

132 Interview with Natia Nazrouzov, 28 August 2023.

133 Yazda, *From Resistance to Rubble: The Stories of Ger Zarik, Siba Sheikh-Kheder and Tel Azer*, July 2023, p. 58.

134 Human Rights Watch, *Iraq: Looming Camp Closures in Kurdistan*, 13 May 2024.

135 UN Security Council, Resolution 2379 (2017), UN Doc. S/RES/2379 (2017), 21 September 2017, § 2.

136 UNITAD further helped the Medico-Legal Directorate start the process to obtain the ISO/IEC 17025 accreditation, a key accreditation "for compliance with this international quality standard and crucial for criminal justice processes". UNITAD, *For the first time in Iraq: Medico-Legal Directorate Forensic DNA Laboratory Works to Obtain ISO/IEC 17025 Accreditation*, 26 October 2023.

137 UNITAD, *Supporting National Authorities* webpage, available at https://www.unitad.un.org/content/supporting-national-authorities (last accessed 1 December 2024).

138 Ibid.

In parallel, at the domestic level, the Iraqi Council of Representatives enacted the Yazidi [Women] Survivors Law No. 8 of 2021 on 15 March 2021. Article 5 provides that:

> The Directorate [General for Female Yazidi Survivors' Affairs] is responsible for achieving [the Law's] goals[139] through the following means:
>
> ...
>
> Seventh: Search for the kidnapped Yazidis, Turkmen, Christians and Shabak men, women and children, whose fate remains unknown, in coordination with the competent authorities inside and outside Iraq and the victims' families ...
>
> Eighth: Coordinate with the Mass Graves Directorate of the Martyrs Foundation in regard to mass graves, to complete all procedures related to the search, investigation, opening of mass graves, revealing the identity of the remains and returning them to their families in order to bury them in a manner that recognises their sacrifice.[140]

At time of writing, according to Yazda, 60 mass graves have been exhumed by the Mass Graves Directorate and UNITAD since the process started in March 2019, leaving around 20 still to be excavated.[141] Nonetheless, mass graves continue to be found, as Yazidis return to live where the crimes were committed and come across undiscovered sites.[142] The latest exhumation started on 21 May 2024 at the Alu Antar Well mass grave in Tal Afar, which is believed to contain the remains of 600 to 700 individuals.[143] As of September 2022, 145

---

139 Compensation, rehabilitation and guarantees of non-recurrence. Yazidi Survivors Law No. 8 of 2021, art. 4.

140 Yazidi Survivors Law No. 8 of 2021, art. 5. Translation by the author.

141 Yazda, *Statement by Yazda on the Burial Ceremonies of 41 Yazidi Victims of Hardan, Kocho and Qney villages*, 22 January 2024.

142 Asymmetrical Haircuts, *Episode 93*, *supra* note 129.

143 Yazda, *Yazda welcomes the exhumation of the Alu Antar Well mass grave in Tal Afar*, 22 May 2024.

Yazidis had been identified and returned to their families.[144] Ahead of their return, official ceremonies were held in Baghdad.[145]

As UNITAD recognised that exhumations were "painful processes that are likely to trigger a wide range of difficult emotions such as sadness, anxiety, anger, loneliness or fear", it requested the International Organisation for Migration and Yazda to support in dispatching psychologists and psychosocial workers to care for victims present on site during the exhumations.[146]

When mass graves in Ger Zarik, in Kurdistan/Northern Iraq, were exhumed in November 2022, Yazda welcomed the process and found that it was a "crucial step towards affording family members human rights and dignity".[147] Nonetheless, the Yazidi community was not always satisfied with how the exhumations, identification and return of remains processes were undertaken. Some exhumations took place during Yazidi religious holidays, and relatives were not always informed on time that an exhumation would take place nor were they given clear information about the identification process and timeline.[148] Furthermore, the choice of which mass grave to exhumed followed UNITAD's lines of enquiry as the Investigative Team's main objective was to collect, preserve and store evidence, rather than the Yazidi community's priorities.[149]

In September 2023, Iraq asked the UN Security Council, as the body in charge of renewing UNITAD's mandate, to do so for a final year until September 2024.[150] On 15 September 2023, the UN Security Council followed Iraq's request[151] and UNITAD's mandate ended on 17 September 2024. However, the Iraqi Mass Graves Directorate is understaffed and under-resources and will not be able to take on exhumations and identifications without UNITAD sup-

144 UNITAD, *Eighth report of the Special Adviser and Head of the United Nations Investigative Team to Promote Accountability for Crimes Committed by Da'esh/Islamic State in Iraq and the Levant*, UN Doc. S/2022/434, 26 May 2022, § 71; Yazda, *The Unknown Fate of Missing Yazidis 8 Years On and Still Waiting*, September 2022, p. 9.

145 UNITAD, *Families Bid Solemn Farewell to Identified Yazidi Victims of ISIL Genocide in Sinjar*, 24 January 2024.

146 UNITAD, *Government of Iraq Resumes Exhumation Activities; Opens Two New Yazidi Mass Graves from ISIL*, 28 October 2020.

147 FYF, *Commencement of the exhumation process in Ger Zarik*, 17 November 2022.

148 Interview with Natia Nazrouzov, 28 August 2023.

149 Ibid.

150 Security Council Report, *Iraq: Vote on UNITAD Mandate Renewal*, available at https://www.securitycouncilreport.org/whatsinblue/2023/09/iraq-vote-on-unitad-mandate-renewal-2.php (last accessed 1 December 2024).

151 UN Security Council, *Resolution 2697 (2023)*, UN Doc. S/RES/2697 (2023), 15 September 2023, § 2.

port.[152] The Iraqi government itself recognised that it did not have enough resources, including financial, for exhumations,[153] so the closure of UNITAD could entail the end of exhumation, identification and return of the remains for the Yazidis, despite mass graves and unidentified bodies remaining. Some mass graves urgently need to be excavated and the bodies they contain need to be exhumed, as they are particularly vulnerable to the weather, for example, the ones in valleys – over time, rain will wash away the remains – or mass graves that are exposed to the elements, unprotected and are thus at risk due to exposure to the weather, animals and human activity.[154]

4 Conclusion

As developed in this chapter, the search for, exhumation, identification and return of the remains of a person who has been victim of enforced disappearance are crucial because, if done pursuant to a victim-centred approach, they allow relatives to get closure about the disappeared's fate, put an end to the uncertainties about their possible death, and allow them to perform funeral rites according to their religious and cultural practices. They further restore the disappeared's and their community's dignity. Nevertheless, as a satisfaction measure, they are not sufficient. In the case of enforced disappearance, States should provide a wide range of reparation measures including financial compensation, psychological and medical support, public apologies and commemorations and non-repetition, as well as investigation capable of leading to the identification and prosecution and eventual punishment of the perpetrators of such crimes. Regarding the disappeared Yazidis and the remaining mass graves and unidentified remains, one can only deplore that UNITAD's mandate has ended in September 2024, as victims deserve and have a right to see their relatives' remains exhumed, identified and returned to them.

152 Asymmetrical Haircuts, *Episode 93*, *supra* note 129.

153 Yazda, *From Resistance to Rubble*, *supra* note 133, p. 57.

154 Ibid; Interview with Natia Nazrouzov, 28 August 2023.

CHAPTER 6

Is There Room for Creative Reparations in International Criminal Law?

Marina Aksenova[1]

1 Introduction

This chapter discusses reparations with creative value in the context of international criminal law. The subject matter of the discussion is thus limited to the context of individual criminal prosecutions of war crimes, crimes against humanity, genocide, and aggression. The purpose is to outline some benefits and pitfalls of engaging with creative reparations in international criminal adjudication. Some of the findings may resonate across the field of international justice more generally.

Reparations, typically implemented later in legal proceedings, aim to mitigate the harm caused by the original violations. Some reparations include an aspect of creative expression when a specific solution is tailored to address the unique circumstances of each case and the collective interests of victims as a group. Including creativity in the practice of reparations, however, requires careful balancing of the formal legal structure of a judicial process with the complexities and traumas that underlie the transgressions.[2] While legal outcomes like guilt or responsibility are often binary ('yes' or 'no'), reparations operate in a more nuanced space, seeking to acknowledge multiple perspectives and provide limited but meaningful relief to victims.[3] Art and creativity are naturally fitting companions for the practice of reparations precisely because of this feature. Reparations have capacity to reflect the deeper yearnings inherent in human condition – these considerations often evade binary characterizations of the legal jargon.

1 Associate Professor, International and Comparative Criminal Law at IE University (Madrid).

2 M Aksenova and A N Rieff, 'Setting the Scene: The Use of Art to Promote Reconciliation in International Criminal Justice', (2021) 33 (2) Leiden Journal of International Law, 495.

3 UN Office of the High Commissioner for Human Rights (OHCHR), 'Rule of Law Tools for Post-Conflict States: Reparations Programmes' (2008) HR/PUB/08/1 (OHCHR Rule of Law Report); Aksenova and Rieff (n 1).

 | DOI:10.1163/9789004716742_007

Creativity for the purposes of this chapter refers to the ability to innovate, transcend conventional solutions, and work with imagination. What is deemed 'creative' therefore depends on the context of each individual case. Within the ambit of law, creative engagement can enliven multiple perspectives by embracing uncertainty and an outsider's observational standpoint.[4] Maks del Mar's framework on legal imagination emphasizes the multifaceted nature of thinking within a legal context. By highlighting the four cognitive abilities rooted in imagination – thinking in possibilities, relating to others' perspectives, generating insightful mental images, and envisioning multiple scenarios – he underscores the importance of empathy and creativity in legal practice.[5] This approach not only allows for a deeper understanding of the law but also fosters a more compassionate inquiry, enabling legal professionals to navigate complex situations while considering the diverse interests and viewpoints of all parties involved.

Reparations that include a creative dimension are often (but not always) termed 'symbolic' by international courts, such as the International Criminal Court (ICC). It is essential to note that the term 'symbolic' in common parlance is often synonymous to 'insubstantial' and may not accurately capture the essence of reparations with creative value discussed in this chapter. Yet international courts, such as the ICC, use this term to refer to other (innovative) types of reparations beyond more traditional 'restitution, compensation, and rehabilitation'.[6] Symbolic reparations with creative aspects can be seen as an 'expressive tool' in the field of international law because they allow courts to empathetically transmit an intended message.[7] Tangible objects, such as monuments, ordered as symbolic reparations solidify the event in collective memory, signalling to future generations the devastating effects of abuse suffered by the victims. In contrast, intangible objects, such as commemoration ceremonies or artistic performances, work more with the present moment by invoking art's healing potential to bring to the surface, relive, and let go of trauma.[8]

---

4 J B White, 'The Legal Imagination' (University of Chicago Press 1973).

5 M del Mar, 'Imagining by feeling: a case for compassion in legal reasoning' (2017) 13 (2) International Journal of Law in Context, 143. See also M del Mar, 'Artefacts of Legal Inquiry: The Value of Imagination in Adjudication' (Hart 2021).

6 Article 75(1) of the Rome Statute of the International Criminal Court, July 17, 1998.

7 OHCHR Rule of Law Report (n 2).

8 Aksenova and Rieff, (n 1); M Aksenova, 'Creative Potential of Reparations at the Inter-American Court of Human Rights and the International Criminal Court', (2020) 43 (1) Suffolk Journal of Transnational Law, 1.

This chapter examines creative reparations at the ICC. The goal is to reveal their transformative dimension as well as potential pitfalls and benefits of engaging with creativity in international criminal proceedings. It must be noted that the ICC's practice of creative reparations is less developed than that of some human rights courts dealing with state responsibility for gross violations of fundamental rights – the Inter-American Court of Human Rights (IACtHR) being the primary example.[9]

Due to historical factors, the IACtHR is quite innovative when it comes to the form and intended meaning of its reparation orders.[10] The IACtHR is particularly skilled in measures aimed at public commemoration to honour both individual victims and groups of victims, especially in case of violations against a large number of persons, such as massacres. Article 63(1) of the American Convention on Human Rights provides that '...the consequences of the measure or situation that constituted the breach of [a Convention] right or freedom be remedied and that fair compensation be paid to the injured party'.[11] The legislative history of this provision reveals that the drafters expressly intended to give the Court broad powers to order reparations, which explains why the IACtHR resorted to many distinct forms of creative reparations, often termed 'symbolic'.[12] Throughout the last twenty-five years, the Court has been ordering the construction of monuments,[13] churches, and parks as a form of reparation to memorialize traumatic events, such as the massacre by the Guatemalan Army of the indigenous Mayan people[14] and the forced disappearance of children in El Salvador, perpetrated by the armed

9 Aksenova (n 6).

10 A Hunneus, 'International Criminal Law by Other Means: The Quasi-Criminal Jurisdiction of the Human Rights Courts', (2013) 107 (1) American Journal of International Law, 1; See also C Medina-Quiroga, 'The Battle of Human Rights: Gross, Systematic Violations and the Inter-American System' (Martinus Nijhoff Publishers 1988), 58.

11 Article 63(1) of the American Convention on Human Rights, 22 November 1969, 4477 U.N.T.S. 123 (American Convention on Human Rights).

12 J M Pasqualucci, The Practice and Procedure of the Inter-American Court of Human Right (Cambridge University Press 2003), 233.

13 See, e.g. *Barrios Altos v. Peru*, Series C No. 87 (IACtHR Reparations and Costs Judgment, 30 November 2001) para. 44(f); *Mapiripán Massacre v. Colombia*, Series C No. 134, (IACtHR Reparations, and Costs Merits Judgment, 15 September 2005) para. 315; *Moiwana Community v. Suriname*, Series C No. 124, (IACtHR Reparations, and Costs, Preliminary Objections, Merits, Judgment, 15 June 2005) para. 218.

14 *Plan de Sánchez Massacre v. Guatemala*, Series C No. 105, (IACtHR Merits, Judgment, 29 April 2004) para. 49.

forces in the course of counter-insurgency operations.[15] The reception of these measures has been somewhat mixed, but this does not undermine their importance as a form of acknowledgement of past abuses. At times, the respondent states displayed significant delays in the construction of monuments.[16] Other times, segments of the local population expressed negative sentiment towards such symbolic measures.[17] Yet all these events created an opening for further dialogue without the finality of a traditional legal judgment. Thus, there is overall culture of acceptance of reparations with creative value at the IACtHR.

The ICC has significantly less experience with reparations primarily because it processes fewer cases and was created more recently than the IACtHR. Despite these factors, the ICC has strong international resonance. Therefore, the eyes are now on the Court as it develops its unique approaches to reparations in the context of the fight against impunity and its core function of assigning individual criminal responsibility for mass atrocities. Based on the available case law, the ICC's reparation orders appear as early examples of a broader vision of justice encompassing symbolization and creativity. For instance, in *Prosecutor v. Lubanga Dyilo* – a case dealing with the recruitment of child soldiers – the judges expressly upheld the value of symbolic reparations.[18] In particular, the ICC ruled that 'rehabilitation measures ought to include the means of addressing the shame that child victims may feel', and may take the form of 'commemorations and tributes'.[19]

Section two of the chapter offers a broad overview of the reparations' regime at the ICC. It focuses on several key cases that laid down the overall framework of reparations applicable at the Court. Section three outlines a few essential features of the emerging reparations practice and ponders the relevance of creativity to the development of reparations at the ICC. Part four offers concluding thoughts as to the future of creative reparations in international criminal law.

15 *Rochac Hernández v. El Salvador*, Series C No. 285, (IACtHR Reparations and Costs, Merits, Judgment, 14 October 2014) para. 49.

16 *Barrios Altos v. Peru* (n 12) paras. 9–11.

17 *Miguel Castro-Castro Prison v. Peru*, Series C No. 160 (IACtHR Merits, Reparations, and Costs, Judgment, 25 November 2006) para. 142.

18 *Prosecutor v. Lubanga-Dyilo*, Case No. ICC-01/04-01/06-3129-AnxA (ICC Order for Reparations, 3 March 2015) paras.46, 67–69 (Lubanga Reparations Order).

19 Ibid.

2 Overview of the Reparations' Regime at the ICC

2.1 *The Overall Framework*

While the old generation of international criminal courts and tribunals placed little emphasis on reparations and victim participation, the ICC together with the Extraordinary Chambers in the Courts of Cambodia (ECCC) are pioneering the idea of inclusivity of victims' concerns in international criminal proceedings.[20] This is done by expressly including reparations' regimes in the institutional frameworks of these courts. Pursuant to Article 75(1) of the Rome Statute of the ICC, the Court may order reparations to victims in the form of 'restitution, compensation, and rehabilitation'.[21] Additionally, the Court may impose reparations with symbolic, preventative, and transformative value.[22] The nature of reparations is thus to be defined on a case by case basis. For this reason, the Court is not limited to ordering a specific type of reparations expressly mentioned in the Rome Statute, such as financial compensation.[23]

The reasons for such flexibility in the field of reparations lie in the drafting history of the Rome Statute of the ICC. The records reveal that the inclusion of reparations in the Court's institutional architecture was not the result of an overarching conception of justice but rather stemmed from considerable pressure by the human rights community advocating for a more victim-oriented ICC.[24] Competing narratives of justice – present at the time of the negotiations – resulted in a compromise limiting the Court's ability to engage with state responsibility. The same tensions granted the ICC judges the power to define a reparatory mechanism addressing victims directly.[25] The outcome of a complex negotiation practice meant that some legal ambiguity regarding the meaning and form of reparations was necessary and many practical issues relating to the scope and implementation of the mandate were deliberately

20 For a detailed account of reparations practice at the ECCC please see C Sperfeldt, 'Practices of Reparations in International Criminal Justice' (Cambridge University Press 2022).

21 Article 75(1) of the Rome Statute of the International Criminal Court, July 17, 1998.

22 *Prosecutor v. Katanga*, Case No. ICC 01/04-01/07 (ICC Order for Reparations Pursuant to Article 75 of the Statute, 24 March 2017) para. 297 (Katanga Reparations Order).

23 *Prosecutor v. Lubanga Dyilo*, Case No. ICC-01/04-01/06 (ICC Judgment on the Appeals Against the 'Decision Establishing the Principles and Procedures to be Applied to Reparations' of 7 August 2012 with Amended Order for Reparations (Annex A) and Public Annexes 1 and 2, 3 March 2015) para. 216 (Lubanga Reparations Judgment); See also See also *Prosecutor v. Bemba Gombo*, Case No. ICC-01/05-01/08-3444, (Submission by QUB Human Rights Centre on Reparations Issues Pursuant to Article 75 of the Statute, 17 October 2016) para. 41.

24 Sperfeldt (n 19) 64.

25 Ibid, 65.

pushed into the future.[26] As a result, the Rome Statute includes a relatively broad human-rights inspired concept of reparations placed within a rather legalized criminal justice framework. This was done without specifying the content of reparations or the scope of beneficiaries. Such a malleable implementation mechanism allows the ICC to continue refining and developing its reparations practice, while testing various specific modalities.

Where appropriate, the ICC may order that the award for reparations be made through the Trust Fund for Victims (TFV).[27] Article 79 of the Rome Statute refers to the TFV, which is a body established by the Assembly of State Parties.[28] Within Article 79 is the mandate to serve as an intermediary between victims and the ICC.[29] This particularly applies to matters relating to accumulating fines or forfeiture ordered by the ICC to be later used for reparations.[30] While the ICC orders symbolic reparations in abstract terms, it is up to the implementing body – the TFV – to ensure the practical execution of the order. Rule 98 of the ICC Rules of Procedure and Evidence specifies that the ICC may order reparations to be deposited with TFV when it 'is impossible or impracticable to make awards directly to each victim', or when the number of the 'victims and the scope, forms and modalities of reparations makes a collective award more appropriate'.[31] The precise role of the TFV in managing reparations is defined on a case by case basis, with the judges normally retaining their supervisory function over the TVF.[32]

The reparation practice of the ICC is still at its early stages of development. It is therefore impossible to make generalized claims about the potential of symbolic reparations ordered in specific cases to reflect group interests. The *Ntaganda* order on reparations expressly highlighted victims wish *not* to be granted any form of memorialization or other forms of symbolic reparations unless they serve practical purposes.[33] The Chamber stressed the significance – for its final determination on the form of reparations – of victims'

26 Ibid.

27 Article 75(2) of the Rome Statute of the ICC.

28 Article 79 of the Rome Statute of the ICC.

29 Ibid.

30 Ibid.

31 Articles 98(2) and 98(3) of the ICC Rules of Evidence and Procedure (2019), available at https://www.icc-cpi.int/iccdocs/PIDS/legal-texts/RulesProcedureEvidenceEng.pdf.

32 *Prosecutor v. Al Mahdi*, Case No. ICC-01/12-01/15 A (ICC Judgment on the Appeal of the Victims Against the 'Reparations Order', 8 March 2018) para. 34 ('*Al Mahdi* Reparations Order').

33 *Prosecutor v. Bosco Ntaganda*, Case No. ICC-01/04-02/06 (ICC Order for Reparations, 8 March 2021) para. 9 ('*Ntaganda* Reparations Order').

desire to receive reparations supporting sustainable and long-term livelihood and well-being as opposed to measures meeting their needs on a short-term basis. The judges thus settled on collective reparations with individualized components. There is, however, an important caveat as to how 'symbolic' is understood in the context of *Ntaganda*. The Chamber noted that reparations must be effective in meeting victims' needs in order to be truly transformative instead of merely 'symbolic' or 'charitable' in nature.[34] In line with this argument, the Chamber instructed the TFV to consider building a community centre as a memorialization effort with a practical purpose of reconciliation between different sectors of community.[35] It is therefore clear that *Ntaganda* does not rule out creative reparations but rather stresses the need for effectiveness and victim participation in designing the measure.

2.2 *The Lubanga Case*

In contrast, the earlier *Lubanga* Reparations Order expressly emphasized the importance of symbolic reparations in the form of commemorations and tributes as well as the significance of addressing 'the shame felt by some former child soldiers' and preventing 'any future victimization'.[36] The ICC's first ever conviction in *Lubanga* concerned the war crimes of enlisting and conscripting of children under the age of fifteen years and using them to participate actgively in hostilities. Mr. Lubanga was found to be responsible for these crimes committed in the Ituri region of Eastern Congo, while he fulfilled his role as a local militia commander. He was sentenced to fourteen years of imprisonment.[37] *Lubanga* is known to be the first international criminal law case laying down the detailed definitions of crimes of enlisting and conscripting children. The *Lubanga* Reparations Chamber was thus called to innovate as it developed a proto-framework for collective reparations in working with the interests of protected groups (children, in this case).[38] The order explicitly stated that 'reparations should aim at reconciling the victims with their families and the affected communities'.[39] The actual implementation of the *Lubanga* Rep-

34 Ibid, para. 91.

35 Ibid, para. 208.

36 Lubanga Reparations Order (n 17) para. 67.

37 ICC Case Information Sheet, Situation in the Democratic Republic of the Congo: The Prosecutor v. Thomas Lubanga Dyilo, ICC-PIDS-CIS-DRC-01-017/21_Eng, updated July 2021, available at https://www.icc-cpi.int/sites/default/files/CaseInformationSheets/LubangaEng.pdf.

38 Lubanga Reparations Order (n 17).

39 Ibid, para. 46.

aration Order allowed for some further fine-tuning of this foundational framework for collective symbolic reparations.

The TFV, tasked with implementing the order, faced a real challenge in explaining how reconciliation and reintegration should be understood for the purposes of symbolic reparations initiatives in the specific context of this case. This explains why its implementation plan submitted to the Trial Chamber was rejected due to lack of specificity.[40] In its original Draft Implementation Plan, the Trust Fund proposed memorialization projects that would be community-driven and 'take a range of forms, including written, audio, artistic, events or other mediums'.[41] Furthermore, it suggested 'symbolic reparations include public condemnation of the crimes of enlisting' children as soldiers.[42] The Chamber, while being supportive of TFV's proposals for programs aimed at the 'reintegration of former child soldiers into society' demanded more details.[43]

Based on this prompt, the TFV experts undertook additional research in the affected regions and concluded in their revised plan that crimes against children are often committed with the 'acceptance of the broader community'.[44] Thus, they suggested, what is really needed in terms of 'memorialization or symbolic initiative' is to raise awareness 'within the broader community' about the harm inflicted on children as a result of their inscription in the armed forces.[45] This is, in part, to fight the social stigma attached to the former child soldiers.[46] Consequently, the TFV suggested that activities and events 'may include [...] a combination of community dialogue, artistic, cultural, and theatrical activities to promote awareness-raising about the convicted crimes and the harms suffered by child soldiers'.[47] When it comes to a more permanent structure, the TFV proposed the building of three community centers that serve as a '"living" space [...] for symbolic activities.'[48] For exam-

40 *Prosecutor v. Lubanga Dyilo*, Case No. ICC-01/04-01/06 (ICC Order Instructing the Trust Fund for Victims to Supplement the Draft Implementation Plan, 9 February 2016) para. 10.

41 *Prosecutor v. Lubanga Dyilo*, Case No. ICC-01/04-01/06 (ICC Filing Regarding Symbolic Collective Reparations Projects with Confidential Annex: Draft Requests for Proposals, 19 September 2016) para. 10.

42 Ibid.

43 Ibid, para. 17.

44 Ibid, para. 15.

45 Ibid.

46 Ibid, para. 23.

47 Ibid, para. 41.

48 Ibid, para. 35.

ple, '[t]he interior of the building could [...] be utilized to exhibit pictures and artwork created by former child soldiers that depict the past, present, and their hopes for the future. The structures may also host music, dance, drama, and cultural events'.[49] In addition, the TFV came up with a plan to launch a mobile program featuring activities to reduce stigma and discrimination that former child soldiers continue to face in the communities where they reside.[50]

The Trial Chamber approved this revised plan for symbolic reparations and requested updates every three months on its implementation.[51] It is interesting to note that this point in time marked the division in the jurisprudence of the ICC of reparations into two parts: symbolic reparations and collective service-based reparations, meant to complement each other.[52] The Trial Chamber expressly highlighted the existence of these two types of reparations in its order. Both types of reparations were viewed as tenets of a comprehensive response to the harms suffered by the victims. For the service-based collective reparations, the Trial Chamber approved the Trust Fund's plan to provide physical and psychological rehabilitation, as well as vocational training and income-generating activities.[53] A more recent *Ntaganda* Reparations Order adopted a slightly different classification distinguishing between symbolic reparations with transformative value, such as a community centre, and rehabilitative measures aimed at helping victims to process emotions such as shame. The latter category includes various levels of mental care and measures of socio-economic support, such as access to schooling.[54]

As is clear from the case law, the precise role of the TFV in managing reparations is defined on a case-by-case basis. For instance, in *Prosecutor v. Al Mahdi*,[55] the Appeals Chamber fully upheld the discretion of the trial chambers under Article 75(1) of the Rome Statute when making reparations orders.[56] Furthermore, the judges confirmed their supervisory role over the

49 Ibid.

50 Ibid, para. 63.

51 *Prosecutor v. Lubanga Dylio*, Case No. ICC-01/04-01/06 (ICC Order Approving the Proposed Plan of the Trust Fund for Victims in Relation to Symbolic Collective Reparations, 21 October 2016) paras. 17, 81, 117.

52 Ibid, para. 12.

53 *Prosecutor v. Lubanga Dylio*, Case No. ICC-01/04-01/06 (ICC Information Regarding Collective Reparations with Three Public Annexes, One Confidential Annex, and One Confidential Ex-Parte Annex, 13 February 2017) para. 22.

54 Ntaganda Reparations Order (n 32) paras. 203, 208.

55 Al Mahdi Reparations Order (n 31) para. 60.

56 Ibid.

TFV.[57] This discretion was fully exercised in *Ongwen*, when the Trial Chamber took the lead in establishing the priority of implementing various reparations considering the limitations of the TVF and the nature of victims' requests. The judges prioritized paying symbolic monetary awards of 750 euros over rehabilitation and other symbolic measures, which are scheduled to follow later.[58]

2.3 *The Ongwen Case*

In 2021, the ICC convicted Mr. Ongwen of murder, rape, and sexual slavery as crimes against humanity and war crimes. Mr. Ongwen was sentenced to twenty-five years of imprisonment.[59] The Court rendered a guilty verdict despite the fact that Mr. Ongwen started as a child solider in the Lord's Resistance Army (LRA) in Uganda at the age of ten, subsequently rising up its ranks.[60] Being recruited as a child effectively blurred the line between the roles of a perpetrator and a victim in this case, inviting questions about the robustness of a legal structure aimed solely at personal accountability.

It is significant that the ICC was created as an institution deciding on individual criminal responsibility. As a result, its formal reparations are linked to the finding of guilt and are primarily responding to the offending by an individual.[61] The process of attributing guilt excludes broader communal factors, and the practice of reparations aims to mirror this overall design inspired by the criminal justice paradigm. Thus, the ICC grants reparations to direct victims, indirect victims, individuals who are family members of the direct victims, or those who suffered personal harm as a result of the offences.[62] For the purposes of reparations, there needs to be a causal link between the crime within the jurisdiction of the ICC and the harm suffered by the victim.[63] This framework automatically excludes survivors affected by violence, which has

---

57 Ibid, para. 34.

58 *The Prosecutor v. Dominic Ongwen*, Case No. ICC-02/04-01/15 (ICC, Reparations Order, 28 February 2024), para. 638 (Ongwen Reparations Order).

59 *Prosecutor v. Dominic Ongwen*, Case No. ICC-02/04-01/15 (ICC Final Decision on the Reparations Proceedings, 4 February 2021) para. 3116.

60 *The Prosecutor v. Dominic Ongwen*, Case No. ICC-02/04-01/15 (ICC Trial Judgment, 4 February, 2021); *The Prosecutor v. Dominic Ongwen*, Case No. ICC-02/04-01/15, (ICC Sentence, 6 May 2021); *The Prosecutor v. Dominic Ongwen*, Case No. ICC-02/04-01/15 A and ICC-02/04-01/15 A2, (ICC Judgment on the appeal of Mr Ongwen against the decision of Trial Chamber IX of 4 February 2021 entitled 'Trial Judgment' and Judgment on the appeal of Mr Dominic Ongwen against the decision of Trial Chamber IX of 6 May 2021 entitled 'Sentence', 15 December 2022).

61 Lubanga Reparations Judgment (n 22) para. 216.

62 Ibid, para. 6.

63 Ibid, para. 81.

not been specifically addressed during a criminal trial. While the rule of causality makes sense from a legal and logistical standpoint, excluding individuals and communities from the ambit of reparations based on the selectivity of prosecutions has strong divisive potential. Selectivity may lead to the formation of hierarchies of victims and re-victimization caused by the under-acknowledgement of the harms suffered.[64] This problem exemplifies somewhat myopic nature of international criminal justice to the extent that it excludes from its purview structural factors breeding collective criminality, such as poverty or lack of security.[65] The latter point does not aim to discredit the system of international criminal justice as a whole but rather it points at its Achilles heel, namely the seeming inability to 'fit' collective societal factors into the individual criminal justice paradigm.

The case of a child soldier, Dominic Ongwen, is an acute demonstration of a degree of short-sightedness of international criminal justice system. The moral ambiguity of prosecuting someone socialized into atrocities as a child certainly received attention in the courtroom, but it failed to get full expression in the eventual legal judgment due to the inherent limitations of the legal process, both in its form and substance.[66] The categories of victims and perpetrators are rather solid within the realm of international criminal law. It is true that Article 31 of the Rome Statute of the ICC lists grounds for excluding criminal responsibility, such as mental disease or qualified duress. Yet these grounds do not include prolonged suffering, such as lifelong traumatization. The reality is more complex than what the current legislative framework permits:[67] with time and consistent exposure to violence, child soldiers transition from the role of victims to the role of perpetrators.[68] Some form of post-

64 K Fisher, 'The Barlonyo Massacre, Ongwen's Trial, and ICC Reparations: Reflections on the Dynamics of Expectations and Disappointment', (2024) 00 Journal of International Criminal Justice, 1.

65 M Burgis-Kasthala and B Sander, 'Contemporary International Criminal Law After Critique: Towards Decolonial and Abolitionist (Dis-)Engagement in an Era of Anti-Impunity', (2024) 22 (1) Journal of International Criminal Justice, 127.

66 M Drumbl, 'The Ongwen Trial at the ICC: Tough Questions on Child Soldiers' (Open Democracy, 14 April 2015), available at https://www.opendemocracy.net/openglobalrights/mark-drumbl/ongwen-trial-at-icc-tough-questions-on-child-soldiers; L G Minkova, 'Expressing what? The stigmatization of the defendant and the ICC's institutional interests in the Ongwen case' (2021) 34 (1) Leiden Journal of International Law, 223.

67 S Rigney, 'Building An Abolition Movement for International Criminal Law?' (2024) 22 Journal of International Criminal Justice, 211.

68 A L Nistor, A Merrylees, and B Holá, 'Spellbound at the International Criminal Court: The Intersection of Spiritualism and International Criminal Law', in J Fraser and B McGonigle Leyh (eds) *Intersections of Law and Culture at the International Criminal Court*

conviction adjustment may still have occurred. Mr. Ongwen received his guilty verdict without much consideration given to his past, but he was subsequently transferred to Norway to serve his sentence. Norway is known for its penal leniency.[69] The decision to move Mr. Ongwen to Norway for serving his sentence may be perceived as a form of mitigation to account for his childhood trauma.

Engaging with art and aesthetics – either through the practice of reparations or as a form of contemplation – contextualizes law by adding a much-needed experiential dimension. Augmenting one's sense of empathy and positive sympathy may not only involve explaining the nature of an internationally recognized prohibition (e.g. of murder) but also by creating a direct experience of what it means to be alive with all its nuances.[70] In the *Ongwen* case, the ICC ordered, *inter alia*, community-based satisfaction and symbolic measures in the form of memorial centres, monuments, memorial prayers as well as reconciliation and cleansing ceremonies.[71] The Chamber underlined that these measures are meant to be transformative in nature as they tackle structural issues and cultural understanding of violence.[72]

The *Ongwen* Trial Chamber strongly gravitated towards collective and community-based reparations.[73] The terminology used was 'collective community-based reparations focused on rehabilitation and symbolic/satisfaction measures'.[74] The judges highlighted considerations of timing, efficiency, and transformative value of collective reparations.[75] Transformative value was explained as an ambition to tackle the cultural meaning of violence and structural barriers leading to victims' stigmatization. Furthermore, the judges expressly recognized the mammoth *Ongwen* conviction and sentencing judg-

(Edward Elgar 2020), 147–168. See also E Baines, 'Buried in the Heart: Women, Complex Victimhood and the War in Northern Uganda' (Cambridge University Press 2016), 3.

69 'Dominic Ongwen transferred to Norway to serve his sentence of imprisonment' (ICC Press Release, 18 December 2023), available at https://www.icc-cpi.int/news/dominic-ongwen-transferred-norway-serve-his-sentence-imprisonment.

70 Aksenova and Rieff (n 1); S O'Sullivan, 'The Aesthetic of Affect: Thinking Art beyond Representation', (2001) 6 Angelaki Journal of the Theoretical Humanities, 125; J Dewey, 'Art As Experience' (Capricorn Books, 1958).

71 Ongwen Reparations Order (n 57) para. 635.

72 Ibid, para. 637.

73 Ibid, para. 663.

74 Ibid, para. 613.

75 Ibid, paras. 613, 637.

ments of 2021,[76] convicting Mr. Ongwen of sixty-one counts of crimes against humanity and war crimes committed in Northern Uganda between 2002 and 2005, as its own satisfaction measure. These documents acknowledge and publicly recognize the harms resulting from Mr. Ongwen's crimes.[77] In line with the efficiency goal, the *Ongwen* reparations judgment expressly rejected costly infrastructure projects, such as museums or hospitals, noting that it is the responsibility of the Government of Uganda. In contrast, the judges instructed the TFV to consider – in consultation with the victims – smaller scale endeavours, such as memorials and reconciliation ceremonies, which were expressly endorsed as some possible forms of symbolic measures.[78]

3 Integrating Creative Reparations in the Practice of ICC

There are several features of the modern practice of reparations at the ICC that simultaneously invite and challenge creative approaches to reparations. This section aims at mapping some major themes accompanying reparatory practice at the ICC.

3.1 *Transformative v. Transitional Justice*

The notion of transformative justice as a way of responding to mass atrocities is quickly gaining traction.[79] The language of transformation is also entering the reparations practice of the ICC as can be seen in the *Ongwen* Reparations Order.[80] Transformative justice places emphasis on restoring broken social bonds and addressing relational rupture caused by systemic violence. The roles of victims and perpetrators are often interchangeable – being severely traumatized as a child can lead to offending as an adult. If the entire society is undergoing significant structural challenges, such as civil war and other forms

76 *The Prosecutor v. Dominic Ongwen*, Case No. ICC-02/04-01/15 (ICC Trial Judgment, 4 February 2021); *The Prosecutor v. Dominic Ongwen*, Case No. ICC-02/04-01/15, (ICC Sentence, 6 May 2021).

77 Ongwen Reparations Order (n 57) para. 636.

78 Ibid, paras. 619, 635.

79 N Wentholt and N L Immler, 'How Tort Can Address Historical Injustice Exploring the Momentum for the Slavery Justice Movement in Dutch Civil Courts' in (2023) 52 Netherlands Journal of Legal Philosophy, 2; Rigney (n 66).

80 Ongwen Reparations Order (n 57) para. 637.

of rupture, then the cycle of violence keeps perpetuating itself unless and until the pattern is interrupted.[81]

The ambition of transformative justice therefore goes further than an outcome-oriented model of justice centred around punishment and accountability. It aims to address social ills underlying the structural violence. Is it possible to incorporate at least some transformative justice elements in a more traditional (criminal) justice model? The practice of reparations bridges these two visions of justice by serving as a conduit for the relational dimension of collective harm. In other words, reparations recognize victims and affected communities in a way that the legal judgment does not.[82] It appears that symbolic reparations with creative value may be able to reflect this complexity in a nuanced way, thereby complementing a legal judgment pronouncing on the guilt or innocence of the accused in a trial.

3.2 *Relationality*

Creative reparations propose an alternative vision of justice that is focused on restoring relationships through extra-criminal law forms of accountability. This shift of perspective is a welcome exit from the cyclical nature of victim-perpetrator dynamics characteristic of mass violence.[83] A criminal trial is not always an escape from this pattern because the formal adjudication of individual criminal responsibility is not fully suited to address all the complexities of collective and individual trauma and ensuing (re-)victimization. Engaging with broader communal factors contributing to societal ruptures (e.g. the feelings of shame the child soldiers may feel) is rewarding as it transcends the individualistic focus of a penal process and speaks to the collective nature of offending and victimization. The shadow side of this development is that the focus on the wider context of mass violence inadvertently results in the 'economy of expectation', whereby reparations validate some victims and not others. The selective nature of international criminal justice enables this uneven distribution of legal attention.[84] Thus, the mere fact that some instances of mass violence fall within the ambit of prosecutions and subsequent

81 M Aksenova, S Parmentier and E Van Sliedregt (eds), 'Breaking the Cycle of Mass Atrocities: Criminological and Socio-Legal Approaches in International Criminal Law' (Hart 2019).

82 Fisher (n 63); Baines (n 67).

83 Aksenova et al (*eds*) (n 80).

84 Fisher (n 63).

reparations and others do not, may lead to the feelings of disappointment, comparison, and exclusion.[85]

Sperfeldt observes that the very nature of reparatory and outreach interventions of the ICC and ECCC in the Democratic Republic of Congo (DRC) and Cambodia, respectively, produced expectations that needed to be 'managed'.[86] It was important to consult the survivor communities to refine intervention tools to fit with the requirements of the legal proceedings. At the same time, such consultations left out genuine two-way communication channels that would have revealed deeper insights about the needs and wants of these communities.[87] To that effect, the *Katanga* Trial Chamber observed that – when consulting victims – 'first and foremost, [...] it is critical that victims' expectations should be managed with extreme care [...]'.[88]

3.3 *Superficiality*

The limited scope for engaging with a complex web of actors affected by violence as part of a criminal trial results in relational challenges in a sense of many voices feeling excluded or unheard. The other aspect of the same process is feeling like the type and nature of reparative or outreach measure is too abstract to address the rupture underlying violence. This remoteness challenge is particularly pronounced when it comes to more creative or educational measures that may appear far removed from people's lives. The distance can also generate unrealistic expectations of what international courts can deliver.[89] Sperfeldt observes that the initial promise of a more victim-oriented justice through reparations has been realized only superficially.[90] The core reason for this is the subjugation of reparative logic to the jurisdictional and legal demands of a criminal trial.[91] While victim-oriented rhetoric is omnipresent in the judicial discourse, the 'victim' remains an amorphous category constructed and regulated through legal logics.[92] This observation is particularly acute when one talks about creative reparations as they may appear significantly detached from the actual concerns of the affected communities. The

85 Ibid.

86 Sperfeldt (n 19) 304.

87 Ibid.

88 *Prosecutor v. Katanga*, Case No. ICC-01/04-01/07-3508 (ICC Order Instructing the Registry to Report on Applications for Reparations, Trial Chamber II, 27 August 2014) para. 9; Sperfeldt (n 19) 137.

89 Sperfeldt (n 19).

90 See also Fisher (n 63).

91 Sperfeldt (n 19), 14.

92 Ibid, 306.

symbolic aspect of reparations addressing the collective and systemic nature of harm may ring hollow in the most critical phase of recovery in the aftermath of mass atrocity.

3.4 *Temporality*

The Preamble to the Rome Statute of the ICC stipulates that putting an end to impunity of perpetrators of mass atrocities contributes to the prevention of such crimes.[93] This aspiration can be read in light of the overall deterrence punishment rationale – the potential perpetrator perceives the threat of punishment as inevitable and is therefore deterred from offending.[94] Deterrence is future-oriented and stands in contrast to retributive approaches focused on past offending and the level of culpability of individual offenders.[95] There are significant limitations of deterrence in international criminal law due to the inherent lack of enforcement and the practice of selective prosecutions.[96] It is thus fair to suggest that by integrating symbolic reparations into the framework of international criminal justice, the system can enhance its deterrent effect via alternative means. For instance, artistic memorialization projects not only commemorate victims but also actively engage communities in a dialogue about justice, responsibility, and the prevention of future crimes.

This multifaceted approach offers a way to address the limitations of a traditional deterrence paradigm and promote a more robust understanding of accountability in an international context. Cultural dialogue through memorialization initiatives has potential of reinforcing societal norms against violence and human rights violations, contributing to a collective commitment to prevent future atrocities. This way, engaging with creative reparations may be seen as connecting the past and the future as various initiatives crystalize the impetus towards learning the lessons from the past and not repeating the same mistakes in the future. This is done not through the vehicle of fear-generating sanctions (as in deterrence-based thinking) but rather through holistic approaches based on understanding of the mechanisms of criminalization and connecting to the broader community.

---

93 Preamble of the Rome Statute of the International Criminal Court.

94 C Beccaria, 'On Crimes and Punishments and Other Writings', (1764) (A Thomas and J Parzen, trans., University of Toronto Press 2009), 49–50.

95 See A von Hirsch, A Ashworth, J V Roberts, 'Principled Sentencing Readings on Theory and Policy' (Hart 2009).

96 K Cronin-Furman, 'Managing Expectations: International Criminal Trials and the Prospects for Deterrence of Mass Atrocity', (2013) 7 (3) International Journal of Transitional Justice, 434.

3.5 *Agency*

Creative reparations offer a way of reclaiming local agency through the process of consultations. While it is true that these consultations are often subordinate to the demands of the legal process,[97] they are still indicative of the direction of justice away from some preconceived and predefined outcomes and towards procedural and structural solutions, which are focused on local ownership.[98] The ambition of creative reparations is therefore to reach the deeper layers of societal malfunctioning by highlighting the roots of offending and empowering the affected communities to seek extra-legal solutions to complement juridical processes. Creative reparations may serve as a symbol of empowerment and a promise of a more humane (international) society that no longer relies on purely punitive and retributive approaches to address social harms.[99]

3.6 *Contestation*

Creative symbolic reparations may bring to the surface uneasy questions and complexities that an outcome-driven judgment may not be able to capture. It is well-established that people come to conclusions based on a set of cognitive biases, namely pre-established ideas about certain events.[100] This is particularly true for events with strong traumatic connotations.[101] It may thus prove insufficient to try and overcome someone's cognitive bias with a legal judgment. One may argue then, that art allows contextualization of law by adding an experiential dimension.[102] This consideration is relevant to the work of the ICC, which is an institution dealing with cases of extreme complexity.

Take, for instance, the problem of child soldiers. There was moral ambiguity of prosecuting someone conditioned into atrocities as a child and this nuance was not fully reflected in the final judgment.[103] The prosecutorial strategy of vilifying Mr. Ongwen by amplifying the narrative of brutality took

---

97 Sperfeldt (n 19) 14.

98 P Gready and S Robbins, 'From Transitional to Transformative Justice: A New Agenda for Practice', (2014) 8 International Journal of Transitional Justice, 339.

99 Rigney (n 66).

100 M Milanovíc, 'Establishing the Facts about Mass Atrocities: Accounting for the Failure of the ICTY to Persuade Target Audiences', (2016) 47 Georgetown Journal of International Law, 1321.

101 Ibid, 1329–1330.

102 Aksenova and Rieff (n 1).

103 Minkova (n 60); R Viswanath, and F Li, 'Constructing a Sensory Alternative to the Ongwen Judgment', (2023) 23(5–6) International Criminal Law Review, 804; Rigney (n 66).

precedence during trial. Conscious downgrading of Mr. Ongwen's childhood trauma fulfilled the need for a symbolic figure collectively representing atrocities of the LRA, especially in the absence of more senior figures standing trial.[104] The emphasis on the perpetrator status of Mr. Ongwen largely cancelled out his status as a victim of child abuse, despite the impact of early victimization on offending later in life.[105] The categories of victims and perpetrators are fixed in international criminal law to the degree of being mutually exclusive. This leaves little room for acknowledging the fact that, with time, child soldiers transition from the role of victims into the role of perpetrators.[106]

Symbolic reparations may be able to reflect this complexity in a sufficiently nuanced way. In contrast with a finite legal judgment, there is no need to concretely determine the status of Mr. Ongwen. Symbolic reparations may open space for grieving and coming to terms with the past, which is free from the simplistic evaluations of 'evil' and 'good'. These new spaces – curated via the vehicle of creative reparations – allow room for contestations as they do not insist on one final interpretation of the events. Arguably, there is a strong healing potential in affording space for such complexity and ambiguity.

4 Conclusion

The reparation orders discussed in this paper demonstrate the ICC's ability to work through its own core limitations, which include the discrepancy between the process of attribution of individual criminal responsibility and the need to rectify larger collective wrongs through reparations, as well as financial and budgetary constraints.[107] It is fair to observe that international criminal law is a prisoner of its own ambition.[108] It aims to do the impossible – reduce the complexity of mass atrocities to a narrow confine of individual criminal responsibility.[109] Holding a person accountable for what is ultimately

104 Minkova (n 60); Viswanath and L (n 102) 178.

105 See e.g. S Green, 'Crime, Victimisation and Vulnerability' in S Walklate (eds) *Handbook of Victims and Victimology* (Routledge 2007).

106 Baines (n 67); See also M Aksenova, 'Introduction' in Aksenova et al (eds) (n 80) 3.

107 F Megret, 'The Politics of International Criminal Justice' (2002) 13 European Journal of International Law, 1261.

108 P Akhavan, 'The Rise, and Fall, and Rise, of International Criminal Justice' (2013) 11(3) Journal of International Criminal Justice, 527; M Aksenova, 'Symbolism as a Constraint on International Criminal Law' (2017) 30(2) Leiden Journal of International Law, 475.

109 Megret (n 106).

a collective process does not match perfectly the aspirations of the field to bring about reconciliation, retribution and deterrence.[110] The friction between the goals of international justice and its outcomes produced several generations of critical legal scholarship.[111]

The most recent abolitionist explorations go as far as inviting the audience to radically reimagine traditional models of justice based on individualized retribution.[112] The process of rethinking occurs by generating a more nuanced explanatory model that accounts for intergenerational trauma, structural causes of violence (e.g. extreme poverty), race, global capitalism, imperialism, and human propensity to obedience during the times of societal disintegration and collapse.[113] The practice of creative reparations with transformative value is a bridge connecting the outcome-oriented individualized retributive justice and the broader (non-carceral) view of justice.[114] Despite the multiple challenges of translating the binary criminal legal process into the language of creative reparations, there is a promise of a more humane justice encoded in the aspiration of the drafters of the Rome Statute. There is a reason why the drafters afforded the ICC a wide margin of appreciation in developing the practice of reparations to meet the challenges of the time. There is therefore definitely room for creative reparations in international criminal law provided the space for re-imagination is kept pliable – adaptability and openness are the key elements to sustaining creativity in international criminal law.

110 M Damaška, 'What is the Point of International Criminal Justice?' (2008) 83(1) Chicago-Kent Law Review, 329; Fisher (n 63).

111 For an overview, see B Sander, 'Doing Justice to History: Confronting the Past in International Criminal Courts' (Oxford University Press 2021).

112 Rigney (n 66); See S. Nouwen and W Werner, 'Monopolising Global Justice: International Criminal Law as Challenge to Human Diversity' (2015) 13 Journal of International Criminal Justice, 157.

113 Aksenova et al (eds) (n 80).

114 Rigney (n 66).

CHAPTER 7

A Song to Nature: Traditional Wiwa Music as Relational Reparation to Indigenous Communities and Their Territory

Nina Bries Silva and Laura Triana Gallego

1 Introduction

On April 19, 2003, in the realm of the Colombian internal armed conflict, paramilitaries and public armed forces entered the town of *Guachirimake* (also known as *La Laguna*) in Sierra Nevada of Colombia, home of Wiwa Indigenous[1] communities. In the following days, they bombed and burned the village to the ground, forcing the displacement of the Wiwa community of *La Laguna*. As a result, the community's bounds, their culture and territory were particularly impacted. They lost their musical instruments and their ability and knowledge to build them. Furthermore, elders were killed or displaced and ceased to transmit their traditional knowledge of music. Music is essential to Wiwa communities and its disappearance within the community of *La Laguna* goes beyond the solely cultural loss. Music bridges communication between the Wiwa and the rest of beings living in their territory both in the material and the spiritual world.[2]

The Wiwa have a holistic relationship with territory and all the elements/beings that compose it. Music enables them to communicate with their territory, unite with everything on earth and maintain the equilibrium between human beings and nature. In contrast with the traditional western dichotomy between nature and culture,[3] for the Wiwa, human beings and territory are interconnected and interrelated. In this interconnected world, every being plays a role in maintaining balance and harmony within the social order derived from such connections. However, throughout history, actions of *suntalo* or outsiders to the Sierra have challenged this social, spiritual, and terri-

1 The Spanish term *Pueblo Indigena* is translated in this contribution as Indigenous people and capitalized to underline their distinctness and self-determination.

2 Centro de Investigación y Educación Popular (CINEP) *Olla de Barro: Gobierno propio de los pueblos indígenas de la Sierra Nevada de Santa Marta* (CINEP, 2010) 14.

3 See: Philippe Descola, *Par-delà nature et culture* (Gallimard, 2005).

 | DOI:10.1163/9789004716742_008

torial balance of the Wiwa people, particularly in southern Guajira and Cesár.[4] These interventions namely include the imposition of orphanages during the evangelization period in the early twenties, the efforts towards the erasure of Damana – the Wiwa native language – and later on, all the actions connected to internal armed conflict forcing the displacement of Wiwa populations and ultimately resulting in the disappearance of some of their cultural practices including the knowledge and practice of music for the community of *La Laguna*.[5] Because of their interconnected relationship with nature, the Wiwa consider that the armed conflict did not only affect human beings but also their territory *Abu Senulang* or Mother Earth.

In November 2016, after more than fifty-six years of internal armed conflict, Colombia initiated its transitional justice process, understood as "the full range of processes and mechanisms associated with a society attempts to come to terms with a legacy of large-scale past abuses, in order to ensure accountability, serve justice and achieve reconciliation".[6] In this context, the Special Jurisdiction for Peace (JEP) was established as the judicial organ of this transitional justice process tasked with judging the cases related to internal armed conflict. On September 7, 2022, the JEP opened the so-called *macro-caso 09*,[7] to investigate and prosecute the crimes committed during the armed conflict against Indigenous people and their Territories.[8] Among the regions prioritized by the case, there is the Sierra Nevada de Santa Marta where the Wiwa Indigenous group lives. In the opening statement, the judges of Chambre of Acknowledgment of the JEP[9] heading the case, stated that for Indigenous people, territory

4 CINEP (n 3) 14.

5 CINEP (n 3) 14.

6 Report of the Secretary-General on the Rule of Law and Transitional Justice in Conflict and Post Conflict Societies, UN Doc. S/2004/616 (3 August 2004), parr.8. While there is ongoing debate about the definition of transitional justice, the latest falls outside the purpose of this paper which uses as working definition the broadly accepted one offered by the UN.

7 The JEP has applied a macro-criminality approach to group together multiple human rights violations into so-called macro-cases, either based on their geographical area (territorial case) or like *in casu*, on their similar thematic, here the series of violations committed against Indigenous people and their territory.

8 JEP – Sala de reconocimiento de verdad, responsabilidad y determinación de hechos y conductas, AUTO No. 105, September 7, 2022.

9 The Chambre of acknowledgment is competent to determine the pattern of macro-criminality, identify that conducts that falls within the jurisdiction of the JEP and open consequently open the cases to process. In these cases, after analysing and contrasting this information, the Chamber for Acknowledgement issued a sentence (called '*Auto de determinación de hechos y conductas*') "determining the patterns and policies associated with international crimes and attributing responsibility to the 'most responsible' perpetrators". This '*auto*' (judgement) serves as a formal accusation act against the identified perpetrators.

is "source of life, existence and identity, because when its breath is destroyed and violated, the life and existence of future generations is weakened".[10] Embodying this Indigenous understanding of the territory as a living being, the Chambre of Acknowledgment of the JEP issued a landmark decision on June 25th 2024, recognizing the "ancestral, sacred and collective territory of the Sierra Nevada" as a victim of the armed conflict with its own right to reparation.[11] Consequently, judges at the JEP are currently questioning how these reparations to the territory should look like.

Grounded in the human rights movement and built around western[12] liberal assumptions, transitional justice (TJ) so far, has failed to consider the more than human world. Over the past years, scholars have started pointing out that the origins and assumptions of TJ are Western centric and anthropocentric,[13] reflecting the broader critique of the human rights field. César Rodríguez-Garavito underlines for instance, that the human rights project "partakes in the blind spots of the Anthropocene, including the faith in unlimited growth and the instrumental view of nature".[14] In de Sousa Santos' words, "the concept of human rights lies on a well-known set of presuppositions, all of which are distinctly Western, namely: there is a universal human nature that can be known by rational means; human nature is essentially different from and higher than the rest of reality".[15] Similarly, Janine Natalya Clark argues that traditional TJ systems, arising from the liberal tradition, are incomplete "because they have a predominantly anthropocentric focus that misses (or minimizes) the intrinsic relationality between human and more-than-human worlds – and the entanglement of human stories and experien-

10 JEP, 'Official statement 075 of 2022', September 13, 2022, available at https://www.jep.gov.co/Sala-de-Prensa/Paginas/JEP-abre-caso-09-investigar-crimenes-contra-pueblos-etnicos.aspx. If not provided otherwise, all the translations are the authors' own.

11 JEP –Sala de reconocimiento de verdad, responsabilidad y determinación de hechos y conductas, AUTO SRVBIT-XCBM-NNHC-JJCP-ACHP-01, June 25, 2024.

12 This contribution uses the term 'west' to refers to the set of ideas and values promoted by European Enlightenment thinkers, rather than a specific group of countries. This explain why even if Latin America has been a pioneer in transitional mechanisms, TJ, still western-centric in the sense that it is dominated by Western though and ideas of democracy and justice.

13 See for instance: Rachel Killean and Lauren Dempster, 'Mass Violence, Environmental Harm, and the Limits of Transitional Justice' (2022) 16 Genocide Studies and Prevention: An International Journal.

14 César Rodíguez-Garavito (ed)., *More Than Human Rights: An Ecology of Law, Thought, and Narrative for Earthly Flourishing* (NYU Law, 2024), 32.

15 Boaventura de Sousa Santos, 'Toward a multicultural conception of human rights' (1997) 18 Zeitschrift für Rechtssoziologie 1.

ces within larger ecosystems".[16] In this context, the key human rights and TJ concepts of reparations and victims, commonsensical in western thinking, have been so far, conceived only in anthropocentric terms. The concept of victim is limited to human beings, harm is understood in terms of human rights violations and reparations subsequently designed in an anthropocentric manner. The Western liberal roots of the human right and TJ project not only resulted in their anthropocentrism, but it also led to the exclusion of Indigenous systems of knowledge,[17] and in particular, the failure to adequately engage with Indigenous relational understanding of nature.[18] Despite the progressive recognition of Indigenous rights in International law sphere (including the collective right to reparation), in practice, western thinking still permeating the discipline, establishing a hierarchy between humans and non-humans and reducing Indigenous knowledge systems to "uses and customs", "customary law" or "infra-legal phenomena".[19] Scholars have consequently called on the decolonization of the human rights[20] and TJ field.[21] This "epistemic decolonization"[22] or "decoloniality project"[23] involves challenging the asymmetrical power relations of human rights project and "repudiating the marginalization of non-European modes of knowledge, discourse, and political practice".[24] Regarding Indigenous people, epistemic decolonization within TJ implies respecting the distinctive ways these communities conceive the

---

16 Janine Natalya Clark, 'Harm, Relationality and More-than-Human Worlds: Developing the Field of Transitional Justice in New Posthumanist Directions' (2022) International Journal of Transitional Justice, 11–12.

17 Alexandra Huneeus and Pablo Rueda Sáiz, 'Territory as a Victim of Armed Conflict' (2021) 15 International Journal of Transitional Justice 210.

18 Most Indigenous ontologies are "about a deep relationality that is context-specific" where the notion of reciprocity is central. See: Mihnea Tănăsescu, 'Rights of Nature, Legal Personality, and Indigenous Philosophies' (2020) 9 Transnational Environmental Law 429, 452.; Stefano Varese, 'Los fundamentos éticos de las cosmologías indígenas' (2018) 36 Amérique Latine Histoire et Mémoire. Les Cahiers ALHIM; Eduardo Viveiros de Castro, *The Relative Native: Essays on Indigenous Conceptual World* (HAU Books 2015).

19 Pedro Garzón López, *Ciudadanía indígena: Del multiculturalismo a la colonialidad del poder* (Centro de Estudios Políticos y Constitucionales, 2016).

20 Davinia Gómez Sánchez, 'Transforming Human Rights through Decolonial Lens' (2020) The Age of Human Rights Journal 276.

21 Khanyisela Moyo, *Postcolonial Transitional Justice: Zimbabwe and Beyond* (London, Routledge 2020).

22 Catherine Lu(n 22) 271.

23 Walter D. Mignolo and Catherine E. Walsh, *On Decoloniality*: Concepts, Analytics, Praxis (Duke University Press, 2018).

24 Catherine Lu (n 22) 271.

world, including considering the more than human world and engaging with them to render justice in their terms. In this sense, the JEP has expressly underlined the necessity to treat Indigenous territories as rights-bearing subjects and adopt an intercultural approach that challenges and adapts the universal human rights grammar to these other systems of knowledge, "under the principle of ethnic and cultural diversity".[25] Similarly, this contribution aims at rethinking the human right concept of reparation, from a bottom-up perspective, departing from anthropological data and treating Indigenous ontologies as another, yet equal, system of knowledge and rights, disregarding thereof the traditional "cultural rights language" which reproduces the colonially of knowledge. Within the human rights discourse, Indigenous knowledge systems have been treated as mere cultural representations of the one single possible reality, the western dominant one. Instead, in line with political ontology scholarship, this contribution treats them as a reflection of reality, preferring therefore the use of the term ontology to epistemology.[26]

This contribution stands at the crossroad between these different sets of scholarship and puts them into conversation. The recognition of territory as a victim challenges these western centric and anthropocentric assumptions and invites us to rethink the concept of reparation, in transitional justice and beyond. As noted by Alexandra Huneeus and Pablo Rueda Saíz, "reimagining territory as a victim provides a legal concept through which transitional justice initiatives, in engaging with Indigenous peoples (…), can create ambitious measures that address the ongoing and concurrent harms unleashed by extractive economic models that create pressure on Indigenous territories".[27] In this sense, Janine Natalya Clark, building on Post humanist studies, has also called "for broader conceptualizations of harm within transitional justice that acknowledge deeply entangled human and more-than human worlds".[28] If scholars have stressed the need for TJ to engage with environmental and relational harm, they leave unanswered the question of how to proceed and frame the reparations. This is where this contribution steps in. In their article, Rachel Killean and Lauren Dempster expressly state that "significant further theoreti-

25 Comisión Colombiana de Juristas, *Boletín #62 del Observatorio sobre la JEP* (20th February of 2023), available at https://www.coljuristas.org/observatorio_jep/documentos/documento.php?id=250. See also: JEP –Sala de reconocimiento de verdad, responsabilidad y determinación de hechos y conductas, AUTO No. 105, September 7th, 2022, §20.

26 On this debate, see for instance: Arturo Escobar, 'Sentipensar con la tierra. Las luchas territoriales y la dimensión ontológica de las epistemologías del sur' (2016) 11 Revista de antropología iberoamericana 1, 11–32.

27 Huneeus and Rueda Sáiz (n 17) 226.

28 Clark (n 16) 5.

cal and empirical research is needed to understand how framings of harm, modalities of repair and processes of development and reform might address environmental harms in practice".[29] Based on qualitative data and visual elicitation,[30] collected through fieldwork conducted with two Wiwa communities, *Siminke* and *La Laguna* in the south of La Guajira, in Colombia, this contribution underscores the significance of music for the Wiwa and their relationship with nature and subsequently argues about the potential of music as a new form of reparation to both the communities and their territory. The communities of *Siminke* and *La Laguna* were both affected by the conflict but in a different manner and intensity. In the community of *Siminke*, elders, teachers, and a whole lineage of musicians have kept alive the practice of *shihkakubi* – or the holistic practice of music that includes sounds, symbols, codes, and meanings.[31] In contrast, the community of *La Laguna* has entered a process of total acculturation, given the seriousness of the paramilitarism intervention in the area. In today's peace process, the Wiwa from *La Laguna* aims to revitalize its connection with music. Consequently, it is argued that revitalizing the practice of music, through measures such as the creation of an educational and media archive of the music knowledge, the establishment of an educational centre dedicated to the practice and knowledge of music or the remaking of music instruments, constitutes a reparation to both the Wiwa and their territory or Mother Earth, enabling the restoration of their broken harmonic relationship.

After setting the context of the case study, this contribution explores from an anthropological, political and cultural perspective the significance of the music for the Wiwa people and their relationship with the territory. It then outlines the impact of the armed conflict on the territory and the Wiwa before moving to the Colombian transitional justice process and the concept of reparation. The last section of the article revisits this concept of reparation through music.

---

29 Killean and Dempster (n 13) 60.

30 It refers to a methodology in which participants communicate through photographs different layers or dimensions of information about their experiences and express meanings based on their perception of space and place through self-created narratives. See Melanie Lombard, "Using auto-photography to understand place: reflections from research in urban informal settlements in Mexico" (2013) 45 Royal Geographical Society 1 and Marisol Clark-Ibáñez, "Framing the Social World With Photo-Elicitation Interviews" (2004) 47 American Behavioral Scientist 12.

31 *Shihkakubi* is the term used in Damana language refers to interpretation of traditional Wiwa dances and music. *Shihkakubi* is connected to nature and constitute a spiritual rule expressing regulation, order, norm, path, and respect. See CINEP (n 2).

2 Methodology

This article is the result of a collaboration between two Ph.D. researchers, one in international law and the other one in humanities. Both have been conducting research with Wiwa communities in the Sierra Nevada de Santa Marta, applying anthropological methods, including legal anthropology tools and visual elicitation techniques. The information collected through those two separate, yet connected researches, was then compared, contrasted and complemented to put together this article about reparation and music in the Sierra Nevada.

Following the opening of the macro-case 09 by the JEP, Nina Bries Silva conducted four months fieldwork with the community of *La Laguna* between December 2022 and March 2023, exploring their relationship with territory and their experience of the armed conflict.[32] Applying the participatory action research methodology of Orlando Fals Borda,[33] she sought to understand the impact of the armed conflict on the territory in the Wiwa's own terms and thereby to imagine together the reparation to the territory. Music naturally emerged from these discussions as essential for interacting with the territory, as a great loss of the armed conflict and as a form of reparation.

Laura Triana Gallego has been conducting research for more than a decade with the Wiwa communities living in the Rancheria River basin, particularly the community of *Siminke*. For her Ph.D. dissertation, she explores the Wiwa use of music, based on ethnographic methods, including visual ethnography methods.

It must be noted that none of the authors are Indigenous themselves yet conducting research with Indigenous communities Laura is a Colombian researcher born in the *Altiplano Cundiboyacense* and can trace some of her family origins to an Indigenous belonging, which has driven her studies choice and research. Nina instead was born and raised in a privileged bilingual European environment and has been working for the defense of Indigenous rights for eight years. Given these personal backgrounds, the research process naturally came with a fundamental personal introspection on bias and privileges. Both researchers are completing their Ph.D. in universities from the Global North and collaborate in this context, with Wiwa communities, with the aim of contributing to the "*diálogo de sabere*s" or horizontal knowledge dialogue and co-constructing politico-legal tool, such as this proposal of relational repara-

32 This fieldwork was supported by the 2022 Noria Grant and the EUI ERC Starting Grant.

33 Orlando Fals Borda & Carlos Rodríguez Brandao, *Investigación Participativa* (Montevideo: La Banda Oriental, 1987).

tion.[34] To reach this stage, the two researchers have interacted with Wiwa communities, following, what Samuel Araujo calls, a "politically self-conscious and explicit dialogue", where the modes of negotiation of place and agency of the participants involved in the processes are considered.[35] They have thus engaged in the reflexivity process proposed by Rosana Guber, reflecting on the relationship between the communities' understandings and the realities described in the research, as well as on the researcher's place within these interactions.[36] Mindful of the ethical implications of this type of research, both researchers have complied with the ethical procedures and guidelines of their respective university (i.e., University of Amsterdam and European University Institute), applying consequently cultural sensitive protocols and ensuring the individual and collective informed consent of participants. In this sense, this contribution is also a way to give back to the communities involved and support their judicial process before the JEP.[37]

3 Wiwa Communities of the Sierra Nevada de Santa Marta: Territory, Memory, and Creation

> Everything in music is nature; it is singing and playing; it is whatuku, called whatuku. Because the whole area of the river, the water, the wind stick, the breeze, everything sings, and we also sing to them to be grateful for what we received from nature
>
> Ade Eusebio Conchagüi Sauna, Personal communication, August 2023

The Wiwa are one of four Indigenous groups inhabiting the Sierra Nevada de Santa Marta (together with the Kogui, Arhuaco, and Kankuamo). Their native language is Damana. They are settled in the Caribbean region, in the departments of La Guajira, Magdalena and Cesar. The Wiwa population counts more than 11,500 members, who live mainly in the Sierra's lower zones – between 1000 and 2500 meters above sea level. The Wiwa consider themselves as the caretakers (*cuidadores*) and guardians of the Sierra Nevada, which constitutes

34 Marcelo Sarzuri-Lima (Coord.), "Diálogo de saberes" (2012) 15 *Revista Integra Educativa* 3.

35 Samuel Araujo "Dimensiones políticas del diálogo intercultural. Patrimonios de conocimiento y luchas sociales" in Margarita Chaves, Mauricio Montenegro y Marta Zambrano, (Eds) *El valor del patrimonio: mercado, políticas culturales y agenciamientos sociales* (Instituto Colombiano de Antropología e Historia, ICANH, 2014).

36 Rosana Guber, *La Etnografía: método, campo y reflexividad* (Siglo Veintiuno, 2001).

37 The findings of this contribution were shared with JEP of the Wiwa community of La Laguna to enhance the reparation to the territory in their case.

the *Corazón del Mundo* – the "Heart of the World". The creator Serankua has mandated them to maintain balance and harmony with nature, through offerings or *pagamentos*. In the late 1970s, following the example of the other three groups of the Sierra Nevada, the Wiwa began the political process of their self-organization and in 1993 set up the Wiwa Yugumaniun Buankwanarrwa Tayrona Organization (OWYBT), to interact with the state institutions.

The Wiwa have a holistic understanding of the territory, which is not defined by physical delimitations but rather by the interconnection of several sacred places along an invisible line called the *línea negra* or "black line". To preserve the harmony of humans with their territory, Wiwa communities, particularly their spiritual leaders – the *mamos* – perform a ritual of spiritual payment[38] consisting of two parts: the confession (*aganguashi*) and the offering (*zhonagueshi*) at different points along the black line. This ritual aims to compensate Mother Earth and connect sacred sites to prevent calamities in the territory. It also pays tribute to spiritual guardians ("parents") of local plants, lagoons, mountains, rivers, foodstuffs, and various living beings. Within this spiritual practice, music plays a key role as it constitutes the link that unites the community to all beings on earth. The *mamos* ("elders") transmit such spiritual beliefs and knowledge through songs and myths that reveal a moral code that every Wiwa must implement daily.[39] This holistic view of music and its cultural significance in transmitting knowledge and playing the instruments is called *shihkakubi*.[40]

Within this perspective, music is central to both communities that are the subject of this article: the people of *Siminke* and of *La Laguna*. However, these Wiwa communities have faced different historical circumstances which have negatively impacted their knowledge and practice of music to different degrees. While the community of *Siminke* still practices music, the community of La Laguna has lost its knowledge and practice of music. Since the violent incursions of paramilitaries in the region, where *La Laguna* is located, the upper basin of the Ranchería River, the community has entered a process of total acculturation. In contrast, *Siminke* houses one of the four communities who have been most central to the practice of music historically among the Wiwa.[41] In this community, approximately 95 families, amounting to 400 peo-

38 Mauricio Córdoba Ponce,"Sitios sagrados y territorio wiwa" (2016) Universitas humanística 61, 275.

39 Ibidem.

40 Laura Triana Gallego, "De la Sierra Nevada a Bogotá: La agencia de comunidades indígenas en narrativas visuales" (2018) Desbordes 9, 107.

41 Ibidem. 110.

ple, are for the great majority still performing rituals, music, dances, and spiritual work oriented by the guidance of spiritual (*mamos* and *sagas*) and political authorities.

Mamo or Ade ("father") Eusebio Conchangüi Sauna, an eighty-year-old elder, is the community's spiritual leader and a well-known musician in *Siminke*. He is the son of Abu ("mother") Rosa, an essential reference within the cultural traditions of music and dance until she died in 2020.[42] Ade Eusebio has been guiding the community and teaching traditional music to his sons and grandsons and recently to other Wiwa living in more remote regions who have lost the knowledge and practice of music due to the armed incursions mentioned above.

For the Wiwa, at the creation of the world, there was a void and then music. The mighty father, *Bunkuanarrua* – also the concept for playing the instruments – and mother, *Yugumaiun* – meaning singing – thought there was a need for music to exist and be played. Before the sunrise, when the mighty deities created the world, music helped to organize it. They gave music to all the living sources in nature: bodies of water, rain, plants, trees, mountains, birds, and lastly, humans, so that all have their own songs. Therefore, all the beings must play music to sustain life on earth and in reciprocity, Mother Earth will continue to nourish and protect her children from sickness and calamities.[43] There is a belief that music begins in the sea, goes up the rivers and ends up in the snowy peaks along the sacred points of the abovementioned black line, where the spiritual payments occur. Therefore, music must be part of all spiritual payments. In this way, music fosters respect in the relationship between humans and the earth with the mandate of the creator *Serankua*.[44] According to Ade Eusebio, there is a mandate from the deities to specific families to play and sing to all elements of their territory – the trees, the sun, the moon, the sea, the butterflies, the fish – and all the resources that nurture humans. It is a form of acknowledgement of their work in nature, as he expresses in the following terms:

> You have the mandate *sewá* to sing and play to preserve one's wellbeing. My father was a musician but had not yet passed the mandate to me

42 Personal communication with Ade Eusebio Conchangui (Siminke 17 January 2016).

43 Laura Triana Gallego, *Comunicación audiovisual, cohesión social y memoria cultural del pueblo Wiwa* (unpublished manuscript, 2024).

44 Laura Triana Gallego, *Neoliberalismo y agencia cultural: proyectos musicales y movilización política del pueblo wiwa de la Sierra Nevada de Santa Marta* (MA Thesis., Universidad Nacional de Colombia, 2014).

> when he died. My life was endangered. A spiritual elder told me I should receive the mandate *sewá* if I wanted to live longer, so this elder passed it on to me. I tell my children and grandchildren about this, so they understand and receive the mandate and know how to play music from sunset to sunrise to all living beings.[45]

By knowing the sacred history of music and the meaning of *shihkakubi,* children learn from an early age the values and norms of behaviour that are present in nature. The music played by the Wiwa accompanies all ritual moments and what they call traditional or spiritual work in a specific order during their lifetime: baptism, marriage, and mortuary.[46] Likewise, music protects the seeds before sowing them and in this way purifies them for healthy growth and a good harvest.

Within musical performances, dance is equally essential. The dance moves are connected to each song. For instance, for a good harvest, they sing and dance in circles, making specific movements resembling those of the swallow, an animal representing abundance. If they require water during dry periods, they sing and dance to the water (*dzirra*), or to the frog, an animal that represents this element, by imitating its shape and behaviour. Other songs and dances are meant to teach values to the kids, like the dance of the monkey (*mako*) or the skunk (*mapulo*). Another aspect of music is the active involvement of all community members in its practice, including the construction of instruments. Women play the *kumana* (a hollow drum) and men play the *whatuku* (a reed flute) and *agana* (a maraca). Women and children mainly sing nasal chants. The construction of instruments has its rituals and procedures carefully done by music elders and learners alike. It requires searching for materials in various places of their territory, from the sea to the Ranchería river basin, to get the different parts of the instruments: a reed, a shell, or the wax from a specific tree.[47] In sum, music guidelines for behaviour and harmony are transmitted through musical performance. Ade Ambrosio (another Wiwa elder) says: "We are singing and carrying the rhythm of the reed and dancing in circles; this way, we carry out the spiritual work."[48] Such messages are transmitted from generation to generation, the elders and traditional authorities passing on cultural knowledge of Wiwa history to the young.

---

45 Personal communication with Ade Eusebio Conchangui (Siminke 22 March 2022).

46 Personal communication with Ade Ambrosio Chimosquero (Siminke 11 December 2011).

47 Triana Gallego (n 44).

48 Ibidem.

Ade Eusebio still holds the musical practice and teaching around the Ranchería river basin alive. He has taught three of his sons – Sebastian, Otoniel, and Joselino – everything he knows and to play the instruments, which, to some extent, guarantees the preservation of their cultural memories. However, he is currently worried about the fate of traditional music, considering the ongoing effects of the armed conflict and mining practices, which have disrupted the communities and their practices, as well as the influence of popular music, which has influenced some community members to lose interest in traditional music.[49] Those circumstances will be discussed in the section below.

4 The Armed Conflict in the Sierra Nevada and Its Impact on the Wiwa and Their Relationship with Territory

Wiwa people have historically faced multiple interventions in their territory, the Sierra Nevada, that can be traced back to the colonization and the imposition of orphanages during the evangelization period, resulting in cultural changes and losses.[50] However, in the last three decades of the 20th century, new conflicts have emerged in relation to the control and exploitation of lands that further impacted Wiwa's culture.[51] At the end of the 1970s, several guerilla groups moved to the Sierra Nevada of Santa Marta due to its fertile ground, to cultivate illicit crops, which in turn, increased the level of violence in the region.[52] The expansion of the illicit crops in the region resulted in the displacement of several Wiwa communities to the higher parts of the Sierra Nevada, the recruitment of minors, as well as the destruction and looting of several sacred places.[53] The groups also forbade the *mamos* from carrying out their spiritual work in those sacred places to maintain the equilibrium with nature.[54] Furthermore, in its fight against narcotraffic, the government started

49 Personal communication with Ade Eusebio Conchangui (Siminke 22 March 2022).

50 CINEP (n 2) 14.

51 Ibidem.

52 CINEP, *Identidad cultural y memoria: Investigaciones participativas de jóvenes Wiwa de la Sierra Nevada de Santa Marta* (CINEP, 2018) 20.

53 CINEP (n 2) 9.

54 Based on the semi-structure interviews and informal conversations conducted with members of the community of la Laguna from November 2022 to December 2022 in the Guajira, Colombia.

in 1978 the first aerial sprayings in the region, with devastating effects on the environment.[55]

The conflict particularly escalated in the decade of 2000, with the incursion of paramilitarism in the region.[56] From April 19th to 25th, 2003, helicopters and fighter planes started gun firing the town of *La Laguna*, and troops belonging to both paramilitaries and public forces, entered the territory of *La Laguna*, burning houses, looting and destroying sacred places, committing violences against the population, which resulted in killings and forced displacement of 52 persons to the city and the neighbouring towns of El Colorado and Mamarongo, located in higher parts of the Sierra Nevada.[57] During the same period, similar violations were committed by the state official army and paramilitaries in other Wiwa towns located in the same area: the massacre of El Limón (September 2002), attacks against the communities of Potrerito (December 2002) and Marocazo (May 2003). In 2005, the Inter-American Commission issued provisional measures in favour of those Wiwa communities, underscoring that "during the last two years these Indigenous people have been victims of a series of acts of paramilitary violence including the murder of approximately 50 Indigenous leaders, the forced displacement of more than 800 people and the humanitarian situation of the communities from La Laguna, El Limón, Marokazo, Dudka, Linda and Potrerito".[58]

Despite those dramatic events, part of the Wiwa community from *La Laguna* decided to return to their original town and rebuild it from the ground with their own resources.[59] A member of the community of *La Laguna* explains that the community decided to return to the territory because they are its guardians and it is the only place where they can connect themselves with nature: "The *mamos* consulted with nature herself from the spirituality and told us that we should return to help nature to regenerate as her guardians."[60]

55 Centro Nacional de Memoria Histórica (CNMH), *Ruama shama: desde el corazón y el pensamiento del pueblo Wiwa: Afectaciones al territorio sagrado por el conflicto armado y sus factores subyacentes* (2017).

56 CNMH, Justicia y Paz: Tierras y Territorios en las versiones de los paramilitares (2012).

57 Colombian Constitutional Court, Decision 004 of 2009, available at https://www.corteconstitucional.gov.co/relatoria/autos/2009/a004-09.htm.

58 IACHR, Medida Cautelar No. 21/05, February 4th, 2005 available at the http://www.cidh.org/medidas/2005.sp.htm.

59 Based on the semi-structure interviews and informal conversations conducted with members of the community of *La Laguna* from November 2022 to December 2022 in the Guajira, Colombia.

60 Semi-structured interview with an anonymous member of the Wiwa organisation Golkushe Tayrona, 15/01/2023, Riohacha, Guajira, Colombia.

From their worldviews, the Wiwa do a complex reading of the impact of the armed conflict, which involves a network of elements, human and more than human and cannot be approached solely in terms of human rights violations within a western dualistic vision of nature and culture. A Wiwa community member from *La Laguna* explained for instance that:

> The explosions, the bombings, the sound of the small aeroplanes, the fighting in the territory, the fumigations of glyphosate, all these sounds that are extern to territory, displaced our birds. The armed conflict did not only generate human loss but also caused the displacement of birds and broke the birth process of our birds. In Colombia, the database always talks about how many people were displaced, but it never talks about how many birds were displaced, how many immigrated, which native birds are there, and which are not there anymore.[61]

He added that "these birds were bringing prosperity to the community because there is nothing more beautiful in the Sierra than listening to the birds singing". Hence, the displacement of the birds left the "territory hurt" and "the community scared and sickened".[62]

For the Wiwa people from *La Laguna*, the armed conflict did not only affect human beings but also the more than human worlds; it caused the displacement of the birds but also the guardian spirits of nature. The Wiwa of *La Laguna* explained for instance, that there was a sacred lagoon in their territory with a singing snake, the snake Dordoy, who regulated through his songs the seasons: "as long as this Dordoy snake is there, the river never dries up, the summer passes stronger and it does not dry".[63] The extensive bombings in the territory during the armed conflict killed the snake and the lagoon subsequently resulted in drought. As Wiwa member of *La Laguna* noted, "today the territory is sick, due to all these negative consequences, the territory is malnourished and threatened".[64] Because of their interrelationship, this suffering of the territory in turn generates new disease in the community and prevents the women from giving birth naturally anymore.

---

61 Semi-structured interview with the Wiwa *cabildo gobernador* Fabio Montenegro, 21/12/2022, Riohacha, Guajira, Colombia.

62 Ibidem.

63 Semi-structured interview with an anonymous member of the community of *La Laguna*, 22/11/2022, Guachirimake, Guajira, Colombia.

64 Semi-structure interview with anonymous community members of La Laguna, 22/11/2022.

These examples illustrate that for the Wiwa worldviews, the impact of the armed conflict goes beyond human rights violations or environmental damages but also disrupts the equilibrium between human and nature. The right to reparation in this context, should reflect Wiwa pluriverse understanding of the world and aims at restoring the harmony, within a human rights decolonial perspective.

5 The Armed Conflict in the Sierra Nevada and Its Impact on Music and Sacred Spiritual Places

While the Wiwa have suffered historical conditions of cultural loss and erasure, it worsened in the decade of 2000s, especially due to the combination of two factors: the construction of the Rancheria Dam (known in Spanish as "*La represa*"), a mass extractive project and the escalation of violence due to the presence of the paramilitary groups during the internal armed conflict. Those two situations affected and altered many of the sacred places of the Black line, as Wiwa members could not perform anymore (or insufficiently) the *Shihkakubi* (or the practice of music) and their *pagamento* (offering) rituals.[65] The Wiwas explain that the dam for instance, was constructed on a sacred place that guaranteed the dissociation of health and sickness and consequently generated many health diseases in the region. Additionally, the dam's construction also caused flooding that submerged several locations tied to *Ade/Abu,* the deities of food. This resulted in prolonged drought periods, adversely impacting local crops and harvests in the region.[66] Because of the disconnection among these sacred places, "the lemon, orange, avocado, and coffee have become sick, and even the Mamos are beginning to lose their eyesight".[67] Ade Ambrosio, a spiritual elder who passed some years ago, explained his concern over the construction of the dam and its spiritual impact in the following terms:

> Before the dam was built, the musicians used to sing all the way, without obstacles; when the dam was built in the middle, it was erased; it was like an eraser, the singing did not reach there anymore, up to the mother… the songs were diminished. Those places have them as a mass,

65 Triana Gallego (n 44).

66 Ibidem.

67 Pablo Mora "Linea Negra un tejido para sanar" <https://www.youtube.com/watch?v=8rM4UngTodk >Acceded 14 april 2024.

> gold mines, gases… they can sing, but the message does not reach there.[68]

The armed conflict and the exploitation of the Rancheria rivers altered wiwa's relationship with territory and their practice of music. In some places, like *La Laguna*, they lost their music instruments and their ability and knowledge to build them. Furthermore, elders were killed or displaced and ceased to transmit their traditional knowledge of music. As Ade Ambrosio's statement underscored, the absence of music also has repercussions on the harmony and balance with nature. While the community of *La Laguna* completely lost its knowledge of music, in *Siminke*, some elders survived and could carry, with the support of the political organizations, the process of revitalization of the practice of music.

Ade Eusebio explains that he was warned by his grandfather that the sacred points would disappear when humans began to harm Mother Earth and not defend her.[69] For this reason, since the 1990s, the Wiwa have created different strategies to restore the balance in the region, starting from re-establishing the spiritual order through cultural practices, rituals and, of course, music. They have designed and implemented these strategies under the umbrella of their political organizations in distinct phases. They began in the late 1990s by constructing music teaching centres in *Rongoy, Pozo de Humo* in Cesar, and *Siminke* in La Guajira, where some older musicians still lived and could teach the music cultural knowledge. Unfortunately, due to the paramilitary incursion, the conflict was once again peaking, and some of the political authorities were assassinated by the illegal armed groups; many communities were displaced, and the program was interrupted.[70]

A second stage began in 2006 in articulation with the Center for Research and Popular Education (CINEP),[71] focusing on creating pedagogical materials for schools and music teaching. During this phase, some young Wiwa members were trained in visual communication to register and preserve memories of the project's musical activities.

Lastly, a third phase started approximately in 2019, when new generations took over political positions. Some of them were musicians or had been part of *Zhimashai*. These new authorities resumed Wiwas' cultural and communication projects to strengthen the community's strategies while dealing with new

68 Ibidem.

69 Personal communication with Ade Eusebio Conchangui (Siminke 06 August 2023).

70 Ibidem.

71 The CINEP is a non-profit organisation founded in 1972 for promoting social changes.

armed conflict situations.[72] These various processes of cultural revitalization in music practices can inform the design of the reparative measures to the Territory, as explored in the next sections.

6 Colombian Transitional Justice, the JEP and Its Macro-case 09

On the 24th of November 2016, the Colombian government and the Revolutionary Armed Forces of Colombia (FARC-EP) signed the Final Peace Agreement for the Termination of the Conflict and the Construction of Stable and Lasting Peace, known as the Final Peace Agreement, bringing an end to more than 56 years of internal armed conflict.[73] The Final Peace Agreement set a complex and comprehensive transitional justice framework (known as the Comprehensive System of Truth, Justice, Reparations and Guarantees of Non-Recurrence – SIVJRNR) to deal with the abuses related to armed conflict. Within this system, the JEP was established as the court in charge of resolving cases related to the crimes committed during and in relation with the armed conflict, in particular by the FARC-EP and members of the State's military forces.

Due to their historical conditions of marginality, structural exclusion and dispossession of lands, ethnic minorities in Colombia, including Indigenous people, have "been seriously affected by the internal armed conflict".[74] Against this backdrop, the Final Peace Agreement states that the JEP must adopt in all its resolutions, an ethnic focus, meaning that it must take into consideration that the armed conflict has affected differentially ethnic groups and apply the laws accordingly considering "their aspirations and worldviews".[75] This differentiated experience of the armed conflict and harms also implies that the JEP must adopt "comprehensive differentiated reparations" in relation to Indigenous people and their territories including Indigenous people.[76] Such repara-

72 Triana Gallego (44).

73 While the Colombian armed conflict is rooted in historical situations of violences, it is usually considered that it started in its modern framing in the 1960s with the emergence of the FARC-EP and ELP (For more background, see: CMH, Basta Ya! Colombia: Memorias de guerra y dignidad (2013)). Yet, the exact duration of the armed conflict is contested and some regions of Colombia remain today conflict zone.

74 Final Peace Agreement of 2016, Ethic Chapter, p. 206.

75 Ibidem.

76 JEP Ethnic Affairs Commission, Protocol 001 of 2019 for coordination, inter-jurisdictional articulation, and intercultural dialogue between the Special Indigenous Jurisdiction (JEI) and the Special Jurisdiction for Peace (JEP).

tions should strive for the harmonization and healing of the territory respecting "the autonomy of Indigenous authorities and their political organisations".[77] In this context, to be transformative, reparations should aim at "restoring the balance and harmony of the people, their culture, their territories and their spirituality, that have historically been violated".[78]

In accordance with this ethnic-territorial approach, the JEP decided to open on September 2022, the *macro-caso 09*, to investigate and prosecute the crimes committed during the armed conflict against "ethnic groups" (*grupos etnicos*) including Indigenous people.[79] The ruling recognized that the armed conflict took place principally in regions inhabited by ethnic groups, had deeply affected their territories and with it, transgenerational relationships, including the ability of community members to preserve and transmit their traditional knowledge and systems of knowledge. From the outset, the JEP acknowledged that for ethnic people, the territory is a living subject, a sacred entity endowed with spiritual relationships based on their own cultural processes and with a relationship of interdependence with the natural environment.[80] The JEP also emphasized that adopting an ethnic approach and incorporating Indigenous knowledge systems can challenge the universal and abstract notions of human rights, which should, in turn, be interpreted through the lens of ethnic and cultural diversity.[81] It consequently accredited in June 2024, the "ancestral, sacred and collective territory of the Sierra Nevada" of the Arhuaco, Kankuamo, Kogui and Wiwa peoples as a victim of the armed conflict, with its own right to reparation, underlying the "inseparable relationship and interdependence that exists between the Territory, the

---

77 Protocol 001 of 2019, p. 73.

78 Protocol 001 of 2019, point 5, p. 12. This echoes the 2011 Victims Law –*Ley de Víctimas y Restitución de Tierras*, one of the first transitional justice instruments adopted in Colombia before the Protocol 001 was issued. This law provides a comprehensive reparation framework inclusive of indigenous experience of the conflict and relationship with nature. Article 45 provides that the territory is "a living entity and sustenance of identity and harmony according to Indigenous cosmovision" and that it "suffered damage when the internal armed conflict violated or desecrated it". Consequently, "Spiritual healing" is part of the reparation of the territory (Article 8).

79 JEP –Sala de reconocimiento de verdad, responsabilidad y determinación de hechos y conductas, AUTO No. 105 de 2022, September 7, 2022. See: https://www.jep.gov.co/Sala-de-Prensa/Paginas/JEP-abre-caso-09-investigar-crimenes-contra-pueblos-etnicos.aspx.

80 Ididem.

81 Comisión Colombiana de Juristas, *Boletín #62 del Observatorio sobre la JEP* (20th February of 2023), available at https://www.coljuristas.org/observatorio_jep/documentos/documento.php?id=250. See also: JEP –Sala de reconocimiento de verdad, responsabilidad y determinación de hechos y conductas, AUTO No. 105, September 7, 2022, §20.

Peoples and the multiple systems of life, since for Indigenous Peoples, there are threads of connection, between the physical world and the spiritual world; sacred sites, such as stones, lagoons, snow-capped peaks or the sea, being the intermediary point between those two worlds".[82]

The question remains however, what reparations to the territory should look like. Scholars like Viaene & Belkis Izquierdo,[83] Huneeus & Rueda Sáiz[84] or Ruiz Serna[85] have underlined the potential for the Colombian experience to have an impact on the concept of reparation and damages by bringing an Indigenous perspective into the legal arena but have left the fundamental question of how could these visions be reflected into reparation granted unanswered. The next section explores how restoring the practice and knowledge of music could be a form of reparation to both Indigenous people as a collective and the Territory in itself.

7 Reparation in Colombian Transitional Justice and Beyond

Reparations constitute a fundamental pillar of transitional justice and have become "the leading response in the contemporary wave of political transformation".[86] Reparations aim to address the needs of victims who suffered harm and alleviate their suffering in order to achieve durable peace, justice, and reconciliation.[87] They can include material and symbolic measures, traditionally grouped in five basic categories: restitution, compensation, rehabilitation, satisfaction and guarantees of non-repetition.[88] These reparations can be indi-

82 JEP – Sala de reconocimiento de verdad, responsabilidad y determinación de hechos y conductas, AUTO SRVBIT-XCBM-NNHC-JJCP-ACHP-01, June 25, 2024. See also: JEP, Comunicado 93 (9 of July 2024), avalaible at: https://www.jep.gov.co/Sala-de-Prensa/Paginas/la-jep-acredita-como-victimas-al-territorio-ancestral-sagrado-y-colectivo-de-la-sierra-nevada-de-gonawindua-santa-marta-y-a.aspx.

83 Belkis Izquierdo and Lieselotte Viaene, 'Decolonizing Transitional Justice from Indigenous Territories' 9.

84 Huneeus and Rueda Sáiz (n 17).

85 Daniel Ruiz Serna, 'El territorio como víctima. Ontología política y las leyes de víctimas para. comunidades indígenas y negras en Colombia' (2017) 53 Revista Colombiana de Antropología 85.

86 Ruti G Teitel, 'Transitional Justice Genealogy' in Ruth Jamieson (ed), *The Criminology of War* (Routledge 2017) 127.

87 Olivera Simić, *An Introduction to Transitional Justice* (Routledge, 2021).

88 UNGA, Basic Principles and Guidelines on the Right to a Remedy and Reparation for Victims of Gross Violations of International Human Rights Law and Serious Violations of International Humanitarian Law, 2005).

vidual or collective reparations. Collective reparations refer to "forms of distribution of public goods or services that are designed for the benefit of all members of a [victimised] region, group, or community, rather than for specific individual victims".[89] Because territory and Indigenous people's identity are interconnected, reparations are essential for them, as they are "not only suitable for improving the living conditions of the injured persons, but [they] also [provide] in a more 'metaphysical' sense the basis for reconstructing the link between present and past times, restoring the continuity of the present generations with their ancestors as well as the integrity and 'eternity' of the cultural and spiritual identity of the communities concerned".[90]

Over the past decades, TJ has grown and quickly imposed itself as the leading response to address legacies of past violence.[91] Transitional justice, in its modern framing,[92] emerged in the waves of democratization in Latin America in the late 1970s-1980s, out of the human rights movement, from which it borrowed concepts and paradigms.[93] From its inception, transitional justice has thus been closely tied to the human rights field: its precursors were human rights activists and it used human rights concepts.[94] Consequently, the concept of reparation in TJ has developed through a human rights lens and followed the developments of the human right field. Until now, the dominant underlying assumption has been that the victims of gross human rights' violations or serious violations of international humanitarian law, must necessarily be human beings and that the experience of harm should be localized in human beings. In this context, reparations so far, have been conceived in anthropocentric terms, focusing solely on the needs of, and harms to humans. With this respect, the jurisprudence of the "avant-gardist" Inter-American Court of Human Rights and Commission on reparations is a particularly telling example. While acknowledging the distinctive and special relationship of Indigenous people with their nature, the Inter-American institutions have not

89 Sam Szoke-Burke, 'Not Only "Context": Why Transitional Justice Programs Can No Longer Ignore Violations of Economic and Social Rights' (2016) 50 Texas International Law Journal 3, 486.

90 Frederico Lenzerin, *Reparations for Indigenous Peoples: International and Comparative Perspectives* (Oxford University Press, 2008).

91 Christine Bell, 'Transitional Justice, Interdisciplinarity and the State of the "Field" or "Non-Field"' (2008) 3 International Journal of Transitional Justice 5, 14.

92 Some scholars have argued that transitional justice finds its conceptual historical roots in the Nuremberg Trails (See for instance: Teitel (n 87)).

93 Ibidem.

94 Paige Arthur, 'How "Transitions" Reshaped Human Rights: A Conceptual History of Transitional Justice' (2009) 31 Human Rights Quarterly 321.

yet incorporated it into the concept of reparation, treating territory as an object which can be subject to compensation or property rights. As noted by Doris Farget, reparations granted so far at the international level have not altered the mainstream human rights paradigm that nature and human beings are dual.[95]

A growing scholarship has criticized the narrow and selective approach of TJ towards harm which is frame within a "legalistic and individualistic" perspective[96] and inevitably leads to a restrictive understanding of reparation. "This is largely due to the manner in which it has mirrored the legalistic bias of the human rights discipline, which sees civil and political rights as more justiciable in a court of law."[97] Scholars have argued that as a liberal model, transitional justice has focused on guaranteeing civil and political rights and failed to address the deeper socioeconomic and structural cause and consequence of conflicts.[98] As noted by Simon Gready, in this conceptual landscape of transitional justice, narrow conception of reparations has prevailed and "reparations policies thus far have concentrated on a limited catalogue of civil and political rights".[99] This approach has prevented transitional justice to effectively engage with structural violence and addresses the structural injustice foregrounded in the settler colonial system. In this context, scholars have advocated for a paradigm shift from transitional justice towards "transformative justice" which is not solely concerned with past injustice but also with the transformation of social, economic, and political structures.[100] Transformative reparations aim at "changing the circumstances in which they [victims] lived, and that could have been one of the roots of conflict and that

95 Doris Farget, 'Entre discontinuité et complexité dans la conception de l'environnement des instances interaméricaines et des requérants autochtones revendiquant leur droit au territoire' (2015).

96 Stephanie Vieille, 'Transitional Justice: A Colonizing Field?' (2012) 4 Amsterdam Law Forum 3, 30.

97 Simeon Gready, 'The Case for Transformative Reparations: In Pursuit of Structural Socio-Economic Reform in Post-Conflict Societies' (2022) 16 Journal of Intervention and Statebuilding 182, 182.

98 See for instance: Amanda Cahill-Ripley, 'Foregrounding Socioeconomic Rights in Transitional Justice: Realising Justice for Violations of Economic and Social Rights' (2014) 32 Netherlands Quarterly of Human Rights 183.

99 Gready (n 96).

100 Wendy Lambourne, 'Transitional Justice and Peacebuilding after Mass Violence' (2009) 3 International Journal of Transitional Justice 28.

anyway are in themselves unjust".[101] While traditionally reparations have been designed initially as backwards-looking, collectively distributed transformative reparations constitute a "response to past socio-economic injustices, with forward-looking outcomes for victims".[102] In the authors' opinion, in the case of Indigenous people, to be transformative, reparation should take into consideration their ontological views and engage with the more-than-human world.

The recognition of Territory as a victim of the armed conflict by the JEP in Colombia challenges us to rethink the concept of reparation rooted in the human rights field and reshape it to include the more than human world. While the JEP is not competent as such to order reparative measures,[103] it can impose special sanctions or *sanciones propias* to the perpetrators who have acknowledged truth and responsibility at an early stage of the proceedings. These sanctions constitute an alternative form of punishment to imprisonment as well as a form of reparation for victims, combining punitive and restorative components. For these reasons, the JEP and the macro-case 09, which includes the Wiwa communities and the territory of the Sierra Nevada, still provide an interesting framework of analysis for the discussions on reparation to the territory. Furthermore, these special sanctions are extremely flexible regarding their restorative content which can and should be enlightened by Indigenous relational ontologies. Our discussions with Wiwa on the ground show that music could become one of these creative *special sanctions*. Within this bottom-up perspective, the next section investigates music as a way to repair.

8 Repairing through Music

According to Federico Lenzerini, "the moment in which reparations (i.e. 'substantive redress') are materially granted is the moment in which the idea of justice crystallizes, and only at that precise moment justice is effectively realised".[104] Reparations are thus an essential component of transitional justice and if reconceptualized in a meaningful way, have the potential to address

101 Rodrigo Uprimny Yepes, 'Transformative Reparations of Massive Gross Human Rights Violations: Between Corrective and Distributive Justice' (2009) 27 Netherlands quarterly of human rights 625, 651.

102 Gready (n 96).

103 The issue of reparation is object to a separate chapter in the Final Peace Agreement.

104 Lenzerini (n 89).

environmental damages suffered by Indigenous communities, enhance their relationship with nature and transform socio-economic realities. We argue that in the case of Wiwa people, integrating music to reparation could perform such a role.

Lisa J. Laplante has advocated for a "pluralist approach to reparations", which "necessarily means different results for different intended beneficiaries".[105] She proposed a participatory process to activate this pluralist approach to reparations where victims based on their positionality would guide "the content of this right in a way that embraces local understandings of repair". Against the traditional "one-size-fits-all approach",[106] such "plural account would require that localized considerations shape" reparations and that "hybridity and plural voices" are considered.[107] This is in line with the well-established scholarship that emphasizes the need for a "localized",[108] "locally owned",[109] "from below"[110] and "bottom-up"[111] transitional justice processes. Building on this scholarship, this article places Wiwa voices at the centre of the research and lets them drive the content of the reparative measures. This also means that it is not the authors' intention to draw a general statement regarding the use of music as reparation. It constitutes instead a "localized" form of reparation that emerged out of a process of consultations from below, within Laplante's pluralist approach to reparations. Therefore, this article should rather be read as an invitation to rethink and reshape the concept of reparation based on a pluriverse understanding of the world. It shows that a paradigm shift from the traditional human/nature dichotomy, can catalyse creative measures such as the reappropriation of music that can take into consideration Indigenous relational ontologies and "reflects multiple and pluralized 'life worlds'".[112]

While transitional justice has traditionally aligned itself with human rights paradigms, it enjoys in fact more flexibility (especially the Colombia transi-

105 Lisa J Laplante, 'Just Repair' (2015) 48 Cornell Int'l L. J. 513, 568.

106 Line Engbo Gissel, 'The Standardisation of Transitional Justice' (2022) 28 European Journal of International Relations 859.

107 Laplante (104) 572.

108 Rosalind Shaw, Lars Waldorf and Pierre Hazan (ed.), *Localizing Transitional Justice: Interventions and Priorities after Mass Violence*' (University of Chicago Press, 2012).

109 Adam Kochanski, 'The "Local Turn" in Transitional Justice: Curb the Enthusiasm' (2020) 22 International Studies Review 26.

110 Kieran McEvoy & Lorna McGregor (ed.), *Transitional Justice from Below: Grassroots Activism and the Struggle for Change* (Hart Publishing, 2008).

111 Patricia Lundy and Mark McGovern, "Whose Justice? Rethinking Transitional Justice from the Bottom Up" (2008) 35 Journal of Law and Society 2, 265–92.

112 Clark (n 16) 16.

tional justice framework) and is not bound to follow the human rights paradigms. In Rachel Killean's words, "reparations can take myriad forms and recognize a diverse range of harms. Their flexibility allows them to be sensitive to the nature and context of the crimes that have been committed".[113] Departing from this assumption of flexibility, the article argues that if transitional justice wants to start what some scholars have called, its "decolonizing process" and be truly transformative,[114] it should distance itself from the classical, yet narrow understanding of reparation and design more ambitious and "culturally sensitive reparation" that would be able to reflect Indigenous worldviews. Engaging with Indigenous worldviews as legitimate source of knowledge instead of reducing them to "uses and customs" or "infra-legal phenomena",[115] against the background of the "coloniality of knowledge" that still permeating TJ,[116] constitutes as such, already "a first step towards a transformative reparation for historical harms".[117]

For the Wiwa people, as for most Indigenous communities, nature and humans are not dual but interrelated and interdependent; every being has a function or a role and needs each other to exist. In this context, music plays an essential role in maintain this spiritual and social order, as illustrated by Ade Eusebio's own words about "Everything sings":

> The sound of the river flowing, the birds singing to nature and sustenance deities for a good harvest, (…) the monkey singing to the water when is about to rain; and of course the humans, who are in charge to sing to those beings of living earth as the ultimate acknowledgement for their work and this has to be done in the specific sacred places where the guardians or deities live.[118]

113 Rachel Killean, 'From Ecocide to Eco-Sensitivity: 'Greening' Reparations at the International Criminal Court' (2021) 25 The International Journal of Human Rights 2, 323–347.

114 See, for instance: Augustine SJ Park, 'Settler Colonialism, Decolonization and Radicalizing Transitional Justice' (2020) 14 International Journal of Transitional Justice 260.

115 Garzón López (n 19)

116 Walter Mignolo, The *Darker Side of Western Modernity: Global Futures, Decolonial Options* (Duke University, 2011).

117 Nina Bries Silva, 'Discovering What Is Already Known: The Afro-Colombian Ancestral Justice System before the Special Jurisdiction for Peace' (2024) 9 International Journal of Transitional Justice.

118 Laura Triana Gallego "Neoliberalismo y agencia cultural: proyectos musicales y movilización política del pueblo wiwa de la Sierra Nevada de Santa Marta" (MA Thesis., Universidad Nacional de Colombia, 2014) 57.

According to Ade Eusebio, singing is given from *Serankua* to the Wiwas as a mandate that needs to be passed on to other generations. Singing and playing music enables cohesiveness, order, and organization, providing the means for communication between the material and the invisible world. The Colombian armed conflict altered this harmonical relationship with the territory. It generated harms that go beyond the human sufferings and include the displacement and disappearance of sacred places. As stated by a leader Wiwa: "Because of this violence, we almost do not feel anymore our spiritual fathers who live in water, threes, plants and stones."[119] In this context, reparations should free themselves from the mainstream dichotomy between human and nature and being instead conceived in a relational manner. Rachel Killean has argued for an "'eco-sensitive' approach to the design and implementation of reparations" in case of environmental harm.[120] However, such approach fails to step outside the opposition between human/nature and instead focuses on "greening" reparations within an eco-centric perspective. This article in turn, advocates in the case of Indigenous people, for a relational understanding of reparation. Music can be a tool to reach such "relational reparation" by enabling Indigenous communities to communicate with spiritual beings and restore the harmony and balance between humans and nature, between the tangible and intangible worlds. Through music, songs and *shihkakubi,* the Wiwas can heal the wounds of their territory and prevent future calamities such as droughts and food scarcity.[121]Therefore, music can constitute a reparative measure to both humans and more than human and reflect Indigenous relational ontologies. In Sanne Weber's view, transformative reparations should "move beyond material assistance (or individual redress)" and aim "to strengthen the capacities and respect the agency (and dignity) of victims to the endpoint of empowering themselves rather than relying on the state".[122] Music as a form of reparation can fulfil this goal and have a transformative nature. Likewise, the study case presented by Carlos Muñoz Lopez on music, reparation and post conflict in El Salado, Colombia, indicates that "music became the catalyst for strength, unity and reconstruction", showing how the revitalization of traditional music contrib-

119 Centro de Memoria Histórica (CMH), *Indígenas se reúnen en la Sierra Nevada por sus víctimas y la memoria* (2015) (translated by the author).

120 Rachel Killean, 'From Ecocide to Eco-Sensitivity: "Greening" Reparations at the International Criminal Court' (2021) 25 The International Journal of Human Rights 323.

121 Laura Triana Gallego, unpublished manuscript 2024.

122 Sanne Weber, 'From Victims and Mothers to Citizens: Gender-Just Transformative Reparations and the Need for Public and Private Transitions' (2018) 12 International Journal of Transitional Justice 88.

uted to the post-traumatic healing of the communities.[123] After the massacre of El Salado perpetrated in the 1990s, the community used music as a practice for social restoration. Similarly, the community members of *La Laguna* expressed during the interviews, the need for the State to support their process of reappropriation of music as a form of reparation within an empowerment perspective by financing the specific material for the creation of the instruments or helping to build an education and culture centre.[124] The new generation of Wiwa political leaders already started from their own initiative and often resources too, to coordinate with State institutions in reclaiming music and facilitating interactions among elders, authorities, and community members, to promote cohesion, preserve cultural memory, and enhance visual archiving.[125]

9 Conclusion

For the Wiwa Indigenous people in Colombia, Territory is a living being, it is their Mother Earth, the *Corazón del Mundo* – the heart of the world, which is not defined by physical delimitations but by the connections between sacred places, and the animate and inanimate world. The Wiwa have an intangible comprehension of the world that can hardly be represented in a text and that certainly goes beyond our understanding as researchers, readers, Indigenous rights defenders or more broadly, as a community raised in a western ontology dominated by a dichotomy between nature and culture. While this article cannot fully encapsulate Wiwa worldviews, it treats them as a legitimate and equivalent system of knowledge that should enlighten legal concepts such as reparation. In this sense, the article constitutes an invitation for further research, to collaborate with Indigenous people in identifying their differentiated harms based on their relational understanding of the world and hence design together new forms of reparation that can reflect this pluralization of lifeworld.

---

123 Carlos Muñoz López, 'La música como elemento de reparación integral en el postconflicto armado, caso El salado, Colombia' (2020) 23 Revista Estudios Socio-Jurídicos 2, 61–99.

124 Semi-structure interviews and informal conversations conducted with members of the community of La Laguna from November 2022 to December 2022 in the Guajira, Colombia.

125 Triana Gallego (n 44).

The Wiwa have faced a history of cultural erasure and ongoing conflicts that have generated disbalance and disharmony with and within their territory. Despite the incommensurability of the harms, both in a material and spiritual sense, the Wiwa identify as a form of reparation, the re-appropriation of music and its expressions of order and social organization. While acculturation meant for the Wiwa the loss of connection with their territory, music, as an intangible, endless cultural resource, is still the path to reestablishing order and harmony. The music rituals enable communication with all the beings on earth, the creation of collective bonds, and the re-instauration of harmony and reciprocity. Singing again to the guardians of water, food, and health, according to Mamo Eusebio, may repair the relations with nature; hence, calamities and further environmental and social issues can be prevented.[126] Because in Indigenous ontologies, humans and nature are interconnected, reparation to the wounded territory implies the involvement of human beings (like the performance of music), and in turn, healing the territory will necessarily also heal the interrelated communities that inhabit it.

The Wiwa know and strongly believe that harming nature is an issue that concerns and impacts the entire world, as the Sierra Nevada constitutes the heart of the world and that all humans eat, drink water, and breathe. This perspective should reach further communities and society in general to develop a strong awareness of the relational bonds between humans and nature, for example, by taking care of their water sources, every time scarcer. The urgency of the situation has called on the legal arena to develop new avenues departing from the traditional dichotomy of culture/nature and reflecting on Indigenous relational ontologies to effectively protect nature and ensure adequate reparations to Indigenous communities. In this context, the suggested relational reparations to the territory and inclusive of the more than human world (music being an illustration of it), have a transformative potential that extends beyond transitional justice, to address also harms caused by climate change or mass extractive projects. We hope that this article creates awareness about the necessity for academia, legal and social actors, environmentalists and human rights activists to engage in a *diálogo de saberes* with Indigenous peoples to co-construct such ambitious reparative measures, that include the more than human world and contribute to decolonization of the human rights-based approach to reparation.

---

126 Ibidem.

CHAPTER 8

Human Rights Violations Caused by Climate Change: Who Repairs Whom?

Patricia Grazziotin Noschang[1]

1 Introduction

The European and Inter-American Human Rights Courts have already begun to receive the new claims arising from the effects caused by climate change on people's health. Thus, the climate litigation that was already taking place in the national courts knocks on the door of the regional courts for the protection of human rights. In the exercise of what is called the intergenerational character, four children and two young people filed a lawsuit with the European Court of Human Rights seeking to hold thirty three States Parties to the European Convention on Human Rights[2] responsible for the effects of climate change. This will certainly be the first of other demands put forward by young people against those who were young in 1992 (Rio Declaration and UNFCCC) and until today have done nothing or little to fulfil the commitments signed about climate change.

There is already a precedent that connects children's rights with responsibility States to contain the effects of climate change in the United Nations Committee on the Rights of the Child.[3] Adding to the demand from European young people and children, at the end of 2020, another demand regarding heat waves in Switzerland also reached the European Court of Human Rights. This time, the petition was proposed by a Swiss Association that fights climate change, made up of hundreds of elderly women who report damage to their health caused by heat waves.

The Inter-American System for the Protection of Human Rights also had the opportunity to address climate litigation in the Inuit Case seeking the responsibility of the United States in relation to its actions and omissions

1 International Law Full Professor University of Passo Fundo.

2 European Court of Human Rights. Duarte Agostinho and others vs. Portugal and others (application no. 39371/20). Available on: https://hudoc.echr.coe.int/fre?i=00161188.

3 UN COMMITTEE ON THE RIGHTS OF THE CHILD. CRC/C/88/D/104/2019. Sacchi, et al. v. Argentina, et al. Decided by the Committee in 2021.

 | DOI:10.1163/9789004716742_009

contributing to global warming. The petition was forwarded to the Inter-American Commission on Human Rights in 2005[4] and subsequently rejected. The decision by the European Court of Human Rights is expected to have an impact on the Inter-American System, since there is already a request for an Advisory Opinion on the Climate Emergency and Human Rights to the Inter-American Court of Human Rights of the Republic of Colombia and Republic of Chile which was submitted in 2023. These actions are happening while the General Assembly, by a Resolution,[5] recognised that people should have access to a clean, healthy and sustainable environment,[6] and that climate change and environmental degradation were some of the most pressing threats to humanity's future.[7] The questions to which this paper is looking for answers are: how will human rights courts determine reparations when States are found responsible for the damages caused to the petitioners? Should the decisions exclusively repair the petitioners? Human rights courts facing a new challenge once in such cases it is possible to discern two different types of petitioners that are in need of reparations: on the one hand the envi-

4 INTER-AMERICAN COMMISSION OF HUMAN RIGHTS. INUIT PEOPLE PETITION 1413/05 VS. THE UNITED STATES, December 7, 2005.

5 Based on Human Rights Council Resolution 2021(A/HRC/48/13) 2021, the General Assembly approved the Resolution in 2022. UNITED NATIONS.HRC. Resolution (A/HRC/48/13). Available at: https://documents.un.org/doc/undoc/ltd/g21/270/15/pdf/g2127015.pdf?OpenElement.

6 "At the regional level, the right was included in the African Charter on Human and Peoples' Rights (1981), the San Salvador Protocol to the American Convention on Human Rights (1988), the Convention on Access to Information, Public Participation in Decision-Making and Access to Justice in Environmental Matters (Aarhus Convention (1998)), the Arab Charter on Human Rights (2004), the ASEAN Declaration on Human Rights (2012), and the Regional Agreement on Access to Information, Public Participation and Justice in Environmental Matters in Latin American and the Caribbean (Escazú Agreement (2018)), among others. The right was legally recognised in more than eighty percent of UN Member States (156 out of 193 States), prior to the global recognition by the HRC and the GA." UNITED NATIONS. UNHR; UNEP; UNDP. What is the Right to a Healthy Environment? Information Note. https://www.undp.org/sites/g/files/zskgke326/files/2023-01/UNDP-UNEP-UNHCHR-What-is-the-Right-to-a-Healthy-Environment.pdf (p. 8).

7 UNITED NATIONS. UNHR; UNEP; UNDP. What is the Right to a Healthy Environment? Information Note. https://www.undp.org/sites/g/files/zskgke326/files/2023-01/UNDP-UNEP-UNHCHR-What-is-the-Right-to-a-Healthy-Environment.pdf; UNITED NATIONS. Report of the Special Rapporteur on the issue of human rights obligations relating to the enjoyment of a safe, clean, healthy and sustainable environment, A/73/188 (19 July, 2018). Available at https://documents-dds-ny.un.org/doc/UNDOC/GEN/N18/231/04/PDF/N1823104.pdf?OpenElement.

ronment and the people who suffer from the damage caused firstly to the environment on the other hand.

A second challenge concerns the legal basis to support the possibility to award reparations to the environment, considering that Human Rights Conventions just envisage reparations for persons or group of persons, without any kind of mention to the environment. In this sense it is important to highlight the period these documents have been written, (i.e. the 50s and 60s), which was before the main environment protection declarations were approved. Nevertheless, it is no uncommon to find researches that support the argument that Human Rights Courts can grant reparations to find researches that support the argument that Human Rights Conventions (which do not include environment provisions), since regional human rights conventions date before treaties and documents that enabled environment protection. In such context, it is important to highlight that the Vienna Declaration recognising the interdependence, intergeneration and interconnection character of environment protection was approved in 1993.[8] On the other hand, there are many treaties and resolutions in the international law sphere which consider the responsibility of states to mitigate and repair the environmental damages caused specially by the effects of climate change, such as the Paris Agreement and the soft law resolutions approved by states. Also the ongoing proceedings at the International Court of Justice,[9] of the Advisory Opinion requested by the General Assembly[10] on the Obligation of States in relation to climate change.

The methodology adopted in this study employs the deductive method of approach, which begins with general premises to analyse specific cases, allowing for the logical construction of well-founded conclusions. Regarding procedures, the research is of a bibliographic and documentary nature, relying on the analysis of theoretical works, scientific articles, Court's decisions and documents relevant to the subject under investigation. The bibliographic method provides theoretical grounding, while the documentary research offers concrete and contextualised data, ensuring the study's consistency and depth. This methodological combination ensures a rigorous and well-substantiated analysis aligned with the objectives of the investigation.

8 II, Vienna, 1993.

9 INTERNATIONAL COURT OF JUSTICE. Advisory Opinion. Obligations of States in respect of Climate Change Available at: https://www.icj-cij.org/case/187.

10 UNGA Resolution 77/276. Available at: https://documents.un.org/doc/undoc/ltd/n23/094/52/pdf/n2309452.pdf.

2 Climate Litigation and the Connection with Human Rights

The climate litigation commonly seeks reparation in court for damages caused by obligations imposed on a State that were not fulfilled by either action or omission. States' responsibility to seek alternatives to curb the effects of global warming and its consequences for human life and the environment is first foreseen at the United Nations Framework Climate Change Convention in 1992 and later in the 2015 Paris Agreement. Such obligations are conventional and become mandatory once States sign and ratify the international commitments in their internal legal system. Treaties also provide for various forms of dispute resolution and, in turn, elect a competent international forum when a State Parties intends to appeal against another for breach of the rules foreseen in the signed international commitment, which, more often than not, will be arbitration or recourse to the International Court of Justice.

On the other hand, when transposed in the internal legal system of States, treaties may also be the matter of fact and law in national jurisdiction and States may also be sued. Thus, considering that the effects of climate change result in damages not only to the environment but also to the health and well-being of the population, it is possible for individuals to claim responsibility to the States by omission or inaction in the fulfilment of the obligations provided for in the signed treaties. And when the reparation is not sufficient nor recognised in the internal scope, there is a possibility, after the exhaustion of internal resources – of forwarding a request to the regional committees and courts established for the protection of human rights, once they are recognised by the respondent States.

One of the questions to be made is: do human rights committees and courts have the competence to analyse and judge demands that seek to hold States responsible for non-compliance with the rules established in climate change treaties?

Considering that the argument usually proposed by the parties is directly related to human rights violations caused by the impact brought by the inaction/omission of States to when accomplishing the agreements in force, it is understood that it is, indeed, possible.

It is important to highlight that the relationship between climate change and human rights is not new. We can go back to the 1972 Stockholm Declaration[11] which brought principles relating human beings to the environment. In 1992, the United Nations Framework Convention on Climate Change rein-

11 Stockholm Declaration, 1972.

forced this connection when it adopted the principle of common concern of humankind. Also in 2015, the UNEP report "[...] describes how governments and other actors may address climate change in a manner consistent with their obligations to respect, protect, promote and fulfil human rights".[12]

Therefore, the claims analysed below demonstrate a new movement of climate litigation, that may occur on both internal and international levels. Most of times, these cases are characterised by a demand to protect the environment, and relate either indirectly to the consequences of the effects of climate change (such as deforestation), or directly when the case evokes a violation of the Paris Agreement[13] and its consequences on people's lives,[14] through human rights related harm. In the words of Christina Voigt: "human rights archetypically protect citizens against the state. In other words, they protect humans from each other: they contain no provision to stop humans from exploiting non-humans or from fundamentally changing their conditions of

12 M. Berger & J. Wentz, *Climate Change and Human Rights* (UN Environment Programme (UNEP), 2015), p. 11.

13 The United Nations Human Rights Committee (HRC) analysed the case of Mr. Ioane Teitiota, in 2020, from Kiribati, who had his deportation determined by New Zealand. Teitiota's legal claim was based on ICCPR Article 6, which refers to the right to life. "2.1The author claims that the effects of climate change and sea level rise forced him to migrate from the island of Tarawa in the Republic of Kiribati to New Zealand. The situation in Tarawa has become increasingly unstable and precarious due to sea level rise caused by global warming. Fresh water has become scarce because of saltwater contamination and overcrowding on Tarawa. Attempts to combat sea level rise have largely been ineffective. Inhabitable land on Tarawa has eroded, resulting in a housing crisis and land disputes that have caused numerous fatalities. Kiribati has thus become an untenable and violent environment for the author and his family." UNITED NATIONS HUMAN RIGHTS COMMITTEE – UNHRC; COMMITTEE ON CIVIL AND POLITICAL RIGHTS – CCPR. Views adopted by the Committee under article 5 (4) of the Optional Protocol, concerning communication No. 2728/2016. pp. 10–14.

14 *Chiara Sacchi* et al. *Case,* presented to the United Nations Child Rights Committee (CRC) was based on the violation of Articles 6 (Right to Life), 24 (Right to Health) and 30 (Right to Culture) of the Convention on the Rights of Children. The Committee, when analysing the facts, decided "that states are responsible for the negative effect of carbon emissions on their territory and that the results impact children's rights inside and outside the investigated countries", but declared the complaints inadmissible due to non-exhaustion of domestic remedies.The plaintiffs filed the petition against the five countries that recognise the right of children to petition: Argentina, Brazil, German and Turkey. UN COMMITTEE ON THE RIGHTS OF THE CHILD. CRC/C/88/D/104/2019. Sacchi, et al. v. Argentina, et al.

life. Within this paradigm, environmental degradation is only relevant insofar as it causes a direct and severe violation of individual rights."[15]

3 Regional Human Rights Courts: The State of the Art of Cases That Relate Human Rights Violations and Environmental and Climate Damage

Regional human rights courts have become a possibility to seek compensation for human rights violations due to climate change, and that directly or indirectly affected, at least, the health of people who petitioned, either by heat waves, by air pollution due to smoke caused by fires or water contamination, without considering damage to the environment. It is noteworthy that climate litigation that reaches regional human rights protection systems, after the exhaustion of internal resources within the defending state, should be based on the violation of a human rights treaty. In this sense, the plaintiffs seek to connect human rights with environmental protection.

Thus, most arguments converge on provisions that protect the right to life, health and connect with resolutions and recommendations that recognise the right to a healthy environment as essential and indispensable for human survival on Earth, besides ratified obligations and foreseen in treaties that determine actions to curb the effects of climate change.

3.1 *The Protection of Human Rights and Climate Change at the European Court of Human Rights: Towards a New Recognition but with Some Restrictions*

In 2024, the European Court of Human Rights (ECtHR) heard three cases simultaneously[16] that argued the effects caused by climate change. The first to reach the Court was *Duarte Agostinho and Others v. Portugal and 32 Others*, followed by the cases *Verein KlimaSeniorinnen Schweiz and Others v. Switzerland* and *Carême v. France*.

---

15 Christina Voigt and Evadne Grant, 'Editorial: The legitimacy of human rights courts in environmental disputes' (2015) 6 *Journal of Human Rights and the Environment*, 131–8.

16 The President of the Court decided that in the interests of the proper administration of justice, the case should be assigned to the same composition of the Grand Chamber as that in the cases of *Verein KlimaSeniorinnen Schweiz and Others v. Switzerland* (application no. 53600/20) and *Carême v. France* (application no. 7189/21), which had also been relinquished.

In the *Duarte Agostinho and Others v. Portugal and 32 others* case, six young Portuguese people joined the European Court of Human Rights seeking compensation for damage caused due to intense heat waves that hit Portugal in 2017. The temperature reached 44°C and several regions suffered with fires that caused the death of, at least, one hundred and twenty (120) persons, in addition to the destruction of their homes, health damage caused by smoke, respiratory diseases and sleep disorders. One of the regions that was hit is Leiria, where four of the plaintiffs live.[17]

In the aforementioned petition, submitted in 2020, the plaintiffs claimed that the thirty three (33) States Parties of the European Convention on Human Rights had violated Articles 2 (Right to Life), 3 (prohibition of torture), 8 (Right to Respect for Private and Family Life), 14 (prohibition of discrimination), 34 (individual petitions) of the ECHR and Article 1 of Protocol no. 1 (Property Protection). The petition also includes the States' responsibility for breach of other international instruments such as the 2015 Paris Agreement and the UN Convention on the Rights of the Child, and general reports and expert findings concerning the harm caused by climate change.[18]

One of the questions that may arise pertain to the relationship between the provisions set out in the European Convention on Human Rights and compliance with the Paris Agreement, since the analysis is subject the scrutiny of a human rights court. In this sense, an important question emerges: Can the European Court of Human Rights impose the responsibility on the thirty three respondent States for their non-compliance with the objectives established by the Paris Agreement? According to Article 32 of the European Convention of Human Rights, "the Court's jurisdiction encompasses all matters concerning the interpretation and application of the Convention and its the respective protocols which are submitted to it for consideration", and from this perspective, the answer is affirmative. One of the arguments presented by the parties is based on the case *Dubettska v. Ukraine*, judged by the European Court of Human Rights in 2011, in which the decision states that Article 8 of the European Convention on Human Rights can be interpreted as being violated in circumstances where a grave there is a serious environmental dan-

17 European Court of Human Rights. Duarte Agostinho and others vs. Portugal and others (application no. 39371/20). Available on: https://hudoc.echr.coe.int/fre?i=00161188.

18 NOSCHANG, Patricia. Litigância Climática, direitos humanos e juventude. International Law Agenda. Available at: http://ila-brasil.org.br/blog/litigancia-climatica-direitos-humanos-e-juventude/

ger that results in a significant impairment of the applicants' capacity to enjoy their home, private or family life.[19]

Notwithstanding this interpretation integrating human rights treaties into environmental protection, the European Court declared the case inadmissible due to the no exhaustion of domestic remedies, a prerequisite for accessing regional human rights protection mechanism. In the meantime, the Court understood that "the existence of mere doubts as to the prospects of success of a private remedy which was not obviously futile was not a valid reason for failing to exhaust that avenue of redress".[20]

Furthermore, the Court examined whether it should consider the extraterritoriality of jurisdiction, but understood that it was related to the Court's case law on this matter and that Portugal had their internal jurisdiction to analyse the claim.[21]

In September 2020 the Court received a second complaint from "[...] four women and a Swiss association, Verein KlimaSeniorinnen Schweiz, whose members are all older women concerned about the consequences of global warming on their living conditions and health".[22] They alleged that the Swiss authorities were not acting positively to prevent and mitigate climate change effects, despite their duties under the Convention. Thus, the petitioners argued that the Swiss Confederation failed to fulfil its duties under the Euro-

19 *Duarte Agostinho and others vs. Portugal and others* (application no. 39371/20).Available at: https://hudoc.echr.coe.int/fre?i=00161188. *Dubetska and others vs Ukraine*. 2011.Available at: https://www.elaw.org/content/european-court-human-rights-dubetska and-others-v-ukraine-application-no-3049903–20110210-ec.

20 Duarte Agostinho and others vs. Portugal and others (application no. 39371/20).: https://hudoc.echr.coe.int/fre?i=00161188.

21 It was clear that the applicants' complaints in the present case did not correspond to any of the circumstances which in earlier cases had given rise to a finding of extraterritorial jurisdiction. The existing case-law therefore provided no basis for establishing extraterritorial jurisdiction of the respondent States (other than Portugal, which had territorial jurisdiction). The Court thus examined whether there were valid grounds for developing the existing case-law on extraterritorial jurisdiction as put forward by the applicants in their submissions given their reliance on a number of "exceptional circumstances" and "special features". In so far as the applicants had relied on the "exceptional circumstances" mentioned in M.N. and Others v. Belgium (dec.) [GC], in that case the Court had not established the existence of extraterritorial jurisdiction of the respondent State nor intended to establish a distinct jurisdictional test. The assessment of any "exceptional circumstances" was ultimately one of effective authority or control over the applicants, in line with established case-law. *Duarte Agostinho and others vs. Portugal and others* (application no. 39371/20). https://hudoc.echr.coe.int/fre?i=00161188.

22 EUROPEAN COURT OF HUMAN RIGHTS. *Klima Seniorinnen vs. Switzerland* (Application No. 53600/20). Available at: https://hudoc.echr.coe.int/tur?i=001–233206.

pean Convention on Human Rights to effectively protect life (Article 2) and to ensure respect for their private and family life, including their home (Article 8). In this context, they claimed that the State did neither introduce adequate legislation, nor implement appropriate and sufficient measures to achieve the goals of combating climate change, in accordance with existing international commitments.

Upon analysing Article 34 ECtHR, the Court understood that those who can demonstrate that they are personally and directly affected by government action or inaction may be considered individual victims in lawsuits related to climate change and this depends on two criteria: "(a) high intensity of exposure of the applicant to the adverse effects of climate change, and (b) a pressing need to ensure the applicant's individual protection". The Court established a high level of complexity to admit cases on climate change and will not admit general cases that deal with public interest (*actio popularis*). After analysing the nature and scope of the applicants' individual complaints and the material submitted by them (and other aspects), the Court concluded that the four individual applicants did not meet the criteria for victim status provided for in Article 34 ECtHR. Therefore, they declared their complaints inadmissible. On the other hand, concerning "the standing of associations, the Court held that the special feature of climate change as a common concern of humankind and the need to promote intergenerational burden-sharing rendered it appropriate to make allowance for recourse to legal action by associations in the context of climate change".[23]

Court's ruling analysed Articles 2 and 8 ECtHR jointly, understanding that the right to life is extended and was directly linked to the principles that guarantee respect for private and family life. In this context, the Court's decision understood that "Article 8 of the Convention encompasses a right for individuals to effective protection by the State authorities from the serious adverse effects of climate change on their lives, health, well-being and quality of life" and that the Swiss Confederation failed to take effective measures to reduce the greenhouse gas emissions. According to the Court, the national legislation contained gaps and flaws in quantifying national greenhouse gas (GHG) emissions limits. Furthermore, the Court observed that Switzerland had not met its previous GHG emission reduction targets. Thus, the Swiss authorities did not act adequately to design and implement legislation, neither take relevant measures that would fulfil their positive obligations under Article 8 of the Convention, which were relevant in the context of climate change.

---

23 EUROPEAN COURT OF HUMAN RIGHTS. *Klima Seniorinnen vs. Switzerland* (Application No. 53600/20). Available at: https://hudoc.echr.coe.int/tur?i=001-233206.

The Court's ruling recognises the importance and principle of common concern of humankind, as established in the Convention on Climate Change, and relates it to the intergenerational nature and equity in human rights matters: "This is especially true in the context of climate change, which is a global and complex phenomenon. It has multiple causes and its adverse effects are not the concern of any one particular individual, or group of individuals, but are rather 'a common concern of humankind'[24] (see the Preamble to the UNFCCC). Moreover, in this context where intergenerational burden-sharing assumes particular importance, collective action through associations or other interest groups may be one of the only means through which the voice of those at a distinct representational disadvantage can be heard and through which they can seek to influence the relevant decision-making processes."[25]

In the similar context, the late Brazilian ICJ judge Trindade, emphasises that "the concept of common concern of mankind highlights universally shared values. This conceptual development – which undoubtedly requires further elaboration – serves as a warning of the obstacles to be overcome in the construction, in a larger dimension (not only spatial but also temporal) and pursuant to the same universalist outlook, of the new International Law for humankind, at this beginning of the twenty-first century."[26]

The third case, *Carême v. France*,[27] was brought to the Court in 2021 by MEP Damien Carême of the French Green Party. Carême alleged that France failed to implement adequate measures to prevent climate change, and that such failure constitutes a violation of the right to life and the right to respect for private and family life, also using the violation of Articles 2 and 8 ECtHR. However, the Court ruled the claim inadmissible, as the victim did not meet the requirements of Article 34 ECtHR.

---

24 Acknowledging that change in the Earth's climate and its adverse effects are a common concern of humankind. UNITED NATIONS. United Nations Framework Convention on Climate Change and Article 24 of Paris Agreement. UNITED NATIONS DEVELOPMENT PROGRAM. Available at: <https://www.undp.org/content/dam/brazil/docs/ODS/undp-br-ods-ParisAgreement.pdf>.

25 EUROPEAN COURT OF HUMAN RIGHTS. *Klima Seniorinnen vs. Switzerland* (Application No. 53600/20). Pending judgment. Proposed on 26 November 2020. Available at: https://hudoc.echr.coe.int/tur?i=001–233206.

26 CANÇADO TRINDADE, Antonio Augusto. International law for humankind: towards a new jus gentium (II) – General Course on Public International Law, 317. Leiden/The Netherlands: Brill/Nijhoff, Recueil des Cours de l'Académie de Droit international de la Haye, 2005. pp. 395–396.

27 EUROPEAN COURT OF HUMAN RIGHTS. *Case of Carême vs. France* (Application no. 7189/21).

Some considerations regarding this case are important. First, Carême was mayor of Grande-Synthe 2001–2019 and at that time sought national jurisdiction by requesting French authorities to take measures to reduce greenhouse gas emissions. Here, unlike the *Duarte Agostinho v. Portugal* case, there was an attempt to exhaust domestic remedies. Second, the Court found that Carême no longer had any ties to the city of Grande-Synthe, as he was not a resident and did not have any property there, except for his brother who still lives there. According to the Court, "[...] environmental damage must have a direct impact or repercussions on the applicant's right to respect for his home, family or private life, or directly affect the applicant's home, family or private life. A general deterioration of the environment is not sufficient."[28]

Some additional considerations regarding the case are also pointed out by Torre-Shaub. Firstly, the Carême ruling is the most overlooked of the three climate decisions handed down on April 9, 2024. Because this decision is insufficiently argued, a few thoughts on it deserve to be shared. Secondly, this rejection is a reminder of the arduous road ahead for the protection of environmental human rights. "Finally, the decision cruelly points out the absence of a right to a healthy environment recognised by the Convention. Given that climate change is one of the world's most pressing environmental problems, this judgment serves as a reminder that little has yet been achieved in terms of the human right to a healthy, stable climate. Despite the success of the KlimaSeniorinnen case, there is still a long way to go."[29]

In the three cases judged by the Court, there is recognition of the possibility of receiving petitions related to the effects caused by climate change and the infringement of human rights. However, substantial advancements are still necessary to ensure the protection of the environment and, by extension, human survival.

The Court also faced the challenge of identifying the litigants (or potential ones), the responsible states and whether domestic remedies had been exhausted. These three aspects are crucial for determining the possibility of redress and will be discussed in the next section.

---

28 Marta Torre-Schaub. The European Court of Human Rights' Kick into Touch: Some Comments under *Carême v. France*. Climate Law. shttps://blogs.law.columbia.edu/climatechange/2024/04/19/the-european-court-of-human-rights-kick-into-touch-some-comments-under-careme-v-france/#molongui-disabled-link.

29 Marta Torre-Schaub. The European Court of Human Rights' Kick into Touch: Some Comments under *Carême v. France*. Climate Law. https://blogs.law.columbia.edu/climatechange/2024/04/19/the-european-court-of-human-rights-kick-into-touch-some-comments-under-careme-v-france/#molongui-disabled-link.

3.2 *Climate Change and Human Rights Protection in the Inter-American System*

In 2005 the Inter-American Commission on Human Rights (IACHR) received the Inuit People's Case petition, which sought to hold the United States accountable for the State's actions and omissions that contribute to global warming. The petition was subsequently rejected.[30]

Additionally, since 2013, at the IACHR has been considering a petition filed by Earthjustice on behalf of the Arctic Athabaskan Council,[31] which alleges that Canada's fragmented and lax regulations on black carbon emissions threaten the human rights of the Athabaskan people. The petition describes how the Arctic is witnessing disproportionately large rates of warming and alleges that this warming is having significant adverse impacts on the Athabaskan people.[32] Such impacts include ecological disturbances that make hunting and fishing more difficult and dangerous, alterations in the regional topography of cultural importance, and the compromising of the people's ability to understand their environment for purposes ranging from subsistence to the maintenance of cultural traditions.[33]

According to the petition, Canada's failure in effectively regulating black carbon emissions triggers a causal chain that leads to the violation of the Athabaskan People's rights to culture, property, health preservation, and means of subsistence benefits, as established by the American Declaration of the Rights and Duties of Man.[34] This failure, also allegedly to the petition, results in vio-

---

30 EARTHJUSTICE. Petition to the Inter-American Commission on Human Rights Seeking Relief from Violations of the Rights of Arctic Athabaskan Peoples Resulting from Rapid Arctic Warming and Melting Caused by Emissions of Black Carbon by Canada. Available at: https://earthjustice. org/sites/default/files/AAC_PETITION_13-04-23a.pdf.

31 EARTHJUSTICE. Petition to the Inter-American Commission on Human Rights Seeking Relief from Violations of the Rights of Arctic Athabaskan Peoples Resulting from Rapid Arctic Warming and Melting Caused by Emissions of Black Carbon by Canada. https://earthjustice. org/sites/default/files/AAC_PETITION_13-04-23a.pdf.

32 EARTHJUSTICE. Petition to the Inter-American Commission on Human Rights Seeking Relief from Violations of the Rights of Arctic Athabaskan Peoples Resulting from Rapid Arctic Warming and Melting Caused by Emissions of Black Carbon by Canada. https://earthjusticeorg/sites/default/files/AAC_PETITION_13-04-23a.pdf.

33 EARTHJUSTICE. Petition to the Inter-American Commission on Human Rights Seeking Relief from Violations of the Rights of Arctic Athabaskan Peoples Resulting from Rapid Arctic Warming and Melting Caused by Emissions of Black Carbon by Canada. Available at: https://earthjusticeorg/sites/default/files/AAC_PETITION_13-04-23a.pdf.

34 AMERICAN STATES ORGANISATION. American Declaration of the Rights and Duties of Man. Available at: https:www.oas.orgdilaccess_to_information_human_right_American_Declaration_of_the_Rights_and_Duties_of_Man.pdf.

lations of Canada's duties to prevent transboundary harm and to the environment in line with the precautionary principle.[35]

Although these two petitions did not receive timely and adequate attention, some relevant resolutions were approved by the IACHR and brought important determinations and considerations. Among these, Resolution 3/2021 on "Climate Emergency – Scope and Inter-American Human Rights Obligations",[36] which emphasises in the preamble the lack of necessary actions by States to achieve the goals foreseen in the Paris Agreement and their duty and responsibility of States to apply and promote respect for human rights. In this sense, the preamble of the Resolution vaticinates that the non-fulfilment of the commitments made by the States can bring devastating consequences "[...] especially for millions of people living in poverty, who even in the best of scenarios, would face food insecurity, forced migration, disease and death. This threatens the very future of human rights and would undo the last fifty years of progress in development, health and poverty reduction."[37] The Resolution systematised the obligations of States regarding human rights and the context of the climate crisis, reaffirming once again the interdependence and interrelationship of human rights. These actions represent the steps taken by those taken within the IACHR in relation to the protection of human rights because in light of impacts of climate change.

At the Inter-American Court of Human Rights, the significance of the request for an Advisory Opinion request by Colombia in 2017[38] is noteworthy, once it provided the Court the opportunity to conduct an analysis of the interdependence of economic, social, cultural and environmental human rights, called by the Inter-American Human Rights Protection System as ESCR. Advisory Opinion (OC) no. 23/17 – Environment and Human Rights, highlighted the relationship of interdependence of human rights, particularly in light of decisions that prove the relationship of protection of the right to life, privacy, family and private property, granted by the European Court of Human Rights and

---

35 INTER-AMERICAN COURT OF HUMAN RIGHTS. Advisory Opinion 23/17. https://www.corteidh.or.cr/docs/opiniones/seriea_23_ing.pdf. para. 50.

36 INTER-AMERICAN COMMISSION. REDESCA. Resolution 3/21. Climate Emergency. Scope of Inter-American Human Rights Obligations. Available at: https://www.oas.org/en/iachr/decisions/pdf/2021/resolucion_3-21_ENG.pdf.

37 INTERNATIONAL COURT OF HUMAN RIGHTS. *Comunidades Indígenas Miembros de la Asociación Lhaka Honhat (Nuestra Tierra) Vs. Argentina* Case. Judgement of 6 February 2020 (Fondo, Reparaciones y Costas). 2020.Available on: <http://www.corteidh.or.cr/docs/casos/articulos/seriec_400_esp.pdf.

38 INTER-AMERICAN COURT OF HUMAN RIGHTS. *Advisory Opinion 23/17*. Available at: https://www.corteidh.or.cr/docs/opiniones/seriea_23_ing.pdf.

the African Commission on Human and Peoples' Rights,[39] considering that the environment conducive to development is one that relates to economic, social and cultural rights insofar, once it does not affect the quality of life and safety of people. In addition, this OC was important in marking and reinforcing the interrelation and interdependence of human rights, recognising environmental protection as a fundamental guarantee of the right to life, principle later confirmed in the *Lhaka Honhat v. Argentina* judgement.[40]

In Advisory Opinion 23 of 2017, the Court points out that:

> The human right to a healthy environment has been understood as a right that has both individual and also collective connotations. In its collective dimension, the right to a healthy environment constitutes a universal value that is owed to both present and future generations. That said, the right to a healthy environment also has an individual dimension insofar as its violation may have a direct and an indirect impact on the individual owing to its connectivity to other rights, such as the rights to health, personal integrity, and life. Environmental degradation may cause irreparable harm to human beings; thus, a healthy environment is a fundamental right for the existence of humankind.[26]

At the beginning of 2023, the issue of climate change was brought before the Court in a new Request for Advisory Opinion (Chile and Colombia), with the "[...] purpose of promoting and accelerating responses to the climate emergency by each State, collectively – regionally and globally –, [...]."[41] The request encompassed a series of inquiries designed to guide solutions grounded in human rights with an intersectional perspective.[42] In 2024, the Court con-

39 INTER-AMERICAN COURT OF HUMAN RIGHTS. Advisory Opinion Request. Available at: https://www.corteidh.or.cr/docs/opiniones/soc_1_2023_pt.pdf. para. 207. African Commission on Human and Peoples' Rights, *Case Ogoni Vs. Niger*, Communication 155/96. para. 52 K.SA. Ebeku, The right to a satisfactory environment and the African Commission. African Human Rights Journal. 2003 (3). pp. 149–166.

40 INTER-AMERICAN COURT OF HUMAN RIGHTS. *Advisory Opinion 23/17*. Available at: https://www.corteidh.or.cr/docs/opiniones/seriea_23_ing.pdf. para. 59. INTERNATIONAL COURT OF HUMAN RIGHTS. Comunidades Indígenas Miembros de la Asociación Lhaka Honhat (Nuestra Tierra) Vs. Argentina Case. Judgement of 6 February 2020 (Fondo, Reparaciones y Costas). 2020. Available: <http://www.corteidh.or.cr/docs/casos/articulos/seriec_400_esp.pdf.

41 INTER-AMERICAN COURT OF HUMAN RIGHTS. *Advisory Opinion 23/17*. Available at: https://www.corteidh.or.cr/docs/opiniones/seriea_23_ing.pdfpara. 56.

42 INTER-AMERICAN COURT OF HUMAN RIGHTS. *Advisory Opinion Request* Available at: https://www.corteidh.or.cr/docs/opiniones/soc_1_2023_pt.pdf. p. 2.

vened public hearings to gather insights from various organisations and individuals who submitted comments and sought to contribute to addressing the questions posed to the Court, which subsequently began to evaluate all contributions.

Also in 2023, the Court ruled on the Case of *The Inhabitants of La Oroya v. Peru.*[43] In such case, the petitioners alleged that environmental contamination within La Oroya community stemmed from the operations of the metallurgical complex located there. The La Oroya Metallurgical Complex (CMLO) was installed in 1922 and nationalised in 1974, was operated by the State until 1997, when it was privatised and sold a US-base company. Throughout this period, the CMLO was dedicated to the smelting and refining of polymetallic concentrates containing high levels of lead, copper, zinc, and other metals harmful to human health and the environment. In 2006, La Oroya was identified as one of the ten most polluted cities globally, with 99% of atmospheric pollutants attributed to the metallurgical complex.[44]

According to the concurring vote of judges Ricardo C. Perez Manrique, Eduardo Ferrer Mac-Gregor Poisot and Rodrigo Mudrovitsch, the judgment of this case represents "one of the most important decisions in the era jurisprudence of the direct justice of the DESCA before the Inter-American Court – at a time of special global concern for the future of humanity – which it will certainly be complemented by the IDH Court in the recent Advisory Opinion presented by Colombia and Chile, on Climate Emergency and Humans Rights Humans, in the Inter-American System."[45]

It is clear that there is a new and progressive movement within the Inter-American system for the protection of human rights towards recognising the responsibilities of States in relation to the adverse effects caused by climate change or environmental disasters that cause harm and violate human rights such as the right to a healthy and balanced environment (encompassing water

---

43 INTER-AMERICAN COURT OF HUMAN RIGHTS. *Inhabitants of La Oroya v. Peru.* Available at: https://www.corteidh.or.cr/docs/casos/articulos/seriec_511_esp.pdf.

44 INTER-AMERICAN COURT OF HUMAN RIGHTS. *Advisory Opinion Request.* Available at: https://www.corteidh.or.cr/docs/opiniones/soc_1_2023_pt.pdf. p. 2; SASSEN, Saskia. Expulsion.

45 VOTO CONCURRENTE DE LOS JUECES RICARDO C. PÉREZ MANRIQUE, EDUARDO FERRER MAC-GREGOR POISOT Y RODRIGO MUDROVITSCH. 177. The case of Habitantes de La Oroya is included in one of the most important decisions in the era jurisprudence of the direct justice of the DESCA before the Inter-American Court —at a time of special global concern for the future of humanity—, which it will certainly be complemented by the IDH Court in the recent Advisory Opinion presented by Colombia and Chile, on Climate Emergency and Humans Rights Humans, in the Inter-American System.

availability and air quality) which can directly jeopardise public health. The forms of reparation for such circumstances will be addressed in the following section.

4 Human Rights Reparations for Damage Caused by Climate Change: In Which Court Will This Be Possible?

Regional courts and human rights are tasked with providing reparations for individuals affected by environmental degradation and its subsequent impact on health, as stipulated by human rights treaties. The question that arises is: who holds the responsibility for determining reparations or the return to the status quo ante of the environment?

The responsibility for environmental damage related to climate change may be assessed both in a national[46] or international[47] level, arising from an actions or omissions by a State, which cause a violation of rules and targets set in international.[48]

It is important to highlight that there is a significant development with the Paris Agreement through a provision in which States recognise the existence of loss and damage resulting from the effects of climate change. Furthermore, the Paris Agreement does not acknowledge reservations, thereby obligating all signatory States to be bound by the commitment to repair losses and damages arising from the non-compliance with the goals provided for in the agreement.[49] In other words, it is the first time that a climate treaty determines the responsibility to States for addressing losses and damages that were not avoided either by action or omission, and by disrespecting the rules of the treaties and the goals proposed by the States themselves.[50]

---

46 NETHERLANDS. Urgenda Foundation v. State of Netherlands, Hague District Court, C/09/456689/HA ZA 13–1396 Judgment (24 June 2015).

47 Ioane Teitiota. UNITED NATIONS HUMAN RIGHTS COMMITTEE – UNHRC; COMMITTEE ON CIVIL AND POLITICAL RIGHTS – CCPR. Views adopted by the Committee under article 5 (4) of the Optional Protocol, concerning communication No. 2728/2016.

48 C.Derani, P. G. Noschang. The jurisdiction of the International Court of Justice in cases of territorial damage caused to States by climate change. Revista de Direito Internacional, v. 19, pp. 46–63, 2022.

49 UNITED NATIONS DEVELOPMENT PROGRAM. Available at: <https://www.undp.org/content/dam/brazil/docs/ODS/undp-br-ods-ParisAgreement.pdf>.

50 C.Derani, P. G. Noschang. The jurisdiction of the International Court of Justice in cases of territorial damage caused to States by climate change. Revista de Direito Internacional, v. 19, pp. 46–63, 2022.

An important matter to be stressed is that there is no provision concerning the reparation for damages incurred. In this sense, it is deemed that such matters shall be up to the so-called "climate litigation", which may be pursued either nationally or internationally, depending on the nature of the damage and the party seeking redress. However, when it comes to responsibility for environmental damage, it should be concluded that the simple understanding of a civil liability[51] where it suffices to indemnify the loss is inadequate. As already outlined, such damage goes beyond monetary compensation as it affects the entire ecosystem where the damage occurred, with frequent implications involving the extinction of species, hence violating the prevention, the precautionary, and the intergenerational equity principles set forth in the Rio Declaration of 1992, along with other international covenants. Environmental damage is directly associated with the fundamental right to life.[52]

One must question in which forum a dispute seeking reparation for environmental damage resulting from non-compliance with one of the treaties establishing climate change goals could occur? The Paris Agreement refers to the dispute resolution procedure provided for in the 1992 Climate Convention, which permits claims to be directed to the International Court of Justice or to arbitration.[53]

4.1 *Reparation in European Court of Human Rights: Climate Change Litigation and Human Rights Protection*

It should be noted that this text also seeks to explore the (im)possibility of regional human rights courts, to address human rights violations due to environmental degradation and the effects caused by climate change, to go beyond. In other words, in addition to reparation and compensation for the plaintiffs who suffered the damages, there is a need of also determining environmental restitution resulting from the same harmful actions. Thus, when analysing the cases judged by the European Court of Human Rights, especially the three recent cases, *Verein KlimaSeniorinnen Schweiz and Others v. Switzerland, Duarte Agostinho v. Portugal and Carême v. France*, the latter two were consid-

51 J. E. Viñuales, 'La distribution de la charge de protéger l'environnement: Expressions juridiques de la solidarité', in A. Supiot (ed.), La responsabilité solidaire. Paris: Conérences du Collège de France, 2018.

52 C.Derani, P. G. Noschang. The jurisdiction of the International Court of Justice in cases of territorial damage caused to States by climate change. Revista de Direito Internacional, v. 19, pp. 46–63, 2022.

53 Article 14 of UN Convention on Climate Change and Article 24 of Paris Agreement. UNITED NATIONS DEVELOPMENT PROGRAM. Available at: <https://www.undp.org/content/dam/brazil/docs/ODS/undp-br-ods-ParisAgreement.pdf>.

ered inadmissible by the Court. On the other hand, the judgment in the former case, *Verein KlimaSeniorinnen Schweiz and Others v. Switzerland*, issued by the Grand Chamber, provides detailed considerations of all treaties, resolutions, recommendations, and decisions on climate change, including the domestic legislation of some States and comparative law. The Court acknowledged Switzerland's failure in meeting the goals outlined in the UNFCC and the Paris Agreement and that the country should take the necessary measures to achieve the reduction of greenhouse gas emissions and implement the provisions foreseen in the treaties.[54]

The ECtHR's range of remedies is broad, encompassing binding declaratory judgments, just satisfaction under Article 41 focused on the principle of restitutio in integrum, as well as both individual and general measures, including those issued within or outside of a pilot judgment procedure. However, it is important to note that this remedial framework does have specific limitations: it does not extend to granting punitive damages, imposing EU-style daily penalty payments for non-compliance, or establishing community development funds to address collective harms, as seen in the practice of the Inter-American Court of Human Rights (IACtHR). Additionally, the Court cannot annul domestic laws and does not categorise its remedial actions according to the five types outlined in the Articles on Responsibility of States for Internationally Wrongful Acts, such as restitution, compensation, satisfaction (which includes acknowledgment of the breach or expressions of regret), cessation, and non-repetition.[55]

The case of *Seniorinnen v. Switzerland* represents a significant moment in climate litigation, as it involves a lawsuit filed by a Swiss association of elderly women who are seeking reparations for health damage caused by heat waves

54 In particular, in view of the magnitude of the risks posed by climate change, the clear science, the urgency of the situation and the clear ultimate objective of the UNFCCC, the State had a positive obligation to take all measures that were not impossible or disproportionately economically burdensome with the objective of reducing GHG emissions to a safe level. The situation required the State to do everything in its power to protect the applicants. 320 the State was required to do everything in its power to do its share to prevent a global temperature increase of more than 1.50C above pre-industrial levels. This necessarily included establishing a legislative and administrative framework to achieve that objective. EUROPEAN COURT OF HUMAN RIGHTS. *Klima Seniorinnen vs. Switzerland* (Application No. 53600/20). Pending judgment. Proposed on 26 November 2020. Available at: https://climatecasechart.com/non-us-case/neubauer-et-al-v-germany/.

55 C.Heri. Too Big to Remedy? What Climate Cases Tell Us About the Remedial Role of Human Rights.European Convention on Human Rights Law Review, The. Available at: https://brill.com/view/journals/eclr/5/3/article-p400_007.xml. Vol.5 pp. 400–422, 2024.

exacerbated by climate change. This case highlights the evolving role of human rights law in addressing environmental harm. The plaintiffs argued that the Swiss government's failure to adequately address climate change, specifically in relation to rising temperatures and their adverse impact on public health, has directly harmed the health and well-being of older individuals, particularly those vulnerable to extreme weather conditions. In terms of reparations, the plaintiffs have petitioned the European Court of Human Rights (ECtHR) to recognise Switzerland's failure to safeguard its citizens from the harmful effects of climate change as a violation of human rights, particularly the right to life and health. The petitioners sough reparations for the harm caused by heat waves, which they argue have disproportionately impacted elderly women living in urban areas with insufficient cooling infrastructure.

In *KlimaSeniorinnen*, the ECtHR effectively ruled that ECtHR Member States are required to establish targets and timelines within their domestic regulatory frameworks aimed at achieving net neutrality, ideally within the next three decades. The Court's ruling was both prescriptive and deferential. It pinpointed specific shortcomings in Switzerland's approach, such as the failure to adopt appropriate legislation and set a carbon budget. However, the Court also granted Switzerland a margin of appreciation in choosing the specific measures to implement in order to comply with Article 8, while still subjecting those measures to oversight by the Committee of Ministers. Although the ECtHR continues to treat remedies as secondary, it provided the applicants and others with guidance on how to press the Swiss government for action at the national level. While the decision represented a missed opportunity to directly address remedies related to climate change, it may mark the beginning of future rulings on this critical issue.[56]

The Seniorinnen case is important not only because it highlights the intersection of climate change and human rights but also because it opens up important questions about how reparations are determined in cases where

56 A. Rocha, M. A. Tigre, V. Stoyanova, E. Xavier, C. Martini, M. Cohen. Reparation for Climate Change at the ECtHR Climate Law. Sabin Law Center. Available at: https://blogs.law.columbia.edu/climatechange/2024/05/10/reparation-for-climate-change-at-the-ecthr. EUROPEAN COURT OF HUMAN RIGHTS. *Klima Seniorinnen vs. Switzerland* (Application No. 53600/20).Available at: https://climatecasechart.com/non-us-case/neubauer-et-al-v-germany/. See also: G. Letsas. The European Court's Legitimacy After KlimaSeniorinnen European Convention on Human Rights Law Review 5 (2024) 444–453; V. Stoyanova. Correlativity Between Human Rights and Positive Obligations and Its Role for the Execution of Judgments Delivered by the European Court of Human Rights/. European Convention on Human Rights Law Review 5 (2024) 455–486.

environmental harm disproportionately affects vulnerable groups. It challenges existing legal frameworks by asking whether human rights courts can or should address reparations for environmental damage, especially when the harm is caused by systemic, long-term environmental trends rather than isolated events. The outcome of this case could set an important precedent for future climate litigation, particularly in the European context, and could influence how other regional courts, like the Inter-American Court of Human Rights, address similar claims related to climate change and health.

4.2 *Reparations in the Inter-American Court of Human Rights: An Integrated Perspective on Reparations between Human Rights and Environmental Protection*

The decisions of the Inter-American Court of Human Rights are based on obligations to act, to refrain from repeating harmful acts, to provide reparations, and on the State's duty to widely publicise the rulings within its domestic sphere. The Court also seeks an integrated perspective of reparations, considering, for example, the affected communities, their relationship with nature, and the preservation of the environment,[57] always stipulating that States, when implementing reparative measures, must listen to the affected population/community. This integrated perspective is evident in the cases of *Lhaka Honhat v. Argentina*,[58] the reparations contained in *La*

57 "Las acciones de remediación deberán tomar en cuenta la información científica actualizada en materia de reparación de daños al medio ambiente provocado por metales. Por unanimidad, que: 11. Esta Sentencia constituye, por sí misma, una forma de reparación. 12. El Estado promoverá y continuará las investigaciones respecto de los actos de amenazas y hostigamientos a las víctimas del presente caso, y respecto de la contaminación ambiental en La Oroya, de conformidad con lo establecido en los párrafos 327 y 328 de la presente Sentencia. 13. El Estado realizará un diagnóstico de línea base y un plan de acción para remediar los daños ambientales en La Oroya, de conformidad con lo establecido en los párrafos 333 y 334 de la presente Sentencia. " INTER-AMERICAN COURT OF HUMAN RIGHTS Inhabitants of La Oroya v. Peru. Available at: https://www.corteidh.or.cr/docs/casos/articulos/seriec_511_esp.pdf. para. 334.

58 INTER-AMERICAN COURT OF HUMAN RIGHTS. Comunidades Indígenas Miembros de la Asociación Lhaka Honhat (Nuestra Tierra) Vs. Argentina Case. Judgement of 6 February 2020 (Fondo, Reparaciones y Costas). 2020. Available at: <http://www.corteidh.or.cr/docs/casos/articulos/seriec_400_esp.pdf para. 333–334. 333. In addition to the actions ordered in the previous paragraph, in order to permanently ensure that the provision of basic goods and services is adequate and regular, as well as the reasonable preservation and enhancement of environmental resources, the State shall prepare a study, within a maximum period of one year from the notification of this Judgment, in which it shall outline the actions that must be implemented for: a) the conservation of surface

Oroya v. Peru,[59] and in the ongoing Advisory Opinion[60] request before the Inter-American Court of Human Rights, submitted by Colombia and Chile.

The Inter-American Court of Human Rights, especially in the case of the *Inhabitants of La Oroya v. Peru,*[61] took the same path as the European Court of Human Rights, conducting a broad and complete analysis of human rights

---

or groundwater resources within the indigenous territories of Lots 14 and 55 that are used by the victim indigenous communities, as well as to prevent their contamination or to remedy existing contamination; b) ensuring permanent access to drinking water for all persons belonging to the indigenous communities who are victims in this case; c) preventing the continued loss or degradation of forest resources in the specified territory, and striving for their gradual recovery; and d) ensuring permanent access to adequate nutrition, both nutritionally and culturally, for all persons belonging to the indigenous communities who are victims in the present case. 334. For the preparation of the study mentioned in the previous paragraph, the specialists in charge must possess the specific technical knowledge required for each task. Furthermore, these specialists must always take into account the views of the victim indigenous communities, expressed according to their own decision-making processes.

59 INTER-AMERICAN COURT OF HUMAN RIGHTS *Inhabitants of La Oroya v. Peru.* Available at:https://www.corteidh.or.cr/docs/casos/articulos/seriec_511_esp.pdf. para. 332.

60 "[...] in order to advance and accelerate the responses to the climate emergency by each State, collectively, regionally and globally, we are posing a series of questions to the Court that will allow it to provide guidance towards human rights-based solutions with an intersectional perspective." p. 2. INTER-AMERICAN COURT OF HUMAN RIGHTS. Advisory Opinion Request. Available at: https://www.corteidh.or.cr/docs/opiniones/soc_1_2023_pt.pdf.

61 "333. The Court recalls that in the present case, the international responsibility of the State was determined due to the failure to fulfil the duty of prevention. The international responsibility resulted from the environmental harm caused by the State when Centromin operated the CMLO, in the absence of adequate oversight measures by the State over the activities of the private company Doe Run, and from the adoption of regressive measures regarding environmental protection. These failures constituted a violation of the duty to prevent environmental damage, which was caused by exposure over the years to pollutants present in the air, water, and soil, and which posed a risk to health. According to the information in the file, which has been included in this Judgment, the air, soil, and water of La Oroya still contain pollutants emitted by the CMLO's activities. In light of this, the Court considers that it is the State's responsibility to adopt measures of restitution concerning the environment. 334.In this regard, the Court orders the State to carry out a baseline diagnostic to determine the level of pollution in the air, soil, and water in La Oroya, which must include an action plan to remedy the environmental damage. The State shall define the short, medium, and long-term actions required for the remediation of the affected areas." INTER-AMERICAN COURT OF HUMAN RIGHTS *Inhabitants of La Oroya v. Peru.* Available at:https://www.corteidh.or.cr/docs/casos/articulos/seriec_511_esp.pdf (original in Espanish).

treaties, recognising the international responsibility of the State for failure to comply with the duty of prevention.[62]

In their concurring opinion, Judges Ricardo C. Pérez Manrique (Uruguay), Eduardo Ferrer Mac-Gregor Poisot (Mexico), and Rodrigo Mudrovitsch (Brazil) retrace the entire historical evolution of the jurisprudence of the Inter-American Court of Human Rights and other courts on environmental matters, as well as the international commitments made by States and the Resolutions and Recommendations of international organisations in this area. It also revisits the obligations of States linked to the principles of prevention, precaution, cooperation, access to justice, political participation and access to information; it considers the environment as a common heritage of humanity and "[...] its link with a *jus cogens* norm" that imposes on States the duty of international solidarity, which is directly linked to intergenerational equity.[63]

The Advisory Opinion submitted at the Inter-American Court of Human Rights by the Republic of Colombia and the Republic of Chile, regarding Climate Emergency and Human Rights. In 2023, the States jointly requested an advisory opinion from the Inter-American Court of Human Rights (IACHR) on the climate emergency and its relationship to human rights obligations under the American Convention on Human Rights. This request is a significant development in climate litigation, as it asks the IACHR to clarify the extent to which States are responsible for protecting the environment and mitigating climate change impacts in ways that uphold the human rights of their citizens, especially those most vulnerable to environmental harm.

---

62 INTER-AMERICAN COURT OF HUMAN RIGHTS *Inhabitants of La Oroya v. Peru.* Available at:https://www.corteidh.or.cr/docs/casos/articulos/seriec_511_esp.pdf.

63 "171. The consideration of the environment as a common heritage of humanity and its link with a *jus cogens* norm imposes on States a duty of international collaboration or solidarity – also derived from the OAS Charter – in the formulation of policies, research, control and promotion of the environment. It is also necessary to combine efforts between individuals, companies, and States to achieve a real perspective of sustainable development. 172. One of the dimensions of the principle of intergenerational equity refers to its link with the environment. In this sense, it implies the duty of current generations to manage and administer the environment in a way that delivers to future generations an environment at least in the same conditions in which it was delivered to us by the generations that preceded us. It is similar to the administration of a trust whose beneficiaries are the next generations and is justified by the autonomous protection of the components of the environment, as well as by a duty of solidarity of the species as a human family". INTER-AMERICAN COURT OF HUMAN RIGHTS Inhabitants of La Oroya v. Peru. Voto Concurrente de los Jueces Ricardo C. Perez Marinque, Eduardo Ferrer Mac-Gregor Pisot y Rodrigo Mudrovitsch. Available at:https://www.corteidh.or.cr/docs/casos/articulos/seriec_511_esp.pdf.

While an advisory opinion is not a legally binding decision, it is a powerful tool that can guide States in their duties and obligations under international law. The potential reparations expected from such an opinion would depend on the Court's interpretation of how the right to a healthy environment intersects with other human rights, such as the rights to life, health, and an adequate standard of living. The advisory opinion could set the stage for future cases in which individuals and groups could seek reparations for harm caused by climate change. The key reparations likely to emerge from the advisory opinion can be grouped into two broad categories: preventive measures and remediation for past and ongoing harm.

What is expected by the Court in this advisory opinion is that it recognises the need for States to cooperate with preventive measures both for the environment and to avoid having to provide reparations in the near future to people who suffer from the adverse effects of climate change and environmental disasters. This is because an Advisory Opinion could not reach measures of reparation or compensation for damages caused once it has been requested by States.

However, one of the most significant expectations of the advisory opinion is that it can define the obligations of States in preventing and mitigating the adverse effects caused by climate change on the environment and consequently on human beings, leading to the violation of their rights. Such preventive measures could include: strengthening national environmental legislation in order to avoid the regression that has been occurring; climate change impact assessments; reparation of past and ongoing damages; compensation for victims who have been affected by floods, fires and prolonged droughts.

While the advisory opinion does not directly award individual compensation, it may set the stage for future litigation by affirming that victims of climate-induced harm, such as displaced persons, those suffering from health impacts, and individuals whose livelihoods have been disrupted by environmental degradation, have the right to seek reparations. This could include financial compensation for direct damages and compensation for loss of life, health, or property due to climate events. It also strongly recommends that States seek to restore damaged ecosystems. In this regard, the Court could recommend that States take steps to restore ecosystems that have been severely damaged by environmental degradation, such as deforestation, soil erosion, and biodiversity loss. Such restoration efforts would be considered part of broader reparations for environmental harm, ensuring that the negative consequences of climate change are mitigated for current and future generations. In addition to considering that there must be a guarantee of access to a healthy environment, considering that the right to a healthy environment is intrinsic to the right to life and health under the American Convention on Human Rights and Advisory Opinion No. 17/23. This would mean that States are obliged to ensure that the environment is protected and that individuals, especially vulnerable groups, have access to the resources necessary for survival, such as clean air, water and food. The Advisory Opinion could therefore define reparations as a state obligation to provide a healthy environment as a preventive measure against future harm.

Thus, climate litigation promoted and connected with human rights violations foreseen in treaties ratified by States can be a way for them to take internal measures to contain and reduce greenhouse gas emissions,[64] considering the determinations of regional human rights courts. Judgments that impose positive duties can also determine the implementation of national policies to achieve the goals proposed in the signed commitments and the targets set for climate change. However, perhaps the most effective way to repair environmental damage resulting from the effects caused by climate change is still litigation in national courts[65] and after exhausting domestic remedies.

4.3 *Reparation in the International Court of Justice*

An Advisory Opinion request is currently before the International Court of Justice, in accordance with UNGA Resolution 77/276, concerning the obligations of States with regard to climate change. The oral proceedings concluded at the end of 2024, with the participation of over 96 States and 11 international organisations presenting their arguments before the judges of the Court. Several statements submitted by member states reference the relationship between climate obligations, human rights, sovereignty, as well as the respect for and adherence to agreements made. Many of the submissions also address issues such as reparations, effective remedies, and the differentiation of responsibilities. But it is crucial to mention that the Advisory Opinion on climate change reaches the Court at a time when the Court has already made significant progress in recognising the principles of environmental protection and the possibility of environmental reparations for damages caused by the actions or omissions of States.[66]

64 Posner EA. 2007. Climate change and international human rights litigation: a critical appraisal. Univ. Pa. Law Rev. 155:1925–45.

65 Posner EA. 2007. Climate change and international human rights litigation: a critical appraisal. Univ. Pa. Law Rev. 155:1925–45; Peel J, Osofsky H.M. 2018. A rights turn in climate change litigation? Transnat. Environ. Law 7(1):37–67.

66 P.G.Noschang. The Jurisprudence of International Court of Justice and Environment protection: a long an slow path towards the recognition of the principles of international environmental law. Revista de Direito Ambiental, v. 115, pp. 197–224, 2024.; C.Derani,

It can be demonstrated that the cases adjudicated by the International Court of Justice up until 2010 did not seek to determine violations of international environmental law standards. It was only in the Pulp Mills Case that the International Court of Justice began to establish the necessity for an environmental impact assessment for a project and to recognise the principles of International Environmental Law. It is equally important to highlight that, following the Pulp Mills Case, the Court has progressively advanced in applying the principles of international environmental law. Specifically, the requirement to present an environmental impact assessment is closely linked to the principles of precaution, prevention, and prior notification.[67]

Considering that the Court's jurisprudence has progressively recognised reparation measures when States violate bilateral or multilateral treaties, causing transboundary environmental damage, the path is already open to recognise the responsibility of States for damages caused by climate change. It is worth noting that the effects of climate change are part of international environmental law, although a distinct climate law is already being advocated. In any case, as previously mentioned, it is impossible to understand the effects of climate change without integrating them within the broader context of socio-environmental damage; that is, the right to a clean and healthy environment for all people, while preserving nature.

At this time the questions submitted to the ICJ are:

a. What are the obligations of States under international law to ensure the protection of the climate system and other parts of the environment from anthropogenic emissions of greenhouse gases for States and for present and future generations;
b. What are the legal consequences under these obligations for States where they, by their acts and omissions, have caused significant harm to the climate system and other parts of the environment, with respect to: (i) States, including, in particular, small island developing States, which due to their geographical circumstances and level of development, are injured or specially affected by or are particularly vulnerable

P. G. Noschang. The jurisdiction of the International Court of Justice in cases of territorial damage caused to States by climate change. Revista de Direito Internacional, v. 19, pp. 46–63, 2022.

67 P. G. Noschang. The Jurisprudence of International Court of Justice and Environment protection: a long an slow path towards the recognition of the principles of international environmental law.Revista de Direito Ambiental, v. 115, pp. 197–224, 2024. C. Derani, P. G. Noschang.The jurisdiction of the International Court of Justice in cases of territorial damage caused to States by climate change. Revista de Direito Internacional, v. 19, pp. 46–63, 2022.

to the adverse effects of climate change? (ii) Peoples and individuals of the present and future generations affected by the adverse effects of climate change?"

It should be emphasised that the aim is not to analyse all the statements and observations submitted by the 96 States, but rather to highlight certain points linking the repair of damages caused by the adverse effects of climate change and the protection of human rights. For instance, the Democratic Republic of the Congo underscores the relationship between climate change and human rights when addressing the displacement of people due to droughts or rising sea levels (already recognised by the IOM and the UNSC). It also highlights that "the duty of due diligence must also be linked to respect for human rights. This has a practical consequence: today, the principle of due diligence requires that no harm be caused not only to other States, but also to all individuals who come within their territorial and extraterritorial jurisdiction. Due diligence is thus no longer limited to an inter-state transboundary dimension."

Some Latin American States, such as Colombia,[68] Uruguay,[69] and Costa Rica,[70] refer to the jurisprudence of the Inter-American human rights system, emphasising the integrated perspective of human rights, while Chile highlights the importance of Advisory Opinion 23/17, with a special focus on reparation for harm caused to peoples and individuals of the present and future generations. As the European Union's[71] comments mention, the jurisprudence of the ECtHR in the KlimaSeniorinnen case is also relevant, interpreting the regional human rights regime applicable to the States of the Council of Europe, as in the Duarte Agostinho case.

In the other hand China and United States of America presented other arguments concerning human rights. As stated in Chinas comments:

68 INTERNATIONAL COURT OF JUSTICE. Written Statement of Colombia. Available at: https://www.icj-cij.org/sites/default/files/case-related/187/187-20240311-wri-01-00-en.pdf.

69 INTERNATIONAL COURT OF JUSTICE. Written Statement of the Uruguay. Available at: https://www.icj-cij.org/sites/default/files/case-related/187/187-20240322-wri-16-00-en.pdf.

70 INTERNATIONAL COURT OF JUSTICE. Written Statement of Costa Rica. Available at: https://www.icj-cij.org/sites/default/files/case-related/187/187-20240326-wri-04-00-en.pdf.

71 INTERNATIONAL COURT OF JUSTICE. Written Comment of European Union. Available at: https://www.icj-cij.org/sites/default/files/case-related/187/187-20240719-wri-01-00-en.pdf.

> In general, it is often difficult to define the indirect adverse effects of anthropogenic GHG emissions on human rights as a violation of human rights. First, the main type of GHG emissions, such as carbon dioxide, are inherently harmless and are indispensable for life and the Earth's ecosystem. It is only the historical accumulation of excessive GHG emissions that may result in indirect adverse effects on human rights. Second, according to existing international law and domestic laws, anthropogenic GHG emissions are not illegal activities. Finally, the causal relationship between anthropogenic GHG emissions and their adverse effects on human rights is complex. It is difficult to establish a causal link between the emissions and specific weather and climate events that affect human rights. Given the diverse sources of these emissions, attributing the adverse effects on human rights to specific States is difficult.[72]

According with Mayers discussions on the nature of climate change reparations are likely to contribute to such doctrinal developments. Comprehensive reparations, in the context of climate change, are not only politically unrealistic but also potentially detrimental to friendly relations between nations. Furthermore, the indeterminacy of applicable corrective obligations and the range of demands for comprehensive or expansive reparations schemes have effectively blocked any explicit recognition of responsibility by industrialised states. Given the high risks of admitting responsibility, Western leaders often resorted to a stance of denial – denying any scientific evidence of anthropogenic climate change or (often less subtly) dismissing any form of "fanatical" finger-pointing and any justification for specific obligations of industrial states regarding climate change. As the concept of loss and damage gains traction in international climate change negotiations, and bargaining power shifts in favour of emerging economies and developing states more broadly, an opportunity window may be opening for industrial states to recognise their responsibilities and provide some form of reparations, thus offering a strong economic and political signal for climate change mitigation. In this process, however, the relevance of the international legal principle of liability in the context of climate change can only be advanced on the basis of a differentiated understanding of applicable corrective obligations, recognising valid reasons for a reasonable reduction in reparations. In relation to a continuing wrongful act with the most alarming consequences for civilisation and

72 INTERNATIONAL COURT OF JUSTICE. Written Comments of the United States of America. Available at: https://www.icj-cij.org/sites/default/files/case-related/187/187-20240815-wri-09-00-en.pdf.

humanity, climate change reparations must, above all, be designed to provide a strong incentive for rapid reductions in greenhouse gas emissions.[73]

5 Final Remarks

Thus, it is understood that "discussing this theme before a regional court allows, in addition, to address not only national or regional obligations, but also those related to international cooperation and shared but differentiated responsibilities, from a human rights perspective."[74] It is possible to realise that human rights protection systems and national laws and courts will have an important role in consolidating the right to a healthy environment and combating the effects of climate change that directly and/or indirectly affect the population and the environment.

In the Inter-American human rights protection system, there has been progress and recognition of the causes and consequences of environmental disasters and the effects caused by climate change, especially in recent years. Although the first documents did not link the two themes, they always mentioned the concern and impact of climate change, especially on vulnerable populations. It is worth remembering that the relationship between environmental preservation and sustainable development with human rights is due to the recognition of the intergenerational, interdependent and indivisible nature of human rights approved by the Vienna Action Plan of 1993, but previously connected by the Stockholm Declaration of 1972.

The Court's conclusions clarify the obligations of States regarding human rights in the context of the climate emergency. By emphasizing preventive measures, compensation for damages, and international cooperation, the opinion offers a legal framework for holding States accountable for the impacts of climate change on human rights and guides future climate litigation in the region. Ultimately, the advisory opinion has the potential not only to shape legal standards on climate-related human rights but also to promote a global understanding of the responsibility States have to ensure the

73 B. Mayer. Asian Journal of International Law, v 7, Issue 1, January 2017, pp. 185–216. Available at: https://www.cambridge.org/core/journals/asian-journal-of-international-law/article/climate-change-reparations-and-the-law-and-practice-of-state-responsibility/59BEEB3F2AE39E8A2DA15815B25D3270.

74 INTER-AMERICAN COURT OF HUMAN RIGHTS. **Advisory Opinion Request.** Available at: https://www.corteidh.or.cr/docs/opiniones/soc_1_2023_pt.pdf. p. 2.

protection of vulnerable populations against the devastating effects of climate change.

References

American States Organisation. American Declaration of the Rights and Duties of Man. Available at:www.oas.orgdilaccess_to_information_human_right_American_Declaration_of_the_Rights_and_Duties_of_Man.pdf

Berger, M. & Wentz, J., Climate Change and Human Rights (UN Environment Programme (UNEP), 2015)

Derani, C., Noschang, P. G. The jurisdiction of the International Court of Justice in cases of territorial damage caused to States by climate change. Revista de Direito Internacional, v. 19, pp. 46–63, 2022.

Earthjustice. Petition to the Inter-American Commission on Human Rights Seeking Relief from Violations of the Rights of Arctic Athabaskan Peoples Resulting from Rapid Arctic Warming and Melting Caused by Emissions of Black Carbon by Canada. Available at: https://earthjustice.org/sites/default/files/AAC_PETITION_13–04–23a.pdf.

Ebeku, K. SA., The right to a satisfactory environment and the African Commission. African Human Rights Journal. 2003 (3). pp. 149–166.

European Court of Human Rights. Duarte Agostinho and others vs. Portugal and others (application no. 39371/20). Available at: https://hudoc.echr.coe.int/fre?i=00161188.

European Court of Human Rights. Dubetska and others vs Ukraine. Julgado em Fevereiro de 2011. Available at: https://www.elaw.org/content/european-court-human-rights-dubetskaand-others-v-ukraine-application-no-3049903–20110210-ec.

European Court of Human Rights. Klima Seniorinnen vs. Switzerland (Application No. 53600/20). Available at: https://hudoc.echr.coe.int/tur?i=001–233206.

European Court of Human Rights. Case of Carême v. France (Application no. 7189/21)

Heri, C. Too Big to Remedy? What Climate Cases Tell Us About the Remedial Role of Human Rights. European Convention on Human Rights Law Review, The. Available at: https://brill.com/view/journals/eclr/5/3/article-p400_007.xml. Vol.5 p. 400–422, 2024.

Inter-American Commission. Inuit People Petition 1413/05 vs. The United States, December 7, 2005.

Inter-American Commission. Redesca. Resolution 3/21. Climate Emergency. Scope of Inter-American Human Rights Obligations. Available at: https://www.oas.org/en/iachr/decisions/pdf/2021/resolucion_3–21_ENG.pdf

Inter-American Court of Human Rights. Comunidades Indígenas Miembros de la Asociación Lhaka Honhat (Nuestra Tierra) Vs. Argentina Case. Judgement of 6 February 2020 (Fondo, Reparaciones y Costas). 2020. Available at: <http://www.corteidh.or.cr/docs/casos/articulos/seriec_400_esp.pdf

Inter-American Court of Human Rights. Advisory Opinion Request. Available at: https://www.corteidh.or.cr/docs/opiniones/soc_1_2023_pt.pdf.

Inter-American Court of Human Rights. Advisory Opinion 23/17. Available at:https://www.corteidh.or.cr/docs/opiniones/seriea_23_ing.pdf

Inter-American Court of Human Rights Inhabitants of La Oroya v. Peru. Voto Concurrente De Los Jueces Ricardo C. Pérez Manrique, Eduardo Ferrer Mac-Gregor Poisot Y Rodrigo Mudrovitsch. Available at: https://www.corteidh.or.cr/docs/casos/articulos/seriec_511_esp.pdf

Inter-American Court of Human Rights Inhabitants of La Oroya v. Peru. Available at: https://www.corteidh.or.cr/docs/casos/articulos/seriec_511_esp.pdf

International Court of Justice. Advisory Opinion. Obligations of States in respect of Climate Change Available at: https://www.icj-cij.org/case/187

International Court of Justice. Written Statement of the Democratic Republic of the Congo. Available at: https://www.icj-cij.org/sites/default/files/case-related/187/187–20240304-wri-01–00-en.pdfpara142–145.

International Court of Justice. Written Observation of China. Available at https://www.icj-cij.org/sites/default/files/case-related/187/187–20240322-wri-19–00-en.pdf

International Court of Justice. Written Statement of the Colombia. Available at: https://www.icj-cij.org/sites/default/files/case-related/187/187–20240311-wri-01–0 0-en.pdf

International Court of Justice. Written Statement of Costa Rica. Available at: https://www.icj-cij.org/sites/default/files/case-related/187/187–20240326-wri-04–00-en.pdf

International Court of Justice. Written Comment of European Union. Available at: https://www.icj-cij.org/sites/default/files/case-related/187/187–20240719-wri-01–0 0-en.pdf

International Court of Justice. Written Statement of the Uruguai. Available at: https://www.icj-cij.org/sites/default/files/case-related/187/187–20240322-wri-16–00-en.pdf

Letsas, G. The European Court's Legitimacy After KlimaSeniorinnen European Convention on Human Rights Law Review 5 (2024) 444–453

Mayer, B. Climate Change Reparations and the Law and Practice of State Responsibility. Asian Journal of International Law , v 7, Issue 1, January 2017, pp. 185–216. Available at: https://www.cambridge.org/core/journals/asian-journal-of-internat

ional-law/article/climate-change-reparations-and-the-law-and-practice-of-state-responsibility/59BEEB3F2AE39E8A2DA15815B25D3270

Netherlands. Urgenda Foundation v. State of Netherlands, Hague District Court, C/09/456689/HA ZA 13–1396 Judgment (24 June 2015)

Noschang, P.G. The Jurisprudence of International Court of Justice and Environment protection: a long an slow path towards the recognition of the principles of international environmental law. Revista de Direito Ambiental, v. 115, pp. 197–224, 2024.

J. Peel & H. Osofsky 2018. A rights turn in climate change litigation? Transnatl. Environ. Law 7(1):37–67

OHCHR. General Comment No. 26 (2023) on children's rights and the environment with a special focus on climate change. Geneva, 26 ago. 2023. Available at: https://www.ohchr.org/en/documents/general-comments-and-recommendations/general-comment-no-26–2023-childrens-rights-and.

Posner, EA. 2007. Climate change and international human rights litigation: a critical appraisal. Univ. Pa. Law Rev. 155:1925–45

Rocha, A., Tigre, M. A., Stoyanova, V., Xavier, E., Martini, C., Cohen, M. Reparation for Climate Change at the ECtHR Climate Law. Sabin Law Center. Available at: https://blogs.law.columbia.edu/climatechange/2024/05/10/reparation-for-climate-change-at-the-ecthr/

Sassen, Saskia. Expulsion. Brutality and Complexity in the Global Economy. Harvard University Press, 2014.

Stoyanova, V. Correlativity Between Human Rights and Positive Obligations and Its Role for the Execution of Judgments Delivered by the European Court of Human Rights/. European Convention on Human Rights Law Review 5 (2024) 455–486.

Torre-Schaub, M. The European Court of Human Rights' Kick into Touch: Some Comments under Carême v. France. Climate Law. Available at: https://blogs.law.columbia.edu/climatechange/2024/04/19/the-european-court-of-human-rights-kick-into-touch-some-comments-under-careme-v-france/#molongui-disabled-link

Trindade, A.C, Antonio Augusto. International law for humankind: towards a new jus gentium (II) – General Course on Public International Law, 317. Leiden/The Netherlands: Brill/Nijhoff, Recueil des Cours de l'Académie de Droit international de la Haye, 2005. pp. 395–396.

United Nations Development Program. Available at: <https://www.undp.org/content/dam/brazil/docs/ODS/undp-br-ods-ParisAgreement.pdf>.

United Nations Human Rights Committee – UNHRC; Committee on Civil and Political Rights – CCPR. Views adopted by the Committee under article 5 (4) of the Optional Protocol, concerning communication No. 2728/2016.

United Nations. United Nations Framework Convention on Climate Change and Article 24 of Paris Agreement. United Nations Development Program. Available at:

<https://www.undp.org/content/dam/brazil/docs/ODS/undp-br-ods-ParisAgreement.pdf>.

UN Committee on the Rights of the Child. CRC/C/88/D/104/2019. Sacchi, et al. v. Argentina, et al.

UNGA Resolution 77/276. Available at: https://documents.un.org/doc/undoc/ltd/n23/094/52/pdf/n2309452.pdf

United Nations. Comitê dos Direitos da Criança responsabiliza cinco países por falta de ação climática. Available at: https://news.un.org/pt/story/2021/10/1766152

United Nations. HRC. Resolution (A/HRC/48/13). Available at: https://documents.un.org/doc/undoc/ltd/g21/270/15/pdf/g2127015.pdf?OpenElement.

Viñuales, J. E. , La distribution de la charge de protéger l'environnement: Expressions juridiques de la solidarité, in A. Supiot (ed.), La responsabilité solidaire. Paris: Conférences du Collège de France, 2018.

Voigt, C., Grant, E., 'Editorial: The legitimacy of human rights courts in environmental disputes' 2015) 6 Journal of Human Rights and the Environment, 131–8.

CHAPTER 9

Rethinking Development/Reparations Programmes and the Role of Third States in Transitional Justice

Prosper Simbarashe Maguchu[1]

1 Introduction

The landscape of reparations for survivors of gross human rights violations is undergoing a significant transformation. Historically, reparations were distinct from developmental projects. Reparations are often presented as mechanisms of justice and accountability, aimed at addressing specific harms caused by historical injustices such as colonial exploitation, systemic oppression, or conflict-related atrocities. In contrast, developmental projects typically focus on broader socioeconomic improvements, such as infrastructure development, poverty alleviation, or capacity building, without necessarily addressing past injustices or targeting specific groups. A second question is whether individuals have a right to reparation for a violation of the primary rule of international law. This is not obvious, as within the State-centred framework of international law, it may also only be the States who claim a violation of individual rights on behalf of their citizens.[2] Some international human rights law (IHRL) regimes provide a clear legal foundation for an individual right to reparation. First of all, human rights law offers, on the primary level, rights to individuals where it is applicable. The issue of applicability can, of course, be problematic, especially with regard to the extraterritorial application. Numerous human rights law treaties contain provisions on reparation that oblige the State parties to guarantee effective reparation for violations of the treaties' terms through the domestic legal system. Based on their wording, they do not provide for an individual right under international law to claim reparation but create an obligation for States to act accordingly.[3]

1 Assistant Professor, Vrije Universiteit Amsterdam, p.s.maguchu@vu.nl.

2 See the decision of the German Federal Constitutional Court that took exactly that position: BverfG, 2 BvR 2660/06, inadmissibility decision of 13.8.2013 – Varvarin, esp. paras. 43–47.

3 C Marxen, Unpacking the International Law on Reparation for Victims of Armed Conflict, in: Zeitschrift für ausländisches öffentliches Recht und Völkerrecht, p. 525.

 | DOI:10.1163/9789004716742_010

In addition to this, some human rights regimes offer individuals a clear right to also claim reparation for violations of their rights. Reparation has to be understood broadly here, in the sense defined above. The regional human rights systems all offer individuals a right to claim reparation and establish concrete procedures for realizing this right.[4] This is typically addressed within international forums between states.[5] Moreover, the chapter explores the role of third party foreign states in regard to reparations.

However, a new paradigm is emerging, wherein foreign states play an increasingly crucial role in fulfilling this neglected right through official development aid initiatives, that is, financial assistance provided by governments or international organizations to support the economic development and welfare of developing countries. This trend is particularly relevant for Africa, where low economic development and large numbers of potential beneficiaries have hindered the implementation of comprehensive reparations programs.[6] Africa's unique context challenges the conventional understanding of reparations within transitional justice.[7] States in the region face significant limits in their capacity to implement effective reparations programs.[8] Consequently, driven by a growing recognition of the need for justice and accountability, and the ability to leverage recovered ill-gotten gains from perpetrators, foreign states – acting as third-party actors – are increasingly becoming key facilitators of reparations on the continent.

This chapter argues that this growing involvement of foreign states, through international development aid agencies and civil society organizations, repre-

---

4 *Id.*, p. 526.

5 For instance in the interstate case of Ahmadou Sadio Diallo Guinea filed an Application instituting proceedings against the Democratic Republic of the Congo (DRC) in respect of a dispute concerning 'serious violations of international law' alleged to have been committed upon the person of Mr. Ahmadou Sadio Diallo, a Guinean national. The Court found that it is a general principle of law that every State has the right to require other States to comply with international law in respect of the person of any of its nationals (*Republic of Guinea v. Democratic Republic of the Congo*, ICJ Rep date). However, in the case of *Velásquez-Rodríguez v. Honduras*, Judgment of July 29, 1988 (Merits) the Inter-American Court of Human Rights was the first to articulate the state duty to make moral and material reparations to individual victims.

6 OHCHR, UN Rule of Law Tools: Reparations (2008), p. 32.

7 In this chapter, transitional justice is comprehensively defined as an array of strategies employed by societies to address the legacies of extensive or systematic human rights abuses. These strategies are implemented as societies transition from periods of violent conflict or oppression towards a state of peace, democracy, adherence to the rule of law, and the respect for individual and collective rights.

8 See OHCHR, n(6).

sent a significant shift, as these actors are demonstrating a greater willingness and capacity to address injustices and realizing reparations as a right of victims of human rights at the international level. This development challenges both development and transitional justice practitioners to revisit and integrate the linkages between reparations and development more strategically. By leveraging assets recovered from perpetrators and channelling them through international development aid agencies and national civil society organizations as reparations (or development aid), this approach offers practical and conceptual advantages in the fight against grand corruption and gross human rights violations.

This chapter expands upon the research conducted by Naomi Roht-Arriaza and Katharine Orlovsky, who analysed the connection between reparations programs and development through the lens of social integration theory.[9] While their study primarily emphasizes state capacity as both a prerequisite for and a potential consequence of implementing reparations, this chapter diverges from their approach by investigating the involvement of third-party foreign states[10] Specifically, it examines the role of states not directly implicated in the human rights violations in facilitating reparations for victims of severe abuses. This inquiry focuses on scenarios where the responsible state lacks the capability or willingness to provide reparations due to low governance and corruption.

Furthermore, this chapter contends that the growing involvement of international development agencies in reparations offers a crucial avenue for promoting justice and fostering healing across Africa. It begins by exploring the existing debates surrounding reparations and their relationship to development, as well as the role of third-party foreign states in the individual right to reparations under international human rights law. The chapter then discusses concrete examples of reparations initiatives undertaken by external states, specifically focusing on recent efforts by the UK, US, and France to address grand corruption and gross human rights violations in Africa. This section critically examines the challenges and opportunities associated with this emerging trend, including the need for political will on the part of victim

9 ICTJ, A Complementary Relationship: Reparations and Development, 2009. This project explores the relationship between transitional justice and development, two fields that have traditionally progressed in isolation both academically and in practice. The project aims to identify and analyse specific synergies between justice and development, articulating how these initiatives should be designed and implemented to reinforce their shared goals of citizenship, social integration, governance, and peacebuilding. The project is overseen by Roger Duthie, Research Associate in the Research Unit at the ICTJ.

10 Ibid.

states, navigating the legal complexities involved, and ensuring the effective and equitable distribution of reparations resources. Finally, the chapter concludes with key findings and raises pertinent discussion points to instigate further research and encourage continued practice in this area.

2 The Right to Reparations: Bridging the Reparations-Development Divide and Claiming Reparations in Foreign States

This section explores the reparations-development dichotomy and examines the role of third-party foreign states in facilitating reparations for victims of gross human rights violations. The analysis specifically excludes reparations for historical injustices directly perpetrated by these foreign states, such as colonialism or slavery.[11] Furthermore, the focus is confined to reparations financed by the resources of the perpetrators, rather than those of the third-party states.[12] The following sections will elaborate on these specific aspects.

2.1 *The Age-Old Reparations/Development Dispute*

Conventionally, transitional justice has advocated for a distinct separation between reparations, aimed at redressing past injustices, and development, which concentrates on broader societal advancement.[13] The argument goes that there is a clear distinction between the two: reparations are intended to acknowledge and compensate for past wrongs or harms inflicted upon specific groups or individuals.[14] While development addresses the broader societal

11 See for example T Craemer, 'International Reparations for Slavery and the Slave Trade', Journal of Black Studies 49 (7) 2018, 694–713; R E Howard-Hassmann, 'Reparations for the Slave Trade: Rhetoric, Law, History and Political Realities', Canadian Journal of African Studies / Revue Canadienne Des Études Africaines 41 (3) 2007, 427–454; M Serumaga 'A Call for Reparations for Slavery and Colonisation', Transition 119 2016, 1–5.

12 States can collectively contribute to reparations even when they are not directly responsible for the atrocities. A prime example is the Trust Fund for Victims, which operates independently of the International Criminal Court (ICC). Established in 2004 by the Assembly of States Parties in accordance with Article 79 of the Rome Statute, the Trust Fund's mission is to support and implement programs that address harms resulting from genocide, crimes against humanity, war crimes, and aggression. Similarly, the Extraordinary African Chambers' appeals judges mandated the implementation of reparations through a 'victims' compensation fund,' modelled after the ICC's Trust Fund for Victims. This fund was eventually established under the auspices of the African Union (AU), following a resolution in July 2016 and the adoption of the fund's statute in early 2018.

13 OHCHR, n(6), p. 26.

14 Ibid.

need for essential goods and services that a government has an obligation to provide to all its citizens.[15]

Critics contend that conflating reparations with development programmes, undermines the unique purpose of reparations as targeted compensation for past injustices, leading to several significant implications. First, it undermines the purpose of reparations: by equating reparations with standard development assistance dilutes the acknowledgment and focus on past wrongs.[16] Second, benefits become rights, not compensation: when reparations are presented as simply providing basic goods, victims correctly perceive them as rights to which they are entitled as citizens, thus negating the restorative intent of reparations.[17] Third, transient benefit of development as reparations: it has been argued that development programs framed as reparations can be beneficial only if they prioritize investment in affected areas, leading to those victims receiving basic services before the general population. However, this benefit disappears once those services become widely accessible.[18]

A study conducted by Naomi Roht-Arriaza and Katharine Orlovsky for the International Centre for Transitional Justice (ICTJ), a leading non-governmental organization in the field, reveals that reparations and development are typically conceptualized and approached independently.[19] However, for survivors and victims, the demand for both often arises simultaneously. The findings indicate that, in practice, reparations and official development aid are interconnected in specific ways. This underscores the notion that the distinction between reparations and development may primarily exist within the intellectual discourses on transitional justice by scholars, while for victims and survivors, the delineation between reparations and development is largely inconsequential.

The research by Naomi Roht-Arriaza and Katharine Orlovsky analyses these links within the context of the post-conflict or political transition period.[20] This present contribution uses these findings as a point of departure, acknowledging that transitional justice has evolved beyond its initial transitional settings. It can now be applied in scenarios where repression persists and no

15 Ibid.

16 Ibid.

17 Ibid.

18 Ibid.

19 Naomi Roht-Arriaza and Katharine Orlovsky, 'A Complementary Relationship: Reparations and Development', (2009) International Center for Transitional Justice <https://www.ictj.org/sites/default/files/ICTJ-Development-Reparations-ResearchBrief-2009-English.pdf> accessed 25 January 2025., 1.

20 Ibid, 2.

transition is occurring.[21] This evolution complicates the process for victims seeking reparations for human rights violations under the same administration responsible for these violations, thereby necessitating reliance on third-party foreign states as the only viable option for claiming reparations.

Moreover, this contribution diverges from the aforementioned study by Roht-Arriaza and Orlovsky, which primarily examines the relationship between reparations programs and the state, emphasizing state capacity as both a precondition and a potential by-product of reparations delivery.[22] In contrast, this chapter will focus on the role of third-party foreign states rather than the perpetrator state or the victims of human rights abuses. While this section indicates that this contribution will not address instances where states propose development aid in lieu of reparations – such as in cases where demands for reparations for historical injustices like slavery and colonialism have been refused – the paragraphs below do engage with examples of such instances. These discussions are included to offer a more nuanced understanding of how states balance development aid and reparations within the framework of transitional justice.

The first case involves claims against Germany for war reparations for crimes committed during World War II, claims as well as proceedings by representatives of the Ovaherero and Namaqua indigenous people before a district court in New York for crimes committed by Imperial Germany at the beginning of the 20th century in what is now Namibia.[23] While the German government has acknowledged these atrocities as genocide, the issue of reparations remains contentious. In 2021, Germany pledged €1.1 billion ($1.34 billion) in financial aid over 30 years to support infrastructure, healthcare, and training projects in Namibia.[24] However, this offer has been criticized by the Herero and Namaqua Council of Chiefs, who argue that the funding constitutes development aid rather than reparations and fails to adequately address the historical injustices inflicted upon their ancestors.[25] The Council consid-

21 P De Grief, '2012 Report of the Special Rapporteur on the promotion of truth, justice, reparation and guarantees of non-recurrence', 5–6, paras. 15–16.

22 N Roht-Arriaza and K Orlovsky, n(19), 2.

23 United States District Court, Southern District of New York, Class Action Complaint, Civ. No. 17–0062, New York, 5.1.2017.

24 See the Joint Declaration by The Federal Republic Of Germany and The Republic Of Namibia 'United in Remembrance of Our Colonial Past, United in Our Will to Reconcile, United in Our Vision of the Future' (19 December 2024).

25 Deutsche Welle, 'Ethnic leaders in Namibia reject German genocide apology' (Deutsche Welle, 31 May 2021) <https://www.dw.com/en/namibia-chiefs-reject-insulting-german-aid-offer-over-colonial-killings/a-57731356> accessed 25 January 2025.

ers the amount "insulting" and "unacceptable," emphasizing the need for a direct link between the funds and the concept of reparations.[26]

Paralleling the Ovaherero and Namaqua case, in Kenya the Mau Mau lawsuit filed in against the British government represents another instance of contested reparations for colonial-era abuses.[27] The lawsuit, brought by Kenyan representatives of the Mau Mau uprising, sought compensation for human rights violations perpetrated by British colonial forces during the 1950s. Although the British government recognized and acknowledged historical injustices, the negotiations concerning reparations remained highly contentious. The British reportedly offered an increase in development aid in exchange for the withdrawal of the reparations claim.[28] This proposal, however, was rejected by the Mau Mau representatives.[29]

The contrasting responses to the offers of development aid in the Ovaherero and Namaqua and Mau Mau cases highlight a critical distinction between reparations and development assistance. While both aim to address historical injustices and improve societal conditions, their specific purposes and implications differ significantly. Reparations serve as a form of direct compensation for past wrongs, acknowledging specific harms inflicted upon a particular group or individual. Conversely, development aid focuses on broader, often long-term, economic or social improvements that may not directly address the specific needs arising from historical injustices.

This distinction is crucial in the context of this Chapter, which specifically focuses on reparations for violations caused by the state of the victims nationality, discussed in the following section.

2.2 *Reparations for Human Rights Violations and the Role of Third Party Foreign States*

Although states have instituted reparations programs to address violations of human rights and humanitarian law following periods of conflict or authoritarian rule, these initiatives often fall short of comprehensive justice. One of the most frequently cited examples of reparation in Africa is the South African reparations program implemented by the Truth and Reconciliation Commis-

26 Ibid.

27 *Ndiki Mutua, Paulo Nzili, Wambugu Wa Nyingi, Jane Muthoni Mara and Susan Ngondi v. The Foreign and Commonwealth Office*, [2012] EWHC 2678(QB).

28 Claims from the ICTJ.

29 Ibid.

sion (TRC).[30] While the payment of reparations has been acknowledged as a core mechanism of transitional justice, the South African state has not yet taken significant steps to award reparations to victims of gross human rights violations through its national courts. This raises the pertinent question: do victims have the right to claim reparations in foreign states?

To explore the involvement of third-party foreign states in facilitating reparations for victims of gross human rights violations using South Africa as a case study, one can examine several "apartheid lawsuits" brought outside South Africa under the US Alien Tort Claims Act (ATCA) of 1789.[31] This US statute allows plaintiffs to bring actions based on modern human rights laws in American courts. A notable example is the Khulumani case, initiated by the Khulumani Support Group, which represents victims of apartheid. These plaintiffs, including those who had shared their stories with the TRC and others who had not engaged with the TRC process, sought reparations in the US against multinational corporations that had conducted business with the apartheid government. The US courts ultimately dismissed the Khulumani lawsuit, a decision largely anticipated due to substantial opposition from both South African and US governments.

Historically, the ATCA was employed in cases such as *Filartiga v. Pena-Irala*,[32] which allowed plaintiffs to bring actions based on modern human rights laws in the US. This precedent was affirmed by the US Supreme Court in *Sosa v. Alvarez-Machain*, establishing that foreigners could use the ATCA to sue for human rights abuses committed worldwide.[33] However, recent Supreme Court decisions suggest a shift towards limiting the universality of such claims, reflecting heightened concerns about foreign entanglements. This trend complicates the ability of survivors to seek reparations through this legal avenue. Multinational corporations, backed by several governments

30 The Truth and Reconciliation Commission (TRC) established the Committee on Reparations and Rehabilitation (CRR), which was tasked with identifying victims, soliciting input from civil society regarding appropriate forms of reparations, and designing recommendations for a government-administered final reparations program. Additionally, the CRR undertook the administration of an urgent reparations program, addressing the immediate needs of over 14,000 victims of human rights violations.

31 Three groups of plaintiffs filed lawsuits against multiple multinational corporations that conducted business in South Africa during apartheid. These actions were consolidated and transferred to the District Court of New York. The plaintiffs, comprising the Ntsebeza, Digwamaje, and Khulumani groups, contended that the defendants had violated international law by engaging in business activities in South Africa during the apartheid era and by providing resources to the apartheid government.

32 *Filartiga v Pena-Irala*, 630 F.2d 876, 844 (2d Cir. 1980).

33 *Sosa v Alvarez-Machain*, 542 U.S. 692 (2004).

including those of the US and the UK, have frequently petitioned the US Supreme Court to prevent foreigners from filing lawsuits in America for human rights violations committed elsewhere. The Khulumani case forms part of a broader trend of lawsuits filed by individuals in third-party countries, igniting debate over the jurisdictional scope of the right to reparation. The case highlights the complexities and challenges of seeking reparations through third-party foreign legal systems, especially when facing diplomatic and political resistance.

There remains significant uncertainty regarding whether states are obligated to establish jurisdiction for human rights cases in the absence of explicit treaty provisions. Some states and commentators argue against such an interpretation, arguing that states' obligations are generally confined to their own jurisdiction unless explicitly extended.[34] Nonetheless, states have found ways to grant third-party foreign claimants the right to seek reparations.[35] One effective approach has been leveraging the nexus between corruption and human rights. By linking corruption to human rights violations, practitioners can utilize domestic, regional, and international human rights mechanisms to claim damages for violations related to corruption. This emerging practice illustrates how the transnational nature of anti-corruption efforts has fostered a strong impetus for states to exercise universal or extraterritorial jurisdiction in cases of grand corruption and gross human rights violations.

Moreover, foreign states have developed mechanisms to ensure that reparations/development aids are not redirected to perpetrators or corrupt officials who may still hold power. This is particularly important in contexts where transitional justice mechanisms are implemented even in the absence of a political transition, with perpetrators still in control. Such situations require innovative approaches to ensure accountability and the effective use of resources. Consequently, the distribution of development aid and reparations is often managed through development aid agencies and civil society organizations, which serve as intermediaries. The examples provided below illustrate this emerging trend and the increasing acceptance of such jurisdictional practices.

---

34 See Convention against Torture and Other Cruel, Inhuman or Degrading Treatment or Punishment (adopted 10 December 1984, entered into force 26 June 1987) 1465 UNTS 85 (Torture Convention) art 14.).

35 I Bantekas and L Oette, 'International Human Rights Law and Practice' (3rd edn, Cambridge, 2024), 667.

3 Emerging Practices

Traditionally, ill-gotten assets would default to the ownership of the recovering state. However, this dynamic may be shifting, partly due to the United Nations Convention Against Corruption (UNCAC).[36] Asset recovery is a fundamental principle under Article 51 of the UNCAC, with Article 57 delineating provisions regarding the recovery and the return of assets by the destination country. More importantly, the nexus between corruption and human rights violations has been highlighted in UNCAC which emphasizes a human rights based approach to asset recovery.[37] The human rights approach to the recovery of stolen assets has remained one of most challenging and contentious subjects in the anti-corruption field, it continues to provoke significant debate regarding its effectiveness, implementation, and the potential conflict between asset recovery efforts and the protection of human rights.[38] Nonetheless, corruption and human rights are inherently mutually exclusive, and there are numerous instances where this relationship has been acknowledged and acted upon.[39] For example, following the fall of Ferdinand Marcos, Switzerland changed its laws to facilitate the return of stolen assets to the Philippines.[40] More recent efforts include western governments initiatives in the

36 UN General Assembly, United Nations Convention Against Corruption, A/58/422, 31 October 2003.

37 United Nations Convention Against Corruption (adopted 21 October 2003, entered into force 14 December 2005) 2349 UNTS 41 Chapter V.

38 CecilyRose, 'Human Rights Law and the Return of Stolen Assets' in Niels M Blokker, Daniëlla Dam-de Jong and Vid Prislan (eds), *Furthering the Frontiers of International Law: Sovereignty, Human Rights, Sustainable Development* (Brill Nijhoff 2021)294–306.

39 Since 2011, the Human Rights Council has been examining the detrimental effects of the non-repatriation of funds of illicit origin to their countries of origin on the enjoyment of human rights. Additionally, the Council has emphasized the importance of enhancing international cooperation to address this issue effectively. See OHCHR 'Recommended Principles On Human Rights And Asset Recovery' (2022) HRC/NONE/2022/2/iPub.

40 The Swiss government set a precedent by proactively freezing Swiss bank accounts and subsequently assisting the Philippine authorities in tracing and recovering the funds. This action was facilitated by the passage of a new law permitting mutual legal assistance in criminal matters to countries even in the absence of a bilateral agreement with Switzerland. The legal basis for this action was the foreign affairs power granted to the Federal Council, the executive branch of the Swiss government, under the Swiss Constitution. At the time, this authority was encapsulated in Article 102, which, under the 1999 Constitution, has been renumbered to Article 184. The relevant paragraph of Article 184 now states: 'Where safeguarding the interests of the country so requires, the Federal Council may issue ordinances and rulings. Ordinances must be of limited duration.'

context of the Ukraine Recovery Conference, where sanctioned Russian individuals were allowed to volunteer assets for Ukraine.[41]

This chapter will examine the policies and legislation in the UK, France, and the US that permit the channelling of recovered illicit assets towards reparations. These countries are selected due to their significant roles in shaping this emerging trend. In these countries, victims of human rights abuses have pursued reparations from foreign states through court actions or other human rights advocacy strategies. These efforts leverage funds from properties and assets recovered from corruption, economic crimes, or other forms of criminal activity. While academia has not traditionally classified these efforts as reparations, the field of transitional justice has long anticipated this possibility. For instance, the Office of the High Commissioner for Human Rights (OHCHR) has argued that, legally, it is reasonable to assert that "especially where a State has accepted providing reparations for victims of third parties, nothing should prevent the State from attempting to recover from those parties."[42] This perspective highlights an evolving understanding within transitional justice that acknowledges the potential for states to seek restitution from third-party perpetrators to fund reparations for victims.

This notion challenges the conventional separation between reparations and developmental initiatives, suggesting a more integrated approach that leverages resources from those responsible for human rights violations. By framing these efforts within the context of transitional justice, there is a growing recognition of the legal and moral imperatives that support the pursuit of reparations, through non-traditional means such as recovery from third parties. This approach not only broadens the scope of reparative justice but also aligns with the practical realities faced by states with limited resources, thereby offering a pragmatic pathway to achieving justice for victims.

A caveat is in order: the practice of utilizing international mechanisms to support reparations and development is not entirely novel. For instance, in 1991, the Malian government, through a Mutual Legal Assistance Treaty request, asked Switzerland to finance a Swiss lawyer to represent Mali's interests. This request was accepted and funded by the Swiss Agency for Development and Cooperation, with the subsequent Malian Konaré government allocating the recovered funds to rural development programs.[43]

41 The Russia (Sanctions) (EU Exit) Regulations 2019 (UK).

42 OHCHR (n6), p. 33.

43 Anne Lugon-Moulin, 'Asset Recovery: Concrete Challenges for Development Assistance,' in Mark Pieth (eds), *Recovering Stolen Assets* (Peter Lang Verlag, 2008).

The three case studies below illustrate the recent evolution and significant progress of this practice, highlighting how linking human rights violations to grand corruption is providing new avenues for reparations.

3.1 *United Kingdom*

In 2012 the UK charged the former Nigeria Delta state Governor James Ibori of money laundering which prosecutors estimated to be at \$250m.[44] Ibori pleaded guilty and admitted stealing money from Delta State and laundering it in London through a number of offshore companies. The UK Court convicted him for money laundering, conspiracy to defraud and forgery, and ordered the confiscation of his illicitly acquired assets.

This case is not merely about a foreign politician being convicted of corruption. Firstly, James Ibori, as the governor of Delta State in Nigeria, presided over some of the most egregious human rights violations in the region.[45] Secondly, Ibori enjoyed near-absolute immunity in Nigeria, being a protégé of the then President Olusegun Obasanjo.[46] Thirdly, the UK Department for International Development (DfID), through its subsidiary CDC Group, equity-funded the Proceeds of Corruption Unit, which began investigating Ibori in 2005 alongside Nigeria's anti-corruption unit, the Economic and Financial Crimes Commission (EFCC).[47] DfID invested £5 million in the investigation, not only because it was the world's largest money-laundering case ever prosecuted but also to ensure that the recovered funds would be returned to Nigeria to mitigate the harm caused by Ibori's actions.[48]

The UK has made it clear it seeks the repurposing of frozen assets related to human rights abuses for the benefit of victims. Thus following the conviction of Ibori on his own admission of guilt the authorities quickly made a statement that "we will now be actively seeking the confiscation of all of his stolen assets so they can be repatriated for the benefit of the people of Delta state."[49]

---

44 *R v James Onanefe Ibori* [2013] EWCA Crim 815.

45 Human Rights Watch, *Corruption on Trial? The Record of Nigeria's Economic and Financial Crimes Commission* (Human Rights Watch 2011) 11–12.

46 Ibid p. 28.

47 Peter Marshall, 'UK Aid Funded Firms 'Linked to Nigeria Fraudster Ibori'' *BBC* (16 April 2012) <https://www.bbc.co.uk/news/world-africa-17728357> accessed 26 January 2025.

48 Ibid.

49 The Daily Post, 'Ibori Pleads Guilty to Money Laundering' Daily Post (28 February 2012) <https://dailypost.ng/2012/02/28/ibori-pleads-guilty-to-money-laundering/> accessed 26 January 2025.

As part of its Anti-Corruption Strategy[50] the UK became the first country to publish its principles and policy on international asset returns.[51] This document was written to increase consistency in how proceeds of corruption are returned and sets a legal requirement for transparency in the use of the returned funds – for sustainability of the reparations measures from recovered assets. In addition, to policies and strategies, the UK has other laws such as the *Sanctions and Anti-Money Laundering Act 2018* provides the legal basis for taking sanctions within the UK.[52] This includes the global human rights regime and the global anti-money laundering regime. *The Economic Crime (Transparency and Enforcement) Act 2022* will allow assets frozen under sanctions connected to human rights abuses and corruption to be repurposed for the benefit of the victims of corruption related human rights violations.[53]

3.2 *France*

In 2007, the publication of a damning report titled "The Biens Mals Acquis" or "Ill-Gotten Gains Affair" by the French non-governmental organization *Comité Catholique contre la Faim et pour le Développement* (CCFD) exposed the vast wealth accumulated in Western countries by 23 African dictators and their families.[54] This report led to a criminal complaint against Equatorial Guinea's First Vice President, Teodoro Nguema Obiang Mangue, brought by NGO s dedicated to combating corruption, including Association Sherpa and Transparency International France.[55] By becoming civil parties to the case, these organizations effectively overcame the inertia of the prosecuting authorities.[56] This action set an important legal precedent, potentially paving the way for similar future actions against other despots.

In the first ever case where a high-level official, while in office, is called to account for grand corruption before a foreign court, France convicted

50 HM Government, United Kingdom Anti-Corruption Strategy 2017–2022 (HM Government 2017) <https://assets.publishing.service.gov.uk/media/5a829eb7e5274a2e87dc21f0/6_3323_Anti-Corruption_Strategy_WEB.pdf> accessed 26 January 2025.

51 Home Office, 'UK Sets Global Transparency Standard for Asset Returns'(GOV.UK,13 January 2022) < https://www.gov.uk/government/news/uk-sets-global-transparency-standard-for-asset-returns> accessed 26 January 2025.

52 Sanctions and Anti-Money Laundering Act 2018 (UK).

53 Economic Crime (transparency and Enforcement) Act 2022 (UK).

54 Maud Perdriel-Vaissière, 'France's Biens Mal Acquis Affair: Lessons From a Decade of Legal Struggle'(2017), Open Society Foundations <https://www.justiceinitiative.org/publications/france-s-biens-mal-acquis-affair-lessons-decade-legal-struggle> accessed 26 January 2025.

55 Ibid.

56 Ibid.

Obiang.[57] Although Obiang tried to claim immunity, in two historic decisions, first announced by the 32nd Chamber of the *Tribunal Correctionnel de Paris* and the Examination Chamber of the Paris Court of Appeals in April 2015, that his nomination to the function of Vice-President was "a nomination of circumstance" designed to shield him from accountability.[58] Subsequently, the French Supreme Court (the Court of Cassation) upheld the ruling, dismissing Obiang's immunity claims because "his functions are distinct from those of a head of state, a head of government or a minister for foreign affairs."[59] It held that Obiang could not benefit from functional immunity because "all the offenses of which he was accused [...] were committed for personal purposes."[60] The court ordered seizure of much of the €150 million in assets Obiang holds in France. Equatorial Guinean had brought the case before the International Court of Justice (ICJ) alleging immunity, this case was however dismissed for lack of jurisdiction.[61]

In 2021, following the judgement against Teodoro Nguema Obiang Mangue, French legislators passed a new law relating to solidarity development and the fight against global inequalities – the *Restitution Law*.[62] The law allows for assets confiscated in "ill-gotten gains" cases to be repatriated to the populations in the countries of origin. It is important to note that the Restitution Law does not enable asset confiscation itself. For the law to have effect, the assets must have been already confiscated under French law following a successful criminal prosecution. Furthermore, French laws allow for confiscation of the instruments and proceeds of corruption, as well as assets belonging to a convicted person who has not been able to justify the origin of the money with which the assets were purchased.

---

57 Transparency International France, 'Definitive Conviction of Teodorin Obiag in France Sends Strong Message, Allows Asset Restitution to Equatorial Guinea' (*Transparency International*, 30 July 2021) <https://www.transparency.org/en/press/teodorin-obiang-conviction-asset-recovery-equatorial-guinea-france> accessed 26 January 2025.

58 Angelique Chrisafis, 'Son of Equatorial Guinea's President is Convicted of Corruption in France' (*The Guardian*, 27 October 2017) <https://www.theguardian.com/world/2017/oct/27/son-of-equatorial-guineas-president-convicted-of-corruption-in-france> accessed 26 January 2025.

59 Human Rights Watch, 'France Equatorial Guinea Vice President's Conviction Upheld' (*Human Rights Watch*, 28 July 2021) <https://www.hrw.org/news/2021/07/28/france-equatorial-guinea-vice-presidents-conviction-upheld> accessed 26 January 2025.

60 Cass. crim., 15 December 2015, n° 15–83156.

61 *Immunities and Criminal Proceedings* (*Equatorial Guinea v France*), (Request for the Indication of Provisional Measures: Order), General List No. 163 [2016] ICJ 1148].

62 No. 2021–1031.

As an anti-corruption focused law, the repurposing powers enable the repatriation of assets to the victims from whom the funds were stolen. The proceeds from the sale of confiscated property are allocated to a specific State budget program dedicated to the restitution of ill-gotten gains, administered by the French Official Development Assistance Mission under the Ministry of Foreign Affairs. Although these funds are separated from the French government's general budget, they remain subject to parliamentary oversight. The funds are allocated to development projects in the country of origin to improve living conditions and human rights for the affected population, adhering to principles of transparency and accountability and involving civil society organizations. The Ministry of Foreign Affairs defines the restitution process on a case-by-case basis.

3.3 *United States*

In another case involving the vice president of Equatorial Guinea, the civil forfeiture matter *United States v. One Michael Jackson Signed Thriller Jacket in the Central District of California*,[63] along with related cases, the United States alleged that Obiang Mangue, then Minister of Agriculture and Forestry in 2011 with an official government salary of less than $100,000, amassed over $300 million worth of assets through corruption and money laundering, contravening both US and Equatoguinean law. Mr. Mangue entered into a settlement agreement requiring him to divest a Malibu, California, mansion purchased for $30 million, a Ferrari automobile, and various items of Michael Jackson memorabilia, as well as to contribute $1 million representing the value of other property.[64]

Additionally, the agreement stipulated that $10.3 million of these settlement funds were to be forfeited to the US, with the remaining settlement funds to be distributed to a charity or organization for the benefit of the people of Equatorial Guinea. The Department of Justice pledged to return the forfeited funds for the country's benefit. According to a donor agreement with the UN, $19.25 million in settlement funds will be utilized to procure, store, distribute, and administer COVID-19 vaccines to at least 600,000 individuals in Equatorial Guinea. Furthermore, MCDI, a charitable organization in the US, with a proven track record of implementing programs in Equatorial Guinea,

---

63 *United States v. One Michael Jackson Signed Thriller Jacket* 2:11-cv-03582-GW-SS (US 2014).

64 James V Grimaldi, 'When US Targets Foreign Leaders for Corruption, Recovering Loot is a Challenge' *The Washington Post* (10 October 2014) <https://www.wsj.com/articles/u-s-reaches-34-million-corruption-settlement-with-equatorial-guinea-official-1412948259> accessed 29 January 2025.

received $6.35 million to oversee the acquisition, storage, distribution, and delivery of additional medicines and medical supplies throughout the country.

The aforementioned cases highlight the nexus between reparations and development in transitional justice, facilitated by the linkage of human rights violations to grand corruption. These instances exemplify how the intersection of corruption and human rights now enables victims to seek reparations in foreign states. Thus, it is crucial to further explore the intersection between corruption and human rights within the transitional justice framework.[65]

This concept is not novel. In 2008, the International Journal of Transitional Justice dedicated a special issue to transitional justice and development, featuring contributions advocating for the expansion of transitional justice to encompass developmental concerns. Concurrently, scholars have stressed the importance of addressing accountability for large-scale corruption and economic crimes within transitional justice frameworks to prevent an impunity gap.[66] Despite facing criticism, the integration of corruption into transitional justice is advocated due to its inherent connections to human rights violations.[67]

Two contrasting perspectives exist on this matter. Advocates of an ambitious approach propose broadening the scope of existing transitional justice mechanisms to enable a more proactive role in shaping development policies and post-conflict economic agendas. This entails reconceptualizing the objectives of transitional justice in broader terms, linking them to the intricate landscape of development processes.[68] Conversely, this approach has drawn criticism from various quarters. Some argue that it risks fundamentally altering the priorities of transitional justice, potentially diluting its core focus on investigating and redressing a specific set of violations.[69] Thus, such an approach could blur the lines between transitional justice and develop-

---

65 IsabelRobinson, 'Truth Commissions and Anti-Corruption: Towards a Complementary Framework?' (2015) 9(1) International Journal of Transitional Justice.33; Alexander Segovia, The Relationship between Transitional Justice And Corruption Current State Of The Discussion And Proposal For A Research Agenda, September 2023.

66 Ruben Carranza, 'Plunder and Pain: Should Transitional Justice Engage with Corruption and Economic Crimes?' (2008) 2(3) International Journal of Transitional Justice, 310.

67 Taygeti Michalakea, 'Anticorruption and Transitional Justice: A Distinction Without a Difference' (2022) 22(2) Human Rights Law Review,.

68 Topher L McDougal, 'The Trilemma of Promoting Economic Justice at War's End' in Dustin N Sharp (ed) *Justice and Economic Violence in Transition* (Springer, New York, NY, 2014).

69 Chris Albin-Lackey, 'Corruption, Human Rights, and Activism: Useful Connections and Their Limits' in Dustin N Sharp. (eds) *Justice and Economic Violence in Transition* (Springer, NewYork, NY 2014).

ment policy, particularly concerning reparations.[70] Others contend that even if transitional justice were to become "development-sensitive," the transformative impact of such connections remains debatable.[71]

The argument regarding whether corruption can constitute a human rights violation eligible for individual complaint procedures remains unsettled. Nonetheless, some scholars, such as Anne Peters,[72] contend that corruption can indeed qualify as a human rights violation, albeit with complexities surrounding international state responsibility.[73] Adopting a human rights perspective alongside criminal law approaches opens avenues for enhanced monitoring and litigation, thereby complementing efforts in both anti-corruption and human rights advocacy.[74] Moreover, various grounds for jurisdiction are delineated in relevant anti-corruption conventions, particularly concerning the prosecution of foreign corrupt practices. As evidenced by the case studies discussed in this chapter, some countries have intensified their efforts to prosecute corrupt foreign practices of businesses with territorial or personal ties to those states, leveraging these principles. Consequently, the scope of anti-corruption enforcement and extraterritorial jurisdiction has been expanded, allowing for a lawful exercise of jurisdiction even with a tenuous personal or territorial link – or in some cases, no link at all. This development is promising for human rights defenders, as they can utilize anti-corruption extraterritorial legislation to pursue the right to reparations.

This approach not only provides innovative funding sources for reparations but also serves to combat impunity and deter corruption by depriving wrongdoers of illicit gains. Furthermore, it facilitates development initiatives, addressing the detrimental impacts of grand corruption in developing states.

4 Challenges

The case studies discussed in the previous section stand out as notable examples However, despite the achievements of the highlighted states, various open questions and challenges persist.

---

70 Ibid.

71 Roger Duthie (ed) *Transitional Justice and Displacement* (Social Science Research Council 2014).

72 Anne Peters, 'Corruption as a Violation of International Human Rights' (2018), 29(4) European Journal of International Law, 1251–1287.

73 Anne Peters, 'Human Rights and Corruption: Problems and Potential of Individualising a Systemic Problem' (2024) 22(2) International Journal of Constitutional Law 538.

74 Peters (n71).

4.1 *Political*

There was a general lack of political will from the victim states to cooperate in international asset recovery cases. This is true in most cases as there are a very few developing countries that have the political will to go after the money.[75] Although it varies from country to country one fundamental reason for this is that in many developing countries the political elite is so intertwined that if investigations about illicit finances begin, people still in power are often implicated.[76] Most corrupt politicians do not work alone. They usually have business friends and family members still in government. Efforts to reclaim money from a former president or other high ranking official often leads back to those currently in power who are unwilling to implicate themselves or lose their own ill-gotten assets, as found by a study by the International Centre for Asset Recovery.[77]

Another challenge is the political backlash stemming from countries with weak governance resorting to novel tactics, such as the use of state hostages.[78] Numerous instances of state-sponsored hostage-taking have emerged, with governments employing individuals as bargaining chips in diplomatic negotiations. A pertinent example is Equatorial Guinea's imprisonment of South African oil workers, Potgieter and Huxham, who initiated legal action against Equatorial Guinea's vice president, Nguema Obiang, in South Africa. Van Rensburg contended that, as the de facto head of Equatorial Guinea's security services, the vice president was responsible for his wrongful imprisonment following a failed business deal between the two parties. A South African court ruled in Van Rensburg's favour, ordering Nguema Obiang to pay nearly 40 million rand (approximately $2.8 million at the time), in addition to interest and legal expenses. Concerned about Nguema Obiang's compliance, Van Rensburg sought to seize his South African assets as collateral.[79] The court permitted the sale of furniture from two villas initially and later ordered the attachment of other properties and a luxurious yacht undergoing repairs in

75 Ivan Pavletic, 'The Political Economy of Asset Recovery Processes' (2009) International Centre for Asset Recovery <https://baselgovernance.org/sites/default/files/2019-06/biog_working_paper_07.pdf> accessed 28 January 2025.

76 International Centre for Asset Recovery, Tracing Stolen Assets: A Practitioner's Handbook (Basel Institute on Governance 2009) <https://baselgovernance.org/sites/default/files/2018-12/Tracing%20Stolen%20Assets.pdf> accessed 28 January 2025.

77 Ibid.

78 See Opinions adopted by the Working Group on Arbitrary Detention at its 99th session, 18–27 March 2024: Opinion No. 1/2024 concerning Peter Shane Huxham and Frederik Johannes Potgieter (Equatorial Guinea) A/HRC/WGAD/2024/14.

79 *Van Rensburg v Obiang* (21748/2014) [2021] ZAWCHC 128.

Cape Town. Equatorial Guinea's subsequently arrested and imprisoned Potgieter and Huxham without due process to negotiate for the release of Obiang's seized assets. Political abuses, such as state-sponsored hostage-taking, undermine the credibility and effectiveness of anti-corruption efforts by diverting attention from justice to power struggles. Such tactics discourage whistleblowers and victims of corruption from seeking accountability, as they risk retaliation through politically motivated actions.

4.2 *Legal*

This section explores two key legal challenges in the recovery of assets linked to grand corruption and human rights violations: the issue of immunity for high-ranking officials and the complexities of interpreting international treaty provisions on asset return. These challenges highlight the difficulties in holding perpetrators accountable and ensuring the effective repatriation of stolen assets.

First, perpetrators of grand corruption linked to gross human rights violations often enjoy *de facto* and in some cases *de jure* immunity in their home countries. For instance, in Nigeria, a sitting governor enjoys constitutional immunity while in office.[80] An illustrative example is the case of a Nigerian state governor suspected of money laundering, Diepreye Alamieyeseigha was charged with money laundering in the UK but he jumped bail and escaped back to Nigeria dressed in women's clothes – to face a hero's welcome and presidential pardon.[81] In Nigeria also senior politicians enjoy immunity from prosecution and benefit from the politics of patronage which protected them from any form of accountability. As a result, another Nigerian state governor, mentioned above, James Ibori was never investigated or arrested in Nigeria. He was finally brought to account after he was arrested in Dubai and extradited to the UK.

Second, the interpretation of treaty provisions presents a significant challenge. International anti-corruption treaties often contain vague language, particularly regarding the return of assets to their "state of origin," referring to the state from which the assets were stolen. Those familiar with the drafting of the UNCAC recall that efforts to reach an international agreement on arrangements governing the return of stolen assets were among the most contentious aspects of the treaty negotiations in 2001–2003. While there was uni-

80 Federal Republic of Nigeria Constitution (As amended in 1999) Section 308.

81 BBC, 'Nigeria Pardons Goodluck Jonathan Ally, Alamieyeseigha' *BBC* (13 March 2013) <https://www.bbc.co.uk/news/world-africa-21769047> accessed 28 January 2025.

versal agreement on the principle that funds should be returned, consensus on the methodology proved highly contentious.[82]

For instance, in the case of France discussed earlier, Equatorial Guinea has approached the ICJ seeking the return of assets after France successfully seized assets purchased by Vice President Teodoro Nguema Obiang Mangue with ill-gotten gains.[83] Equatorial Guinea's new case at the ICJ centres on the claim that France has violated the UNCAC by failing to return confiscated property as requested and by generally failing to cooperate with and assist Equatorial Guinea. Equatorial Guinea asserts that France must return all property covered by its request. However, Article 57 of the UNCAC does not adequately address several crucial aspects of asset return, particularly concerning how third-party states can contribute to the payment of reparations from seized assets of corrupt human rights abusers.

4.3 *Technical*

The involvement of development aid organizations and civil society organizations in reparations programs poses a significant challenge, as these initiatives are often not perceived as genuine reparations by victims of gross human rights abuses. This issue mirrors the challenges faced by collective material reparations, which frequently risk being seen as having minimal reparative capacity or not being recognized as reparations at all. A core part of this problem is that such programs do not specifically target victims. Reparations financed by recovered stolen money typically manifest as collective programs distributing material goods, often focusing on "non-excludable goods" – resources that, once made available, are difficult to restrict from broader consumption.[84] For instance, when a collective reparations program funds the construction of a hospital or a road, both victims and non-victims benefit equally. This dilutes the reparative impact intended for victims alone. This challenge is further compounded when these collective programs distribute not only non-excludable goods but also basic necessities, a situation often seen when reparations programs are integrated into broader development initiatives.[85] In developing countries, where demands for reparations are met

82 Phil Mason, Twenty Years with Anti-Corruption. Part 5 (Chr. Michelsen Institute2020) <https://www.u4.no/publications/twenty-years-with-anti-corruption-part-5> accessed 28 January 202.

83 *Immunities and Criminal Proceedings* (*Equatorial Guinea v. France*) (Merits) General List No. 163 [2020] ICJ 300.

84 OHCHR (n6), p. 26.

85 Ibid.

with limited resources, governments are strongly inclined to argue that development initiatives themselves constitute reparations.[86]

5 Concluding Remarks

This contribution argues that without recognizing the conceptual and practical synergies between transitional justice and development, the potential of transitional justice in contributing to sustainable peace will be limited.[87] Moreover, as reparations for large-scale victim populations, as often seen in African countries, necessitate a multi-faceted approach to ensure non-recurrence of violations, the integration of development in securing reparations warrants re-evaluation. Thus the emerging trend of third states playing a significant role in facilitating reparations signifies a promising and innovative approach deserves further analysis and emulation. This development, stemming from the nexus between transitional justice and corruption-related human rights violations, offers a novel avenue for funding reparations. This is particularly crucial given the persistent challenge of financing reparations in developing countries. However, it is important to temper expectations regarding the role of recovered assets in financing reparations and to critically assess the involvement of development actors in asset recovery, repatriation, and management processes. This emerging trend poses a challenge to both transitional justice practitioners and academics to research deeper into the linkages between transitional justice and development, as well as exploring how the intersection of human rights violations and corruption can yield beneficial outcomes.

86 Christopher J Colvin, 'Overview of the Reparations Program in South Africa' in De Greiff Pablo (ed) *The Handbook of Reparations* (Oxford University Press 2006) 176–215.

87 Yvette Selimand Tim Murithi, 'Transitional Justice and Development: Partners for Sustainable Peace in Africa?' (2011) 6(2) Journal of Peacebuilding & Development, 58.

CHAPTER 10

Reparations for Armed Conflict Related Atrocities in Inter-state Proceedings

The Armed Activities (DRC v Uganda) *Judgment on Reparations and Its Legacy*

Sotirios-Ioannis Lekkas[1]

1 Introduction

On 9 February 2022, the International Court of Justice (ICJ or the Court) rendered its Judgment on the Reparations Phase of the *Armed Activities* (*DRC v Uganda*) case.[2] The Judgment concluded a case which had all the hallmarks of a landmark: an exceptionally large-scale, protracted, and complex armed conflict, a key actor as the respondent, and virtually unfettered material jurisdiction of the Court. As a reminder, in 1999, the Court was seized with DRC's claims against Uganda arising from the (then ongoing) Second Congo War.[3] A parallel application against Rwanda failed on grounds of jurisdiction,[4] whereas proceedings against Burundi were discontinued before the Court had an opportunity to pass judgment.[5] In 2005, the Court rendered its Judgment on the Merits, declaring Uganda responsible for violating the principle of non-use of force and non-intervention by the acts of its own forces and by supporting armed groups in the DRC.[6] The Court also found Uganda responsible for breaches of international humanitarian law and international human rights

---

1 Lecturer in International Law, School of Law, University of Sheffield (s.i.lekkas@sheffield.ac.uk). This paper is partly based on research conducted in the context of the project 'The Rules of Interpretation of Customary International Law' (TRICI-Law). This project has received funding from the European Research Council (ERC) under the European Union's Horizon 2020 Research and Innovation Programme (Grant Agreement No. 759728).

2 *Armed Activities on the Territory of the Congo* (*DRC v Uganda*), ICJ Rep 13 (ICJ, Reparations, 2022) (*CO Reparations*).

3 *Armed Activities on the Territory of the Congo* (*DRC v Uganda*) ICJ Pleading 3 (ICJ, Application Instituting Proceedings, 1999).

4 *Armed Activities on the Territory of the Congo* (*New Application: 2002*) (*DRC v Rwanda*), ICJ Rep 6 (ICJ, Jurisdiction and Admissibility, 2006).

5 *Armed Activities on the Territory of the Congo* (*DRC v Burundi*), ICJ Rep 3 (ICJ, Order, 2001).

6 *Armed Activities on the Territory of the Congo* (*DRC v Uganda*), ICJ Rep 168 (ICJ, Merits, 2005) (CO Merits); para. 345 (1).

 | DOI:10.1163/9789004716742_011

law, as well as for plundering DRC's natural resources.[7] The Court concluded that Uganda had to make reparation to the DRC for the injury caused by its internationally wrongful acts and enjoined the parties to enter into negotiations for that purpose.[8] After almost 10 years of sporadic and fruitless discussions, the DRC brought back the case to the Court in 2015 for conclusive resolution.

The *CO Reparations* Judgment brings to the fore fundamental questions about the ways in which inter-state proceedings can lead to the determination of reparations in the aftermath of armed conflict. These questions are by no means unique to the DRC war; in fact, they are salient features of *post bellum* dispute settlement. Contemporary armed conflicts are increasingly complex in that they often involve the participation of multiple states, the interposition of non-state actors, and even the intervention of international organisations.[9] Another marked challenge of post-conflict processes relates to the documentation of the number of harmed individuals and the valuation of damage especially due to the innate difficulty of fact-finding and verification in the fog of war and the passing of time after the conflict has ended.[10] These complications are compounded by broader uncertainties about the holders of a right to a remedy under international law and the unsystematised character of 'general rules regarding payment' in the law of international responsibility.[11] War brings about crippling harms to persons individually and incalculable devastation to communities collectively, as well as seriously strains the economic capacity of states to cater even to critical needs of their population. In this context, the decision as to who will receive payment and how are not mere technicalities or afterthoughts, as they often appear in inter-state proceedings, but entails serious distributional consequences. These vexing questions are only amplified partly because inter-state judicial proceedings on reparations are a relatively rare occurrence.[12] It is telling that the principal judicial organ of the United Nations, the ICJ, has been called upon to decide on the amount of reparation due for internationally wrongful acts only four times in its his-

7 Ibid, paras 345 (3), (4).

8 Ibid, paras 261, 345 (5), (6).

9 E.g. L Moffett, 'Reparations and War: Finding Balance in Repairing the Past' (OUP 2023) 124.

10 E.g. H M Holtzmann and E Kristjánsdóttir (eds), 'International Mass Claims Processes: Legal and Practical Perspectives' (OUP 2007) 210–211.

11 *Factory at Chorzów* (*Claim for Indemnity*) (*Germany v Poland*), PCIJ Ser A No 17 (PCIJ, Merits, 1928), 61; on the issue of remedies see e.g. D Shelton, 'Remedies in International Human Rights Law' (3rd edn OUP 2015) 15–16.

12 L Moffett (n 9) 161.

tory with the CO *Reparations* Judgment far exceeding the scale of any previous case.[13]

This contribution scrutinises the legal findings of the Court in the CO *Reparations* judgment and evaluates its implications for the development of the law of international responsibility on reparations especially as it applies to inter-state proceedings in the aftermath of armed conflicts. The analysis proceeds as follows. Section 2 flags up the legal issues stemming from the complex character of the DRC conflict, namely the participation of multiple states and non-state actors. It discusses the Court's findings with respect to causation and the burden of proof and tries to flesh out the generalisable features of the decision. Section 3 subsequently turns to the strategies employed by the ICJ to deal with the uncertainty surrounding the establishment and valuation of damage. It presents the controversial 'global sums' approach and critically discusses its doctrinal and normative underpinnings. Section 4 contextualises the Court's determination of the beneficiaries of reparation within broader developments relating to an individual right to reparation. It takes note of the discrepancy between the right-holders of certain international rules, the beneficiaries of reparation under the law of state responsibility, and the entitlement to the payment of reparation. Section 5 delves deeper into the issue of payment by focusing on the rules relating to its modalities. It demonstrates how these rules have thus far eluded codification efforts and proper consideration by the Court, notwithstanding their profound distributive implications.

As will be argued, the overarching purpose of the law of state responsibility at each cleavage of reparations proceedings is the 'personalisation' of reparations in a dual sense: reparations should reflect as accurately as possible the responsibility of the wrongdoer and they should also remedy, as far as possible, the harm of the actual victims. Yet, the settlement of cases involving mass claims arising from armed conflict can lead to distortions owing to evidentiary challenges and the need for reconciliation and re-building. In this respect, some of the Court's findings relating to causation, establishment and valuation of damage, and payment are amenable to misinterpretation. The contribution argues against their wholesale generalisation, despite the high profile of the case.

---

13 For previous judgments see *Corfu Channel (United Kingdom v Albania)*, ICJ Rep 244 (ICJ, Assessment of Compensation, 1949); *Ahmadou Sadio Diallo (Republic of Guinea v Democratic Republic of the Congo)*, ICJ Rep 324 (ICJ, Compensation, 2012); *Certain Activities Carried out by Nicaragua in the Border Area (Costa Rica v Nicaragua)*, ICJ Rep 15 (ICJ, Compensation, 2018).

to a particular injury that it was not caused by its failure to meet its obligations of vigilance as an occupying force.[27] For damage occurring outside Ituri, the Court would assess on a case-by-case basis whether Uganda's actions or support was a sufficiently direct and certain cause of the injury suffered.[28] The Court also drew the same distinction for the purposes of the allocation of the burden of proof. The Court concluded that Uganda had to establish that a specific injury occurring in Ituri was not caused by its failure to discharge its obligation as an occupying force.[29] As to other claims, the burden of proof remained in principle with the DRC.[30]

From the outset, whilst the situation of occupation seems to have played a role both in the context of the substantive law of state responsibility and the procedural law of the burden of proof, it is important to point out that the two remain distinct. As a procedural matter, the Court confirmed the principle that a party invoking a fact has normally the burden of proving that fact (*onus probandi incumbit actori*).[31] Yet, this is an open-ended principle; the burden can shift depending on which party is in a better position to furnish relevant evidence, the 'subject-matter and nature of the dispute' and 'on the type of facts which is necessary to establish'.[32] Ultimately, when it comes to deciding who bears the burden of proof, the Court exercises inherent powers relating to the proper administration of justice.[33] In the event, two factors seem to have played a role for the allocation (and partial reversal) of the burden of proof. First, Uganda's prolonged and effective control over Ituri placed it in a better position than the DRC to collect contemporaneous evidence on facts relating to that area.[34] Second, the nature of the dispute implied that Uganda could not avoid an award of reparation by simply denying DRC's claim, because internationally wrongful acts causing injury and the appropriateness of reparation for this injury belonged to the *res iudicata* of the Merits Judgment.[35]

From the perspective of the law of state responsibility, the Court reiterated that an award of compensation requires a 'sufficiently direct and certain causal nexus between the wrongful act [...] and the injury suffered [...] con-

27 Ibid, paras 78, 95.
28 Ibid, paras 84, 97.
29 Ibid.
30 Ibid, paras 118–119.
31 Ibid, para. 115; for a discussion of the practice of the Court affirming that principle see, e.g., C Brown, 'A Common Law of International Adjudication' (OUP 2007) 94–95.
32 CO Reparations (n 2) para. 117.
33 C F Amerasinghe, 'Evidence in International Litigation' (Brill 2005) 75.
34 Ibid, para. 118.
35 CO Merits (n 6) para. 259–260; see, *mutatis mutandis, Diallo* Compensation (n 13) para. 21.

sisting of all damage of any type, material or moral'.[36] In this way, the Court reaffirmed its own jurisprudence on causation in contrast to other international courts and tribunals, which variably refer to notions like 'proximity' or 'foreseeability', but introduced, at the same time, an element of flexibility that approximates these other notions.[37] What constitutes a 'sufficiently direct and certain causal nexus' cannot be determined in the abstract, but it 'may vary depending on the primary rule violated and the nature and extent of the injury'; that is, the other components of the obligation of reparation under customary international law.[38] Crucially, unlike evidentiary matters, the Court's exposition does not include the factual circumstances of the case as a factor bearing on the required causal nexus under the law of state responsibility. Along similar lines, the Court exercised restraint in laying down the principles applicable in situations of causal overdetermination when harm originates from multiple causes.[39] Importantly, the Court affirmed that an award of compensation cannot be precluded solely on the basis that damage is due to multiple concurrent causes if there is a sufficiently direct and certain causal nexus with the internationally wrongful act of the respondent.[40] It also acknowledged that multiple internationally wrongful acts by different actors can lead to a single injury or multiple distinct injuries.[41]

However, the interpretation and application of these principles in light of the applicable primary rules and the complex character of the acts raised several issues. A first issue related to the Court's finding that the causal nexus requirement was satisfied with respect to all injuries occurring in the once occupied Ituri, unless it could be established with respect to a particular injury that it was not caused by Uganda's failure to discharge its obligation of vigilance as the occupying power. As Judge Yusuf pointed out, this obligation is

36 CO Reparations (n 2) para. 93; similarly *Certain Activities Carried Out by Nicaragua in the Border Area (Costa Rica v Nicaragua)*, ICJ Rep 15 (ICJ, Compensation, 2018) para. 32; *Diallo* Compensation (n 13) para. 14.

37 *Final Award–Eritrea's Damages Claims*, XXVI RIAA 512, 529 (EECC, 2009) para. 39; *Final Award–Ethiopia's Damages Claims*, XXVI RIAA 639, 656 (EECC, 2009) para. 39; *Lubanga* ICC-01/04-01/06-3129-AnxA, AC, (ICC, Order for Reparations, 3 March 2015) para. 59; *Katanga*, ICC-01/04-01/07-3728, TC-II (ICC, Ordonnance de réparation en vertu de l'article 75 du Statut, 24 March 2017) para. 162; *Al-Mahdi*, ICC-01/12-01/15-236, TC-VIII (ICC, Reparations Order, 17 August 2017) para. 44; see also V Lanovoy, 'Causation in the Law of State Responsibility' (BYBIL 2022) 47.

38 CO Reparations (n 1) para. 93; see also ARSIWA (n 13) Commentary to Art 31, para. 10.

39 For the notion see: I Plakokefalos, 'Causation in the Law of State Responsibility and the Problem of Overdetermination: In Search of Clarity' (2015) 26 EJIL 471, 471.

40 CO Reparations (n 1) paras 94, 97.

41 Ibid, para. 94.

one of best efforts: the occupying power is obligated to take appropriate measures to prevent certain acts being committed, not to achieve that no such acts are committed at all times and under all circumstances.[42] In the *Bosnian Genocide* case, involving a violation of the obligation to prevent genocide, the Court held that 'such a nexus could be considered established only if the Court were able to conclude…that the genocide at Srebrenica would in fact have been averted if the Respondent had acted in compliance with its legal obligations'.[43] The Court reasoned its departure from this antecedent on the basis that 'the legal régimes and factual circumstances in question are not comparable, given that, unlike the above-mentioned *Genocide* case, the present case concerns a situation of occupation'.[44] The reference to the factual circumstances in the reasoning of the Court gives the false impression that the required causal nexus hinges on purely factual considerations in contradiction to its legal findings in the same part of the decision.[45] A more consistent interpretation of the Court's reasoning suggests that the legally relevant factor was the primary rule involved. In other words, the material scope of the obligation of vigilance of the occupying force to ensure public order––and hence, the scope of its responsibility––is evidently broader than the obligation to prevent only acts of genocide.[46]

A second, and related, issue is how the causal analysis with respect to Ituri compares with the same analysis on injuries committed by groups which Uganda supported in the rest of the DRC. In this respect, the Court was, for the most part, silent as to whether and, if so, what kind of acts committed by groups supported by Uganda outside Ituri would fulfil the required causal nexus. In one part of its reasoning, the Court rejected the claim for 'all damage to property that would not have occurred "but for" the unlawful use of force by Uganda' by recalling its finding on the merits that 'armed groups operating

42 *Armed Activities on the Territory of the Congo (DRC v Uganda)*, ICJ Rep 145 (ICJ, Reparations (Separate Opinion of Judge Yusuf), 2022) para. 19; on terminology see ARSIWA (n 13) Art 14 (3) and Commentary to Art 14, para. 14; also T Demaria, 'Trois observations sur la causalité à la lumière del'arrêt sur les réparations dans l'affaire des Activités armées sur le territoire du Congo (RDC c. Ouganda)' (2022) 53 L'Observateur des Nations Unies 309, 318.

43 *Application of the Convention on the Prevention and Punishment of the Crime of Genocide (Bosnia and Herzegovina v Serbia and Montenegro)*, ICJ Rep 3 (ICJ, Merits, 2007) ('*Bosnian Genocide*') para. 462.

44 CO Reparations (n 1) para. 95.

45 See above n37 and accompanying text; for a similar criticism see A Ollino, 'Causality in the Law of State Responsibility: Considerations on the *Congo v Uganda* Case' (2022) 95 QIL Zoom-In 5, 11.

46 For the general point see: I Plakokefalos (n 38) 478.

outside Ituri were not under the control of Uganda' and, thus, their acts were not attributable to it.[47] On its face, the finding appears to conflate attribution of conduct with the required causal nexus for reparation. It is important to note that the Merits Judgment found that Uganda violated its obligations under international human rights law and international humanitarian law not only by failing to take appropriate measures as an occupying force, but also 'by the conduct of its armed forces, which ... incited ethnic conflict and failed to take measures to put an end to such conflict'.[48] This latter obligation is not one of best efforts, but would be more aptly described as a specific complicity-type rule.[49] In *Nicaragua*, the Court found the US responsible for encouraging violations of international humanitarian law committed by the *contras*, even though there was obviously no situation of occupation.[50] What is more, the Court explicitly ordered the US to make reparation for injury caused by this violation, even though the US did not exercise any strict or effective control over the *contras* for the purposes of attribution of conduct.[51]

What is legally and normatively unsatisfactory is the implication that the required causal nexus would be met in occupied territory by mere omission, but it is not established in unoccupied areas even when there is active support to violations of international human rights and international humanitarian law.[52] However, this contradiction is more apparent than real. As a matter of law, not every form of support to armed groups in violation of the prohibition of the use of force automatically qualifies as encouragement to violations of international humanitarian and human rights law, still less implies a specific link to damage to persons or property.[53] As a matter of fact, the Court's findings in the Merits Judgment are limited to incidents in Ituri which involved 'encouragement and military support' to the seizure of lands by one ethnic

---

47 CO Reparations (n 1) para. 250 citing CO Merits (n 5) paras 160, 177, and 247.

48 CO Merits (n 5) para. 345 (emphasis added).

49 E.g. *Legal Consequences of the Construction of a Wall on the Occupied Palestinian Territory*, ICJ Rep 219 (ICJ, Advisory Opinion, Separate Opinion of Judge Koojimans, 2004), para. 49.

50 *Military and Paramilitary Activities in and against Nicaragua (Nicaragua v US)*, ICJ Rep 14 (ICJ, Merits, 1986) ('*Nicaragua*') para. 255.

51 *Nicaragua* (n 49) para. 292 (9), (13).

52 A Ollino (n 44) 19; on the general point, M Jackson, 'Complicity in International Law' (OUP 2015) 131–132; *contra* O Corten and P Klein, 'The Limits of Complicity as a Ground for Responsibility: Lessons Learned from the *Corfu Channel* Case' in K Bannelier, T Christakis, and S Heathcote (eds), *The ICJ and the Evolution of International Law* (Routledge 2011) 313, 315.

53 See eg the separate treatment in CO Merits (n 5) paras 345 (1), (3); *Nicaragua* (n 49) paras 292 (3), (9).

group against the other and of Ugandan 'troops [standing] by during the killing and [failing] to protect the civilians'.[54] Conversely, the Merits Judgment did not record any such incidents outside Ituri nor did the Court endeavour to do so in the Reparations stage.[55] More importantly, this finding of fact also suggests a stronger causal nexus between Uganda's internationally wrongful acts and harms to persons and property in Ituri. Unlike *Bosnian Genocide,* Uganda's internationally wrongful act did not only consist of a dereliction of a duty to ensure public order as an occupying power, but of its active encouragement and support to violations occurring in Ituri.[56]

A third related issue arising from the decision is whether and how the different categories of Uganda's internationally wrongful acts had a bearing on the quantum (ie amount) of compensation. The Court only raised this issue with respect to injuries caused in the course of hostilities between the Ugandan and Rwandan armies in Kisangani. In the event, the Court found that 'each state is responsible for damage in Kisangani that was caused by its own armed forces acting independently', even though it was unable to apportion to Uganda a specific share of the injury.[57] This seems in line with 'the fundamental principle governing the law of international responsibility: a State is responsible only for its own conduct, that is to say the conduct of persons acting, on whatever basis, on its behalf'.[58] Apart from this finding, the Court limited itself in enumerating a range of possibilities. According to the Court, when 'multiple causes attributable to two or more actors have resulted in injury, a single actor may be required to make full reparation for the damage suffered' or 'responsibility for part of such injury should instead be allocated among those actors'.[59] On the one hand, the open-ended reference of the Court to 'actors' clearly suggests that these considerations are not only applicable in the case of plurality of responsible states, but also when the internationally wrongful act of a state is a concurrent cause of damage alongside the conduct of other (even private) actors.[60] On the other hand, the Court did not

54 CO Merits (n 5) para. 209.

55 CO Reparations (n 1) para. 214; see, on this point, CO Merits (Verhoeven) (n 16) para. 4; *Armed Activities on the Territory of the Congo (DRC v Uganda)*, ICJ rep 361 (ICJ, Merits (Dissenting Opinion of Judge *ad hoc* Kateka) 2005) para. 48.

56 See n(42–45) and accompanying text.

57 CO Reparations (n 1) paras 221, 253; for the contrary view see *Oil Platforms (Islamic Republic of Iran v United States of America)*, ICJ Rep 324 (ICJ, Merits (Separate Opinion of Judge Simma), 2003) para. 76.

58 Bosnian Genocide (n 42) para. 406.

59 CO Reparations (n 1) para. 98.

60 T Demaria (n 41) 320–321.

clarify how these principles applied to the wrongful acts consisting of failure to prevent violations by third parties and support to armed groups in Ituri.[61] What is left unclear is whether these types of conduct constitute 'cumulative' or 'complementary' causes of injury.[62] It is true that violations of obligations to prevent are often characterised as 'complementary' causes in that they are insufficient alone to bring about injury.[63] In turn, this characterisation would imply that the state would be responsible for a separate injury or, more practicably, a portion of the injury caused by the violations of the third party.[64] At the same time, Uganda's internationally wrongful acts in Ituri, consisting of active support in violation of specific complicity-type obligations, could also be viewed in certain circumstances as 'cumulative' causes leading to an indivisible injury.[65] Arguably, for this reason, the Court's finding on causation with respect to Ituri was couched in terms of a rebuttable presumption. With respect to specific injuries, Uganda could still absolve itself by proving that injury would occur even without its conduct.[66]

What emerges from this short exposition is that the complex circumstances of the case called for a certain degree of selectivity and conciseness in the treatment of the legal issues relating to the responsibility arising from the complex wrongful acts in question. With respect to causation, the Court reaffirmed established principles of the law of reparations but avoided key clarifications as to the issue of causal overdetermination and its bearing on the determination of the amount of compensation. However, it would be false to assume that, as a matter of principle, different categories of internationally wrongful acts should be treated indistinctly for the purposes of causation in the context of determination of reparation. Undeniably, the most pressing issue for the Court was the availability of evidence and, most importantly, who would bear the consequences of gaps in the evidentiary record given

61 A Ollino (n 44) 20.

62 For the nomenclature see B Bollecker-Stern, 'La préjudice dans la théorie de la responsabilité internationale' (Pedone 1973) 267 ff.

63 E.g. J E Noyes and B D Smith, 'State Responsibility and the Principle of Joint and Several Responsibility' (1988) 13 YJIL 225, 230; T Demaria (n 41) 321–322.

64 E.g. P D'Argent, 'Reparation, Cessation, Assurances and Guarantees of Non-Repetition' in A Nollkaemper and I Plakokefalos (eds), *Principles of Shared Responsibility: An Appraisal of the State of the Art* (CUP 2015) 208, 224; for an illustrative example from domestic courts see Supreme Court of the Netherlands, *Mothers of Srebrenica Association and ors v The Netherlands*, ECLI:NL:HR:2019:1223, Judgment (19 July 2019).

65 E.g., *mutatis mutandis*, A Nollkaemper et al, 'Guiding Principles on Shared Responsibility in International Law' (2020) 31 EJIL 15, 40–44.

66 See n(26) and accompanying text.

the intricacies of the case. In this respect, the Court's well-reasoned decision clarified the circumstances under which the burden of proof can be allocated more equitably. That said, the analysis of the Court with respect to evidentiary procedure, 'seminal' as it was,[67] was partly overshadowed by its methodology for the establishment of the other constituent element of the obligation to make reparation, namely injury, and, especially, for valuation of compensable damage.[68] The section that follows focuses on these issues in turn.

3 Dealing with Uncertainty: Standard of Proof and the Establishment and Valuation of Damage

Apart from complexity, another vexing problem in situations following an armed conflict is the identification and valuation of damage caused during the armed conflict. In CO *Reparations*, the crux of the contention centred around the deficiencies of the evidentiary record that consisted mainly of secondary sources (ie reports by inter- and non-governmental organisations and expert reports) and an alleged registry of (largely unverified and unverifiable) claims which ultimately did not form part of the public record.[69] This allowed the emergence of two irreconcilable narratives between the parties. On the one hand, Uganda insisted that any damage needed to be sufficiently documented for it to be compensable, arguing that the DRC had time at its disposal to compile evidence.[70] On the other hand, the DRC pointed to the uncontroversial character of the findings of the Court in its Merits Judgment, to the impossibility of collecting contemporaneous evidence due to the devastation caused by the armed conflict, and to the subsequent destruction of evidence on account of the lapse of time since the conflict.[71] To its credit, the Court tried to bridge this gap already during the pre-hearing phase of the reparations proceedings. After the first round of written pleadings, the Court submitted specific questions to the parties relating to the extent and valuation of damage.[72] Also, after receiving and evaluating their responses, it appointed

67 O Pomson, 'The ICJ's Armed Activities Reparations Judgment: A Brave New World?' (*Articles of War*, 4 February 2022), https://lieber.westpoint.edu/icj-armed-activities-reparations-judgment/.

68 Along similar lines, CO Reparations (Yusuf) (n 41) para. 9.

69 CO Reparations (n 1) paras 125, 138, 147.

70 Ibid, para. 113.

71 Ibid, para. 112.

72 Ibid, para. 17.

four experts to assist it with the same issues.[73] Yet, despite these efforts, the evidentiary record of the case remained wanting in several respects, as it transpires from the Court's decision.[74]

In its final decision, the Court tried to remedy the evidentiary gaps by attenuating the applicable standard of proof. Specifically, the Court found that 'the standard of proof required to establish responsibility [ie in the Merits phase] is higher than in the present phase on reparation, which calls for some flexibility'.[75] In support of this finding, the Court took note of the practice of the Ethiopia-Eritrea Claims Commission (EECC) and the International Criminal Court (ICC) as well as the fact that 'a large amount of evidence has been destroyed or rendered inaccessible over the years since the armed conflict'.[76] However, curiously, the Court did not indicate what the applicable standard of proof actually was.[77] In fact, the only indication as to its methodology with respect to the establishment and valuation of damage was the following:

> The Court may on an exceptional basis, award compensation in the form of a global sum within the range of possibilities indicated by the evidence and taking account of equitable considerations. Such an approach may be called for where the evidence leaves no doubt that an internationally wrongful act has caused a substantiated injury, but does not allow a precise evaluation of the extent or scale of such injury.[78]

In the end, the Court decided to award a global sum of USD 325 million broken down into three general heads (damage to persons – USD 225 million; to property – USD 40 million; and to natural resources – USD 60 million).[79] But, as many of the Judges remarked in their individual opinions, it does not transpire from the reasoning what were the specific findings as to the extent and value of damage that led to these numbers.[80]

73 *Armed Activities on the Territory of the Congo* (*DRC v Uganda*), ICJ Rep 264 (ICJ, Order, 2020).

74 CO Reparations (n 1) para. 125.

75 Ibid, para. 124.

76 Ibid, paras 123, 124; e.g. EECC Final Award (Eritrea's Damages) (n 36) para. 36; *Katanga* TCJ Reparations (n 36) para. 38.

77 *Armed Activities on the Territory of the Congo* (*DRC v Uganda*), ICJ Rep 165, (ICJ, Reparations (Separate Opinion of Judge Robinson), 2022) para. 41.

78 CO Reparations (n 1) para. 106.

79 Ibid, para. 405.

80 E.g. *Armed Activities on the Territory of the Congo* (*DRC v Uganda*), ICJ Rep 140 (ICJ, Reparations (Declaration of Judge Tomka), 2022) para. 9; CO Reparations (Yusuf) (n 41)

First, the uncertainty surrounding the applicable standard of proof had an obvious impact on the rejection of entire heads of damage. For instance, with respect to the establishment of damage to civilian persons and property, the Court was at many points unable to lay down even approximately the extent of the damage but nonetheless found these damages compensable.[81] At the same time, it dismissed DRC's claims relating to 2000 killed soldiers and damage to state civilian and military property in their entirety for lack of evidence, even though they were largely substantiated by the same second-hand sources.[82] In essence, the finding implies that Uganda did not cause death or injury to a single soldier or damage to a single piece of state-owned military or civilian infrastructure by unlawfully 'invad[ing] a part of the territory of the DRC of the size of Germany and ke[eping] it under its own control, or that of the various Congolese warlords it befriended, for several years'.[83] This goes to show that what constituted 'substantiated injury' for the Court differed depending on the nature and type of the injury. One might wonder whether the assessment of damages would have been significantly different, had the Court found on the merits that Uganda's activities were justified in terms of *ius ad bellum* (which it did not). A similar criticism can be levelled against the Court's wholesale rejection of DRC's claim of environmental or macroeconomic damage.[84]

Arguably, the discrepancy relating to the applicable standard of proof stemmed from both conceptual and practical reasons. From a conceptual perspective, as will be explained in more detail in subsequent sections, the Court was aware that, with respect to claims relating to international human rights and humanitarian law, the DRC is seeking reparation for injuries sustained

---

paras 22–36; CO Reparations (Robinson) (n 76) paras 2–6; *Armed Activities on the Territory of the Congo (DRC v Uganda)*, ICJ Rep 185 (ICJ, Reparations (Declaration of Judge Salam), 2022, para. 18.

81 E.g. CO Reparations (n 1) paras 181, 193, 206, 257.

82 Ibid, paras 165, 255, 256.

83 *Armed Activities on the Territory of the Congo (DRC v Uganda)*, ICJ Rep 334 (ICJ, Merits (Separate Opinion of Judge Simma), 2005) para. 2.

84 CO Reparations (n 1) paras 350, 384; along the lines of EECC Final Award (Ethiopia's Damages) (n 36) paras 461, 465, 469; for criticisms see CO Reparations (Robinson) (n 76) para. 46; D Desierto, 'The International Court of Justice's 2022 Reparations Judgment in DRC v. Uganda: 'Global Sums' as the New Device for Human Rights-Based Inter-state Disputes' (*EJIL:Talk! Blog of the European Society of International Law*, 14 February 2022), https://www.ejiltalk.org/the-international-court-of-justices-2022-reparations-judgment-in-drc-v-uganda-a-new-methodology-for-human-rights-in-inter-state-disputes/; more modestly A Ollino (n 44) 20–22.

both in fact and in law by individuals and not–strictly speaking–the state.[85] Still, at the very least, one could argue that the right to life under international human rights law is relevant with respect to the killing of enemy soldiers in pursuit of an act of aggression.[86] From a more practical viewpoint, whilst DRC's inability to produce evidence with respect to damage to individuals was justified due to the circumstances of the case, it should have been able to adduce at least some concrete evidence with respect to damage to its own personnel and property (which it did not).[87]

But apart from this point, the Court's open-ended findings with respect to the standard of proof and the applicable methodology pervaded all aspects of the establishment and valuation of damage.[88] One notable feature of the decision is that the Court did not lay down the number of affected persons or property based on which it calculated the amount awarded. At points, the Court established 'the range of possibilities indicated by the evidence'.[89] So, for instance, it identified specific – even if at times wide – margins as to lives lost (10,000 to 15,000), displaced persons (100,000 to 500,000), or child soldiers recruited (1,800 to 2,500).[90] As to other categories of claims, such as injuries to persons or sexual violence, the Court declared that it was impossible to determine, even approximately, the extent of damage.[91] Another such feature is the Court's mercurial approach as to the valuation of damage. As to some heads of damage such as sexual violence or damage to property, the Court took note of proceedings before the Trial Chambers (TC s) of the International Criminal Court (ICC) in cases relating to the DRC and came up with an amount per victim.[92] As to other heads of damage, such as loss of life, injuries to persons, displacements, and recruitment of child soldiers, the Court refused to lay down any monetary value per victim but limited itself to

---

85 CO Reparations (n 1) para. 102; also *Diallo* Compensation (n 12) para. 57; *Ahmadou Sadio Diallo (Republic of Guinea v Democratic Republic of the Congo)*, ICJ rep 391 (ICJ, Compensation (Declaration of Judge Greenwood), 2012) para. 1; G Gaja, 'Is a State Specially Affected When its Nationals' Human Rights are Infringed?' in LC Vohrah et al (eds), *Man's Inhumanity to Man – Essays in Honour of Antonio Cassese* (Kluwer 2003) 373, 379.

86 UNHRC, 'General Comment No 36 – Article 6: Right to life' (3 September 2019) UN Doc CCPR/C/GC/36 para. 70; see e.g. D Akande and M Jackson, 'The Right to Life and *Jus ad Bellum*: Belligerent Equality and the Duty to Prosecute Acts of Aggression' (2022) 71 ICLQ 453, 456.

87 CO Reparations (n 1) paras 165, 255, 256.

88 CO Reparations (n 1) para. 277.

89 Ibid, para. 106.

90 Ibid, paras 162, 204, 223.

91 Ibid, paras 181, 193.

92 Ibid, paras 192, 249.

finding the evidentiary record unconvincing in this respect.[93] This is so notwithstanding the availability of values for most of these heads in decisions of other international mechanisms which lent themselves to comparison or even transfer including those of the ICC in the DRC cases.[94] The reasons for these discrepancies are not apparent. To illustrate this point, with respect to rape and sexual violence, the Court took note with approval a value cited in one expert report submitted to the ICC, even though its authors admit that this is a 'symbolic payment' and not 'full' compensation.[95] Conversely, the Court refused to take into account the amount fixed by the ICC with respect to child soldiers as an '*ex aequo et bono*' pronouncement,[96] even though another TC later confirmed that the amount corresponded to the cost of rehabilitation programmes for child soldiers run by the Trust Fund for Victim in the DRC.[97] Apart from these inconsistencies, it is questionable whether such restrictive approach was even required in line with the Court's own jurisprudence. To the contrary, as the Court has held in multiple occasions, these claims also involve non-material damage which 'can be established even without specific evidence'.[98]

The 'global sums' approach of the Court in this case raises broader normative questions about whether and how inter-state proceedings relating to massive human rights violations in the aftermath of armed conflict can be conducive to the application of the principle of full reparation. On the one hand, as the Court very clearly acknowledged, it was bound to decide 'within the range of possibilities indicated by the evidence'.[99] In this context, recourse to equitable considerations is not a substitute for evidence adduced in the proceedings or would have been adduced if they actually existed; 'equity is not alchemy'.[100] On the other hand, in any case involving reparations, an international court or tribunal '*must* determine, insofar as possible, the appro-

---

93 Ibid, paras 163–164, 180, 205, 224.

94 Ibid, paras 163 *in fine*, 205.

95 Ibid, para. 192 citing *Ntaganda* (Reparations Order) ICC-01/04-02/06-2659, TC-IV (8 March 2021) para. 238 but see idem para. 239 and *Ntaganda* (Experts Report on Reparation) ICC-01/04-02/06-2653-Anx1-Red2, TC-IV (3 November 2020) para. 220.

96 Ibid, para. 205 citing *Lubanga* (Decision Setting the Size of the Reparations Award for which Thomas Lubanga Dyilo is Liable) ICC-01/04-01/06-3379-Corr, TC-II (21 December 2017) para. 259.

97 *Ntaganda* Reparations (n 94) para. 244.

98 *Diallo* Compensation (n 12) paras 21, 23; CO Reparations (n 1) para. 164; along similar lines, *Diallo* Compensation (Greenwood) (n 84) para. 7.

99 CO Reparations (n 1) para. 106.

100 *Diallo* Compensation (Greenwood) (n 84) para. 5.

priate compensation for each violation'.[101] This entails an '*obligation* to determine appropriate compensation, even if the process involves estimation or guesswork within the range of possibilities indicated by the evidence'.[102] The application of a lower standard of proof, still more the equitable allocation of the burden of proof, should have enabled the Court to reach more conclusive figures with respect to the specific harms claimed in the case.[103] As has been explained, the Court could exercise moderation in several cleavages: the identification of victims, the valuation of damage, or the adjustment of the overall amount of compensation due, once reached, as a trade-off for relying on such 'estimation or guesswork'.[104] However, by resorting to the 'global sums' approach, the Court avoided to engage and explain the legal and normative choices involved at each of these steps. In fact, it failed to fully convince even some of the Judges who voted in favour of the *dispositif* in whole or in part.[105] More importantly, such vague approach to calculation of damages makes any personalisation of losses, still more actual reparation to individuals, practically impossible.[106] The next section takes a closer look on this issue in turn.

4 Dealing with Victims: Individual Rights to Reparation under General International Law

The *CO Reparations* Judgment should also be contextualised within broader developments concerning the position of individuals in the law of state responsibility. It is trite that the traditional law of state responsibility views the state as the sole right-holder under international law that claims reparation for any injury caused by the violation including for any harm suffered by its nationals.[107] In this configuration, the individual is cynically reduced to 'a

---

101 EECC Final Award (Eritrea's Damages) para. 37 (emphasis added).

102 CO Reparations (Robinson) (n 76) para. 8 citing EECC Final Award (Eritrea's Damages) 508 (emphasis added).

103 CO Reparations (Robinson) (n 76) para. 41.

104 Ibid, para. 8.

105 See e.g. CO Reparations (Tomka) (n 79) para. 7; CO Reparations (Yusuf) (n 41) para. 42; CO Reparations (Robinson) (n 76) para. 47; CO Reparations (Salam) (n 79) para. 18.

106 *Armed Activities on the Territory of the Congo* (*DRC v Uganda*), ICJ Rep 200, (ICJ, Reparations (Opinion dissident du M. le Juge ad hoc Daudet), 2022) para. 27; CO Reparations (Salam) (n 79) para. 22; D Desierto (n 83).

107 E.g. *Mavrommatis Palestine Concessions* (*Greece v United Kingdom*), PCIJ Ser A No 2, (PCIJ, 1924) paras 11–12; also *Nottebohm* (*Liechtenstein v Guatemala*), ICJ Rep 4, (ICJ, 1955) para. 24.

convenient scale for the calculation of the reparation due to the State'.[108] As will be shown, it is undeniable that this configuration has changed to some extent, albeit ambiguities as to the content of rights of individuals in international law and their implementation through the traditional mechanisms of state responsibility persist. These ambiguities relate to the identification of the rules that establish individual rights or interests under international law, the extent to which these rights correspond to secondary obligations of the state to make reparation directly to individuals, and the rules pertaining the payment of reparations to individuals.

To start, it is no longer in doubt that individuals can have rights under international law.[109] However, apart from international human rights law, it is intensely debated whether some of the rules involved in the context of the CO case entail rights of individuals under international law.[110] Indeed, according to a widely shared view, individuals have certain rights or at least legally protected interests under international humanitarian law entailing a substantive entitlement to reparation under international law.[111] The silence of Article 3 of Hague Convention IV and Article 91 AP-I as to the beneficiaries of the states' obligation to pay compensation for violations of international humanitarian law has been interpreted as affirming this view.[112] Moreover, the antecedent of the UN Compensation Commission constitutes evidence that repa-

108 *Factory at Chorzów* (*Germany v Poland*), PCIJ Ser A No 17, (PCIJ, Claim for Indemnity (Merits), 1928), para. 28.

109 E.g. *LaGrand* (*Germany v US*), ICJ Rep 466, (ICJ, 2001) para. 77; *Jadhav* (*India v Pakistan*), ICJ Rep 418, (ICJ, 2019) para. 115.

110 E.g. ARSIWA (n 13) Commentary to Art 33 para. 3; A Peters, 'Beyond Human Rights: The Legal Status of the Individual in International Law' (Jonathan Huston tr, CUP 2016) 7–8.

111 UNGA, 'Basic Principles and Guidelines on the Right to a Remedy and Reparation for Victims of Gross Violations of International Human Rights Law and Serious Violations of International Humanitarian Law', annexed to UNGA Res 60/147 (21 March 2006) (BPRV) para. 15; ILA, 'Draft Declaration of International Law Principles on Reparation for Victims of Armed Conflict (Substantive Issues)–International Law Association–International Law Committee for Victims of Armed Conflict–Prepared by Professor Reiner Hoffmann' (2010) 74 ILARC 295, 299; T Meron, 'The Humanization of Humanitarian Law' (2000) 94 AJIL 239, 251–253; *contra* e.g. R Provost, 'International Human Rights and Humanitarian Law' (CUP 2002) 27–34; K Parlett, 'The Individual in the International Legal System' (CUP 2011) 225.

112 E.g. *Jurisdictional Immunities of the State* (*Germany v Italy; Greece intervening*, ICJ Rep 291, (ICJ, Dissenting Opinion of Judge Yusuf, 2012) paras 13–14; F Kalshoven, 'State Responsibility for Warlike Acts of the Armed Force' (1991) 40 ICLQ 827, 833 and 850; C Greenwood, 'International Humanitarian Law (Laws of War)' in F Kalshoven (ed), *The Centennial of the First International Peace Conference* (Nijhoff 2000) 161, 250; BPRV (n 110) preamble 1.

ration provided by a state may also accrue to individuals in cases of violations of the *ius ad bellum*.[113] On the one hand, in the absence of special rules, the implementation of the international responsibility of the state for the violations under discussion remains primarily an inter-state affair.[114] On the other hand, as a matter of principle, 'it is scarcely necessary to point out that the capacity to possess civil rights does not necessarily imply the capacity to exercise those rights oneself'.[115] As the Court has enunciated, 'the duty to make reparation is a rule that exists independently of those rules which concern the means by which it is to be effected'.[116]

The existence of individual rights under international law should also entail in principle that the obligation of reparation should 'accrue' to individuals under the general law of international responsibility.[117] Notably, in *Wall*, the Court found 'that Israel also has an obligation to compensate, in accordance with the applicable rules of international law, all natural or legal persons having suffered any form of material damage as a result of the wall's construction'.[118] However, as one commentator has suggested, 'Israel's duties towards individuals [might] have been affirmed by the Court only to circumvent the difficult question of Palestinian statehood'.[119] In this latter respect, according to the International Law Commission, even when the secondary obligation of reparation exists towards a state, reparation does not accrue necessarily or exclusively to that state.[120] The ILC notes that when a state exercises diplo-

113 E.g. A Fischer-Lescano, 'Subjektivierung völkerrechtlicher Sekundärregeln' (2007) 45 AdV 299, 330–331; A Gattini, 'The UN Compensation Commission: Old Rules, New Procedures on War Reparations' (2002) 13 EJIL 161, 170–171; see e.g. Governing Council of the UNCC, 'Criteria for Expedited Process of Urgent Claims' (2 August 1991) S/AC.26/1991/1; more generally: Y Dinstein, 'War, Aggression and Self-Defence' (5th edn CUP 2011) 111 ('the obligation to indemnify the victims of aggression').

114 P D'Argent (n 14) 580–581.

115 *Appeal from a Judgment of the Hungaro/Czecoslovak Mixed Arbitral Tribunal (The Peter Pázmány University) (Czechoslovakia v Hungary)* PCIJ Ser A/B No 61, 231.

116 *Jurisdictional Immunities of the State (Germany v Italy; Greece intervening)* ICJ Rep 99, (ICJ, 2012) para. 94.

117 Cf. ARSIWA (n 13) Art 33 (2).

118 *Legal Consequences of the Construction of a Wall on the Occupied Palestinian Territory* (Advisory Opinion), ICJ Rep 136, (ICJ, 2004) para. 153; also *Legal Consequences of the Policies and Practices of Israel in the Occupied Palestinian Territory, including East Jerusalem*, (ICJ, Advisory Opinion, 2024), https://www.icj-cij.org/sites/default/files/case-related/186/186-20240719-adv-01-00-en.pdf, paras 269, 271.

119 P D'Argent, 'Compliance, Cessation, Reparation and Restitution in the Wall Advisory Opinion' in P-M Dupuy et al (eds), *Common Values in International Law—Essays in Honour of Christian Tomuschat* (Engel 2006) 463, 475.

120 ARSIWA (n 13) Commentary to Art 33, para. 3.

matic protection over its nationals, it 'do[es] so in its own right or that of its national – or both'.[121] As a result, reparation for the injury suffered by the individual should be made for the benefit of the injured individual.[122] The Court essentially alludes to these antecedents in the CO Reparations Judgment when it states that 'the reparation awarded to the DRC for damage to persons and to property reflects the harm suffered by individuals and communities as a result of Uganda's breach of its international obligations'.[123]

What remains an open question is how reparation can benefit the injured individuals as a practical matter. In this respect, the ICJ in *Jurisdictional Immunities* did not accept – albeit in *obiter* – 'a rule requiring the payment of full compensation to each and every individual victim as a rule accepted by the international community of States as a whole as one from which no derogation is permitted'.[124] The Court pointed to post-war agreements between formerly warring parties involving lump-sum settlements, waivers, and set-offs as examples.[125] On its face, the Court's pronouncement only stipulates that there is no *jus cogens* rule imposing on a responsible state an obligation to pay compensation to individuals. However, if individuals had a right under general international law to claim reparations directly from the responsible state independently from their state of nationality, then, by logical implication, their state of nationality could not waive or set off that right.[126] Also, the ICJ in the same case has indicated that if the receiving state uses these funds to rebuild its economy or infrastructure instead of distributing them to the individual victims, these individuals do not have a claim against the state responsible for the internationally wrongful act.[127] Importantly, the Court left open the possibility that individual victims may have a claim against the receiving state. The ILC had previously put forward such a 'recommended practice', but

121 ILC, 'Draft Articles on Diplomatic Protection with commentaries' (2006) II(2) YbILC 26 (DADP), Commentary to Art 1, para. 5.

122 *Diallo* Compensation (n 12) para. 57; *Diallo* Compensation (Greenwood) (n 84) para. 1; G Gaja, 'Quel préjudice pour un état qui exerce la protection diplomatique?' in D Alland et al (eds), *Unity and Diversity – Essays in Honour of Professor Pierre-Marie Dupuy* (Brill 2014) 487, 489; A Pellet, 'The Second Death of Euripide Mavrommatis? Notes on the International Law Commission's Draft Articles on Diplomatic Protection' (2008) 7 LPICT 33, 56–57.

123 CO Reparations (n 1) para. 408.

124 *Jurisdictional Immunities* (n 115) para. 94; similarly, A Gattini, 'Le riparazioni di guerra nel diritto internazionale' (CEDAM 2003) 668; S Furuya, 'Waiver or Limitation of Possible Reparation Claims of Victims' (2018) 78 ZaöRV 591, 594.

125 *Jurisdictional Immunities* (n 115) para. 94.

126 Gattini (n 123) 628–631; Furuya (n 123) 593.

127 Ibid, para. 102.

cautioned that it was 'not susceptible to transformation[n] into [a] rul[e] of law in the exercise of progressive development'.[128] The European Court of Human Rights has found in two cases involving multiple violations of human rights that the applicant government exercising diplomatic protection has an international obligation to distribute the amount awarded to individual victims.[129] By contrast, the Appeals Chamber of the International Criminal Court has held that 'there is [no] internationally recognized right to a consideration of individual applications for reparations, in cases where the applicable law provides for both individual and collective awards for reparations and a collective award is made'.[130] In the *CO Reparations* Judgment, the Court stopped short from favouring any particular development. Rather, it only took note of 'the undertaking given by the Agent of the DRC…according to which the compensation to be paid by Uganda will be fairly and effectively distributed to victims of the harm'.[131] At the same time, the Court 'encouraged' the DRC to consider the possibility of adopting measures 'for the benefit of the affected communities as a whole'.[132] At the time of writing, there is no official information as to how the DRC actually used the amounts paid by Uganda.

The *CO Reparations* judgment continues a line of jurisprudence that is increasingly receptive to the rights of individuals under international law including their interest to benefit from reparations from internationally wrongful acts. At the same time, it also attests to the reality that interstate proceedings in the aftermath of armed conflicts strain the capacity of existing institutions to implement such a 'personalised' approach to reparations without losing sight of the collective aspects of war-related harms. In the *CO Reparations* judgment, the tension underlies the entirety of the Court's reasoning relating to causation and establishment and valuation of damage.[133] However, ultimately, the most conspicuous, but still incipient, consequence of individual rights under the law of state responsibility appears to be at the stage of payment. Yet, the law pertaining to payment has been mostly over-

128 DADP (n 120) Art 19 (c) and Commentary to Art 19, para. 1.

129 *Cyprus v Turkey* (Just Satisfaction) [GC] App no 25781/94 (ECtHR, 12 May 2014) para. 58 citing Compensation (n 12) para. 57; *Georgia v Russia* (Just Satisfaction) [GC] App no 13255/07 (ECtHR, 31 January 2019) paras 77–79; see also Governing Council of the UNCC, 'Distribution of Payments and Transparency' (24 March 1994) S/AC.26/Dec.18.

130 *Lubanga (I)* (Judgment on the appeals against the 'Decision establishing the principles and procedures to be applied to reparations' of 7 August 2012) ICC-01/04-01/06-3129, AC (3 March 2015) para. 155.

131 CO Reparations (n 1) para. 408.

132 Ibid.

133 See n(84) and accompanying text.

looked by international courts and tribunals and scholars alike. The section that follows turns briefly to this issue.

5 Dealing with Payment: 'Personalisation' of Reparation and Economic Capacity of the Responsible State

Almost a century ago, the Permanent Court of International Justice, the predecessor institution of the ICJ, proclaimed the principle of full reparation as innate in the notion of the wrongful act.[134] Less famously, the PCIJ affirmed its jurisdiction to determine the method of payment of reparation including 'to whom the payment shall be made, in what place and at what moment; in a lump sum or maybe by instalments; where payment shall be made; who shall bear the cost etc.'[135] According to the PCIJ, this is a question of applying the 'general rules regarding payment'.[136] These general rules have not yet been codified in a systematic way and they appear still in flux in several respects. As has been shown in the previous section, general rules of payment, technical as they might be, entail serious distributional consequences. The present section expands upon this issue by drawing upon another aspect of the *CO Reparations* decision, namely, the role of the economic capacity of the responsible state to pay war reparation and the modalities of payment.

A constant theme in *post bellum* settlements is whether and, if so, how the capacity of the responsible state to pay compensation without compromising its ability to meet its people's basic needs bears on the determination of war reparations.[137] In the *CO Reparations* case, the amount claimed by the DRC, which totalled over USD 11 billion, and Uganda's economic situation as a developing state brought the issue to the fore.[138] The Court recalled the findings of the EECC as to whether the economic condition of the responsible state bears on the determination of the amount of compensation.[139] In that decision, the EECC found that basic human rights norms had a bearing on the law on state responsibility in that 'in no way may a people be deprived of its own means of

134 *Factory at Chorzów* (n 10) para. 47.

135 Ibid, para. 61.

136 Ibid.

137 For one famous iteration of the argument: J Maynard Keynes, 'The Economic Consequences of the Peace' (1919, reprinted Harcourt, Brace and Howe 1920) 113–225.

138 CO Reparations (n 1) para. 109; e.g. D Desierto (n 83); B Mageste Castellar Campos, 'War Reparations as a Financial Burden to the Responsible State: The Congo v Uganda Case' (2022) 95 QIL Zoom-In 43, 43.

139 CO Reparations (n 1) para. 110.

subsistence'.[140] On this basis, the EECC proceeded to 'conside[r] whether it was necessary to limit its compensation awards in some manner to ensure that the ultimate financial burden imposed on a Party would not be so excessive, given its economic condition and its capacity to pay, as to compromise its ability to meet its people's basic needs'.[141] That said, the ICJ stopped short from rubber-stamping this antecedent, nor did it take into account the economic situation of Uganda, explicitly at least, in determining issues of causation, establishment of injury, or valuation of damage.[142] Besides, there is no indication that these circumstances had any influence on the fixing of the total amount due.[143] At the same time, the CO *Reparations* Judgment introduces a certain degree of novelty with regards to the modalities of payment which lessens in fact the financial impact of an award of compensation on the responsible state. In this respect, it is possible to argue that Uganda's economic capacity to pay the award had a limited and implicit impact on the issue of payment.[144]

In particular, the Court ordered that the total sum will be paid in five annual instalments of USD 65 million from 2022 to 2026.[145] The Court provided no reasons for this finding, whereas there is no antecedent for such a modality in the decisions of the ICJ or its predecessor institution, the Permanent Court of International Justice. Practice relating to peace settlements varies considerably as to the issue of payment and spans from no specific arrangements to complex regimes of schedules of payment and financing.[146] The rationale of the ILC in adopting ARSIWA can be instructive as to the legal considerations that underlie an award involving specified modalities of payment. The late Judge Crawford, then acting as ILC's special rapporteur on state responsibility, drew a distinction between 'the quantum [ie amount] of compensation, which by definition reflects the actual losses suffered as a result of the breach, and the mode of payment'.[147] The capacity of the responsible state to pay without depriving the population of its means of subsistence only

140 EECC Final Award (Eritrea's Damages) (n 36) para. 19.

141 Ibid, para. 22.

142 CO Reparations (n 1) para. 407.

143 Castellar Campos (n 137) 54.

144 Castellar Campos (n 136) 57.

145 Ibid, para. 406.

146 See, e.g., Castellar Campos (n 137) 56–57; P D'Argent, 'The Conversion of Reparations into Sovereign Debts' in M Erpelding, B Hess, and H Ruiz Fabri (eds), *Peace Through Law: The Verseilles Peace Treaty and Dispute Settlement after WWI* (Nomos 2019) 205, 206–209.

147 J Crawford, 'Third Report on State Responsibility' (15 March 2000) UN Doc A/CN.4/507, para. 41.

related to the latter and could elicit delayed payment, if a circumstance precluding wrongfulness existed, or rescheduling in line with the practice of international financial institutions.[148] It is also possible to draw similarities in reasoning with findings in the context of individual responsibility under international law. In *Al-Mahdi*, a Trial Chamber of the ICC decided that the indigence of the accused has no bearing on the liability to make reparation, but rather can be taken into account in enforcing a reparations order 'by affording an option to make reasonable payments in instalments'.[149] However, the correlation between economic capacity and modalities of payment remains implicit in the reasoning of the *CO Reparations* judgment.[150]

The provision for payment of the total sum in annual instalments was not, however, the only novelty of the decision. What was truly unique was the Court's finding that 'post-judgment interest at an annual rate of 6 per cent on each instalment will accrue on any overdue amount from the day which follows the day on which the instalment was due'.[151] It is true that the 1882 treaty constituting the background of the *Russian Indemnities* case laid down a principal sum payable to Russia in annual instalments without interest.[152] However, in the rare occasions that international courts and tribunals specify payment in instalments, interest continues to accrue annually on the principal sum still due.[153] In doctrinal terms, the Court's categorical pronouncement as to post-judgment interest raises questions as to the applicable rule at play. According to the ILC, whereas the award of pre-judgment interest requires the application of the customary rule reflected in Article 38 ARSIWA, post-judgment interest is a matter of procedure of each international court or tribunal.[154] Yet, the reason for relegating post-judgment interest to a procedural matter is not at all clear.[155] From a normative perspective, if an international court or tribunal is bound to consider retrospectively the impact of time on the value of compensation in the time between the wrongful act and the judg-

148 Ibid, para. 42; also M Paparinskis, 'A Case Against Crippling Compensation in International Law of State Responsibility' (2020) 83 MLR 1246, 1255–1256 (although criticises this view).

149 *Al-Mahdi* (n 36) para. 114.

150 CO Reparations (n 1) para. 407.

151 CO Reparations (n 1) para. 406.

152 *Affaire de l'indemnité russe (Russia/Turkey)* [1912] XI RIAA 421, 435.

153 E.g. *Velásquez Rodríguez Case (Compensatory Damages)* Ser C No 7 (IACtHR, 21 July 1989) para. 57; also ARSIWA (n 13) Commentary to Art 38, para. 5.

154 ARSIWA (n 13) Commentary to Art 38, para. 12; J Crawford, 'State Responsibility: The General Part' (CUP 2013) 533.

155 R Silvestre J Martha, 'The Financial Obligation in International Law' (OUP 2015) 471.

ment, it should also bear the responsibility to take the necessary measures to preserve such value prospectively.[156] This is not a mere technicality, but can potentially have real distributional consequences. As Judge Tomka observed '[t]his decision...does not take into account that, with the passage of time, the real value of the compensation awarded and still remaining to be paid in instalments, will diminish...by up to US$39,000,000'.[157] Besides, even if Uganda's economic capabilities had an implicit bearing in the determination of modalities of payment, due account must also be given to the availability of adequate means of subsistence for the beneficiaries of the reparation. In extreme situations where both parties are in dire financial situation, reparation, 'rather than depriving one people of their own means of subsistence, [...] would rather require the return to another people of *their* means of subsistence, wrongfully taken'.[158] At any rate, the implication that international courts and tribunals operate *in vacuo* on this important issue should be resisted.

6 Conclusion

The CO case tested and exposed the practical and logistical restrictions that the ICJ faces as an institution with limited resources, notwithstanding its unparalleled standing within the legal profession. On the one hand, the Court reaffirmed key principles of the law of international responsibility and clarified important aspects of its procedure including the crucial issue of the allocation of burden of proof. On the other hand, the ICJ resorted to a nebulous 'global sums' approach which left little space for the 'personalisation' of reparation, namely, the consideration of the specific character of the wrongful act, the nature of the harm, and the identity and needs of the real victim. In this respect, the decision blurs the line between substantive and procedural law, between legal reasoning and factual determination, and, ultimately, between law, equity, and expediency.[159] At the very least, this ambiguity should have implications for the relevance of the Court's decision for future cases.

156 Ibid 472.

157 CO Reparations (Tomka) (n 79) para. 10.

158 Crawford, Third Report (n 146) para. 39.

159 On the notion of 'expediency' see M Bedjaoui, 'L'opportunité dans les decisions de la Cour International de Justice' in L Boisson de Chazournes and V Gowlland-Debbas (eds), *The International Legal System in Quest of Equity and Universality – Liber amicorum Georges Abi-Saab* (Nijhoff 2001) 563–589.

At the same time, the *CO* case provides an opportunity to reflect more broadly about the ways in which inter-state proceedings can provide redress to the victims of armed conflict through the fusion of the law of state responsibility with fundamental principles of international human rights law. The law on reparations seems to evolve on the basis that the real victims of internationally wrongful acts, but also the real payers of reparations, are human beings of flesh and blood whose rights and interests ought to be protected under international law. One neglected aspect of this development is the gradual elaboration of general rules of payment that take into account this tension. At this stage of the development of international law, general rules of payment appear still in flux and it is important to identify potential pitfalls. First, the increasing focus to the harms of individuals may lead to preclusion or serious curtailment of compensation, unless individual victims can be identified.[160] Ultimately, a 'personalised' approach to reparation should be complemented by a realistic way to offset evidentiary problems and, most importantly, to address the harm to collective goods. The key take-away is that personalised and collective approaches to reparations are not mutually exclusive, but complementary and address different harms. Second, due account must be given to the distributional aspects of payment which so far have been completely overlooked. The implication that international courts and tribunals and, ultimately, states operate in a legal vacuum with unfettered discretion should be resisted.

---

160 See, e.g., *Cyprus v Turkey* (n 128) para. 47; *Georgia v Russia (I)* (n 128) para. 70; CO Reparations (n 1) para. 107.

CHAPTER 11

Fitting a Square Peg in a Round Hole?

Challenges and Prospects of Inter-State Human Rights Complaints as (Overlapping) Avenues for Individual Reparations

Veronica Botticelli[1]

1 Introduction

A brief *tour d'horizon* of contemporary inter-state dispute settlement practice reveals a sharp increase in complaints regarding human rights and fundamental freedoms before international courts, tribunals, and quasi-judicial monitoring bodies, regardless of whether these mechanisms are assigned general or specific human rights competence.[2] An inter-state complaint is a formal legal action initiated by one or more States against another before a treaty-based body, whether judicial or quasi-judicial, alleging non-compliance with one or more provisions included in an international human rights treaty.[3] While not unprecedented, this development departs from earlier practice, historically constrained by the political and economic costs of initiating proceedings. Inter-state human rights cases have fre-

1 Postdoctoral Research Fellow in Public International Law, Department of International, Legal, Historical and Political Studies, University of Milan, Milan, Italy; veronica.botticelli@unimi.it. All references to case law are current as of February 28, 2025. Later decisions have not been considered.

2 On the topic of inter-state complaints in the field of international human rights law, see extensively S Leckie, 'The Inter-State Complaint Procedure in International Human Rights Law: Hopeful Prospect of Wishful Thinking?' (1988) 10(2) *Human Rights Quarterly* 249; PH Kooijmans, 'Inter-State Dispute Settlement in the Field of Human Rights' (1990) 3(3) *Leiden Journal of International Law* 87; more recently, M Lawry-White, 'Inter-State Human Rights Disputes: Mapping Dispute Resolution Options Including Conciliation' (2024) 13(1) *International Human Rights Law Review* 5.

3 For the purpose of this contribution, 'complaint', 'communication', 'application', 'case', 'claim', 'petition', and 'proceeding' will be used interchangeably, even though – in the very reality of international (quasi-)adjudication practice – they reflect significant variations in competent bodies, judicialization, jurisdiction, admissibility, procedure, legal standards, outcomes, and remedies. For a terminological taxonomy, see I Risini and G Ulfstein, 'Human Rights, State Complaints' (2022) *Max Planck Encyclopedia of Public International Law* [MPEPIL], para. 2, <https://opil.ouplaw.com/display/10.1093/law:epil/9780199231690/law-9780199231690-e817> accessed 28 February 2025.

 | DOI:10.1163/9789004716742_012

quently been perceived as unfriendly acts,[4] or as 'Trojan horses' for claims that relate only peripherally or pretentiously to human rights.[5] Furthermore, instituting such complaints often serves as a litigation strategy to adjudicate multiple aspects of a broader dispute by segmenting it into claims under different legal rules.[6]

Consequently, inter-state proceedings are increasingly burdening the dockets of courts, tribunals, and quasi-judicial monitoring mechanisms instituted under regional and universal human rights treaties. These bodies primarily discharge their (quasi-)adjudicatory functions through the examination of individual claims, widely recognized as the 'cornerstone' of human rights protection frameworks.[7] The exercise of this procedural right allows individuals to access international justice without the 'mediation' of the State of nationality acting as a *parens patriae*, as was intended through diplomatic protection. However, individual applications are not the sole (quasi-)judicial avenue for safeguarding fundamental rights. Notably, there has been a resurgence in inter-state applications as a mechanism for adjudicating disputes over the interpretation, application, and enforcement of human rights obligations. Human rights treaties also authorize their monitoring bodies to address inter-state complaints through various procedural frameworks.[8]

4 See D Shelton, *Remedies in International Human Rights* (3rd edn, OUP 2015) 60; I Risini and G Ulfstein (n 3), para. 33.

5 See, *inter alia*, Leckie (n 2), at 266; PH Koojimans (n 2) 90, 97; as regards inter-state complaints under the UN Convention for the Elimination of All Forms of Racial Discrimination, see instead P Thornberry, 'The Committee on the Elimination of Racial Discrimination (CERD)' in F Mégret and P Alston (eds), *The United Nations and Human Rights: A Critical Appraisal* (OUP 2020) 321; R Garciandia and P Webb, 'The UN's Work on Racial Discrimination: Achievements and Challenges' (2022) 25(1) *Max Planck Yearbook of United Nations Law* 228.

6 See BI Bonafé, 'Parallel Human Rights Proceedings Before International Courts and Monitoring Bodies' (2021) 15(2) *Diritti umani e diritto internazionale* 369. On the (ongoing) 'multiplication' of inter-state disputes between Ukraine and Russia before different courts and tribunals, see L Hill-Cawthorne, 'International Litigation and the Disaggregation of Disputes: Ukraine/Russia as a Case Study' (2019) 68(4) *International and Comparative Law Quarterly* 779.

7 AA Cançado Trindade, *The Access of Individuals to International Justice* (OUP 2001) 35. While the individual complaints procedure was a groundbreaking development in judicial human rights protection, the recognition of *locus standi* in other areas of international law dates back to, at least, 1907. On this matter, see F Orrego-Vicuña, 'Individuals and Non-State Entities before International Courts and Tribunals' (2001) 5 *Max Planck Yearbook of United Nations* 53, 54–55.

8 For a comprehensive overview of all inter-state human rights complaints procedures, see R Reilly and H Trout, 'Inter-State Complaints in International Human Rights Law' (*British Institute of International and Comparative Law*, 27 April 2022) <https://www.biicl.org/docu

At the regional level, inter-state procedures are outlined in Article 33 of the European Convention on Human Rights (ECHR), Articles 45 and 61 of the American Convention on Human Rights (ACHR), and Articles 47 to 53 of the African Charter on Human and Peoples' Rights (ACHPR). Almost all international human rights treaties concluded under the auspices of the United Nations system do provide for several inter-state complaints mechanisms.[9] Illustrative examples of such procedures can be found, *inter alia*, in Articles 11–13 of the Convention for the Elimination of All Forms of Racial Discrimination (ICERD), Article 41 of the International Convention on Civil and Political Rights (ICCPR), and Article 21 of the Convention Against Torture (CAT). In a manner analogous to the proceedings before the International Court of Justice (ICJ),[10] the overwhelming majority of inter-state procedures are optional, necessitating that State parties deposit additional declarations to indicate their consent to be subject to the inter-state dispute settlement mechanism as delineated in the pertinent treaty instrument.[11] Furthermore, the effective functioning of such optional jurisdiction clauses, if adopted, typically depends on a reciprocity requirement: States can hold each other accountable for violations only if they are prepared to face comparable risks themselves. Thus, it is no coincidence that specialized courts and quasi-judicial monitoring bodies

---

ments/153_inter-state_complaints_in_international_human_rights_law_-_event_report.pdf> accessed 28 February; L Lixinski, 'On the Circumscribed and Problematic Resurgence of Inter-State Human Rights Cases' (2022) 3 *European Convention on Human Rights Law Review* 174, at 176–177.

9 For an analysis of inter-state complaints procedures in *core* UN human rights conventions and their interaction with ICJ dispute settlement, see A Zimmermann, 'Human Rights Treaty Bodies and the Jurisdiction of the International Court of Justice' (2013) 2 *The Law & Practice of International Courts and Tribunals* 5. The *only* 'core' UN treaty lacking an internal inter-state complaint mechanism is the Convention on the Elimination of All Forms of Discrimination Against Women, which instead provides a traditional dispute settlement clause granting the ICJ jurisdiction over treaty interpretation and application. See MA Freeman, C Chinkin, B Rudolf, 'Article 29', in *The UN Convention on the Elimination of All Forms of Discrimination Against Women: A Commentary* (OUP 2012) 597. Though not strictly a core human rights treaty, the Genocide Convention similarly omits a specialized treaty-based enforcement mechanism, relying instead on the ICJ's jurisdiction via a compromissory clause. On the *ratio* of this significant omission, see C Tams, L Berster, B Schiffbauer (eds), *Convention on the Prevention and Punishment of the Crime of Genocide: A Commentary* (Hart Nomos 2014) 26, 294.

10 MI Papa, 'Litigating Collective Obligations Before the International Court of Justice: Progress, Challenges and Prospects' (2024) 23(1) *The Law and Practice of International Courts and Tribunals* 36, 42–43.

11 In support of the need for 'a system of general compulsory and binding dispute settlement procedures', see further M Brus, *Third Party Dispute Settlement in an Interdependent World* (Martinus Nijhoff 1995) 182.

currently engaged in inter-state human rights proceedings are vested with compulsory jurisdiction. In this regard, it is no surprise that the European Convention on Human Rights (ECtHR) has served as an authentic pioneer, having been the inaugural human rights supervisory mechanism to receive and consider inter-state cases before both the European Commission of Human Rights (ECommHR, 'Commission') and the European Court of Human Rights (ECtHR).[12] After that, from early 2000s onwards, the African Commission for Human and Peoples' Rights ('African Commission') initiated the examination of three inter-state communications, rendering a merits decision in one case and elected to discontinue the adjudication of the more recent ones. Ultimately, in 2023 the African Court for Human and Peoples' Rights ('African Court') has received its first-ever inter-state application.[13] The expansion of inter-state human rights litigation has also extended, albeit in a limited (yet significant) manner, to quasi-judicial monitoring mechanisms established under United Nations human rights treaties and related protocols. Notably, the Committee on the Elimination of All Forms of Racial Discrimination (CERD Committee) has received three communications, marking the first – and, thus far, only – inter-state cases ever brought before UN treaty bodies.[14]

Conversely, a resurgence of inter-state human rights complaints has taken place before general courts adjudicating State disputes between States. The

---

12 On the inter-state case law developed within the framework of the European system on human rights, see extensively I Risini, *The Inter-State Application in the European Convention of Human Rights: Between Collective Enforcement of Human Rights and International Dispute Settlement* (Brill 2018); I Risini and T Eicke, 'Inter-State Applications under the European Convention on Human Rights – Situating the Instrument in the Current Human Rights Landscape' (2024) 13(1) *International Human Rights Law Review* 41.

13 K Van Hout, 'Landmark Inter-State Dispute Filed With the African Court on Human and Peoples' Rights', (Oxford Human Rights Hub, 7 February 2024) <https://ohrh.law.ox.ac.uk/landmark-inter-state-dispute-filed-with-the-african-court-on-human-and-peoples-rights/> accessed 28 February 2025; S Nxumalo, 'DRC v. Rwanda: The African Court's First Interstate Case' (Oxford Human Rights Hub, 21 February 2025) <https://ohrh.law.ox.ac.uk/drc-v-rwanda-the-african-courts-first-interstate-case/> accessed 28 February 2025.

14 For more information, see Office of the High Commission for Human Rights, 'Inter-state Communications: Committee on the Elimination of Racial Discrimination' <www.ohchr.org/en/treaty-bodies/cerd/inter-state-communications> accessed 28 February 2025. For a discussion of this practice, see further J Eiken and D Keane, 'Towards an Amicable Solution: The Inter-State Communications Procedure under ICERD (2022) 21(2) *The Law & Practice of International Courts and Tribunals* 302; R Garciandia, 'Inter-State Communications before United Nations Human Rights Treaty Bodies: Distinctive Features and Evolving Aims' (2025) 28 *Austrian Review of International and European Law Online* 1, 5.

expanding field of international human rights law has indeed modified, without fully overturning, the pre-World War II'bilateral' understanding of law among sovereign States, leading to the 'rising' of shared collective interests within the international community. In this regard, as reiterated by Brown Weiss,[15] the concept of the 'international community' does not anymore consist of sole States. It nowadays encompasses other important non-state actors, such as international organizations, but also, and more significantly, individuals, groups of persons, and minorities. Building on some progressive sparks developed in the case law of the Permanent Court of International Justice (PCIJ) concerning minority rights, the ICJ could not overlook the evolution of international law regarding individual rights, even in the context of claims not strictly related to human rights.[16] Therefore, after an initial reluctance, inter-state proceedings in the field of human rights have now become the new 'business as usual',[17] with the ICJ's docket currently bustling with the examination of a plethora of cases lodged under some of the most significant human rights treaties.

Inter-state human rights litigation emerges from complex contexts where human rights protection often intersects with broader economic, territorial, and legal disputes, including international crimes in armed conflicts. Unlike individual applications, which directly address alleged human rights treaty violations, inter-state cases frequently engage with broader dimensions of international law. Therefore, a State must have a compelling incentive to invoke such proceedings against another's domestic actions. Motivations for inter-state complaints can significantly vary, ranging from a genuine commit-

---

15 E Brown Weiss, 'Invoking State Responsibility in the Twenty-First Century' (2002) 96 *American Journal of International Law* 798, 804.

16 M Scheinin, 'The ICJ and the Individual' (2007) 9 *International Community Law Review* 123; MW Janis, 'Individuals and the International Court', in AS Muller, D Raic, M Thuranszky (eds), *The International Court of Justice: Its Future Role After 50 Years* (Kluwer Law International 1997) 205.

17 For an early discussion of the ICJ's approach to human rights issues, see V Gowlland-Debbas, 'Judicial Insights into the Fundamental Values and Interests of the International Community', in AS Muller, D Raic, M Thuranszky (n 8) 327; R Higgins, 'Human Rights in the International Court of Justice' (2007) 20 *Leiden Journal of International Law* 745; B Simma, 'Human Rights Before the International Court of Justice: Community Interest Coming to Life?', in CJ Tams and J Sloan (eds), *The Development of International Law by the International Court of Justice* (OUP 2013) 301; B Simma, 'Mainstreaming Human Rights: The Contribution of the International Court of Justice' (2012) 3(1) *Journal of International Dispute Settlement* 7; V Gowlland-Debbas, 'The ICJ and the Challenges of Human Rights Law', in M Andenas and E Bjørge (eds), *A Farewell to Fragmentation: Reassertion and Convergence in International Law* (CUP 2015) 109.

ment to addressing grave and systematic human rights violations to strategic political considerations shaped by cross-border dynamics and geopolitical interests.[18]

Against this backdrop, scholars have broadly categorized the practice of inter-state human rights proceedings into 'pure' and 'impure' cases.[19] This distinction is partly reflected in the terminology used to describe this phenomenon, with labels such as 'collective', 'community', or 'public' interest litigation, 'strategic litigation,' and 'lawfare'.[20] As Bruno Simma observed, most inter-state proceedings involve human rights' considerations as an 'accessory' to a wider dispute, somewhat hindering the 'purity' of the claims.[21] Conversely, a 'pure' human rights dispute is characterized by two key elements. First, the applicant State must advance a human rights claim against another State, alleging a violation of its the latter's human rights obligations toward its own nationals, thus echoing diplomatic protection. Second, the claim must not be (mis)used as a tool for political leverage or to express dissent within a broader conflict. To maintain its integrity, it must avoid invoking compromissory or jurisdictional clauses in human rights treaties to address disputes that, as concerns their ratione materiae, extend

18 S Leckie (n 2), at 254; SC Prebensen, 'Inter-State Complaints under Treaty Provisions – The Experience under the European Convention on Human Rights', in G Alfredsson, J Grimheden, BG Ramcharan and A Zayas (eds), *International Human Rights Monitoring Mechanisms: Essays in Honour of Jakob Th. Möller* (2nd Revised Edition, Martinus Nijhoff Publishers), 441, 460.

19 For a reference to the concepts of 'pure' and 'impure' as applied to inter-state human rights cases, see P Palchetti, 'I ricorsi interstatali in materia di diritti umani: uno strumento da maneggiare con cura' (2021) 15(2) *Diritti umani e diritto internazionale* 361, 363; As concerns the ECtHR's inter-state case law, see D Spielmann, 'The European Court of Human Rights as guarantor of a peaceful public order in Europe', 7 November 2014, available at: www.echr.coe.int; C Tomuschat, *Human Rights between Idealism and Realism* (OUP 2008) 242; P Leach, 'On inter-state litigation and armed conflict cases in Strasbourg' (2021) 2(1) *The European Convention on Human Rights Law Review*, 1, 30–33.

20 Although often considered synonymous, these terms have subtle semantic differences. Public interest litigation (where 'public' may be replaced by 'collective' or 'community') is generally viewed positively, while strategic litigation is considered neutral. In contrast, lawfare carries a negative connotation. For an exemplification and a non-exhaustive taxonomy, see I Venzke, 'Public Interests in the International Court of Justice – A Comparison Between Nuclear Arms Race (2016) and South West Africa (1966)' (2017) 111 *American Journal of International Law Unbound* 68.

21 See further B Simma, 'Human Rights Before the International Court of Justice: Community Interest Coming to Life?' in CJ Tams and J Sloan (eds), *The Development of International Law by the International Court of Justice* (OUP 2013) 320.

beyond the specific human rights violations in question.[22] Along the lines of this taxonomy, another scholar has further identified three distinct categories of inter-state human rights claims: diplomatic protection claims, direct claims, and mixed claims.[23] These classifications depend on the exact nature of the alleged wrongdoing. Diplomatic protection claims arise when the applicant State invokes the responsibility of another State for an internationally wrongful act that has harmed one or more of its nationals or other people under its jurisdiction. Direct claims, by contrast, assert a violation of the applicant State's rights without necessarily involving its nationals or other people under its jurisdiction. Mixed claims combine elements of both the two aforementioned 'categories', involving the co-existence of individual and State interests in the dispute.

Regardless of whether inter-state human rights cases are considered 'pure' or 'impure', or whether they involve 'diplomatic protection', 'direct' or 'mixed' claims, several scholars have questioned the appropriateness of using the forms and methods of general public international law for the creation and enforcement of human rights treaties in discussing recent practices.[24] This has led to the identification of an inherent 'mismatch' between the procedural framework and the substantive content of inter-state human rights litigation.[25]

As an increasing number of States intend to pursue reparations claims for human rights violations, either alongside or independently of individual complaints that have been previously lodged or remain pending, it is timely to address and further discuss the advantages and shortcomings of this phenomenon. This is particularly relevant considering the possible (and frequent) overlaps between individual and inter-state proceedings to obtain reparations, as these mechanisms may, as argued, serve distinct objectives.

22 F Fontanelli, 'The Disputes Between Armenia and Azerbaijan: The CERD Compromissory Clause as a One-way Ticket to Hague' (*EJIL:Talk!*, 11 November 2021) <https://www.ejiltalk.org/the-disputes-between-armenia-and-azerbaijan-the-cerd-compromissory-clause-as-a-one-way-ticket-to-hague/> accessed 28 February 2025; M Papadaki, 'Complex Dispute and Narrow Compromissory Clauses: Ukraine's Institution of Proceedings against Russia' (*EJIL:Talk!*, 7 March 2022) <https://www.ejiltalk.org/complex-disputes-and-narrow-compromissory-clauses-ukraines-institution-of-proceedings-against-russia/>.

23 J Howley, *Overlapping Interstate and Individual Claims in International Law* (OUP 2024), at 40–41.

24 L Lixinski (n 8), at 174; I Risini (n 12), at 70.

25 M Benzing, 'Community Interests in the Procedure of International Courts and Tribunals' (2006) 5(3) *The Law & Practice of International Courts and Tribunals* 217.

Next to this introductory section, this contribution unfolds in four main parts. Section 2 explores the legal framework governing inter-state and individual claims for the purpose of State responsibility, focusing on their possible intersection in seeking reparations for human rights violations. Section 3 analyses relevant case law, particularly from the ECtHR, to assess how courts navigate overlapping claims and allocate reparations in practice. Section 4 evaluates the potential of friendly settlements as a mechanism for balancing State and individual interests for reparations claimed in the context of an inter-state human rights complaint. Finally, Section 5 offers some concluding remarks on the challenges and prospects of inter-state litigation as a viable avenue for securing reparations for human rights violations.

2 Overlapping Inter-State and Individual Complaints in Seeking Reparation for Human Rights Violations: A (Re)Appraisal of the Relevant Legal Framework

Reparation is fundamentally integrated into the general international legal framework, as reflected in the Latin phrase *ubi jus ibi remedium*, i.e. «where there is a right, there is a remedy».

In the context of an inter-state human rights dispute, both the approaches and objectives of the applicant State in seeking reparations could deviate significantly from those of affected individuals. For instance, the claimant State might regard a comprehensive damage assessment as impractical, time-consuming, or counterproductive, due to an absence of or insufficient evidence, especially in cases of grave and widespread human rights violations having occurred, or where significant time gaps might complicate evidence collection. In such contexts, the evaluation of estimating suitable reparations will be contingent upon a protracted and time-consuming fact-finding process that can often be temporally detached from the merits phase of the case.[26] Furthermore, the magnitude of reparation, particularly whenever conspicuous compensation is at stake, may be influenced by the economic (in)capacity

26 In the event that the assessment of reparations is not contextual to the decision on the merits, the time-lapse between the judgment on the merits and the judgment on reparations can significantly change. See *Armed Activities on the Territory of the Congo (Democratic Republic of the Congo v Uganda)*, Reparations, Judgments, I.C.J. Reports 2022, p. 13 (merits judgment: 2005); ECtHR, *Cyprus v Turkey* [GC] 25781/94, Judgment (Just Satisfaction), 12 May 2014 (merits judgment: 2001); *Georgia v Russia (I)* [GC] 13255/07, Judgment (Just Satisfaction), 31 January 2019 (merits judgment: 2014); *Georgia v Russia (II)* [GC] 38263/08, Judgment (Just Satisfaction), 28 April 2023 (merits judgment: 2021).

of the responsible State. In this regard, the existence of a customary international rule ensuring that the financial burden imposed on a State does not become excessively punitive remains uncertain.[27] In such scenarios, an injured State may decide to adopt a conciliatory approach to maintain or restore diplomatic relations with the responsible State or to offset pre-existing financial obligations.[28] Similarly, strategic considerations may lead an injured State to forgo reparation claims or decline to initiate proceedings altogether, even in response to serious breaches of international law.[29]

Under general international law, reparation – alongside cessation and guarantees of non-repetition – constitutes the primary consequence of an internationally wrongful act. Reparation may take the form of restitution, compensation, and satisfaction, either singly or in combination with each other, depending on the nature of the wrongful act and the extent of the damage caused.[30]

This general rule was first articulated by the PCIJ in its landmark *Chorzów Factory* case. In its judgment on jurisdiction, the PCIJ remarkably asserted that «[…] it is a principle of international law, and even a general conception of law, that any breach of an engagement involves an obligation to make reparation in an adequate form».[31] In its subsequent judgment on the merits issued in the same case, the PCIJ further elaborated this general rule, adding that:

27 Some authors have supported the possibility of recognizing such a customary rule, particularly in cases regarding States' responsibility for the violation of the prohibition of the use of force and their obligations under international humanitarian law. See, *inter alia*, I Brownlie, *International Law and the Use of Force by States* (OUP 1963) 147; B Graefrath, 'Iraqi Reparations and the Security Council' (1995) 55 *Zeitschrift für ausländisches öffentliches Recht und Völkerrecht* (*ZaöRV*) 1, 64; E David, *Principes de droit des conflits armés* (5th edn, Bruylant 2012) 735. *Contra*, see M Paparinskis, 'A Case Against Crippling Compensation in International Law of State Responsibility' (2020) 83(6) *Modern Law Review* 1246.

28 C Ferstman, 'The Relationship Between Inter-State Reparations and Individual Entitlements to Reparation: Some Reflections' (2018) 78 *Zeitschrift für ausländisches öffentliches Recht und Völkerrecht* (*ZaöRV*) 561.

29 A Bufalini, 'On the Power of a State to Waive Reparation Claims Arising from War Crimes and Crimes Against Humanity' (2017) 77 *Zeitschrift für ausländisches öffentliches Recht und Völkerrecht* (*ZaöRV*) 447.

30 ILC, Articles on the Responsibility of States for Internationally Wrongful Acts, 'Artic of the International Law Commission on the Work of its 53rd Session' (23 April–1 June and 2 July–10 August 2001) UN Doc A/CN.4/SER.A/2001/Add.1 (ARS) Article 31, reflecting *Chorzów Factory* (Germany v. Poland) (Jurisdiction) [1927] PCIJ Rep Series A No 9, 21.

31 *Chorzów Factory* (n 30) 47.

> […] the essential principle contained in the actual notion of an illegal act – a principle which seems to be established by international practice and in particular by the decisions of arbitral tribunals – is that reparation must, as far as possible, wipe out all consequences of the illegal act and re-establish the situation which would, in all probability, have existed if that act had not been committed.[32]

The International Law Commission (ILC), which began codifying State responsibility from 1949 onwards, incorporated this general principle into Article 31 of the Draft Articles on the Responsibility of States for Internationally Wrongful Acts (ARSIWA, Draft Articles). This provision establishes that any injury resulting from an internationally wrongful act necessitates full – and no more –[33] reparation as an automatic and inherent consequence of the recognition of a State's responsibility.[34]

However, general international law on State responsibility does not explicitly determine whether entities *other* than States are entitled to reparation for violations, nor does it clarify whether injuries suffered by individuals are encompassed within the damages claimed by a State when its nationals or other people under its jurisdiction have been harmed as a result of a wrongful act. In the context of diplomatic protection, the injured individual does not possess independent rights separate from those of their State of nationality. Instead, the claim is exercised at the discretion of the State, which asserts its own right under international law rather than vindicating the personal rights of the affected individual.[35] As Tomuschat also argued, the bilateral nature of a State's obligation to provide reparation to another State for the harm caused to one or more of its nationals merely 'supplements' situations where an indi-

32 *Chorzów Factory* (Germany v. Poland) (Merits) [1928] PCIJ Rep. Series A, No. 17, 29.

33 There is no clear authority for punitive damages in international law, and this scarcity of practice emphasizes that, at present, punitive damages are certainly not a generally accepted remedy in international law. In this sense, see S Wittich, 'Punitive Damages' in J Crawford et al. (eds), *The Law of State Responsibility* (OUP 2010) 667. For a different assessment, especially as regards States responsibility for grave and serious breaches, see NHB Jørgensen, *The Responsibility of States for International Crimes* (OUP 2000) 187.

34 ILC, *Draft Articles on Responsibility of States for Internationally Wrongful Acts*, Supplement No. 10 (A/56/10), Chp.IV.E.1, November 2001, para. 4, p. 224.

35 See R Provost, *International Human Rights and Humanitarian Law* (CUP 2002) 45; N Ronzitti, 'Access to justice and compensation for violations of the law of war' in F Francioni (ed), *Access to Justice as a Human Right* (OUP 2007) 100; C Tomuschat, 'State responsibility and the individual right to compensation before national courts' in A Clapham and P Gaeta (eds), *The Oxford Handbook of International Humanitarian Law in Armed Conflict* (OUP 2014) 811.

vidual's rights appear to be violated by their own State of nationality.[36] Before the rise of international human rights law, issues regarding reparations for damages suffered by individuals were solely handled within domestic legal systems, which were anticipated to deliver an effective remedy.[37] By contrast, in contemporary international law, the legal relationship arising from a State's commission of an internationally wrongful act does not necessarily adhere to the principle of reciprocity. Therefore, it is not inherently confined to a strictly traditional bilateral framework requiring the existence of a 'special affected' claimant State and a respondent State as a prerequisite.[38]

The determination of whether reparation is owed – either concurrently or exclusively – to an entity other than the directly injured State depends on the structure and content of the breached obligation. In terms of structure, alongside bilateral obligations, international law recognizes a distinct category of so-called 'integral' or 'interdependent' obligations, which are owed to the international community as a whole rather than to one or more specific States.[39] This critical shift towards the recognition of community interests has also influenced, though inconsistently, the case law of the ICJ since its famous *obiter dictum* in the *Barcelona Traction* judgment.[40] Over the years, scholars have further identified a distinct 'sub-category' of community inter-

---

36 M Zwanenburg, 'The Van Boven/Bassiouni Principles: An Appraisal' (2006) 24 *Netherlands Quarterly of Human Rights* 654, 655; C Tomuschat, 'Reparation in Favour of Individual Victims of Gross Violations of Human Rights and International Humanitarian Law' in MG Kohen (ed), *Promoting Justice, Human Rights and Conflict Resolution Through International Law: Liber Amicorum Lucius Caflisch* (Martinus Nijhoff 2007) 569, 577–581.

37 Other scholars affirm that States should always recognize an effective remedy for the breach of international human rights; see D Shelton (n 4) at 103.

38 «[…] International justice stands beyond the *inter*-state dimension, and a wide range of international tribunals nowadays adjudicate cases that take place at both *inter*-state and *intra*-State levels, to the benefit of human beings and the international community as a whole […] The truth is that the strictly *inter*-state outlook has an ideological content and is a product of its time, a time long past», AA Cançado Trindade, 'Reflections on the Realization of Justice in the Era of Contemporary International Tribunals' (2020) 408 *Collected Courses of The Hague Academy of International Law* 33.

39 LA Sicilianos, 'The Classification of Obligations and the Multilateral Dimension of the Relations of International Responsibility' (2002) 13(5) *European Journal of International Law* 1127, 1133–1134; T Ruys, 'Legal Standing and Public Interest Litigation – Are All Erga Omnes Breaches Equal?' (2021) 20(3) *Chinese Journal of International Law* 457, 458.

40 *Barcelona Traction, Light and Power Company, Limited* (Belgium v. Spain) (New Application: 1962), (Judgment, Preliminary Objections) I.C.J. Reports 1970, p. 3, p. 32, para. 33. On the legacy of this dictum, see CJ Tams and A Tzanakopoulos, 'Barcelona Traction at 40: The ICJ as an Agent of Legal Development' (2010) 23 *Leiden Journal of International Law* 781.

ests that pertain to a specific group of States that are parties to a given multilateral convention, i.e. obligation *erga omnes* (*partes*). These obligations arise when all contracting State parties to a multilateral treaty share a common legal interest in ensuring compliance with the rules enshrined therein.[41]

During the *travaux préparatoires* of the ARSIWA, the ILC took stock of the increasing 'multilateralization' of international responsibility. The existence of a 'common ground' of shared interests and values was reflected in the version of the Draft Articles adopted on first reading in 1996, in two ground-breaking provisions that, for their era, were remarkably forward-thinking: Article 19, addressing international crimes of States, and Article 40, which expanded the definition of the 'injured State' to include, in the case of State crimes and certain other situations, all States.[42]

The final version of the ARSIWA significantly revised the 1996 draft. eliminating Article 19 and replacing it with Articles 40 and 41, which regulate breaches of obligations arising from *peremptory norms*. Such provisions distinguish between obligations *erga omnes*, owed to the international community, and obligations *erga omnes partes*, owed to a limited group of treaty parties. A crucial aspect of the ILC's work was incorporating non-bilateral obligations into State responsibility, differentiating between claims by *directly* injured States (Article 42) and other States with a legal interest (Article 48), often referred to as *indirectly* or *specially* affected States. As James Crawford has emphasized, Article 48 is a provision grounded on the need to qualify, in the event of a violation, the position of States, other than the injured one(s), that are parties to a multilateral convention imposing obligations *erga omnes partes*, as is the case for human rights treaties.[43] While the Draft Articles mostly reaffirmed existing law on the consequences arising from internationally wrongful acts, they also broke new ground in strengthening broader community interests in international legality. Furthermore, given the unsuccessful attempt, in the late 1950s, to codify general norms on State responsibility for

41 *Questions relating to the Obligation to Prosecute or Extradite* (Belgium v. Senegal), Judgment (Merits), I.C.J. Reports 2012, p. 422, para. 68; PYS Chow, 'On Obligations Erga Omnes Partes' (2021) 52 *Georgetown Journal of International Law* 469.

42 J Crawford, *State Responsibility: The General Part* (CUP 2013) 365.

43 J Crawford, 'Responsibility for Breaches of Communitarian Norms: An Appraisal of Article 48 of the ILC Articles on Responsibility of States for International Wrongful Acts', in U Fastenrath, R Geiger, DE Khan, A Paulus, S Von Schorlemer and C Vedder (eds), *From Bilateralism to Community Interests: Essays in Honour of Bruno Simma* (OUP, 2011) 224, 225; more recently, JA Hofbauer, 'Erga Omnes (Partes)' in C Binder, M Nowak, JA Hofbauer and P Janig, *Elgar Encyclopedia of Human Rights* (Edward Elgar Publishing 2022), 89, 96.

injuries to aliens,[44] it is not surprising that the ILC carefully avoided any explicit (or implicit) reference to primary obligations concerning individuals.

Instead, reparations for the benefit of non-state entities, including under procedures such as those established under human rights treaties, were ultimately excluded from the final draft. However, at the very last moment, the ILC opted to include a clause in Article 33(2), stipulating that all provisions in the second part of the ARSIWA – devoted to the *content* of the international responsibility of the State – were adopted without prejudice to any rights, arising from the international responsibility of a State, which may accrue directly to any person or entity other than the State.[45] Two significant findings follow from this statement. On the one hand, this provision, although couched in terms of a 'without prejudice' clause, seems to be taking for granted the existence of reparation rights in favour of non-State entities.[46] On the other hand, the 'last-minute' inclusion of this provision in the third part of the ARSIWA as a *panacea* for the inter-state structure of international responsibility seems to have had some underestimated side effects.[47] In providing further analysis on this sibylline reference, the ILC's Commentary to Article 33 ARSIWA remarked that, when an obligation of reparation exists towards a State, «reparation does not necessarily accrue to that State's benefit».[48] More-

44 This was first noted by Roberto Ago in his First Report on the Responsibility of States, YbILC, 1969-II, paras. 88 ff.; see also YbILC, 1963-II, at 227 and 252. See further R Kolb, *The International Law of State Responsibility* (Edward Elgar Publishing 2017), at 7.

45 Article 33 of the International Law Commission (ILC) Articles on the Responsibility of States for Internationally Wrongful Acts provides as follows: «1. The obligations of the responsible State set out in this part may be owed to another State, to several States, or to the international community as a whole, depending in particular on the character and content of the international obligation and on the circumstances of the breach. 2. *This part is without prejudice to any right, arising from the international responsibility of a State, which may accrue directly to any person or entity other than a State* (emphasis added)».

46 J Crawford, 'The ILC's Articles on Responsibility of States for Internationally Wrongful Acts: A Retrospect' (2002) 96(2) *American Journal of International Law* 874, 887: «[...] In form a saving clause, it nonetheless clearly envisages that some 'person or entity other than a State' may be directly entitled to claim reparation arising from an internationally wrongful act of a state».

47 A Gattini, 'Alcune Osservazioni sulla tutela degli interessi individuali nei progetti di codificazione della Commissione del diritto internazionale sulla responsabilità internazionale e sulla protezione diplomatica' in M Spinedi, A Gianelli and ML Alaimo (eds), *Codificazione della responsabilità internazionale degli Stati alla prova dei fatti* (Giuffré 2006) 431, 432.

48 ILC, *Draft Articles on Responsibility of States for Internationally Wrongful Acts, with commentaries*, YbILC, 2001, 95, para. 3.

over, whenever a State is held responsible for human rights violations, « [...] the individuals concerned should be regarded as the ultimate beneficiaries, and in that sense as the holders of the relevant rights».[49] Consequently, all States may invoke the responsibility of the wrongdoing State and seek reparations for the benefit of the victims.

Nevertheless, the ILC rapidly shifts attention to the *mise en oeuvre* of the regime of international responsibility, stating that, whenever an international obligation is established to the benefit of a subject other than the State, international law envisages specific procedures that the person or the entity can activate to establish the State responsibility without any active involvement of the national State acting as a proxy, as happens in the field of human rights law, where individuals are the holders of fundamental rights and freedoms and, therefore, the chief and ultimate beneficiaries of the protection. As scholarship appeared to be rather fragmented at the time of the *travaux préparatoires* of the ARSIWA, the ILC could have seized the opportunity to further investigate the problem, addressing the question of whether and to what extent the typologies of reparation enumerated in Article 34 ARSIWA should be applied differently in the context of a breach of an obligation owed to an individual, or whether there might be *other* forms of reparation better tailored to redress the harm suffered by individuals.

While the ILC provided a broad framework, many uncertainties still persist. Whenever a State invokes another State's responsibility for human rights violations, issues arise regarding the relationships among the responsible State, the claimant State, and the victims, whether viewed individually or as a group.

The Draft Articles do not explicitly address the sensitive interplay between State responsibility claims and individual claims arising from the same wrongful act, nor do they clarify whether the nature, amount, and methods of awarding reparations differ when the injured party is an individual or when a claim is brought by a non-injured State.[50]

It is well established that individuals may invoke the responsibility of States for human rights violations through treaty-based complaint mechanisms, as most human rights conventions provide access to judicial or quasi-judicial bodies empowered to determine alleged breaches and to grant reparations.

Given that a considerable number of international human rights treaties include provisions for both individual and inter-state complaints, there is

49 Ibid.

50 D Shelton, 'Righting Wrongs: Reparations in the Articles on State Responsibility' (2002) 96(4) *American Journal of International Law* 833.

a theoretical – and, as will be shown, also a concrete – potential for overlap between these two types of claims. This is particularly evident under the theory positing that inter-state claims frequently «originate from injuries to private individuals».[51] However, as with the ILC's Draft Articles, no human rights treaty explicitly delineates the relationship between individual and inter-state claims – whether in terms of their respective admissibility requirements or, for present purposes, from the perspective of reparations.[52]

In the absence of a treaty-based rule addressing this issue, recourse has often been made to general principles of international law, such as *res judicata, lis pendens*, and the rule precluding double jeopardy.[53] Most human rights treaties prohibit multiple (individual) claims, preventing supervisory bodies from hearing cases already submitted,[54], settled,[55] or pending[56] before another procedure of 'international investigations' or settlements, provided

51 H Lauterpacht, *International Law: Being the Collected Papers of Hersch Lauterpacht* (Elihu Lauterpacht ed, CUP 1970), at 293–294; see also G Gaja, 'Is a State Specially Affected When Its Nationals' Human Rights Are Infringed?' in L Chand Vohrah et al. (eds), *Man's Inhumanity to Man: Essays on International Law in Honour of Antonio Cassese* (Kluwer 2003) 382.

52 See I Risini (n 12), at 208; See further E Carpanelli, 'Il rapporto tra ricorsi interstatali e individuali dinanzi alla Corte europea dei diritti umani, (2021) 15(2) *Diritti umani e diritto internazionale* 389, 392; A Cannone, 'Ricorsi individuali e casi interstatali nella pratica passata e recente della Corte europea dei diritti dell'uomo' (2022) *Ordine internazionale e diritti umani* 581, 582.

53 On these general principles, see H Chand, *Treatise on the Law of Res Judicata: Including the Doctrines of Jurisdiction, Bar by Suit and Lis Pendens* (W. Clowes & Sons 1894); B Cheng, *General Principles of Law as Applied by International Courts and Tribunals* (CUP 2006); A Reinisch, 'The Use and Limits of *Res Judicata* and *Lis Pendens* as Procedural Tools to Avoid Conflicting Dispute Settlement Outcomes' (2004) 3 *The Law & Practice of International Courts and Tribunals* 37.

54 E.g. Article 35(2)(b) ECHR: «The Court shall not deal with any application submitted under Article 34 that [...] is substantially the same as a matter that has already been examined by the Court or has already been *submitted* to another procedure of international investigation or settlement and contains no relevant new information (emphasis added)».

55 E.g. Article 56(7) AfCHPR: «Communications relating to Human and Peoples' rights referred to in Article 55 received by the Commission, shall be considered if they [...] do not deal with cases which have been *settled* by those States involved in accordance with the principles of the Charter of the United Nations, or the Charter of the Organisation of African Unity or the provisions of the present Charter (emphasis added)».

56 E.g. Article 5 (2) of the Optional Protocol to the International Covenant on Civil and Political Rights: «The Committee shall not consider any communication from an individual unless it has ascertained that: (a) The same matter is not being *examined* under another procedure of' international investigation or settlement' (emphasis added)».

that the second claim shares the same parties, cause of action, and object as the first one.

However, as is evident, the application of the 'triple identity' test to overlapping inter-state and individual applications would require a flexible interpretation of each criterion.[57] For example, identity of parties is complicated by the fact that, in inter-state claims, the State acts as *parens patriae* for its citizens or other people under its jurisdiction. This gives rise to particular difficulties in mixed claims, where the distinction between general interests and diplomatic protection is not always readily apparent. With regard to the identity of cause of action, a central issue arises from the distinction between the rights of the State and those of the individual. Traditionally, in diplomatic protection cases, a State claims reparation for a violation of its own rights under international law, irrespective of whether the individual concerned has access to a remedy. Conversely, when the individual is the direct rights-holder, the State's claim to reparation may be regarded as merely residual and procedural in nature. However, a non-formalistic approach has been advanced, interpreting the 'cause of action' as referring to the factual circumstances giving rise to relief, thereby rendering two claims identical if there are the same in essence, in accordance with the doctrine of 'issue estoppel' or 'collateral estoppel'.[58] Regarding the identity of object, the situation varies depending on the scope of the inter-state claim. If the State seeks reparation for the harm suffered by individual victims, then its object may align with that of an individual claim. Conversely, if the inter-state complaint merely alleges the existence of an administrative practice or a pattern of conduct, then individual cases may serve as illustrative examples, validly distinguishing the inter-state claim from that brought by an individual applicant. As is evident, the complexities of inter-state human rights litigation thus require a context-sensitive interpretation of the triple identity test, rather than a formalistic approach, to account for the intersection between State and individual claims.

Regardless of how strictly or flexibly the 'triple identity' test is applied, international law prohibits double recovery, even when multiple different claimants bring actions against the same defendant. Indeed, in its seminal advisory opinion issued in the *Reparations for Injuries* case, the ICJ held that,

57 Y Shany, *The Competing Jurisdictions of International Courts and Tribunals* (OUP 2003), 26, where the author discusses the desirability of applying a «degree of flexibility» in the application of these criteria.

58 See further W Dodge, 'National Courts and International Arbitration: Exhaustion of Remedies and Res Judicata Under Chapter Eleven of NAFTA' (2000) 23 *Hasting International and Comparative Law Review* 357, 366–67.

while no rule establishes a 'hierarchy' between diplomatic and functional protection claims arising from an individual injury, «[i]nternational tribunals are already familiar with the problem of a claim in which two or more national States are interested, and they know how to protect the defendant State».[59] The Commentary to Article 46 of the ILC's Draft Articles, when addressing multiple injured States, quotes this as evidencing that States claiming reparation in respect of the same alleged wrongful act should coordinate their claims to avoid double recovery.[60]

Difficulties arise in direct (or 'pure') inter-state complaints, where the applicant State – whether directly or indirectly affected – does not seek reparations on behalf of individuals but, instead, it asserts its own rights. Mixed claims, by contrast, engage both State and victim interests, with reparation potentially covering both. This overlap can generate legal complexities, particularly in ensuring that compensation is neither duplicated nor insufficient. In both contexts, the absence of a strict treaty-based rule governing the relationship between inter-state and individual claims compounds the challenge. Nonetheless, even where a State pursues a claim, victims retain *locus standi* to seek reparations through individual proceedings.

Confronted with these normative gaps, human rights bodies have developed jurisprudence to allocate reparations, prevent double compensation, and coordinate parallel claims, thereby enhancing the effectiveness of international protection mechanisms. The following section examines how these bodies apply general principles -such as *res judicata, lis pendens*, and the prohibition of double recovery -in practice. It explores the methods employed to reconcile State interests in initiating proceedings with the fundamental rights of victims to obtain reparation. Rather than enforcing these principles rigidly, human rights bodies have displayed deference to the procedural classification of inter-state complaints, adapting their application to distinct procedural and substantive contexts. Consequently, the *Chorzów Factory* test, rooted in the bilateral structure of classic international law, warrants reconsideration to accommodate the specificities of human rights adjudication.[61]

---

59 *Reparations for injuries suffered in the service of the United Nations* (Advisory Opinion), I.C.J. Reports 1949, 174, 175.

60 ILC's Commentary to Draft Articles (n 48) 271.

61 FE Torres, 'Revisiting the Chorzów Factory Standard of Reparation – Its Relevance in Contemporary International Law and Practice' (2021) 90(2) *Nordic Journal of International Law* 190; See also D Shelton, 'Reparations', in *Max Planck Encyclopedia of Public International Law* [MPEPIL], August 2015, para. 3, <https://opil.ouplaw.com/display/10.1093/law:epil/9780199231690/law-9780199231690-e392?prd=MPIL> accessed 28 February 2025.

3 Overlapping Claims, Competing Rights: Addressing Reparations amidst Inter-State and Individual Human Rights Cases in Practice

As the resurgence of inter-state human rights litigation can be regarded as a relatively recent phenomenon, it is not surprising that overlaps between inter-state and individual claims have remained infrequent in practice, particularly regarding compensation claims.

It must nonetheless be acknowledged that a number of inter-state claims brought before non-human rights courts and tribunals have intersected with individual proceedings within the human rights framework. For instance, in the *Avena* case, Mexico instituted proceedings against the United States before the ICJ, alleging breaches of the Vienna Convention on Consular Relations (VCCR) in respect of nearly fifty Mexican nationals.[62] Simultaneously, individual petitions were submitted under the American Convention on Human Rights (ACHR) on behalf of at least eight of those individuals.[63] Similarly, France's nuclear testing, challenged by New Zealand before the ICJ in the *Nuclear Tests* case,[64] led to concurrent individual complaints before the ECommHR and the UN Human Rights Committee, stemming from the same factual circumstances.[65] Overlaps have also emerged before the European Court of Human Rights (ECtHR), as in *Bankovic and Others v. Belgium and Others*,[66] where individual victims of NATO air operations alleging human rights violations arising from acts of war that were also subject of inter-state proceedings – the ten *Legality of Use of Force* cases-brought by Yugoslavia against various NATO member States.[67] Additionally, the Eritrea-Ethiopia

---

62 *Case Concerning Avena and Other Mexican Nationals* (Mexico v. United States of America) (Judgment) [2004] I.C.J. Reports 12.

63 See, among others, *Medellin v. United States of America*, Case 12.644, Rep. 90/09 (IACHR, 7 August 2009) (Medellin/Cardenas/Garcia); *Arias v. United States of America*, Pet. 15/12, Rep. 73/12 (IACHR, 17 July 2012); *Rodriguez v. United States of America*, Pet. 1672/11, Rep 63/ 12 (IACHR, 29 March 2012); *Diaz v. United States of America*, Pet. 259/11, Rep. 133/11 (IACHR, 19 October 2011).

64 *Examination of the Situation in Accordance with Paragraph 63 of the Court's Judgment of 20 December 1974 in Nuclear Tests* (New Zealand v. France) [1995] I.C.J. Reports 288.

65 *Bordes and Others v. France*, Communication No. 645/1995, UN Doc CCPR/C/57/D/645/1995, Human Rights Committee (HRC), 22 July 1996; *Tauira v. France* [ECommHR], App. No. 28204/95, 4 December 1995.

66 *Bankovic and Others v. Belgium and Others* [ECtHR], App. No. 52207/99, 12 December 2001.

67 *Legality of Use of Force* (Serbia and Montenegro v. Belgium, Canada, France, Germany, Italy, Netherlands, Portugal, United Kingdom, and United States of America) (Preliminary Objections) [2004] I.C.J. Reports 279.

Claims Commission (EECC) – an *ad hoc* inter-state arbitration mechanism instituted to adjudicate claims for loss, damage, or injury resulting from violations of international humanitarian law or other violations of international law during the Eritrean-Ethiopian armed conflict of May 1998[68] – has witnessed parallel individual complaints before the African Commission on Human and Peoples' Rights.

An examination of this practice reveals that overlaps have been generally managed relying upon the inherent differentiation of jurisdictional mandates. The IACHR has emphasized that its jurisdiction differs significantly from that of the ICJ, primarily because the ICJ adjudicates inter-state disputes, whereas the IACHR handles individual petitions against States. Moreover, the rights at issue and the remedies provided by the IACHR are directly linked to the individuals concerned, thereby allowing for the coexistence of distinct forms of reparation: one awarded to Mexico by the ICJ and another granted for the benefit of affected Mexican nationals by the IACHR, as ultimately occurred in the *Avena* context.[69] Similarly, in assessing alleged violations of human rights obligations, the EECC recognized that certain claims advanced by both States were submitted in the exercise of diplomatic protection, leading to an overlap with individual human rights complaints before the AfCommHPR. In response, the EECC emphasized the need to prevent double recovery wherever possible.[70] As for the human rights proceedings initiated in the context of the *Nuclear Tests* dispute, these cases were ultimately dismissed due to a lack of jurisdiction or standing, thereby preventing any potential overlap from becoming a legal issue.

The evolving landscape of inter-state jurisprudence, particularly within the ECtHR, further illustrates this trend. Notably, overlaps between proceedings under Articles 33 and 34 have become increasingly frequent, especially in cases arising from armed conflicts. In such instances, applicant States often allege multiple human rights violations, leading to complaints that serve a twofold purpose: addressing systemic issues in the respondent State's legal framework while simultaneously resembling diplomatic protection, whereby a State seeks reparations on behalf of affected individuals.

---

68 N Klein, 'Eritrea-Ethiopia Claims Commission', *Max Planck Encyclopedia of Public International Law* [MPEPIL], March 2013, para. 7, <https://opil.ouplaw.com/display/10.1093/law:epil/9780199231690/law-9780199231690-e1774> accessed 28 February 2025.

69 See *Rodriguez v. United States of America* (n 63), para. 55; *Arias v. United States of America* (n 63), para. 44.

70 Ethiopia's Damages Claims (Final Award) (2009) XXVI UNRIAA 631 [329], [366].

Determining appropriate remedies in inter-state applications presents significant legal and practical challenges. The sheer number of victims often complicates both identifying and quantifying reparations, thus increasing the risk of overlapping individual and inter-state claims. More critically, inter-state cases often involve complex political sensitivities, where high-value compensation awards may hinder the enforcement of judicial decisions.

As a result, even before addressing the issue of implementation, the formulation of effective and practicable reparations remains a major challenge, as demonstrated in *Cyprus v. Turkey (IV)*, *Georgia v. Russia (I)*, and *Georgia v. Russia (II)*.[71] Further developments are expected in *Georgia v. Russia (IV)*[72] and *Ukraine v. Russia (re Crimea)*,[73] where the ECtHR has deferred its determination on just satisfaction, considering the matter not yet ready for adjudication.

Although not directly related to the question of just satisfaction, the Court has previously addressed the issue of overlapping individual and inter-state cases in *Ireland v. United Kingdom*.[74] That case raised concerns about potential interference with an individual complaint – *Donnelly and Others v. United Kingdom* – lodged before the ECommHR prior to the Commission being seized of the inter-state application.[75] Both complaints alleged specific acts

---

71 ECtHR, *Cyprus v. Turkey (IV)* [GC], no 25781/94, Judgment (Just Satisfaction), 12 May 2014; *Georgia v. Russia (I)* [GC] no 13225/07, Judgment (Just Satisfaction), 31 January 2019; *Georgia v Russia (II)* [GC], no 38263/08, Judgment (Just Satisfaction), 28 April 2023.

72 *Georgia v Russia (IV)*, no 39611/18, Judgment (Merits), 9 April 2024; on the main findings of the judgment, see V Botticelli, 'Beyond the divide: the human rights cost of borderisation in the ECtHR's Georgia v Russia (IV) merits judgment European Court of Human Rights (Second Section): Judgment of 9 April 2024' (2024) 6 *European Human Rights Law Review* 542.

73 *Ukraine v Russia (re Crimea)* [GC], nos. 20958/14 and 38334/18, Judgment (Merits), 25 June 2024; for a comprehensive analysis of the ECtHR's decision, see K Dzehtsiarou, 'Ukraine v Russia (re Crimea): The European Court of Human Rights Goes All-In' (*EJIL: Talk!*, 27 June 2024) <https://www.ejiltalk.org/ukraine-v-russia-re-crimea-the-european-court-of-human-rights-goes-all-in/>; M Milanović, 'Some Additional Comments on the ECtHR Crimea Judgment: Occupation, Sovereignty and "Law"' (*EJIL:Talk!*, 27 June 2024) <https://www.ejiltalk.org/some-additional-comments-on-the-ecthr-crimea-judgment-occupation-sovereignty-and-law/>.

74 *Ireland v United Kingdom*, no. 5310/71 (Judgment), 18 January 1978, Series A, No. 25; Series B, Vol, 23 (I–II); on the matter, see further M O'Boyle, 'Torture and Emergency Powers Under the European Convention on Human Rights: Ireland v. United Kingdom' (1977) 71 (4) *American Journal of International Law* 674.

75 *Donnelly and Others v. United Kingdom*, nos. 5577–83/72 (Decision), 15 December 1975, DR 4, 4, 88, 87. This case is not the only one related to the Northern Ireland Conflict. A detailed list of all individual complaints lodged before both the ECommHR and the

contrary to Article 3 of the ECHR, as well as the existence of an administrative practice violating the prohibition of torture and other inhuman or degrading treatment. In its admissibility decision in *Donnelly*, the ECommHR rejected the United Kingdom's objection that the individual application was 'identical' to the inter-state proceeding previously declared admissible by the Commission.[76] Indeed, the ECommHR, holding that the inter-state claim had not yet been 'examined', remarked that the parties and claims were 'different'.[77] Hence, the ECommHR found no violation of the then-in-force Article 27(1)(b), a provision now reflected almost verbatim in the current Article 35(2)(b). However, in a subsequent ruling, the ECommHR terminated its examination of the individual applications associated with the inter-state complaint due to the applicants' failure to exhaust domestic remedies, particularly with regard to the alleged administrative practice. Consequently, the merits of the individual case were never adjudicated. Ireland, moreover, did not claim just satisfaction from the Court in the context of the inter-state proceeding, although it referred to the situation of certain individual applicants as examples of the alleged administrative practice.[78]

The judgment on just satisfaction rendered in the *Cyprus v. Turkey* (*IV*) inter-state case marked a significant milestone, as it was the first instance in which the ECtHR addressed the applicability of Article 41 in the context of inter-state applications. The case arose from Turkey's military occupation of Northern Cyprus in 1974, which led to the division of the island sovereign territory and the establishment of a *de facto* administration, the so-called 'Turkish Republic of Northern Cyprus' (TRNC). These events resulted in a series of grave and systematic violations of the Convention, including enforced disappearances and severe restrictions on the rights of the enclaved Greek Cypriots. In its 2001 judgment on the merits, the Court identified numerous violations, acknowledging, *inter alia*, breaches of the rights to life, liberty, property, and family life, among others.[79] In a groundbreaking decision, the ECtHR ordered Turkey to pay a lump sum of €90,000,000, with €30,000,000 allocated to the families and relatives of missing persons and

ECtHR is available in B Dickson, *The European Convention on Human Rights and the Conflict in Northern Ireland* (OUP 2012), 377–396.

76 *Donnelly and others v. United Kingdom*, nos. 5577–83/72 (Decision), 5 April 1973, CD 41, 122, paras. 262–266.

77 Ibid., para. 266.

78 Ibid.

79 *Cyprus v. Turkey* (*IV*) [GC], App. No. 25781/94, Judgment (Merits), 10 May 2001, ECHR 2001–IV.

€60,000,000 to be distributed among the enclaved Greek Cypriots residing in the occupied Karpas Peninsula.

At the outset, the ECtHR was required to determine whether Article 41 applies to inter-state cases. In addressing this question, the Court draws extensively upon general international law. While asserting that Article 41 operates as *lex specialis*,[80] it maintained that the provision was originally conceived to align with «the principles of public international law relating to State liability»,[81] and thus «has to be construed in this context». Citing the *Chorzów Factory* principle and the ICJ's case law,[82] the ECtHR held that the Convention, though containing its own specific provisions on State responsibility, should not be regarded as a self-contained regime but must be interpreted as part of general international law.[83] The ECtHR also relied on the textual reference to an 'injured party' in Article 41–written with a lowercase 'p'- interpreting it as encompassing any party entitled to bring proceedings, including States. Accordingly, it dismissed Turkey's argument that the pronouns *his* or *her* in Rule 60(1) of the Rules of Court confines just satisfaction applies only to individuals, as its rationale is to account for physical and psychological suffering, which inherently pertains to natural persons.[84] As Judges Pinto de Albuquerque and Vučinić also noted in their concurring opinion, in this case «the teleological interpretation of the Convention reinforces the conclusion already imposed by the textual, historical and systemic construction of both the Convention and the Rules of Court».[85]

In *Cyprus v. Turkey*, the ECtHR emphasized that the applicability of Article 41 ECHR to inter-state applications depends on the nature of the complaint brought by the applicant State. The ECtHR established a twofold typology of Article 33 cases: the first category concerns abstract and systemic violations of the Convention, while the second involves concrete violations affecting iden-

80 *Cyprus v Turkey* (*IV*) (n 71) para. 42.

81 Ibid para. 40.

82 *Chorzów Factory* (n 29) at 21; *Fisheries Jurisdiction Case* (Federal *Republic of Germany v Iceland*), Judgment (Merits), I.C.J. Reports 1974, paras. 71–76; *Gabčíkovo-Nagymaros Project* (*Hungary v Slovakia*), Judgment, I.C.J. Reports 1997, para. 152, all cited in *Cyprus v. Turkey* (*IV*) (n 71) para. 41.

83 The ECtHR has often contended that the European Convention «should so far as possible be interpreted in harmony with other rules of international law of which it forms a part» (see *Al-Adsani v. United Kingdom* [GC], App. No. 35763/97, Judgment (Merits), 21 November 2001, para. 55).

84 *Cyprus v Turkey* (*IV*) (n 79) para. 38.

85 Ibid, Concurring Opinion of Judge Pinto De Albuquerque, joined by Judge Vučinić, para. 5.

tifiable individuals.[86] In the case at hand, the ECtHR held that when a Contracting Party complains *in abstracto* about a general failure by another State to comply with the Convention, just satisfaction «may not be appropriate»,[87] since «the primary goal of the applicant Government is that of vindicating the *public order of Europe* within the framework of collective responsibility under the Convention».[88] Conversely, the alleged violations concern specific rights of identifiable individuals who could themselves have brought an individual application under Article 34, the Court likened the applicant State's role under Article 33 to that of diplomatic protection. In such cases, just satisfaction may be awarded «having regard to the particular circumstances of the case»,[89] provided the claim relates to a sufficiently precise and objectively identifiable group of victims.[90] In *Cyprus v. Turkey* (*IV*), the ECtHR further outlined three criteria for determining the appropriateness of damages in inter-state cases.[91] First, the complaint must concern violations of fundamental human rights affecting the applicant State's nationals or other victims. Second, individual victims must be identifiable. Third, the primary purpose of the proceedings must be assessed to determine whether the claim pursues an individual or collective aim.[92]

However, this approach raises both legal and practical challenges. The categorization of claims as abstract or concrete remains contested. For instance, the analogy to diplomatic protection in cases involving missing persons or residents of specific areas has been criticized, as reflected in the dissenting opinion of Judge Karakaş[93] and the partly concurring and partly dissenting opinion of Judge Casadevall.[94] Determining both the amount and function of just satisfaction under Article 41 of the ECHR also poses challenges. While that provision aims to compensate for the lack of full reparation at the domestic level, as established in *Varnava and Others v. Turkey*,[95] some judges, including Pinto de Albuquerque and Vučinić, have argued that compensation

86 I Risini (n 12) 63; Spielmann (n 19) 7.
87 *Cyprus v Turkey* (*IV*) (n 71) para. 42.
88 Ibid para. 44.
89 Ibid para. 45.
90 Ibid para. 47.
91 Ibid para. 22.
92 Ibid.
93 *Cyprus v Turkey* (*IV*) (n 71), Dissenting Opinion of Judge Karakaş, 52–53.
94 *Cyprus v Turkey* (*IV*) (n 71), Partly Concurring and Partly Dissenting Opinion of Judge Casadevall, 45.
95 *Varnava and Others v Turkey*, Apps. Nos. 16064–16066/90 and 16068–16073/90, Judgment (Merits and Just Satisfaction), 18 September 2009, para. 244.

awarded in certain cases resembles punitive damages rather than strictly just satisfaction.[96]

These complexities are further reflected in the ECtHR's treatment of overlapping inter-state and individual applications. The Court has consistently emphasized that the object and scope of such proceedings may differ, even when they arise from the same factual matrix. This distinction was particularly evident in *Varnava*, where individual applications concerning disappearances linked to Turkish military operations in Northern Cyprus were lodged *after* the conclusion of the inter-state proceeding in *Cyprus v. Turkey*. Although the Court had already found violations affecting missing Greek Cypriots and their families in the inter-state case, it declined to strike out the individual applications, emphasizing that compensation for individual damage could lead to different outcomes.

Admittedly, in the *Varnava* case, the ECtHR concluded that Article 35(2)(b) of the Convention required complaints to be introduced by the same persons, thereby preventing States from depriving individuals of the right to bring or pursue their own claims through an inter-state application.[97] Although this formulation appears to require identity of parties, the Court also considered the possibility of striking out claims under Article 37(1)(c), which allows dismissal when further examination is no longer justified.[98] It nevertheless declined to do so, observing that the inter-state judgment had not identified the specific missing persons involved and, therefore, could not be regarded as having disposed of the individual claims.[99] Since different remedies might be awarded, the Court concluded that the individual applicants' interests had not been subsumed by the inter-state judgment. Rather than strictly applying *res judicata*-like principles under the Convention, the ECtHR demonstrated flexibility in managing overlapping claims, only barring reconsideration when the same individual injury had already been specifically addressed and remedied.

While the ECtHR did not initially exclude individual claims in *Cyprus v. Turkey*, it adopted a different approach in *Georgia v. Russia (I)*, deferring to findings in individual cases when determining inter-state reparation. This evolution suggests that inter-state claims seeking compensation for individual harm function analogously to diplomatic protection, consistent with human rights principles that prioritize individual redress.

---

96 *Cyprus v Turkey (IV)* (n 71), Concurring Opinion of Judge Pinto de Albuquerque, joined by Judge Vučinić, para. 13.

97 *Varnava* (n 95), para. 118.

98 Ibid, para. 119.

99 Ibid.

Georgia v. Russia (I) involved allegations of an administrative practice of arresting, detaining, and expelling Georgian nationals from Russia. In 2014, the ECtHR found that Russia had implemented a 'coordinated policy' of such expulsions in violation of the Convention, but postponed its decision on damages, anticipating a negotiated settlement.[100] When negotiations failed, Georgia submitted a claim for just satisfaction in 2015, prompting the Grand Chamber to address whether it could award damages in inter-state cases and whether Georgia's claims were justified and substantiated. Russia argued that only directly affected individuals could claim damages and that Georgia's failure to individually identify most victims precluded it from seeking compensation.[101] In its judgment on just satisfaction, the ECtHR, relying on its prior findings, confirmed that Article 41 permits awarding reparation in inter-state cases, provided the claims pertain to Convention violations.[102] The Court did not apply *res judicata* to bar the inter-state claim but deferred to findings in individual cases once they were rendered. Unlike in *Donnelly* or *Varnava*, where State and individual applicants pursued distinct claims, *Georgia v. Russia (I)* involved a shared object, as Georgia sought damages on behalf of individuals. Thus, inter-state reparation was excluded whenever an individual case had already been adjudicated. The Court's reasoning reflects the principle that direct victims have the stronger interest in vindicating their rights, while indirect victims are more likely to be barred from relitigating. Diplomatic-protection-type actions similarly seek reparation for individual injury, sharing the same objective of redressing personal harm. In *Georgia v. Russia (I)*, the ECtHR declined to consider an inter-state reparation claim where an individual case had already been determined, acknowledging their identity in purpose. This approach has influenced other tribunals to dismiss subsequent claims on res judicata or similar grounds, even if the parties were not identical.

Nonetheless, the individual dimension remains central to the Court's jurisprudence. In *Cyprus v. Turkey*, the ECtHR distinguished between diplomatic protection-like inter-state applications and broader claims addressing systemic issues or administrative practices. Even when a large number of nationals are affected, such claims remain oriented toward individual redress. Similarly, in *Georgia v. Russia (I)*, the Court found that an administrative-practice

100 *Georgia v. Russia (I)* [GC], App. No. 13255/07, Judgment (Merits), 3 July 2014. For an analysis of the judgment, see B Arp, 'Georgia v. Russia (I)' (2015) 109(1) *American Journal of International Law* 167.

101 *Georgia v. Russia (I)* (n 100), paras. 16–18, 29–47.

102 Ibid, paras. 19–20.

claim could resemble diplomatic protection when it seeks compensation for affected individuals, thereby reinforcing the continuing overlap between inter-state litigation and the protection of individual rights.

In its 2023 judgment on just satisfaction delivered in *Georgia v. Russia (II)*, the ECtHR awarded nearly €130 million in compensation for grave and systematic human rights violations committed during the Russo-Georgian War in Abkhazia and South Ossetia, which had taken place between 1 and 16 August 2008.[103] In its judgment on the merits of 21 January 2021, the Court had found that the Russian Federation had engaged in administrative practices in violation of Articles 2, 3, 5, and 8 of the Convention and Article 2 of Protocol No. 4. Furthermore, the ECtHR held that Russia had failed to comply with its obligations under Article 38.[104] In its just satisfaction judgment concerning the *Georgia v. Russia (II)* case, the ECtHR finally clarified the necessity of precision in identifying victims, thereby intercepting the criticism voiced by Judge Casadevall in *Cyprus v. Turkey (IV)*.[105] The compensation allocated for victims of killings, torture, arbitrary detention, and property destruction reflected the ECtHR's acknowledgment of large-scale violations and the need for substantial reparations. The categories of beneficiaries included were as follows: at least 50 victims of civilian killings in South Ossetia and the 'buffer zone' (€65,000 each);[106] at least 166 victims of inhuman and degrading treatment and arbitrary detention by South Ossetian forces (€16,250 each);[107] at least 16 victims of torture among the group of Georgian prisoners (€4,000 each); at least 23,000 victims prevented from returning to their homes (€5,000 each);[108] and at least 412 victims of Russia's failure to conduct an effective investigation into deaths occurring during active hostilities (€20,000 each).[109] Relying on the principles outlined in Article 38 ECHR and Rule 44A of the Rules of Court, as well as the methodology developed in *Georgia v. Russia (I)*, the ECtHR reviewed the lists of alleged victims identified

103 *Georgia v Russia (II)* (n 71).

104 *Georgia v Russia (II)* [GC], App. No. 38263/08, Judgment (Merits), 21 January 2021.

105 *Cyprus v. Turkey (IV)* (n 71), Partly Concurring and Partly Dissenting Opinion of Judge Casadevall, para. 5: «[...] it would have been appropriate to award an individual sum – on a *per capita* basis – to each of the victims rather than awarding a lump sum to the Cypriot State without indicating any criteria for distribution. The reality is that in practice all the awards made by the Court to date by way of just satisfaction have been granted directly to individual applicants» (emphasis added).

106 *Georgia v. Russia (II)* (n 71) para. 40.

107 Ibid para. 42.

108 Ibid para. 44.

109 Ibid para. 45.

in the merits judgment. It assessed the plausibility of the applicant government's factual submissions and the sufficiency of its just satisfaction claims, ensuring that awards were grounded in substantiated and verifiable evidence.[110]

4 Friendly Settlements as a Panacea for the Janus-Faced Dilemma of the Co-existence of State and Individual Reparations Claims?

The ECtHR's case law underscores that, even in inter-state proceedings, the individual – and not the applicant State – is the ultimate beneficiary of any just satisfaction award. Consequently, any monetary compensation received by a State must be transferred to victims through a distribution mechanism established by the recipient government. Regarding overlapping reparation claims brought through individual applications, such claims remain admissible provided they seek reparations distinct from those pursued by the claimant State. This distinction is critical, as diplomatic-protection-type claims, where a State seeks reparation on behalf of individuals, preclude separate individual claims for the same damages.

This leads to two conclusions. First, claimant States cannot seek reparation for themselves, as they are not human rights holders under the Convention. Second, any form of reparation deriving from a State's *status* as a High Contracting Party is effectively precluded, given the exclusively monetary nature of just satisfaction. Whether a State acts on behalf of its nationals or denounces systemic violations to uphold the *ordre public de l'Europe*, it remains barred from claiming compensation for itself.

However, the distinction between State and individual damage also considers the difference between individual and collective claims. Inter-state proceedings may at times resemble class actions, aggregating claims that could correspond to similar reparation claims potentially brought by affected individuals. In other cases, they assume a broader or collective aspect, focusing on systemic violations rather than personal injury. This distinction reinforces the idea that a State's own 'moral' interest is engaged when grave human rights violations affect its citizens on a widespread scale. In such circumstances, a State's action extends way beyond mere diplomatic protection, embodying a broader commitment to maintaining international legal standards and protecting its citizens from large-scale harm.

110 Ibid para. 37.

In consideration of the rigid structure of the just satisfaction scheme, integrating both State and individual interests in awarding reparation has proven to be a challenging task. As a result, alternative means to settle inter-state disputes have developed, especially when strict adherence to traditional just satisfaction principles would be impractical or inadequate to tackle the broader aspects of a case.

In this context, friendly settlements have increasingly been recognized as a viable mechanism of reconciling the diverging interests of States and individual victims. While traditionally regarded as a marginal aspect of the ECHR framework, particularly in inter-state applications – earning the label of the 'sleeping beauty' of the Convention –, friendly settlements have gained a more prominent role in individual cases.[111] Certainly, although the aim of 'chilling out' disputes is identical in both inter-state and individual cases – as some authors wisely noted, 'to avert an authoritative ruling that might attract extensive publicity and media scrutiny'[112] – friendly settlements have taken on a more significant role in individual cases. Beyond this pragmatic function, friendly settlements also serve to correct the structural imbalance between applicants and respondent States and to alleviate the Court's ever-increasing workload.[113]

In the context of inter-state cases, however, their use has been the exception rather than the rule, as illustrated by cases such as *France, Norway, Denmark, Sweden, Netherlands v. Turkey* and *Denmark v. Turkey*.[114] This limited application is understandable given the nature of the issues often involved in such cases. Systemic and large-scale human rights violations, which typically constitute the basis of inter-state claims, do not lend themselves easily to negotiated resolutions. The idea of 'bargaining' over funda-

111 N Wenzel, 'Rethinking Friendly Settlements under the European Convention on Human Rights: Why We Should Design a New Friendly Settlement Procedure for Inter-State Cases' (*Völkerrechtsblog*, 28 April 2021), https://voelkerrechtsblog.org/rethinking-friendly-settlements-under-the-echr; H Keller and R Piskóty, 'Friendly Settlements as the Sleeping Beauty in Inter-State Cases: Opportunities and Risks for the European Court of Human Rights' (*Völkerrechtsblog*, 28 April 2021), https://voelkerrechtsblog.org/friendly-settlements-as-the-sleeping-beauty-in-inter-state-cases/.

112 See in general H Keller, M Forowicz and L Engi, *Friendly Settlements before the European Court of Human Rights: Theory and Practice* (OUP 2010).

113 See M Forowicz, 'Friendly Settlement', *Max Planck Encyclopedia of International Procedural Law* [MPEiPro], June 2017, para. 24, <https://opil.ouplaw.com/display/10.1093/law-mpeipro/e3196.013.3196/law-mpeipro-e3196?prd=OPIL> accessed 28 February 2025.

114 *France, Norway, Denmark, Sweden and the Netherlands v. Turkey*, Apps. Nos. 9940–44/82, Report of the Commission, 7 December 1985 (Friendly Settlement), DR 44 (1985); *Denmark v. Turkey*, Apps. Nos. 34382/97, 5 April 2000 (Friendly Settlement) ECHR 2000 IV.

mental rights and freedoms may appear incongruous, if not inappropriate, particularly when the principal achievement of the ECHR has been to remove human rights issues from the realm of political compromise and entrust them to judicial adjudication, thereby affirming the ECtHR's role as the ultimate *arbiter* of Convention rights.[115] This gives rise to a pertinent question: why should States endeavour to achieve a friendly settlement when judicial decisions appear to offer a more authoritative resolution?[116]

The legal basis for friendly settlements under the ECHR is outlined in Article 39, which sets out procedural and substantive criteria for their implementation.[117] Friendly settlements may occur at various procedural stages. The earliest opportunity arises once an application has been registered, though negotiations at this stage are rare given the uncertainty surrounding admissibility. The likelihood of settlement increases following a declaration of admissibility, when the 'contours' of the case are defined more clearly. A further opportunity arises post-merits, when the ECtHR defers its decision on just satisfaction under Article 41. In such cases, settlements may focus solely on financial reparations, as the substantive violations have already been adjudicated. Conversely, the probability of settlement decreases once a case is relinquished to the Grand Chamber, where the parties are more likely to seek a definitive judicial ruling. Additionally, individual applications arising from inter-state complaints may be settled independently of the principal inter-state proceeding. The case law indicates that friendly settlements in inter-state claims depend on the specific circumstances of each dispute. Notably, settlements have been reached in both typologies of inter-state cases, reflect-

115 V Fikfak, 'Against settlement before the European Court of Human Rights' (2022) 20(3) *International Journal of Constitutional Law* 942, 958.

116 For a discussion of the practice of friendly settlement in the context of the Inter-American Court of Human Rights, see extensively J. Contesse, 'Settling Human Rights Violations' (2019) 60 *Harvard International Law Journal* 317, 346–347; N Saltalamacchia Ziccardi et al., 'Friendly Settlements in the Inter-American Human Rights System: Efficiency, Effectiveness and Scope' in P Engstrom (ed) *The Inter-American Human Rights System: Impact Beyond Compliance* (Springer 2018) 59, 65.

117 Article 39 ECHR provides as follows: «1. At any stage of the proceedings, the Court may place itself at the disposal of the parties concerned with a view to securing a friendly settlement of the matter on the basis of respect for human rights as defined in the Convention and the Protocols thereto. 2. Proceedings conducted under paragraph 1 shall be confidential. 3. If a friendly settlement is effected, the Court shall strike the case out of its list by means of a decision which shall be confined to a brief statement of the facts and of the solution reached. 4. This decision shall be transmitted to the Committee of Ministers, which shall supervise the execution of the terms of the friendly settlement as set out in the decision.»

ing their differences and specificities. This demonstrates the flexibility of the mechanism and dispels the assumption that it exists solely to provide reparations for individual victims. Instead, it can also serve broader State interests in upholding human rights compliance.

A prominent example is the settlement facilitated by the former European Commission on Human Rights in *Denmark, France, Netherlands, Norway, and Sweden v. Turkey*.[118] This case involved allegations of widespread and systematic human rights violations by the Turkish military regime. The settlement brokered through the ECommHR, included commitments by Turkey to prevent future violations, lift martial law, and improve transparency in its human rights practices. Although criticized for not fully redressing the violations at issue, the settlement achieved substantial political significance by prompting Turkey's subsequent acceptance of the individual application procedure under the Convention. This outcome produced a milestone in Turkey's engagement with the Convention system, arguably yielding a more impactful outcome than a mere judicial declaration of violations.

A comparable – if not more compelling – result was reached in the case of *Denmark v. Turkey*, where the applicant State alleged that a Danish national of Kurdish origin had been subjected to torture at the hands of Turkish authorities.[119] The settlement reached in this case incorporated both preventive measures and compensatory elements, demonstrating a balanced approach to addressing human rights violations. Significant aspects of the settlement included commitments to legislative and administrative reforms, official apologies, and an enhanced political dialogue on human rights issues. Additionally, the agreement included *ex gratia* monetary compensation, which Denmark was not required to transfer directly to the victim. Despite the lack of direct victim compensation, the ECtHR removed the case from its docket, underscoring its flexible and pragmatic approach under Article 39. This outcome highlights the Court's willingness to prioritize effective resolutions of disputes over rigid procedural requirements, while ensuring the integrity of its processes. This flexibility enables the Court to foster negotiated outcomes that remain consistent with the Convention's object and purposes,

118 'European Commission of Human Rights: Report on the Applications of Denmark, France, Netherlands, Norway, and Sweden Against Turkey and the Conclusion of a Friendly Settlement' (1986) 25(2) *International Legal Materials* 308.

119 For a brief comment on the specific content of the settlement, see 'European Court of Human Rights (ECHR): *Denmark v. Turkey* (Friendly Settlement)' (2000) 39(4) *International Legal Materials* 788.

particularly in inter-state cases where complex political and legal considerations are at play.[120]

The practice of friendly settlements thus aligns closely with the broader remedial objectives of the Convention. While Article 41 ECHR generally contemplate just satisfaction in the form of monetary compensation, settlements often extend beyond financial relief to encompass structural and preventive measures addressing systemic violations. They often may encompass structural measures designed to address systemic violations and prevent their recurrence, including institutional reforms or modifications in policy. Consequently, such settlements present a more comprehensive approach to redress, thereby enhancing the Convention's ability to deliver significant and forward-looking remedies that purely judicial determinations alone may fail to attain.

5 Conclusive Remarks

The examination of inter-state complaints in human rights litigation reveals an evolving intersection between traditional state responsibility and individual-centric reparative justice. While the ECtHR and other judicial bodies have made significant progress in addressing these challenges, as seen in *Cyprus v. Turkey* (*IV*), *Georgia v. Russia* (*I*) and (*II*), fundamental gaps remain. The continued reliance on bilateral adjudicatory systems within a multilateral human rights framework complicates the fair distribution of reparations, the adequacy of just satisfaction awards, and the recognition of collective rights harm.

Beyond judicial decisions, friendly settlements emerge as a pragmatic yet underutilized mechanism for addressing inter-state disputes. By fostering structural reforms and promoting compliance with human rights norms, these settlements have the potential to achieve reparative justice beyond financial compensation. However, their effectiveness depends on balancing state-driven priorities with the rights of individual victims, reaffirming the centrality of human rights in inter-state litigation.

Ultimately, the evolving practice of inter-state human rights complaints underscores the need to reconcile procedural frameworks of state responsibility with substantive human rights protection. A more holistic approach – integrating judicial rulings, friendly settlements, and innovative reparations

120 M Galanter and M Cahill, '"Most Cases Settle": Judicial Promotion and Regulation of Settlements' (1994) 46 *Stanford Law Review* 1339, 1351.

mechanisms – can strengthen accountability, address large-scale human rights violations more effectively, and enhance the capacity of international courts and monitoring bodies to deliver justice. Only through such advancements can human rights litigation fully realize its mandate to uphold justice, dignity, and the rule of law on a global scale.

Index

www.ingramcontent.com/pod-product-compliance
Lightning Source LLC
Chambersburg PA
CBHW051357240926
51852CB00001B/53
9789004716735